This is the latest volume to appear in the successful 'Cambridge History of Modern France', and is the most authoritative account available in English of the presidency of Georges Pompidou. Pompidou consolidated the constitutional changes made by de Gaulle, to the extent that he is now regarded as the Fifth Republic's second founding father, and continued de Gaulle's haughty attitudes to foreign policy. He also launched a programme of modernization and industrialization: under Pompidou France saw both the climax and the end of the post-war boom. Serge Berstein and Jean-Pierre Rioux analyse the politics of the period, and also give an overview of France's economy, culture and society. Their comprehensive study contains all the standard features, such as maps, chronology and tables, which have helped this series to establish itself as the premier multi-volume account of modern France. Students, scholars and teachers in history and political studies will find this volume invaluable.

SERGE BERSTEIN is Professor of History at the Institut d'Etudes Politiques, Paris, and the author of *The Republic of de Gaulle, La République sur le fil* and numerous other books on modern French history.

JEAN-PIERRE RIOUX is Director of Research at the Institut d'Histoire du Temps Présent, Paris. His many books include *The Fourth Republic, 1944–1958* and *Pour une histoire culturelle*.

9   The Pompidou Years, 1969–1974

This book is also part of the Cambridge History of Modern France, a multi-volume textbook series on the history of France from 1815 to the present day, co-published with the Maison des Sciences de l'Homme. Each volume is a translation of a title or titles from the series 'Nouvelle histoire de la France contemporaine' which has been in the course of publication by Editions du Seuil, Paris, since 1972. Authors are either historians at the top of their profession, but actively writing works of research, or younger scholars keenly involved with the topics concerned. Each shows a clear awareness of work currently being undertaken in the field, in English as well as in French. The series as a whole forms a comprehensive, coherent and up-to-date history of France since 1815.

For a list of titles in the series, please see end of book

The Pompidou Years, 1969–1974

SERGE BERSTEIN
Professor of History, Institut d'Etudes Politiques, Paris
and
JEAN-PIERRE RIOUX
Director of Research, Institut d'Histoire du Temps Présent, Paris

Translated by
CHRISTOPHER WOODALL

 CAMBRIDGE
UNIVERSITY PRESS
EDITIONS DE
LA MAISON DES SCIENCES DE L'HOMME
Paris

PUBLISHED BY THE PRESS SYNDICATE OF THE UNIVERSITY OF CAMBRIDGE
The Pitt Building, Trumpington Street, Cambridge, United Kingdom

CAMBRIDGE UNIVERSITY PRESS
The Edinburgh Building, Cambridge CB2 2RU, UK http://www.cup.cam.ac.uk
40 West 20th Street, New York NY 10011–4211, USA http://www.cup.org
10 Stamford Road, Oakleigh, Melbourne 3166, Australia
and Editions de la Maison des Sciences de l'Homme
54 Boulevard Raspail, 75270 Paris Cedex 06, France

Originally published in French as *La France de l'expansion, 2: L'apogée Pompidou 1969–1974* by Editions du Seuil 1995 and © Editions du Seuil.

First published in England by Editions de la Maison des Sciences de l'Homme and Cambridge University Press 2000 as *The Pompidou Years, 1969–1974*

English translation © Maison des Sciences de l'Homme and Cambridge University Press 2000

First published 2000

Printed in the United Kingdom at the University Press, Cambridge

Typeset in 10/12pt Plantin [CE]

A catalogue record for this book is available from the British Library

Library of Congress cataloguing in publication data
Berstein, Serge.
[Apogée Pompidou. English]
The Pompidou Years, 1969–1974 / Serge Berstein and Jean-Pierre Rioux.
  p. cm.
Includes bibliographical references and index.
ISBN 0 521 58061 7 (hardback)
1. Pompidou, Gèorges, 1911–1974.
2. France – Politics and government – 1969–1974.
3. Presidents – France – Biography.
I. Rioux, Jean-Pierre, 1939– II. Title.
DC421.B4713 2000
944.083'7'092–dc21 99–23268 CIP

ISBN 0 521 58061 7 hardback
ISBN 2 7351 0839 2 hardback (France only)

The first part of this book was written by Serge Berstein and the second by Jean-Pierre Rioux.

Contents

Illustrations

Tables

Abbreviations

BEP	brevet d'études professionelles
CAL	comités d'action lycéens
CAP	certificat d'aptitude professionnelle
CCU	Comité consultatif des universités
CDP	Centre Démocratie et Progrès
CEA	Commissariat à l'énergie atomique
CEG	collège d'enseignement général
CERC	Centre d'études des revenus et des coûts
CERES	Centre d'études, de recherche et d'éducation socialistes
CES	collège d'enseignement secondaire
CFDT	Confédération française et démocratique du travail
CFP	Compagnie française des pétroles
CFTC	Confédération française des travailleurs chrétiens
CGT	Confédération générale du travail
CID–UNATI	Centre d'information et de défense–Union nationale des associations de travailleurs indépendants
CIR	Convention des institutions républicaines
CNESER	Conseil National de l'Enseignement Supérieur et de la Recherche
CNIP	Centre national des indépendants et paysans
CNJA	Centre national des jeunes agriculteurs
CNPF	Conseil national du patronat français
CPU	Conférence des présidents d'université
CREDOC	Centre de Recherches, d'Etudes et de Documentation sur la Consommation
CREP	Centre de Recherche Economique sur l'Epargne
DATAR	Délégation à l'aménagement du territoire et à l'action régionale
DEA	diplôme d'études approfondies
DESS	diplôme d'études specialisées
DEUG	diplôme d'études universitaires générales

DGRST	Délégation générale à la recherche scientifique et technique
EDF–GDF	Electricité de France–Gaz de France
EEC	European Economic Community
ENA	Ecole nationale d'administration
EPCSC	Etablissements publics à caractère scientifique et culturel
ERAP	Entreprise de recherches et d'activités pétrolières
FDES	Fonds de développement économique et social
FEN	Fédération de l'Education nationale
FGDS	Fédération de la gauche démocrate et socialiste
FNSEA	Fédération nationale des syndicats d'exploitants agricoles
GAEC	Groupement agricole d'exploitation en commun
GDP	gross domestic product
GNP	gross national product
HLM	Habitation à loyer modéré
IFOP	Institut français de l'opinion publique
INED	Institut national d'études démographiques
INSEE	Institut national de la statistique et des études économiques
IUT	Institut universitaire de technologie
JAC	Jeunesse agricole chrétienne
JOC	Jeunesse ouvrière chrétienne
MLAC	Mouvement pour la Libéralisation de l'Avortement et de la Contraception
MODEF	Mouvement de défense des exploitants familiaux
MRJC	Mouvement rural de la jeunesse chrétienne
MRP	Mouvement républicain populaire
NATO	North Atlantic Treaty Organization
OECD	Organization for Economic Cooperation and Development
ORTF	Office de radio-télévision française
PCF	Parti communiste français
PDM	Progrès et démocratie moderne
POS	Plans d'occupation des sols
PS	Parti socialiste
PSU	Parti socialiste unifié
RATP	Régie autonome des transports parisiens
RPF	Rassemblement du Peuple Français
SAFER	Société d'aménagement foncier et d'établissement rural
SDAU	Schéma directeur d'aménagement et d'urbanisme

SEREB	Société pour l'étude et la réalisation de l'engin balistique
SESAME	Système d'étude du schéma d'aménagement
SFIO	Section française de l'internationale ouvrière
SMIC	Salaire minimum interprofessionelle de croissance
SMIG	Salaire minimum interprofessionelle garanti
SNCF	Société nationale des chemins de fer
SNECMA	Société nationale d'études et de construction de moteurs d'avions
SNES	Syndicat national de l'enseignement secondaire
SNI	Syndicat national des instituteurs
SNIAS	Société nationale industrielle aérospatiale
SOFRES	Société française d'enquêtes par sondage
UCRG	Union des clubs pour le renouveau de la gauche
UDR	Union des démocrates pour la république
UER	Unités d'enseignement et de recherche
UGCS	Union des groupes et clubs socialistes
UNEF	Union nationale des étudiants de France
ZAC	Zone d'aménagement concerté
ZUP	Zone à urbaniser en priorité

Chronological summary

1969

29 April	Georges Pompidou and Gaston Deferre announce their candidatures for the presidency
30 April	The Independent Republicans declare their support for Pompidou
12 May	Alain Poher announces his candidature
22 May	Jacques Duhamel declares his support for Pompidou
1–15 June	Presidential elections
20 June	Jacques Chaban-Delmas becomes prime minister
2 July	Formation of parliamentary club Présence et action du gaullisme
4 July	Formation of Centre démocratie et progrès
1–13 July	Foundation of Parti socialiste under the leadership of Alain Savary
20 August	The franc is devalued by 12.5 per cent
16 September	Prime minister Chaban-Delmas launches *Nouvelle Société* project
19 October	Maurice Faure becomes president of the Parti radical
October	*L'Anti-de Gaulle* by Louis Vallon
13 November	Pompidou declares position on nuclear industry
November	Liberalization of ORTF
1–2 December	Conference at The Hague on EEC enlargement
10 December	EDF signs up to first *contrat de progrès*
15 December	Pompidou decides to create a centre for the contemporary arts in Paris
19 December	The American press reveals Franco-Libyan negotiations on arms sales
24–9 December	The 'Cherbourg gunboats' affair

1970

7 January	Law introducing SMIC
14 January	Chancellor Brandt sets forth his *Ostpolitik* to the Bundestag
21 January	Law providing for the sharing out among Renault's employees of a part of the company capital
	The parliamentary UDR group question the objectivity of the first TV channel
28 January	Jean-Jacques Servan-Schreiber publishes his radical manifesto, entitled *Ciel et Terre*
8 February	Georges Marchais becomes assistant general secretary of the PCF
23–9 February	Visit of Pompidou to United States
Feb–March	Clashes at Nanterre and Assas. The dean of Nanterre, Paul Ricœur resigns from his post on 14 March
8–15 March	Cantonal elections
March	Creation of the Institut pour le développement industriel
March–April	Lorry drivers block roads; protests by farmers; demonstration of mayors outside Hôtel Matignon
4 April	Roger Frey calls on the majority to seek broad alliances for the municipal elections
20 April	Agreement between CNPF and trades unions on monthly basis for wages payment
20 May	Roger Garaudy is expelled from PCF
27 May	Disbandment of the Gauche prolétarienne
4 June	*Anti-casseurs* law
18 June	Victory of Conservatives in Great Britain. Edward Heath becomes prime minister
25–7 June	Chaban-Delmas attacked at UDR Conseil national
28 June	Servan-Schreiber elected parliamentary deputy for Nancy
9 July	Agreement reached on right to training leave
16 July	The Conseil Constitutionnel removes several clauses from the Pleven law on the creation of associations
10 August	German–Soviet treaty recognizing the Oder–Neisse border
20 September	Chaban-Delmas re-elected deputy of Bordeaux, defeating Servan-Schreiber
6–13 October	Visit of Pompidou to Moscow

9 November	General de Gaulle dies
December	The Senate opens an enquiry into irregularities in the administration of public affairs in La Villette

1971

7 January	Government reshuffle; René Tomasini becomes UDR general secretary
19 February	Demonstration by lycée students following the 'Guiot affair'
24 February	Colonel Boumédienne nationalizes French oil companies operating in Algeria
26 February	Pierre Messmer becomes minister for overseas departments and territories
14–21 March	Municipal elections
20–1 May	Heath–Pompidou talks in Paris
16 June	François Mitterrand becomes first secretary of the PS
12 July	The five UDR chairmen of National Assembly committees issue a criticism of the government
16 July	Laws on the reform of apprenticeship, the upgrading of technical education, and on job training
19 July	'Garantie foncière' scandal and charging of UDR deputy Rives-Henry
August	Michel Poniatowski launches the idea of a federation of centrists
20 September	Senate elections
12 October	The PCF publishes its election manifesto, *Changer de cap* ('Changing course')
17 October	Servan-Schreiber becomes president of the Parti radical
3 November	Creation of Mouvement réformateur
18 November	Dega affair
13–14 December	Pompidou meets Nixon in the Azores

1972

19 January	*Le Canard enchaîné* publishes Chaban-Delmas' tax form
22 January	EEC membership treaty signed by Great Britain, Ireland, Norway and Denmark
March	PS programme, *Changer la vie*, published

1 April	Senate report on clandestine advertising on television
23 April	Referendum on EEC enlargement
17 May	Chaban-Delmas is authorized to call for a vote of confidence in the National Assembly 'if he deems it useful'
23 May	National Assembly approves confidence motion
16 June	Parti radical splits
26 June	Socialist party and communist party sign a *programme commun de gouvernement*
5 July	Law on regional public authorities; Chaban-Delmas resigns; Pierre Messmer becomes prime minister
12 July	Arthur Conte becomes director general of ORTF
5 September	Alain Peyrefitte replaces René Tomasini as UDR general secretary
6 September	Pierre Messmer outlines general policy to National Assembly, but does not request a vote
4 October	Foundation of the Mouvement des radicaux de gauche
8 October	Valéry Giscard d'Estaing declares that 'France wants to be governed from the centre'

1973

7 January	Messmer sets out the majority's programme in a speech in Provins
10 January	Visit of Pompidou to Minsk
27 January	Vietnam peace accord signed in Paris
12 February	Second devaluation of the dollar
4–11 March	Legislative elections
6 March	Messmer–Lecanuet electoral agreement on candidate withdrawals
2 April	Edgar Faure elected president of National Assembly; Roger Frey becomes president of UDR group
3 April	Pompidou's message to parliament announcing a reform to reduce the presidential term to five years
5–12 April	Second Messmer government formed
22 April	Henry Kissinger proposes a new Atlantic Charter
31 May–1 June	Pompidou meets Nixon in Reykjavik
12 June	The Lip watchmaking firm at Besançon goes bankrupt and closes: the workers occupy the factory

28 June	Disbandment of Ligue communiste and Ordre nouveau
10 July	Michel Debré criticizes the government's economic policy
14 August	The police clear the Lip factory
11–17 September	Pompidou travels to China
6 October	Outbreak of Yom Kippur war. Alexandre Sanguinetti elected UDR general secretary
16 October	Arthur Conte replaced by Marceau Long as director general of ORTF; the Arab countries reduce their oil exports by 25 per cent and increase the price by 17 per cent
16–19 October	The National Assembly and the Senate vote in favour of the introduction of five-year presidential terms
24 October	Plan to introduce five-year presidential terms shelved
17–18 November	UDR conference in Nantes
4 December	Alleged bugging of *Le Canard enchaîné* offices
December	Jean Charbonnel entrusts Claude Neuschwander with the task of turning Lip around
14 December	EEC summit in Copenhagen, including three new member states
20 December	Approval of the Royer law restricting the opening of large-scale retail outlets

1974

5 January	Pierre Messmer declares: 'Lip, c'est fini!'
19 January	The Conseil des ministres decides to float the franc
11 February	At the summit of industrialized countries in Washington, France opposes the creation of an organization of oil-consuming nations
28 February	Government reshuffle
12 March	Visit by Pompidou to USSR
2 April	Death of Georges Pompidou

Part 1

The republic of Georges Pompidou

1   Change and continuity

A decisive test for the Fifth Republic

The resignation of General de Gaulle on 28 April 1969 did not clear the ground for a seamless succession, and there were many reasons for this. Above all, his resignation came at the end of a convoluted crisis and seemed to represent its logical conclusion. Foreshadowed by the poor election results of 1965 and 1967 which had revealed the gulf that now separated public expectations from government policy, followed by the convulsive crisis of 1968 that appeared to call into question the very foundations of society and cause the state to totter, the resignation was the culmination of a gradual process of erosion in public support for de Gaulle's republic.[1] It was logical to wonder whether the departure of the founder of the Fifth Republic would mean a change of regime or merely a change of personnel.

This indeed was what was at stake in the succession process that got under way that 28 April. The creation of the Fifth Republic had been the personal achievement of General de Gaulle, who had never ceased to fashion as he saw fit, with piecemeal additions and adjustments, both the letter and the spirit of its institutions. From the constitutional reform of 1962, which had introduced presidential elections by universal suffrage, to a style of government that came close to direct democracy by vesting most of the decision-making power in the president, the regime had steadily strayed ever further from the parliamentary system laid down in the founding text of 1958.

This drift, which was deplored by many politicians especially on the left, seemed clearly linked to the personality of the founder of the Fifth Republic, to his pre-eminent historical role, to his charismatic personality and to the imperious style that inclined him to the view that once the ritual of universal suffrage had been celebrated, power was to be exercised by hierarchical, indeed military, command. Many of those engaged in politics felt that the departure of General de Gaulle ought to mark a resumption of normality, returning the regime to the letter of the constitution: that is, to parliamentary government. With the removal of the larger-than-life personality whose massive shadow had seemed to crush French politics ever since 1958, the era of 'personal power' that the left and a section of the right imputed to de Gaulle would be at an end. The new president of the republic, as one politician among others, would be forced, whatever his personal qualities, to negotiate with his peers, using the institutions in a way more in keeping with the constitution's founding text. Moreover, the notion that Gaullism could not survive the disappearance of its founder was shared by the General's own followers and perhaps by de Gaulle himself, firm in the conviction that he had had no predecessor and could have no genuine successor either. After all, just two days prior to the 27 April referendum, André Malraux, the most loyal of all de Gaulle's followers, speaking at the final meeting of the General's supporters, had stated that the post-de Gaulle era could not be built on the ruins of Gaullism. Malraux had thus pitched the future of the regime into the referendum balance and declared that de Gaulle's republic could not outlive de Gaulle.

But if, for contrasting reasons, this analysis was shared by de Gaulle's opponents and by his diehard supporters, it failed to take account of a number of other facts that were pulling in the opposite direction. First, there was the vast majority that the General had won in the June 1968 legislative elections, each component of which displayed its attachment to the Fifth Republic, even if some, like Valéry Giscard d'Estaing and his Independent Republicans, had opposed the General in the April referendum. Second, with its massive 'yes' vote in the 1962 referendum, the French electorate had ratified the constitutional changes and expressed a clear desire that the Fifth Republic should endure. Third, there was increasing support for the regime's institutions among a section of the opposition that had taken on board the clear shift in public opinion, which was now firmly convinced, contrary to the view taken by the majority of French electors prior to 1958, that a democratic republic and strong executive power could after all coexist. François Mitterrand, the candidate of the united left in 1965, was attempting to win over to this presidential approach a section of those who had previously given him their backing. Meanwhile, in the centre, the managers who supported Jacques Duhamel, Joseph Fontanet or René Pleven sought to distance themselves ever more sharply from those who, like Jean Lecanuet and Pierre Abelin, remained frozen in unwavering opposition to any form of anti-European Gaullism.

It was around this issue that the various political forces, faced with the need to find a strategy and select candidates for the unexpected presidential election that de Gaulle's resignation had triggered, would now group.

The candidature of Georges Pompidou

The twenty-eighth of April 1969 did not turn out to be the day of chaos that General de Gaulle and his loyal supporters had at every election warned would follow any result hostile to the ruling majority. On the contrary, everyone could now assess for themselves the ability of the institutions to weather a crisis. In view of the fact that the outgoing president of the republic had declared that his resignation would take effect at noon, Alain Poher, president of the Senate, who was entrusted under the constitution with the interim period, moved into the Elysée palace the same day at 3 p.m. There was doubtless some friction between the interim president, who was regarded as the true victor of the referendum, and the government, which after all had been appointed by de Gaulle and was still engaged in day-to-day business, but there was no threat of any real constitutional crisis. The Fifth Republic prepared calmly, if not placidly, to find a successor to Charles de Gaulle.

In actual fact, the name of this successor was already on everybody's lips. Georges Pompidou, prime minister from 1962 to 1968, the man who could take most credit for the June 1968 election triumph, and the potential leader of a parliamentary majority that in the main was quite ready to support him, had let it be known repeatedly during the first few months of 1969 that he intended to stand for president. It was believed that General de Gaulle had decided to resign in 1970 on his eightieth birthday and Pompidou was expecting to announce his candidature on that occasion.[2] Be that as it may, public opinion was in no doubt as to Pompidou's willingness to stand. One might of course object that in the tacit hierarchy of the Fifth Republic the second-ranking officer of state, and as such the heir apparent, was the current prime minister. But even if Maurice Couve de Murville could have been prevailed upon to stand, there were many reasons for him to stand aside. First, his political stature, after serving as prime minister for only a matter of months, was less substantial than that of his predecessor at the Hôtel Matignon (the residence of the prime minister). Second, there was a deep-seated enmity between the two men, since Pompidou remained convinced that, in an attempt to wreck his political career, de Murville had connived at slanders regarding his private life that were spread at the time of the Markovic affair.[3] Lastly, if some of de Gaulle's supporters, angry with Pompidou for contributing to the failure of the referendum by presenting himself as a potential successor to the General, certainly felt tempted to block his path, this applied neither to the vast bulk of UDR deputies who saw Pompidou as their true leader, nor to the political grouping as a whole, which the former prime minister had reorganized around his own handpicked men at the Lille conference in 1967.[4]

Pompidou moved fast to head off any manoeuvre on the part of possible Gaullist rivals. On the 28th itself, in a message to de Gaulle expressing his loyalty and the regret he felt about the General's resignation, Pompidou informed him that, as he had already announced, he intended to present his candidature to succeed him. Early the following morning his parliamentary secretary officially announced Pompidou's decision to run. This received the immediate endorsement of the political office of the UDR, which recommended that the party should give its official support to Pompidou, as a candidate who had emerged from its own ranks. That evening both the parliamentary grouping and the executive committee of the UDR swung behind him.[5]

To the party that had governed France since 1958, Pompidou presented himself as de Gaulle's natural successor, emphasizing the thread of continuity that he intended to make the main theme of his appeal to the electorate. But Pompidou was too shrewd a politician to overlook the fact that the General had lost his referendum as a result of dissent among the centre right, following the decision by Valéry Giscard d'Estaing and the majority of centrists to join the 'no' camp. To secure the presidency Pompidou knew that he had to attract back into the majority fold all those who had withdrawn their support from the General, while persuading the UDR to forgo taking revenge on its former allies for breaking the solidarity pact that had held since 1962. Pompidou therefore told the UDR deputies, reminding them of the elementary rules of electoral arithmetic, that in order to reach the decisive threshold it was essential to practise 'ouverture' or openness, i.e. to form political alliances. Indeed, Pompidou was willing to extend this embrace to include all those who did not back the communist candidate.[6] It remained to be seen whether those whose support he sought would be willing to enter into the alliance that he was offering.

Support from the right and 'opening' to the centre

Nothing could have appeared less certain than the backing of Giscard d'Estaing for Georges Pompidou's candidature. The young leader of the moderate right – he was forty-three at this time – had never concealed his ambition one day to succeed General de Gaulle. He knew, however, that on this occasion his chances were limited not only by his relative youth but also by the fact that he had no time to do the vital pre-campaign groundwork. But his inability to enter the fray did not mean that he had to jettison any kind of personal strategy. If he could not himself stand, he could at least work to ensure that the transition he desired to see from Gaullists to moderates be effected by someone congenial to him, while he figured in the role of both stage director and designated successor. Thus, on 28 April, Giscard immediately mooted the idea of a 'candidature of reassurance', to be entrusted to a 'man of experience' – someone who had remained free of involvement in the political battles between majority and opposition. It was a portrait that one could hardly fail to recognize as that of Antoine Pinay. This was a clever move, since Pinay, who had served as prime minister under the Fourth Republic, might hope to attract a sizeable portion of the non-communist left to his candidature. Just one vital ingredient was missing: the agreement of Pinay himself. But, as in 1965, Antoine Pinay again side-stepped the challenge, declaring that he would only stand as a candidate of last resort in the event of a national emergency which, he added, did not then exist.[7] Giscard's efforts to discover an alternative 'candidate of reassurance' who would be prepared to participate in the proposed venture proved vain, since on 30 April the parliamentary grouping of his party, the Independent Republicans, resolved to back Pompidou, leaving their leader, Giscard, with no choice but to fall into line. Pompidou had thus managed to secure the support of the same majority coalition that until April 1969 had backed General de Gaulle.

But Pompidou wanted to go still further, gnawing into support for the centrists whom he knew to be split over the prospect of joining the government coalition. Ever since the 1967 elections, Jacques Duhamel, Joseph Fontanet, Pierre Sudreau and others had been seeking a dialogue with the government and, as prime minister, Pompidou had developed contacts with them. In May 1969 Pompidou renewed these contacts and, having undertaken, if elected, to preside over a politically open style of government and to relaunch European policy, he finally won the support of this centre ground. On 22 May, at the end of a radio debate, Jacques Duhamel, chairman of the parliamentary grouping Progrès et démocratie moderne, pledged his support for Pompidou's candidature, thereby adding his voice to those of René Pleven and Joseph Fontanet who had both already taken this step. The presidential majority taking shape was thus tri-polar, adding a section of the centre to the Gaullists and the moderates.

Pompidou's candidature looked all the more impregnable, given the utter prostration of his adversaries.

The left in tatters

In 1965, pitted against General de Gaulle, the Left, with François Mitterrand as its candidate, had gained an unexpectedly high vote that had restored its credibility. But the 1969 presidential election could hardly have come at a worse moment. Still reeling from the impact of the *événements* of 1968, the left was deeply divided. The communist party, which was isolated following the Soviet invasion of Czechoslovakia and exposed to the violent attacks of the *gauchistes*, wanted a single left-wing candidate who, as in 1965, would relieve it of the need to assess its numbers and would deprive the right of the ever effective electoral weapon of anti-communism. Any such move, however, would favour François Mitterrand, whose name would go forward as unity candidate. However, the Fédération de la gauche démocrate et socialiste (FGDS), which might have drawn strength from a second Mitterrand candidature, had collapsed in the aftermath of the 1968 events, while Guy Mollet, general secretary of the SFIO, was now worried by Mitterrand's openly declared ambition to lead the left. While the former partners of the non-communist left engaged in a trial of strength, a move by Gaston Defferre put an end to any notion of a single left-wing candidature. On 29 April, Defferre, deputy and mayor of Marseille, unexpectedly sought and won SFIO backing for his own bid for the presidency. The centrist image that Defferre had gained as parliamentary deputy and city mayor, following his attempt to form a 'broad federation' in 1965,[8] set off a chain reaction. Defferre's candidature was rejected first by Mitterrand's Convention des institutions républicaines and then by Jean Poperen's Union des groupes et clubs socialistes, at their conference in Saint-Gratien. The PCF also rejected the centrist strategy implicit in Defferre's candidature, and chose as its own preferred candidate – not its general secretary Waldeck-Rochet, but Jacques Duclos, an old leader of good-natured and reassuring appearance. These two candidates of the left were quickly joined by two candidates of the extreme left, as the Parti socialiste unifié (PSU) rallied behind their national secretary Michel Rocard, and the Trotskyists of the Ligue communiste presented their leader Alain Krivine.[9]

With the left split, and its public support eroded by the fright felt by the French as they cast their minds back to the 1968 crisis, Pompidou had very little to worry about. Indeed, for Pompidou the only real danger was from the opposition centrists, with the candidature of the interim president of the republic, Alain Poher.

The candidature of Alain Poher

Whereas the candidature of Pompidou had long been expected, that of Alain Poher was the outcome of chance. He had become president of the Senate in October 1968 following the withdrawal, and with the backing, of Gaston Monnerville, but was virtually unknown to the French public. Since the existence of the Senate as an independent legislative chamber had been called into question by the reform put to referendum in April 1969, Alain Poher had found himself spearheading a rebellion of notables against General de Gaulle. The victory of the 'no' camp and Poher's resulting elevation to the Elysée suddenly transformed this discreet and unassuming senator into a prominent personality in French political life and therefore, at a stroke, made him a potential president in the eyes of French public opinion. This prospect, however, appeared to leave Poher cold. When questioned about his intentions, he replied that he would not stand. He stuck to this position even when Valéry Giscard d'Estaing urged him to take the place of the faltering Antoine Pinay. But two circumstances intervened to overcome the reluctance of the interim president. First, the opposition centrists, as well as a sizeable section of the non-communist left, saw him as the man best able to stop Pompidou. Pierre Abelin, Jean Lecanuet and the radical Félix Gaillard therefore urged Alain Poher to throw his hat into the ring. Rather more discreetly, Guy Mollet appealed for a candidate to step forward around whom socialists could rally without misgivings. The other factor that influenced Poher's decision was the findings of the opinion polls. Well before he had reached any decision on the matter, a growing number of electors were stating their determination to vote for him. This shift in public opinion towards Alain Poher culminated in mid-May when SOFRES credited him with 39 per cent of voting intentions in the first round of the election, while IFOP gave him 37 per cent. Either percentage would have placed him as runner-up to Pompidou. The projections for the second round of voting were of even greater interest: the Senate president was forecast to win with 56 per cent of the votes, leaving the former prime minister with 44 per cent.[10]

These encouraging prospects clinched the decision for Alain Poher. Having declared on 7 May, 'I am in no way a candidate, I do not wish to be, but I might perhaps be forced into it', by 12 May he had decided to take the plunge. The list of candidates was completed by a seventh man, Louis Ducatel, who represented nobody but himself. On 16 May 1969, the election campaign got under way.

The 1969 election campaign

What, in mid-May 1969, were the hopes and expectations of the French electorate that had just forced General de Gaulle to resign?[11] Opinion polls show that, as implicit in their 'no' vote in the April referendum, the French wanted a clean break from the politics of the past. A resounding 51 per cent of French people, as against 31 per cent, wanted the new president to introduce far-reaching change in the way that power was exercised. With the exception of foreign policy, where 51 per cent of French people as against 29 per cent wanted previous policies to be pursued, the desire for change touched every major area of French politics. Unsurprisingly, it was in the field of economic and social policy that expectations were highest, with 64 per cent of respondents as against 18 per cent hoping for a change in direction. The same desire for change was expressed (45 per cent as against 20 per cent) with regard to higher education. On the other hand, if the majority of French people wanted to see a fresh approach to constitutional issues, this was much less clearcut, with 39 per cent as against 30 per cent calling for change in this area. Looking closer, it is clear where concerns were focused and therefore easier to interpret the 'no' vote in the April 1969 referendum: 57 per cent of French people wanted their future president to act as an arbiter, above the fray, while just 32 per cent wanted him, like de Gaulle, to take personal charge of all the main planks of policy. The French people had not handed the General his notice inadvertently but out of a clear desire for change. Obviously the question was who, of the available candidates, could best fulfil this expectation. Until mid-May, opinion favoured Alain Poher over Pompidou.

Given their desire for a president who could act as arbiter, 51 per cent of French people felt that Alain Poher was better placed to play such a role than Pompidou. Poher was also thought more capable than Pompidou of being a 'president for all French people' (44 per cent as against 31 per cent for Pompidou); of 'healing the rifts that had emerged between the two camps at the April referendum' (43 per cent as against 20 per cent); and of addressing the interests of wage-earners (39 per cent as against 22 per cent), of farmers (30 per cent as against 24), and of small shopkeepers (40 per cent as against 18 per cent). Here again, one can see why the mid-May polls predicted a victory for Alain Poher. Pompidou, on the other hand, was viewed as a man of the right by 76 per cent of French people, whereas only 39 per cent attributed this label to Alain Poher, and as a 'representative of capital' by 55 per cent of respondents. To this was added a long list of terms that sketched in a rather unappealing picture of the majority grouping's candidate: among other things, Pompidou was thought to be self-important, overbearing, pretentious, sardonic and devoid of convictions.

Despite this catalogue of liabilities, all the opinion polls predicted that Pompidou would win the first round with 41 or 42 per cent of the vote. There was obviously a mismatch between the somewhat theoretical desires of the French as revealed in the opinion polls, and their voting intentions. They liked Alain Poher but regarded Pompidou as the man most capable of occupying the highest office of state. The polls showed that the French saw Pompidou as a true statesman who had demonstrated his ability during the crisis of 1968. They could see that he had a set of policies and the backing of a majority coalition to see them through, whereas support for the Senate president was at best patchy. Finally, Pompidou had the advantage of a shrewd election campaign and a cleverly worded slogan, *le changement dans la continuité* ('change within continuity'). If 'continuity' guaranteed him the approval of the overwhelming majority of UDR Gaullists (90 per cent), 'change' secured him 60 per cent of Independent Republican and at least a third of centrist votes. With characteristic skill, Pompidou ran a campaign that highlighted those of his strong points that set him apart from the Senate president.

Well aware of the expectations of French people, Pompidou, like his main rival, promised to bring forward policies to address their day-to-day concerns. In a specific pitch to the middle class, whose numbers and influence had been boosted by economic growth, Pompidou pledged to give industrialization special priority. But he also demonstrated his awareness of the difficulties facing shop-keepers and small businesses, whose recent campaigns had led to the setting-up of an association for the self-employed, the CID–UNATI (Centre d'information et de défense–Union nationale des associations de travailleurs indépendants). Turning to the centrists, Pompidou stated his commitment to broader cooperation in Europe and to the lifting of de Gaulle's veto on Great Britain's entry into the European Economic Community (EEC). Distancing himself from the April referendum, he pledged that the powers of the Senate would not be curtailed in any way. On television Pompidou proved a highly impressive performer and the straightforwardness of his message and the smoothness of the UDR political machine enabled him to reach a very broad section of the electorate. But above all he laid great emphasis on the one point that distinguished him fundamentally from Alain Poher, the constitutional issue. While adopting the stance of defender of the constitution of the Fifth Republic and warning that Alain Poher's proposals could lead to a crisis of government, Pompidou nevertheless acknowledged, bowing to the desire for change, that the way in which power was exercised had to be modified. 'I am not General de Gaulle', he declared on 15 May during a debate broadcast on the radio. 'I shall necessarily be more persuasive, more conciliatory.' The left-wing Gaullist Léo Hamon interpreted this in his own fashion, asserting that 'the time [had] come to move away from epic, if not mystic, Gaullism to a political Gaullism which, provided it is well balanced, can stand the test of time'.[12] But the success of Pompidou in the first round of voting was ensured not only by his personal qualities and the skill of his campaign, but also by the evident weaknesses of his opponents.

Of all the presidential campaigns held under the Fifth Republic, the 1969 campaign stands out for its moderation or, more precisely, for its lack of drama. Since the two most credible candidates were both of the right, the choice put to the voters involved no overarching social project. Moreover, the character and pragmatic views of the principal candidates made it impossible to stimulate any far-reaching public debate over the choices before the electorate. Lastly, the low-key way the campaign unfolded made any real shift in power appear increasingly unlikely. The real danger for Pompidou would be if the left achieved an outstanding result in the first round and if Poher also did well. In this scenario, when it came to the second round, Poher might be able to ride an anti-Gaullist tide. In the event, nothing of the kind happened. On the left Gaston Defferre conducted a relatively lacklustre campaign, his television appearances revealing his lack of charisma and the failure of the Parti socialiste (PS) to give him its firm backing. Moreover, he seemed to place himself at the margins of the new political game by announcing on 15 May that, if elected, he would appoint Pierre Mendès France as his prime minister: indeed, from that point on the two men appeared together at every campaign event. This had the effect of pushing Gaston Defferre even further into the shadows, while causing the public quite rightly to question just who, under such an arrangement, would be the true head of the executive. As for Mendès France, although he still retained considerable prestige in the eyes of many intellectuals who remembered the promise he had embodied in 1954–5, he no longer held much sway with the broader public who saw him as a man of a dim and distant past who had set his face against the Fifth Republic. As a result, the polls registered a steady decline in support for Defferre's candidature from about 24 per cent of voting intentions at the beginning of May to 5 per cent of votes actually cast on 1 June. Support for Poher's candidature, though it did not fall so far, was also severely eroded. As we have seen, as long as Alain Poher remained out of the race, the French entrusted him with their growing confidence. But as soon as he announced his candidature and was forced to campaign and expound his ideas on concrete issues, his uncertainties were exposed. There were three main unanswered questions. Would Alain Poher, if elected to the Elysée, seek the backing of the right or of the left? What would be his conception of the function of the president? Would he have to dissolve the Assembly and appeal to the French people to provide him with a new majority or would he agree to govern with the majority produced by the 1968 elections, which left parliament in the hands of the UDR?[13] On all three points, Pompidou could supply clearcut answers and it is easy to see why he chose to concentrate on an agenda that quickly focused attention on the nature of the regime itself. Many observers took the view that the election of Alain Poher would return the country to a parliamentary system, undermining the pre-eminent role of the president – that is, the mould-breaking characteristic of the Fifth Republic. Realizing that on this issue Pompidou's advantage was beyond dispute, Alain Poher made a late attempt to shift from his earlier position, thereby confirming his image as a waverer. On the issue of the parliamentary majority, Alain Poher remained non-committal, visibly hesitating between a dissolution that would force him to specify the direction in which he would turn for support, and the preservation of an inherited majority, which would leave the Gaullists in control of parliament. If, to these handicaps, one adds the mediocrity of his television performances and the weakness of the party apparatus that supported him, one can see why the polls that had been so favourable to him before he entered the race registered so sharp a downturn the moment he started campaigning. Whereas in mid-May he had enjoyed 37 or 39 per cent of voting intentions, on 1 June he obtained only 23.4 per cent of votes cast. The collapse of the non-communist left and the shrinkage of the opposition centre placed Pompidou in the best possible position, also boosting the communist candidate, Jacques Duclos.

Making great play of his gravelly man-of-the-soil accent, his humble origins and his resulting store of good sense, Jacques Duclos ran a shrewd and reassuring campaign. Drawing a veil over his lengthy Stalinist past, he presented himself as a spokesman for the working classes, attracting the votes of a large chunk of the non-communist left that had remained unconvinced by Gaston Defferre's candidature. So although the polls in early May only attributed him with 10 per cent of voting intentions, when it came to the actual 1 June vote, Duclos achieved a 21.5 per cent score for his party. Indeed, most analysts took the view that if the campaign had lasted any longer Duclos would have taken Alain Poher's place as first-round runner-up. Be that as it may, the

Table 1. *Presidential election of 1 June 1969: first round*

		Percentage of electorate	Percentage of vote
Electorate	28,774,041	100	
Votes	22,492,059		
Abstentions	6,281,982	21.8	
Spoilt papers	287,372	0.9	
Pompidou	9,761,297	34.0	43.9
Poher	5,201,133	18.1	23.4
Duclos	4,779,539	16.6	21.5
Defferre	1,127,733	3.9	5.0
Rocard	814,051	2.8	3.6
Ducatel	284,697	0.9	1.2
Krivine	236,237	0.8	1.1

way the first-round campaign had developed seemed to make the victory of Pompidou a foregone conclusion (see table 1).

Georges Pompidou's electoral victory

By the evening of 1 June, the verdict of the electorate was decisive: Pompidou had won a clear victory and the chances of his triumphing in the second round were overwhelming. He had broken through the 42 per cent vote share forecast by the polls, whereas every other candidate except Duclos had seen his support collapse. Ahead in every department except one, and with an outright majority of votes in sixteen departments, Pompidou could now be defeated in the second round only if all his opponents formed a coalition against him, a highly improbable scenario. With his election to the presidency a foregone conclusion, all that now mattered to Pompidou were its precise circumstances. Looking to the future, he appealed to Alain Poher to withdraw from a battle that was in any case hopeless, so that he could put himself forward as the candidate of a national majority, confronting the communists head-on. But despite pressure from his closest advisers, from a section of the centre and even from Pierre Sudreau, whom he had thought of appointing prime minister had he won the presidency, Alain Poher now refused to quit the field that he had so long hesitated to enter. Yet it was clear that Poher was about to launch himself into a losing battle. Gaston Defferre withdrew from the race, urging those who had supported him, a paltry 5 per cent, to switch their allegiance to Poher. But Defferre's example was followed neither by the extreme left candidates, Rocard and Krivine, both of whom withdrew from the race without stating their

Table 2. *Presidential election of 15 June 1969: second round*

		Percentage of electorate	Percentage of vote
Electorate	28,761,494	100	
Votes	19,854,087		
Abstentions	8,907,407	31.0	
Spoilt papers	1,295,216	4.5	
Pompidou	10,688,183	37.0	57.5
Poher	7,870,688	27.4	42.4

preference for the second round, nor, more importantly, by the communist party, whose decision could have clinched the outcome, given that a transfer to Poher of their 21.5 per cent of first-round votes would have put him ahead of Pompidou, perhaps enabling him to mobilize the left behind his candidature. The communists, however, took the view that Pompidou and Poher were as alike as Tweedledum and Tweedledee, and therefore urged their supporters to abstain *en masse*. Viewed objectively, this worked in Pompidou's favour. Indeed, the communist party was clearly determined to ensure the failure of Poher, a staunch supporter of the Atlantic Alliance, far preferring a man who was heir to de Gaulle's foreign policy. They were also resolved to do all in their power to avert the formation of a new 'broad federation' which would bring together socialists, radicals, centrists and moderates, isolating them in the ghetto from which they were trying to escape.

For Alain Poher the game was up. He sharpened up his campaign, lambasted the Gaullist 'clan' that had governed France for twelve long years and, in an effort to woo left-wing voters, even promised constitutional changes to confine the president to a role as arbiter. Nothing worked. Assured of victory, Pompidou now felt free to emphasize the *ouverture* of his political approach, inviting on to his platform those centrists and moderates who supported his bid for the presidency.

In the run-up to the second-round vote, opinion polls gave Pompidou a steady 56 per cent of voting intentions, leaving Alain Poher with just 44 per cent. On the night of 15 June, the gap turned out to be even wider (as shown in table 2).

Pompidou's victory was overwhelming. Not only had he crushed his opponents but, in spite of considerable abstention, which was much more widespread than in the second round of the 1965 election, he had scored a higher overall percentage than de Gaulle himself on that occasion. Having remained silent throughout the election campaign, even making a trip to Ireland during the vote itself, the General now sent the new president a brief but cordial message of congratulation. Try as the communists might to christen Pompidou 'Mister One Third', pointing to the number of abstentions, the new president could clearly take pride in securing a huge vote of confidence from the electorate. Rather than risk a leap into the unknown, the French had preferred the option held out to them by Pompidou: 'openness within continuity'. Yet the exact meaning of what was still just an electioneering buzzphrase remained unclear. What policies did Pompidou intend to pursue?

Georges Pompidou's conception of government

The man who moved into the Elysée palace on 20 June 1969 saw himself as the unchallengeable heir to Charles de Gaulle. Yet when responding to questions from the press he repeatedly stated 'I am not General de Gaulle', as if to stress that neither his background, nor his historical stature, nor his character were in any way comparable to those of de Gaulle. For although the new president of the republic claimed to draw on the Gaullist view of politics, he brought to public service a temperament and an approach that were very much his own.

There is no doubt that Gaullism lay at the heart of Pompidou's outlook: after all, Pompidou had spent his entire political career since 1945 in collaboration with the General.[14] It was quite evident that he shared de Gaulle's view as to the ultimate goal of policy: to ensure the grandeur of France through its role in the world and, accordingly, to reject the politics of opposing blocks as a form of subjugation to the United States, safeguarding the independence of the French nation through an independent defence capability, founded on its nuclear *force de frappe*. Equally, Pompidou was convinced that this goal could not be achieved unless France possessed a strong state under the direction of the president of the republic. Whatever ambiguities he had allowed to persist during his election campaign, this belief was the cornerstone of his faith. As he expressed it during his press conference on 10 July 1969: 'the president is at one and the same time the supreme head of the executive, the guardian and guarantor of the constitution, the person charged with setting the government's course and shaping its basic policies, while ensuring and monitoring the smooth operation of public powers: he is both the nation's arbiter and its highest officer.' In *Le Nœud gordien*, a book he wrote after his departure from the Hôtel Matignon in 1968, Pompidou went even further, writing about the successor to de Gaulle, a role he intended for himself: 'lacking the charisma of the man who founded the Fifth Republic, the head of state will have to intervene in the management of the state in a constant and permanent way, and through his day-to-day activity maintain the supremacy that universal suffrage will not of itself automatically confer.'

Yet, like de Gaulle, Pompidou had no wish to see the development of a presidential regime. Here again, *Le Nœud gordien* provides evidence of his loyalty to the constitutional settlement of 1958:

In a multi-party regime, where ruling majorities are formed by coalition, the National Assembly is by its very nature a source of division and instability. This being the case, it is vital to safeguard every provision in our constitution that vests executive power in a head of state who is unaccountable to the Assembly. As for the government, though formed by the president, it is nevertheless appointed in accordance with the need to secure majority backing in the Assembly, and therefore acts as a link. At the same time, the power to dissolve the Assembly, a vital means of pressure, enables the government to follow policies that are acceptable to the majority, though not of its making.

It is quite clear that on this issue Georges Pompidou did indeed represent continuity, holding firmly to the fundamental views of Gaullism.

Yet, even if their objectives were identical, the methods employed by Pompidou differed quite markedly from those used by de Gaulle. In the book that he wrote on the political ideas of Pompidou,[15] Stéphane Rials took care to bring out the contradictions within Pompidou's personality, which were the outcome not only of his background but also of the age in which he lived. Born in 1911 at Montboudif in the Cantal department, Pompidou was an unalloyed product of the republican culture of the first half of the twentieth century. Attached to his rural roots, he clung loyally to the peasant virtues of sound sense, sturdy reliability and hard work but he also shared the peasant's dread of the kind of upheavals that could bring hardship and suffering in their wake. This background gave him both an instinctive distrust for the grand abstract schemes of intellectuals cut off from the day-to-day life of ordinary men and women, and a deep-seated conservatism that became increasingly marked with the passing years. As the son of a primary school teacher, he was a strong believer in the republican ideal of self-advancement through education. It was a path that his own life vividly illustrated. After doing brilliantly at school, he had won a place at the Ecole normale supérieure, which he left with an *agrégation* in French, the highest competitive qualification for those wishing to teach. This complex background formed the framework of Pompidou's life until the outbreak of the Second World War, and provided him with one of the features that most distinguished his behaviour – a pragmatism that inclined him to favour material improvements in individual lives, as long as the beneficiaries fulfilled their part of the bargain by making the required effort, and a taste for practical reforms that was far removed from the resolve to transform the structures of society that the Marxist left advocated. These character traits, which inclined Pompidou towards compromise and conciliation – provided the essentials were not lost in the process – made him shy away from the high-profile outbursts and drama that had constituted de Gaulle's style, favouring instead a calmer way of conducting political business that still left plenty of room for firmness. It is doubtful whether such character traits really justify the 'radical' label that has often been applied to him. After all, he shared little of what was specific to radicalism. On 3 June 1966, when the future president of the republic was asked to outline his political convictions in an interview for the daily newspaper *Paris-Presse*, he gave his article the title: 'Why I am in the centre'. Having rejected the notions of the centre as either 'marshland' morass or pivotal 'hinge', Pompidou supplied the traditional definition of the centre as a 'happy medium':

If, on the other hand, to be in the centre means to take account of people's needs and aspirations, if it means to weigh both the need for movement and change that is obvious in France, and at the same time the need to avoid destroying everything in an old country which has, after all, amassed a lot of intellectual, moral and material goods, then, yes, I am in the centre.[16]

Rather than calling to mind any version of radicalism, with its cult of the small-scale, the political behaviour of the new president was more likely to conjure up François Guizot.

This humanist man of letters, who had compiled an *Anthologie de la poésie française*, had a post-war career that diverged sharply from his experience as a young man. Although a Gaullist, Pompidou had never been a member of the Resistance and he displayed great irritation with the kind of Resistance mythology nurtured by the 'barons' of Gaullism, most of whose careers had been forged in the 'Free French' or internal Resistance crucible. Above all, the years 1945–69 had provided Pompidou with two fundamental experiences that transformed the political culture of his youth and provided him with the convictions that were to characterize his politics as president of the republic: first, the lengthy collaboration with de Gaulle when Pompidou was a member of his cabinet in the post-war provisional government; his thoughtful loyalty during the General's chairmanship of the RPF; the contribution he made as head of cabinet when de Gaulle served as the last prime minister of the Fourth Republic in 1958; and finally the long period of over six years during which he acted as President de Gaulle's prime minister. Closer to de Gaulle than anyone else throughout this entire period, Pompidou had a vision of the grandeur of France and the strong state that accorded perfectly with the General's own views, and was far removed indeed from the notions dear to individualistic radicalism.

Second, Pompidou had pursued a post-war career in banking that had opened his eyes to the economic realities of the modern world, leaving him with the profound conviction that there could be no powerful state and no national grandeur without economic prosperity, the key to which, in a world dominated by market economics and free-market values, was industrialization. Thus, both as prime minister and later as president of the republic, Pompidou laid insistent stress on what came to be known as the 'industrial imperative', a thoroughgoing attachment to free-market liberalism and an admiration for profit that inclined him to favour industrial concentration and the development of large-scale profitable enterprises. In this area one would be hard put to detect the legacy of any radicalism devoted to the defence of the 'small-scale'.

It was with this background of ideas and convictions that on 20 June 1969 Georges Pompidou prepared to govern France, a nation still troubled by the repercussions of the 1968 events, and which in the recent elections had expressed its desire for change.

The Chaban-Delmas government takes shape

On 20 June 1969, the new president of the republic appointed Jacques Chaban-Delmas to serve as his prime minister. Chaban-Delmas had been president of the National Assembly ever since 1958 and his appointment as prime minister had long been expected. Nobody appeared better placed to implement the 'openness within continuity' that the head of state had promised. On the continuity side, Chaban-Delmas was a Gaullist 'baron' who had played a major role in the internal Resistance, rising to the rank of brigadier general at the age of twenty-nine. As mayor of Bordeaux since 1947 and a prominent personality first of the RPF and then of the UDR, the depth of his Gaullism was beyond question. But of all the Gaullists, the new prime minister was without doubt the man who best symbolized political *ouverture*. While loyal to de Gaulle, his loyalty had never been blind or unconditional, and indeed he had refused to fall into line with the General on several occasions: during the 1951 elections over the ban placed by de Gaulle, then president of the RPF, on electoral alliances; again, over the General's refusal to allow Gaullists to participate in government under the Fourth Republic;[17] and then in 1958 over de Gaulle's wish to see Paul Reynaud become president of the National Assembly. Chaban-Delmas had spearheaded that wing of Gaullism that had participated in the government of Mendès France in 1954–5, had joined the Republican Front at the 1956 elections and had exercised power in coalition governments right up until 1958. Moreover, since 1958, in his position as president of the National Assembly, Chaban-Delmas had been anxious to protect parliamentary rights that de Gaulle's style of government frequently eroded – a concern that underscored his proximity to such centrists as the Independent Republicans.[18] Finally, he displayed a degree of social awareness by including within his inner circle such senior civil servants who had been influenced by Mendès France as François Bloch-Lainé or Simon Nora, and even Jacques Delors, a trade unionist of Christian socialist convictions. Yet on constitutional issues Chaban-Delmas, like Pompidou, shared de Gaulle's concept of presidential pre-eminence and on this vital matter he never expressed the slightest doubt. However, owing to the temperaments of the new president and his prime minister, the impression would often be given that, as compared to de Gaulle's time in office, the roles had been reversed. All the drive, creativity and imagination seemed to come from Matignon while at the Elysée the taste for reason, order and balance served to minimize and rein in some of the government's initiatives.[19]

The government that Chaban-Delmas proceeded to form, under the watchful eye of the president, fulfilled Pompidou's desire for greater political inclusiveness within a context of continuity. There were two key government appointments that illustrated and symbolized this approach. Michel Debré, the very embodiment of unconditional loyalty to Gaullism, became minister of defence. The new minister for foreign affairs, Maurice Schumann, on the other hand, while he was an eminent Gaullist Resistance figure, had been one of the leaders of the Christian Democrats at the time of the MRP. The same balancing act was performed in the allocation of ministerial portfolios. The UDR, in control of twenty-seven ministries, found itself in a position of strength with three ministers of state: flanking Michel Debré were Edmond Michelet, succeeding Malraux at cultural affairs, and Roger Frey, who was entrusted with relations with parliament. Indeed, all the different currents within the Gaullist party were represented, with Robert Boulin at health and social security, Henri Duvillard with responsibility for war veterans, Olivier Guichard in charge of education, Robert Galley at post and telecommunications, Albin Chalandon at housing and equipment, and Henri Rey placed in charge of overseas departments and territories. To these should be added François-Xavier Ortoli, a former aide to Pompidou, who became minister for industrial development and scientific research.

But the government also threw its doors open to those who had backed Pompidou's candidature. The centrists, now the third pillar of the majority, were well represented, though less in numerical terms than in the importance of the ministries placed in their charge. René Pleven became minister of justice, Jacques Duhamel minister of agriculture, and Joseph Fontanet minister of labour, employment and population. It was the Independent Republicans and especially their leader Valéry Giscard d'Estaing who were left with the meanest pickings, paying the price for supporting the 'wrong' side in the April referendum. Indeed, Pompidou only allowed Giscard d'Estaing to return to the ministry of finance after Antoine Pinay had turned down the position. Meanwhile, Raymond Mondon became minister for transport, Raymond Marcellin minister of the interior and André Bettencourt minister for national and regional development – but then both Marcellin and Bettencourt were well known for their reservations regarding Giscard d'Estaing's leadership of their party.[20]

Whereas the selection of ministers clearly entailed Pompidou's approval, the prime minister seems to have had his hands free to appoint the particularly numerous (twenty or so) junior ministers who appeared to be chosen on the basis of a form of political carve-up that Pompidou found infinitely irritating.[21]

However, the president was convinced, as he had written in *Le Nœud gordien*, that 'the only alternatives before us are to accept the well-camouflaged but swift return of an Assembly-dominated regime or to accentuate the presidential character of our institutions'. Having decided, for his part, to pursue the second of these two courses, Pompidou reorganized the Elysée departments accordingly, abolishing the duality inherent in the existence of both a general secretariat and a cabinet by upgrading the former. The president appointed Michel Jobert, a former supporter of Mendès France who had switched his allegiance to Pompidou, as secretary general, with Edouard Balladur as his assistant, and he placed around them a team of men most of whom had been his close collaborators at Matignon. Whereas this team welcomed and supported the appointment of Chaban-Delmas, two other presidential advisers did not. Pierre Juillet, a conservative diehard, strongly disapproved of the new prime minister's reformist streak, while Marie-France Garaud nurtured a fierce hostility towards him. Both advisers were to prove tireless in their efforts to open up a gulf between Pompidou and Chaban-Delmas, laying insistent emphasis on what they saw as the excess of parliamentary zeal apparent in the conduct of the prime minister whom they also reproached for his progressive views and for adopting an attitude reminiscent of prime ministers under the Fourth Republic.[22]

For the time being, however, it was up to the new team to prove its ability, and in fact, until the end of 1971, its initiatives seemed to be crowned with success.

2   The 'New Society', 1969–1971

Following the election of Georges Pompidou, the process of forming a government together with the parliamentary recess placed the new president firmly in the driving seat of decision-making. But with the return of parliament, the wide-ranging programme outlined by Jacques Chaban-Delmas in his speech on 16 September, and the spate of initiatives that he then launched, a question was posed that had never before arisen under the Fifth Republic: who governed France? Was it the president, who was unaccountable to parliament, or was it the prime minister, as leader of a government whose task was, in the words of the constitution, 'to determine and conduct the politics of the nation'? A more parliamentary view of government thus regained ground, even though, as we have seen, Pompidou had given his unambiguous backing to the presidentialist view. From 1969 to 1972 this remained a live political issue and the spectre of split-power 'diarchy' stalked the regime, driving a wedge between the Elysée and Matignon, while the president's stated or implicit reservations fuelled a permanent revolt against the prime minister, gradually undermining his position. Yet the logic of the Fifth Republic, fully supported by Chaban-Delmas, left no trace of a doubt: it was the president who governed the nation. Nowhere was this clearer than in the field of foreign policy.

Foreign policy: holding the line

If there is one branch of politics that forms an incontestable presidential *domaine réservé*, it is foreign policy. Like de Gaulle before him, Pompidou devoted much of his time to this policy area, with the assistance of Maurice Schumann whom he met for talks several times a week. In fact, the line that Pompidou followed did not differ substantially from that pursued by de Gaulle, though the new president's temperament and the views of his minister for foreign affairs (who did not always see eye to eye with Pompidou) helped to soften its implementation and to avoid either crises or sensational outbursts.

French foreign policy appeared to proceed precisely as before. Pompidou had no intention whatever of questioning either of its two main planks: the drive for national independence backed by the *force de frappe*, or relations between France and the two superpowers. The desire to build on de Gaulle's legacy was particularly apparent in Pompidou's attempt to give France an independent Mediterranean policy. Despite the misgivings of a section of the public, Pompidou confirmed the stance adopted at the time of the Six Day War, when de Gaulle had supported the Arabs and voiced hostility towards Israeli policy, accusing the Jewish state of acting in a domineering manner towards the Arab world. In concrete terms, this line had led to an embargo on arms shipments to the Near East.[1] Pompidou was strongly influenced in this area of foreign policy by the pro-Arab lobby, whose principal representatives were a former left-wing Gaullist, Philippe de Saint-Robert, and a former Vichy collaborator, Jacques Benoist-Méchin.[2] Indeed, it was on Benoist-Méchin's initiative that France not only sought to improve its relations with Morocco, leading to the visit of King Hassan II to France in February 1970 but also, in spite of Schumann's reluctance, tried to forge links with Colonel Gaddafi, who had just seized power in Libya. When talks began on supplying French military planes and tanks, Pompidou argued that Libya was not after all involved in the war with Israel and that, if France did not deliver the weapons requested, the Colonel would surely turn to the Soviet Union. The president's initiative raised a general outcry both abroad and in France. Israel accused France of committing a one-sided violation of the arms embargo and in the United States the Jewish community organized a protest against the French decision. In France itself, Michel Poniatowski, general secretary of the Independent Republicans and loyal lieutenant to Valéry Giscard d'Estaing, called Michel Debré, the minister for defence, an 'arms dealer', comparing him to Sir Basil Zaharof, a famous early twentieth-century arms trafficker.[3]

Indeed, Mediterranean policy presented France with one setback after another and damaged the president's reputation. In December 1969, the news leaked out that five gunboats that the Israeli navy had ordered from France, and which had been impounded in Cherbourg under the terms of the embargo, had in fact left the port bound in theory for Norway but in fact for Haifa, where they arrived several days later. This made the French government look ridiculous and revealed that the president's pro-Arab policy had the active disapproval of a section of the French civil service that had gone along with a clear breach of the embargo.[4] The soaring ambitions of Colonel Gaddafi also became apparent, persuading the French government to stagger its arms

deliveries to Libya in order to prevent them from being used in the
Arab–Israeli conflict.

Yet Pompidou's greatest setback was in relations with Algeria.
Although, in his broadcast address on 15 December 1969, Pompidou
had announced 'a forthcoming re-establishment of all our relations with
Northern Africa', tension with Algeria mounted steadily. On 13 June
1970, Colonel Boumédienne suspended the negotiations that were
under way to reassess the fiscal reference price for crude oil produced by
French companies, and on 21 July he decided unilaterally to increase by
50 per cent the crude oil base price on which the companies' tax bills
were calculated. Pompidou insisted on playing things down, considering
Franco-Algerian relations to be so important as to render this forced
takeover of secondary importance. The Quai d'Orsay and the prime
minister's office resumed talks. In the autumn, however, Pompidou
moved to place François-Xavier Ortoli, minister for industrial development, in charge of the talks. But it was in vain. On 24 February 1971,
Boumédienne nationalized French oil companies and in April he
demanded that France pay for its oil supplies in advance, suspending
loading until his demands were met. France could merely acknowledge
the collapse of its policy and resolve that the 'privileged relationship'
between France and Algeria was now finally at an end.[5]

Relations with the two superpowers revealed the same continuity and
the same disappointment. In February 1970, Pompidou made an official
visit to the United States, during the course of which he intended to
restate France's reservations regarding American policy in Vietnam and
the international role of the dollar, while moving away from the crude
and visceral anti-Americanism that France had displayed since 1965.
The conversations with the Americans went very smoothly, even if
Nixon's and Pompidou's views turned out to be diametrically opposed
on almost every issue. It was the French president's Middle Eastern
policy that in the end turned the trip into something of a fiasco. On 28
February 1970 in Chicago, the French head of state was booed by a
crowd of pro-Israeli demonstrators whom the local police made very
little effort to restrain. The incident prompted Madame Pompidou's
immediate return to France and cast a shadow of failure over the entire
trip, rendering yet harsher any analysis of French relations with the
United States.[6]

Following the pattern set by de Gaulle, the refusal to fall into line with
United States policy went hand in hand with cordial relations with the
Soviet Union, though without any political *rapprochement*. Apart from
underlining the importance of France's role on the world stage,
Pompidou could not expect much from his trip to Moscow in October

1970, especially in view of his misgivings regarding Chancellor Brandt's *Ostpolitik*, which he feared might eventually, in the event of an American withdrawal from Europe, bind Germany to the Eastern bloc. On his arrival in Moscow, the French president immediately outlined the limits of his policy, declaring that, 'France is a Western country and intends to remain so without restriction'. In these circumstances, nothing very substantial could be expected to result from the visit. The final communiqué, with its statement of the need to put an end to the 'policy of opposing blocs' (just two years after the Soviet intervention in Czechoslovakia) and its expression of approval for the German–Soviet treaty of August 1970 (which Pompidou evidently did not care for) demonstrated the limitations of the exercise. The only really positive outcome was the decision that the French and Soviet foreign ministers would henceforth meet on a regular basis (in theory twice a year), which gave the French the sensation that their country was a world player.[7]

In fact, Pompidou had now realized that France, a middle-ranking power, could no longer play a major independent world role and that, having eschewed the verbal fireworks and make-believe drama that the stature of de Gaulle had managed to transform into historical events, it could no longer delude itself on this score. The only remaining means for France to play an international role commensurate with its ambitions was its European policy.

The enlargement of the EEC

On the European issue, the views of Georges Pompidou differed only slightly from those of his predecessor. What de Gaulle saw as a means for his country to open itself up to international trade and find a market for its agricultural produce, Pompidou viewed as a 'necessity' flowing from the very existence of a European civilization and people.[8]

Of course, the new president would have no truck with any notion of a supranational Europe. He shared the General's conviction that Europe could be nothing other than an association of its member states, since the state was the only concrete expression of the nation. Also, Europe must be 'European', that is, not dependent on the United States, and 'balanced', that is, prepared to enter into political cooperation with Eastern Europe, China and the Third World.[9] On this point, there was not the slightest divergence between Pompidou and de Gaulle.

Nor were there any striking differences in terms of policy implementation. It is true that, whereas de Gaulle had twice created a sensation by vetoing moves to enable the United Kingdom to join the Common Market, Pompidou smoothed the way for British membership. Circumstances, however, had changed. Germany had emerged as an economic power, the Deutschmark appeared able to lay down the financial law in Europe, and *Ostpolitik* had demonstrated that the Federal Republic now intended to shake off the tutelage of the victors of the Second World War and act as a major power. British entry might now provide a counterweight to German power in Europe, helping to re-establish a sense of balance and thus shore up French influence.[10]

Yet Pompidou would only entertain an enlargement of the Common Market on certain conditions. Before any new members could join, European integration would have to be completed and deepened and France's partners would have to undertake not to increase the powers of the European Commission. On this basis, Pompidou was willing to take the initiative of opening discussions with the four countries that had applied for membership (the United Kingdom, Ireland, Denmark and Norway). This was the position that the French president advocated at the six-member EEC summit that met in The Hague on 1 December 1969 and, by and large, he got his way. France gave the go-ahead for negotiations on EEC enlargement in exchange for her partners' adoption, by 1 January 1970, of the final financial ruling on the Common Agricultural Policy.[11]

The victory of the Conservatives in the British general election of 18 June 1970 facilitated matters by placing at the helm of the country a convinced European in the person of Edward Heath. It also prompted the French president, speaking in Strasbourg on 27 June, to issue a passionate plea for the *construction* of Europe. Negotiations nonetheless proved long and hard, becoming ensnared on the international status of the pound and the fate of the Commonwealth. It was not until Prime Minister Heath and President Pompidou met in Paris in May 1971 that the most serious stumbling-blocks could be removed. Finally, on 22 January 1972, the United Kingdom, Denmark, Ireland and Norway signed their treaty of Common Market membership, to take effect on 1 January 1973. In the case of Norway, however, owing to the 'no' result in the referendum held to decide the issue, EEC membership was shelved.[12]

Success on the European stage, casting Pompidou as the guiding light of European politics, enabled him to ride out the poor results of his Mediterranean policy and the disappointments of his trips to the United States and the Soviet Union. To illustrate the president's new prestige, when he met President Nixon in the Azores in December 1971, it was in Pompidou's capacity as representative of a nascent Europe that the president of the United States confided to him his decision to devalue the dollar, even though in August Pompidou had sharply criticized

American financial policy following the decision to suspend the convertibility of the dollar.

When it came to assessing Pompidou's foreign policy, the French seemed to be particularly struck by the change in style introduced by the new president, regarding his approach as a renunciation of the grand global goals of General de Gaulle. When asked the question, 'at present, would you say that the influence that France exerts in the world is very great/great/rather slight or very slight?', 75 per cent of those polled in April 1968, under de Gaulle's presidency, had replied either 'great' or 'very great'. By January 1970, this had fallen to 59 per cent. On the other hand, public opinion took the view that, compared with de Gaulle, Pompidou had achieved a *rapprochement* with the 'Anglo-Saxons'. Asked in January 1970 whether they felt that since the time of de Gaulle their country's relations with Britain and the United States had improved, 45 per cent and 40 per cent respectively said they had. However, 35 per cent and 42 per cent respectively of those questioned replied that relations with these countries had remained virtually unchanged.[13]

While retaining complete control over French foreign policy, Pompidou also made his mark on the economic choices facing the country, in many respects pursuing the policy he had introduced as prime minister.[14]

A buoyant economy amid danger signals

No judgement can be delivered on an economic policy without taking into consideration the economic circumstances to which it is applied: after all, government can only go along with, temper or try to correct world economic trends. It would therefore be absurd artificially to cordon off the five years of Pompidou's presidency from the preceding period during which he played a vital role as prime minister. Besides, in any free-market economy one has to take account of the strategies pursued by business, which do not simply translate top-down political decision-making.

The Pompidou years marked the high point in a boom that the French economy had been enjoying ever since the 1950s. It was a global phenomenon with considerable impact on France and more so during Pompidou's presidency than previously, since it was at this time that industry became an engine for growth. Between 1969 and 1973, French industrial productivity increased by 7 per cent a year, as against 5.5 per cent between 1960 and 1968, and the investment rate approached 30 per cent of GNP. During these years France experienced a rate of expansion that placed it immediately behind Japan but ahead of both the United States and the Federal Republic of Germany.[15] These figures bore witness to the success of France's policy of rapid industrialization, the aim of which was to catch up with competitor countries. Yet this choice of policy ushered in dramatic changes, transforming the structure of the working population. Between 1969 and 1974, the number of miners fell by 9.2 per cent a year, agricultural workers by over 6 per cent, and farmers by 5.6 per cent. Meanwhile, the percentage of middle-ranking and senior managers in the economy rose by 3.9 per cent and 5.6 per cent a year respectively. Between 1969 and 1974, the drive to industrialize achieved a spectacular 90 per cent increase in exports.[16]

While in part this was certainly the outcome of international economic circumstances, it also sprang from a deliberate policy choice in favour of a high growth rate, regardless of resulting inflationary tensions. Whereas Germany opted to rein in its growth in order to maintain stability in its balance of payments, hold down prices and ensure the currency was strong, even if this meant a slowdown in industrial production and a slight rise in unemployment, France under Pompidou took the opposite path. Breaking with General de Gaulle's resolve not to devalue the franc in spite of strong inflationary pressures resulting from the sizeable salary increases agreed under the Grenelle accords, Pompidou, in agreement with finance minister Valéry Giscard d'Estaing, decided to devalue by 12.5 per cent on 20 August 1969 in order to place the country on a sounder financial footing. This was followed on 28 August by a plan intended to reduce state spending and so return the balance of payments to the black, to encourage private saving, implement a credit squeeze, freeze prices and encourage exports. But having implemented this package of measures, Pompidou plumped for growth, aiming for an annual 7.5 per cent increase in industrial output – lower than Japan's, but much higher than that of any other major industrial nation. The clear goal was to modernize the country by loosening financial constraints. There followed a spate of wage increases to stimulate consumption and a monetary and fiscal policy tailored to encourage investment through low interest rates and easy credit. As a result, however, inflation stuck at the relatively high rate of 6 to 7 per cent a year.[17]

Introduced against the background of a favourable world economic climate, French policy (unlike German policy, for example) ignored the danger signals that were just beginning to make themselves felt internationally and which would soon compromise growth and make Pompidou's presidency the last chapter in the thirty-year-long boom that with hindsight was celebrated as the *trente glorieuses*. In the end, these signs of imbalance, perceptible as early as 1967, called into question the foundations of the global boom that had lasted since the 1950s. The first evidence of the looming crisis was the exhaustion of American economic growth, owing to a slowdown in labour productivity and a concomitant increase in the United States' foreign trade deficit. In Europe, the imbalances partly stemmed from the growth in unemployment caused by the arrival on the jobs market of the immediate post-war baby-boomers. The main factor, however, was a rash of salary claims that kept alive social conflicts that had arisen from the desire to see the fruits of growth shared more equally between wages and profits. These strains combined to produce turbulence within the international monetary system, registering the dysfunctions of the world economy and their attendant inflationary phenomena. The first warning sign was the devaluation of the pound in 1967, followed in 1968 by the United States' decision to suspend the covertibility of dollars into gold by private dollar holders. In what turned out to be a vain attempt to halt speculation against the dollar, the United States created new international liquid assets with special drawing rights intended to pose no competitive threat to the dollar. The devaluation of the franc in August 1969 and the revaluation of the Deutschmark in October 1969 failed to restore balance. While France went for growth, other countries raised interest rates and restricted credit in an effort to squeeze inflation out of the system.[18] It was against this background of severe monetary instability and threats to world growth that President Pompidou decided to pursue his expansionist policy with renewed vigour, convinced that growth was vital to the maintenance of social peace in France. This rested on the notion that the turbulence experienced would be short-lived. It turned out to be a false assumption.

The economic policy of Georges Pompidou

Given that Pompidou's overriding aim was to modernize France through rapid industrialization and make French companies competitive in the world market, the 'industrial imperative' was inevitably at the heart of his economic policy. With the assistance of Bernard Esambert, his technical adviser on industrial issues, and François-Xavier Ortoli, his minister for industrial development, Pompidou took charge of this field of policy, personally drafting the introduction to the Sixth Plan in 1971, setting out the main planks of the country's economic policy.

One of the principal components of Pompidou's industrial policy was the emphasis placed on large-scale technological and industrial projects. Their purpose was not only to guarantee France's independence by placing her at the forefront of the latest technologies (electronics, computers and the nuclear industry), but to tighten the security of her strategic supplies (oil and uranium), and to provide her with a national defence capability (aeronautics and space). In all these areas the French state intervened directly, either by acting as project manager through its own research laboratories or publicly owned companies, or by offering contracts or special deals to private firms or to public–private partnerships. For Pompidou this represented a major personal commitment.

In civil aviation, it was as prime minister at the end of the 1960s that Georges Pompidou had promoted the merger of Nord-Aviation, Sud-Aviation and SEREB into SNIAS (Société nationale industrielle aérospatiale). From 1967 onwards, Pompidou had advocated cooperation between the French, German and British aviation industries, which culminated in 1969 with the launch of the Franco-German Airbus project. The year 1969 also saw the unveiling of the Mercure project. Finally, cooperation between SNECMA and General Electric enabled French industry to make major progress in civilian reactors, with the launch in 1973 of the CFM 56. Rather less successful was the decision to pursue the Concorde project, whose commercial profitability was already in considerable doubt.

In the field of space, it was Pompidou's stubborn determination that convinced his more wary partners to pursue European cooperation and, even after the failure of the Europa rocket, to agree in 1972 to consider the creation of a European space agency and the start of the Ariane programme.

The issue that arose at this time in the civilian nuclear industry was whether the generation of French natural uranium graphite-gas reactors should be continued or scrapped. Marcel Boiteux, managing director of EDF, recommended that it should be scrapped, arguing that research had not made sufficient progress and that the electricity it generated would be too costly. He therefore advocated the adoption on licence from Westinghouse of the American enriched-uranium model. In November 1969, Pompidou arrived at the decision that the Commissariat à l'énergie atomique (CEA) should press on with research into the French model, while also giving EDF the go-ahead to launch in 1970 a programme entailing the construction of several massive power stations following the American design. Then in 1971 the government floated the idea of building a European uranium enrichment plant, to be named Eurodif, at Tricastin, south of Montélimar. Reorganized under the direction of André Giraud, the CEA became the project manager of a concerted programme designed to make France self-sufficient in energy via the nuclear option.[19] It was the same thinking that had led

Pompidou as prime minister in 1966 to decide on the merger of the numerous state-owned oil companies to create the ELF-Aquitaine group under the chairmanship of Pierre Guillaumat, a process that was pursued throughout Pompidou's term as president.[20]

Lastly, Pompidou's interest in advanced technologies acted as a stimulus to computer science and telecommunications. In the former field, CII (Compagnie internationale d'informatique), which had hitherto specialized in scientific and military computers, joined Philips and Siemens to manufacture computer systems. In the field of telecommunications, investments made by the DGT (Direction générale des télécommunications) paved the way for the industrial expansion of electronic communications technology by the CIT-Alcatel group.

This determination that France should embrace the latest technologies was further illustrated by the construction from 1970 onwards, with financial backing from the state, of the Fos-sur-Mer steel complex. Using the Japanese water-based steel-making process, with output earmarked for export, Fos provided yet further proof – if proof were needed – of the government's belief in the pursuit of a growth-led economy.[21]

If, as part of a drive to modernize, the acquisition of ground-breaking technologies was one of the main planks of Pompidou's economic policy, the other, which he had previously pursued as prime minister, was the promotion of business concentration. The objective was to make French industry competitive by enabling French firms to reach a size that would give them scale economies in manufacturing, research and marketing. Particular emphasis was laid on heavy industry and plant manufacturing. In the majority of cases, the state did not intervene directly in company mergers, contenting itself with encouraging them with various financial measures and tax breaks: loans from the public revenue department through the intermediary of FDES (Fonds de développement économique et social), financial assistance for exporters, support for French industrial and commercial investments abroad, tax incentives to help companies undergoing merger to revalue their assets, a consolidated profit tax system for companies investing abroad, etc. While mergers were usually initiated by the companies themselves or by the commercial banks that increasingly controlled them, the state still had to give its go-ahead and the president thus retained a crucial influence. For example, in order to safeguard national independence, he intervened to prevent the purchase by Westinghouse of shares held by the Belgian group Empain in Jeumont-Schneider, a company entrusted with the construction of French nuclear power stations. Similarly, in 1971, Pompidou stepped in to block the merger between Rhône-Poulenc and Saint-Gobain-Pont-à-Mousson.[22]

The fruits of this policy of providing state encouragement, and sometimes even a positive lead for mergers, form an impressive list. In the steel industry, as a response to state-led investment, large-scale mergers occurred around the Usinor and Sidelor groups. In metallurgy, the production of aluminium, alloys, titanium and zirconium was brought together by the merger of Saint-Gobain, Pont-à-Mousson and Péchiney-Ugine-Kuhlmann. In the chemicals industry, Rhône-Poulenc took over the chemical divisions of Péchiney, Saint-Gobain and Naphtachimie. A further regrouping process involved Péchiney-Ugine-Kuhlmann and the new chemicals group ATO, which included both the CFP (Compagnie française des pétroles) oil companies and ELF, and to which the chemical division of Charbonnages de France was added. The publicly held potassium mines of Alsace and the national industrial nitrogen 'Office' were merged to form the state-run Entreprise minière et chimique (EMC). In the construction materials sector, the main development was the merger of Saint-Gobain (glass and fibres) and Pont-à-Mousson (cast iron). In the field of mechanical and electrical systems, restructuring occurred around Schneider (with the creation of the Creusot-Loire group) and the Compagnie générale d'éléctricité. In electronics, it was the Thomson-Brandt group that acted as magnet. Large-scale mergers also occurred in the cement, timber, paper and rubber industries.[23]

This resolute pursuit of the mergers policy that he had first championed as prime minister now raised a key issue for Pompidou as president, namely the fear that such far-reaching changes might trigger dramatic upheavals within French society. First and foremost, Pompidou feared that the restructuring that he was promoting might lead to factory closures, thereby compounding regional imbalances, with an increase in industrial concentration in the more dynamic regions, contrasting with the desertification of parts of the country deemed less suitable for the siting of industrial plants. He was also fearful that the productivist logic of his policy might lead to the destruction of the environment, spurring into action the green opposition that the 1968 crisis had revealed in all its vigour. Lastly, the president was worried by the potentially fatal threat to the small and medium-sized businesses that he regarded as important for the preservation of the social fabric and which he was determined to sustain in those sectors where he believed they had an economic future.

In these three areas, Pompidou's economic policy therefore incorporated measures designed to mitigate any negative repercussions resulting from the promotion of high-tech industry and the encouragement of large-scale industrial conglomerates. In terms of regional policy,

Pompidou continued to support the work of DATAR (Direction de l'aménagement du territoire et de l'action régionale) which, as prime minister, he had created in 1963. DATAR served to place a brake on the growth of the Paris region, while overseeing the balanced development of other major conurbations as well as medium-sized towns. It also sought to attract business to regions that were suffering severe population loss. Brittany thus became home to the electronics industry, Toulouse and the south-west specialized in aerospace, while tourism was developed along the Aquitaine and Languedoc coastlines.

A growing awareness of environmental issues led to the creation in January 1971 of a ministry for the environment, headed by Robert Poujade, until then the general secretary of the UDR. Poujade quickly introduced a series of measures to combat industrial pollution, setting up catchment agencies to prevent river pollution, building water purification systems, and monitoring landfill sites and industrial polluters.

Lastly, the desire to preserve a network of small and medium-sized firms led to the creation of a junior ministry for small and medium-sized business, headed by the UDR deputy Gabriel Kaspereit. Equally – given the banks' reluctance to extend credit to small and medium-sized firms – it was largely with a view to providing them with investment finance that IDI (Institut de développement industriel) was set up in 1969.[24]

The overall economic policy that Pompidou implemented was crystal clear. The goal was to achieve strong growth in order to modernize the nation's industrial base and secure international competitiveness, while addressing imbalances arising from rapid industrialization and thus preventing French society from falling to pieces under the impact of all the upheavals that such a process entailed. This policy obviously went hand in hand with social measures designed to win broad popular support for the president's goals. But a difference in emphasis soon emerged between the president and his prime minister, whose role in this area was of the greatest significance.

The 'New Society'

On 16 September 1969, before an extraordinary session of the National Assembly, in a speech that was to create huge interest, the prime minister Chaban-Delmas laid out his general political stance.

The first thing to be remarked upon was that the prime minister's style brought to mind Mendès France rather than General de Gaulle, and the second was that his analysis owed a great deal to the Club Jean-Moulin and to the sociologist Michel Crozier. The approach taken in the speech was clearly left-wing and bore the imprint of the prime minister's principal private secretary, the inspector of finances, Simon Nora, a former associate of Mendès France. In concrete terms, the statement presented a diagnosis of the state of French society that pulled no punches: France was industrially backward, saddled with a fragile economy, organized around archaic and conservative institutions, and subject to a sprawling and ineffective state machine. To address French society's many logjams (the speech included a veiled analysis of the crisis of May 1968), the prime minister called for the creation of a *Nouvelle Société* that would be 'prosperous, young, generous and liberated'. With this in mind, he outlined a number of proposals, which he grouped under four headings: training and the provision of information, the transformation of the role played by the state, the improved competitiveness of the French economy, and the rejuvenation of social structures. He immediately set out the first measures he intended to take: the liberalization of the ORTF (Office de radio-télévision française), the granting of managerial independence to nationalized companies like SNCF and EDF–GDF, the development of training programmes, the creation of the Industrial Development Institute, the extension of holidays and increases to both the minimum pension and the national minimum wage (SMIG).[25]

This ambitious and wide-ranging programme, tracing the outlines of a modern democracy that Mendès France himself would not have repudiated, opened up an unbridgeable gulf between, on the one hand, the prime minister and, on the other, the president of the republic and the parliamentary majority, though the latter two positions remained distinct throughout.

Tensions with the president were of two types. First, there was Pompidou's irritation with what he viewed as a deplorable switch in roles. He held that it was up to the president to set out the main goals of policy and that the prime minister's job was to find ways of achieving them. Chaban-Delmas had just assigned his government a set of objectives that he had underpinned with a far-reaching philosophy of social relations within a modern industrial state. As a result, the president's second press conference just six days later, on 22 September, seemed distinctly prosaic and uninspired. It cannot have been pleasant for the head of state to read the comment penned by Jacques Fauvet in the following day's *Le Monde*: 'the prime minister having delivered a presidential address to the National Assembly last week, the head of state was condemned to make a prime-ministerial declaration to the press'.[26] Pompidou's irritation was made all the more acute by the fact that he had not been able to read Chaban-Delmas' speech before it was delivered to the National Assembly: first the prime minister had forgotten to submit it to him, and then he had submitted it too late for the head of state to peruse it before it was delivered.[27] In Pompidou's eyes this offhand attitude was compounded by the fact that the offending speech made only one brief and passing mention of the president of the republic.

But the second and more substantial grounds for presidential displeasure lay in the content of Chaban-Delmas' speech, and indeed the whole notion of a 'New Society'. It was not as if the majority of the reforms proposed by the prime minister were rejected by the president. Indeed, industrialization, an attack on red tape, improvements in training and providing people with information, and liberalization were all policies that chimed with Pompidou's own ideas. What shocked the president was the manner in which they were presented, the generalizing, abstract and intellectual discourse that the prime minister adopted to frame his proposed reforms, poles apart from Pompidou's desire to base action on good peasant common-sense. The mere mention of the 'New Society' was enough to make him bristle with irritation, and indeed the term elicited from him nothing but sarcastic remarks and a stream of jibes that the various members of his entourage then obligingly repeated. Pompidou underscored his opposition to Chaban-Delmas' approach by repeatedly stating that it was real people who interested him, not an abstract society. Yet for all this, Pompidou did nothing to undermine his prime minister's desire for reform, since it was after all perfectly consistent with his own.

Relations between the prime minister and the majority in the National Assembly were a rather different matter. While the Independent Republicans and the centrists belonging to Jacques Duhamel's Centre Démocratie et Progrès did nothing to hide their pleasure at the prime minister's stance, the same could not be said for the majority of the UDR group. After all, they had been elected, it should be remembered, in June 1968 on a tide of conservatism, and they viewed as a form of betrayal not only the prime minister's left-leaning speech, couched in a style that could not fail to offend them, but also his attempt to respond to the issues raised by the events of 1968 by establishing a 'New Society'. Indeed, many UDR members saw the prime minister's speech as an attempt at wooing the left that threatened to marginalize the UDR – or at least a section of it – by building a majority around the centre-left. There was certainly some truth in this: Chaban-Delmas' aim was in effect to isolate the communists and their allies, while securing the support of the reformist left. The reservations of UDR members, moreover, were shared by the president, even if Pompidou was not clearly identified with UDR conservatism. On 17 September, the National

Assembly backed the programme that Chaban-Delmas had set out in his speech by 369 votes to 85. But the foot-dragging among the UDR was so self-evident that François Mitterrand, without any fear of contradiction, could tell the prime minister: 'When I look at you, I have no doubt as to your sincerity; but when I look at your majority, I doubt your success.'

Be that as it might, as long as the 'New Society' remained the prime minister's programme, and concrete improvements in people's actual lives continued to be the president's line, the two men could agree on the implementation of a social policy involving sweeping reforms. And, whatever name one chose to give them, this amounted to an attempt to adapt French society to the new conditions thrown up by economic growth, while also seeking to respond to the crisis of 1968.

Policies for social progress

The Chaban-Delmas government oversaw the introduction of a set of bold social and industrial relations policies, the three main planks of which were 'contractual' policy, the implementation of procedures for tackling low wages, and measures on training and education.

The key to the new approach was contractual policy. It was the government's clear aim to replace class struggle and widespread industrial conflict, along with its litany of strikes and lost production, with a culture of negotiation, making it possible to resolve labour disputes through balanced compromise. This seemed all the more feasible in a situation where continued strong growth made it appear reasonable to imagine that a more equitable division of the fruits of growth might pave the way for far-reaching change in the nature of social relationships. To show the way, the state would set an example of collective negotiation in the area under its direct control: the public sector. This was not embarked upon without careful consideration. Indeed the idea of placing relationships between the state and public-sector companies on a contractual footing had been launched in 1967 in a report by Chaban-Delmas' own principal private secretary, Simon Nora. Yet the policy that was implemented in 1969 went further than the proposals set out in Nora's 1967 report, introducing two innovative and complementary procedures: *contrats de programme* and *contrats de progrès*. 'Programme contracts' were to be negotiated between the state and public companies, eventually granting autonomy to the EDF–GDF, SNCF and RATP. 'Progress contracts', on the other hand, were to be reached between the newly autonomous company and the unions, with the state thus withdrawing from the business of determining salary levels. This new approach produced widely differing agreements in different companies, though all entailed an increase in the overall wages bill. Salaries, though now indexed either to GNP or to the company's own output, were ringed round with let-out clauses that could be activated by excessive price rises. These contracts cleared the path for the introduction of wages policies, most of which included clauses on the abolition of low wages, reductions in working hours, employment security guarantees to cover restructuring programmes, and training. Finally, the need to monitor the implementation of the agreements reached by the 'social partners' produced a form of joint administration, obliging the two sides to adopt procedures that entailed ongoing collaboration, and to defend the contractual agreements before their respective constituencies. The objective of contractual policy was to bring about a fundamental shift in the way that the two sides of industry related to one another. This was also why the unions, even though they had all signed contractual agreements, were reluctant from 1970–1 onwards to enter into collective negotiations that might undermine their identity as bulwarks of opposition to bourgeois society or coopt them into the system they were intent on fighting by leading them down the path of collective negotiation.[28]

The second thrust in implementing the new social policy related to the lifting of low wages in line with the decision to increase incomes as French growth proceeded, in order to achieve a fairer division of its fruits. In this area, the government's approach is well illustrated by two fundamental measures: the payment of wages on a monthly basis, and the introduction of a national minimum wage indexed to growth (SMIC). Unlike contractual policy, the monthly payment of wages was originally the president's idea, even if it fell to the prime minister to implement it. It was during his election campaign that Pompidou, no doubt on the advice of Georges Levard, former general secretary of the CFDT, had introduced the idea in order, as he stated, to reduce 'the gulf that somehow separates the elite, paid monthly, from the infantry, the rank and file, paid by the hour'. In the eyes of the president, distrustful of grand theoretical constructions tailored for intellectuals, the payment of wages on a monthly basis was just the kind of concrete measure that, in practice, could improve the life of the most disadvantaged. Instead of being paid by the hour or on the basis of their output, they could now rely on a monthly salary including the payment of holidays and, if they fell ill, took maternity leave or suffered an accident at work, they would receive benefits that took account of how long they had been with the firm, a factor also taken into consideration if they were sacked or when they reached retirement. Having cleared the plan with a 'committee of wise men', on 11 March 1970 the council of ministers recommended that the social partners open negotiations with a view to implementing the reform. Accordingly, on 20 April 1970, the CNPF (Centre national du patronat français) and the unions signed an accord, followed by discussions in the various union branches, culminating in 1971 in more than forty separate agreements on the monthly payment of wages.[29]

No less important was the law passed on 11 January 1970 which replaced the SMIG (salaire minimum interprofessionnel garanti), a price-indexed minimum income introduced in 1952, with the SMIC (salaire minimum interprofessionnel de croissance) which, as its name indicated, was indexed to growth, i.e. to increases in output and average wages. In the economic climate of the time, the objective of the SMIC was to give the purchasing power of wage-earners a significant boost.

To this effort to improve the conditions of wage-earners, one should probably add the decision by Renault under the law of 21 January 1970 to allocate to its workers a small portion of its capital – even if the results of this measure were limited. This scheme had in fact been provided for by the 1967 law on profit-sharing, which the president viewed as an experiment. Regarded with distrust by trades unionists, with hostility from the most conservative wing of the UDR, and with trepidation by employers, it was a measure that proved short-lived.

The third area of social policy to be addressed by the new government, relating to the provision of training and information, was enacted by laws passed on 16 July 1971. These aimed to reform the process of apprenticeship, raise standards in the teaching of technical subjects, grant technical diplomas an equal status with mainstream qualifications and, above all, launch vocational training. The small print broadened the entitlement to training leave that had been introduced in a union–employer accord of July 1970, and specified that costs were to be covered by the employers.

Despite Pompidou's manifest distrust for theoretical statements of doctrine, the measures taken in the first years of his presidency clearly sought to transform industrial relations, replacing class struggles with contractual agreements befitting a democratic society governed by the laws of free-market capitalism. Arousing the hostility of those who nurtured a revolutionary vision of industrial relations (left-wing parties and trades unions), the presidency set itself the ambitious goal of changing society and, indeed, for several months it seemed capable of doing so. Yet the 'New Society' was clearly the project of the prime minister, whose role it was, in the overall allocation of governmental responsibilities, to implement social and industrial relations policy and who, in any case, had claimed paternity of the project in his 'New Society' speech on 16 September 1969. The well-known jibe attributed to Pompidou and recounted by Jacques Julliard – 'Chaban? He thinks he's been prime minister for three years. Not a bit of it! He's been minister of labour for three months'[30] – neatly illustrates the fact that public opinion attributed the 'New Society' project to Chaban-Delmas alone. In fact this is rather unfair: such a project could hardly have been implemented without the consent of the president who, moreover, took an active part in it. It was equally misleading to the extent that the 'New Society' project was not in fact confined to the industrial relations arena, but included a plan to liberalize the exercise of power.

A drive for political liberalization

The desire for *ouverture* that Pompidou had expressed during his election campaign amounted, as far as he was concerned, to the return of Giscard d'Estaing and his supporters and the incorporation of a swathe of centrists into the majority camp dominated by the Gaullists of the UDR. Doubtless going far beyond the president's intentions, Chaban-Delmas seemed determined that 'openness' should symbolize a broader liberalization of the way power was exercised, moving away from the personalized and authoritarian character it had assumed under General de Gaulle. This liberalization agenda focused on three main areas: relations between president and parliament, the reorganization of the ORTF, and the attempt to restore greater autonomy to local bodies through a programme of regionalization.

In the profession of faith that Pompidou wrote prior to the first round of the presidential election, he clearly stated his desire to introduce a new style into presidential relations with parliament: 'Openness has first of all to be achieved in relations with parliament, both the National Assembly and the Senate: seeking a dialogue between government and elected representatives, a more trustful cooperation in the drafting of legislation, and a systematic provision of information regarding every aspect of the government's policy, thus enabling parliament to perform its monitoring to the full, while avoiding government by assembly'. Both the selection as prime minister of Chaban-Delmas, a deputy since 1946, president of the National Assembly since 1958 and a man of dialogue, and the appointment, in the shape of Roger Frey, of a minister for relations with parliament, a position accorded senior status, bore witness to the president's determination to see these intentions were carried out. A further demonstration of openness was provided by the government's decision, for the first time since 1962, to seek the deputies' approval for the prime minister's general policy statement. The desire for cooperation that the president and his prime minister had expressed led to the appointment of twenty junior ministers, all of them members of parliament, to be replaced at regular intervals in order to create a 'pool of future ministers'. The same spirit of cooperation informed the establishment of a 'liaison committee' of the parliamentary majority, entrusted with the task of consulting regularly with the prime minister from autumn 1969 onwards. The Senate, which de Gaulle had viewed with suspicion, emerged from its ostracism. Ministers resumed their trips to the Palais du Luxembourg to answer senators' questions, and joint parliamentary commissions strove, usually with success, to agree on the wording of bills. Finally, as a further indication at least of a relative rehabilitation of the role of parliament, the practice of denying parliament the right to amend legislation and forcing it to vote on an all-or-nothing basis, a procedure very frequently used under de Gaulle (eleven times in 1966, sixteen times in 1967, seven times in 1968), became much rarer (used twice in 1970 and 1971, but not used at all in either 1969 or 1972). Having restated his principled opposition to any return to government by assembly, the new president thus moved to restore in part the monitoring role of parliament, returning to it a degree of power that had shrunk steadily throughout the de Gaulle years.[31]

It was also during his presidential campaign that Pompidou had pledged to liberalize radio and television broadcasting, which was previously so firmly under the thumb of government that TV news programmes in the past had often been put together in the office of the minister for information, who would not hesitate to hand out instructions or reprimands to ORTF managers. Such practices had come in for fierce denunciation during the 1968 crisis and Chaban-Delmas now intervened to make a number of changes, once again appearing to take reform rather further than the president intended. Significantly, the Chaban-Delmas government had no minister for information, but merely a minister of junior rank, dubbed 'the government spokesman': Léo Hamon.

In November 1969, the prime minister introduced a series of measures designed to implement the planned liberalization of broadcasting. He decided to create independent news units within each television network and in radio, headed by directors appointed for two-year periods, whose independence would be underwritten by the ORTF board of directors. One of these appointments, that of the journalist Pierre Desgraupes, who was placed in charge of the main TV channel, created a scandal. This single decision was ample proof that the policy of liberalizing news coverage was taken seriously, given the new director's renown for independence both of mind and language. The appointment, an outcome of presidential lobbying by Desgraupes' friend Pierre Lazareff, caused an outcry on the conservative wing of the majority. Pierre Juillet, political adviser to the president, did not hesitate to accuse the prime minister of 'handing television over to our worst enemies'. This anger, echoed by numerous right-wing deputies and senators, prompted Pompidou to consider reversing his decision. After a tempestuous row between Pompidou and Chaban-Delmas, the prime minister succeeded in securing the confirmation of Desgraupes' appointment. From this point on, television, which many Gaullists still saw as 'the voice of France', was a divisive issue within the government.[32]

The third area in which the prime minister's liberalizing inclinations collided with the president's caution was regional policy. The defeat of the April 1969 referendum had left this issue unresolved. Although the new government issued many public statements in favour of granting local bodies broader scope for independent action, it was much more circumspect when it came to adopting concrete measures. Indeed, during a speech in Lyon in October 1970, the president made known his refusal to see the region as a new territorial authority, stating that it should be no more than 'the concerted expression of the departments it comprises'. Under such circumstances, regional policy achieved but scant results: relaxation of control over local council budgets; the 1971 law that made it easier for councils to merge or regroup; and, lastly, the July 1972 law that established regional bodies as straightforward public institutions with exclusively economic powers. The assemblies that had been planned – the regional councils and the economic and social committees – were to be manned not by people directly elected by the constituents but by local representatives and appointees. Having been rejected by Pompidou, regionalization as a genuine form of decentralization was shelved for the remainder of his presidency.[33]

Moreover, the image of liberalism and social openness that the prime minister had wished to impart to the 'New Society' became tarnished by the government's need to maintain order against a background of great social and political upheaval.

Maintaining order and fighting the remnants of leftism

By reinforcing the Gaullist majority, the 1968 legislative elections had brought the political phase of the May '68 events to a halt: in the end the 'system' that had seemed bound to fall apart was in fact confirmed in power. Yet the elections had not waved a magic wand, instantly calming social turmoil. On the contrary, unrest was fomented by the pursuit of growth and the resulting scramble for its 'fruits'. Also, the government's social and industrial relations policies, with the 'New Society' procedures that it implemented, had the effect of legitimizing this process of bid and counter-bid. Indeed, Pompidou presided over a period of unceasing social agitation stoked by vigorous inflationary expansion: the road-blocks organized by truck-drivers unhappy with the ban that prevented them from using the country's main roads and motorways over the 1970 Easter weekend; the anger of farmers over deep structural changes affecting their profession; protests by shop-keepers and small business people belonging to Gérard Nicoud's CID–UNATI, a demonstration outside the Hôtel Matignon by hundreds of mayors complaining about the financial situation that central government had imposed on local councils in April 1970; not to mention the spate of strikes afflicting all sectors of both manufacturing industry and the civil service. Added to this, student agitation rumbled on. In February and November 1970, Nanterre was the site of serious incidents that led to the intervention of the police and the resignation of the dean, Paul Ricœur. In March 1970, fights broke out at the Assas faculty. In February 1971, it was the turn of high school students to demonstrate, following the conviction of a fellow student for 'violent demonstration': the *affaire Guiot*.

This climate of turmoil was fuelled and exploited by leftist organizations who had not yet given up the hope of unleashing the revolution by forcing the government to engage in the spiral of provocation and repression that had proved so effective in May 1968. Alive to this risk, the government sought to defuse tension through its reforming policies, though obviously this could only show results over the medium term. Chaban-Delmas and his ministers therefore strove to avoid any trial of strength, taking care not to inflame conflicts. Accordingly, Olivier Guichard, minister for education, tried to keep the lid on student agitation by tolerating certain centres of militancy, realizing that to use violent repression would be to put a match to the powder-keg. This softly-softly approach, however, greatly annoyed the parliamentary majority, who could not bear to see the authority of the state held up to ridicule. Raymond Marcellin, minister of the interior, found Guichard's low-key approach hard to endure, and argued for a no-nonsense clamp-down. No one, however, was more irritated than the president himself. Indeed, Pompidou never tired of goading the prime minister and pressing him to impose order, above all by deciding, in March 1971, to find a replacement for Maurice Grimaud as chief of police. Since May 1968, Grimaud had succeeded in tackling social agitation with cautious skill, maintaining law and order and avoiding bloodshed. With Grimaud gone, Chaban-Delmas soon found himself forced to adopt repressive measures. Under such circumstances, he strove to focus his crackdown on leftists and on those who deliberately sought to destabilize the government and to bring about the failure of his 'New Society'.

In April 1970, following a hard-hitting speech in Albi by President Pompidou in which he stated that he would not tolerate people resorting to violence, Chaban-Delmas unveiled a bill designed to force those who incited clashes to pay for any damage caused. He summed up this approach in a shock slogan: *il est nécessaire que les casseurs soient les payeurs* or 'those who smash up will have to pay up'. In June 1970, despite the reluctance of the Senate, parliament voted through the *loi anti-casseurs*, making it illegal to participate in a banned demonstration and assigning to its organizers collective liability. Meanwhile, the minister for the interior lashed out at leftist *groupuscules* which he alleged (in some cases quite unfairly) were behind every disturbance. In particular, he trained his sights on one of the active revolutionary organizations, the Gauche prolétarienne, which in May 1970 was therefore disbanded, while its principal leader, Alain Geismar, who during the 1968 crisis had led the SNE-SUP (Syndicat national de l'enseignement supérieur), was arrested and put on trial. The editors of the newspaper *La Cause du peuple*, Le Bris and Le Dantec, were also brought before the courts and convicted for incitement to commit a number of crimes and misdemeanours, as well as for inciting violence. The defendants' lawyers, however, turned the trial into a platform which Jean-Paul Sartre then used to arraign bourgeois society. Sartre's action was supported by the philosopher Simone de Beauvoir and the writer Jean-Edern Hallier who created a spectacle by selling *La Cause du peuple* at the tops of their voices.

However, the crackdown on leftist militancy never went beyond the provisions of the law. This was clear when, in an attempt to prevent the disbanded Gauche prolétarienne from reforming as an underground organization – an association calling itself the 'Amis de la Cause du peuple' had attempted to register with the chief of police – the minister of justice, René Pleven, presented a bill to parliament that would have made the setting-up of new associations subject to the authority of police prefects, who would be empowered to refer individual cases to the courts if they deemed the aims of the association to be in breach of the law. Though the National Assembly approved the bill at its first reading on 24 June 1970, the Senate threw it out on a point of order made by senator Marcilhacy. After the final passage of the bill but before its enactment, Alain Poher, the Senate president, referred it to the Constitutional Council. Then, on 16 July, to the surprise of everyone, especially René Pleven, the Constitutional Council, hitherto regarded as a docile auxiliary of the state, declared that the main article of the bill was unconstitutional.

Order was thus maintained not in a climate of out-and-out repression, as the opposition claimed, but in compliance with democratic freedoms: the constitution had instituted sturdy protective barriers to restrain any possible government excess.[34]

Policies crowned with success

Overall it is fair to say that until the end of 1971 the policies that President Pompidou and his prime minister pursued were crowned with success. While failing to match the approval rating achieved by General de Gaulle, Pompidou's foreign policy was certainly to the liking of the French people. The pursuit and acceleration of growth likewise met with the wishes of most people, who hoped to see further improvements in their standard of living. The 'New Society' project, though the butt of left-wing criticism, embodied a social-democratic reformist plan for managing free-market capitalism attracting broad public support. Lastly, the policy of liberalization was well received and helped to marginalize leftism, which by now seemed confined to tiny groupings, the repression of which aroused no particular emotion in the public at large, especially since it took a relatively mild form.

This success registered strongly on every available index of public opinion. The public remained virtually unaware of any disagreements between the Elysée and Matignon and made hardly any distinction in its approval of the president and of his prime minister. Throughout the five years of his presidency, Pompidou enjoyed a popularity rating that remained constantly 'in credit', with those satisfied with his performance amounting on average to almost 60 per cent, while those who were unhappy remained below 30 per cent. It was in 1970, after his visit to the Soviet Union and following the death of de Gaulle, that his popularity peaked, with 67 per cent of respondents 'satisfied' and just 20 per cent 'unhappy' (see figure 1). French people were expressing a feeling that Pompidou was now implementing with concrete measures his policy of 'openness within continuity', preserving the positive aspects of Gaullism while remedying its flaws.

In September 1971, when French people were asked the question, 'Do you think that Georges Pompidou has followed policies similar to or different from those of General de Gaulle?', an overwhelming majority of those polled answered 'similar', whether on day-to-day politics (72 per cent as against 18 per cent), on industrial relations and *participation*

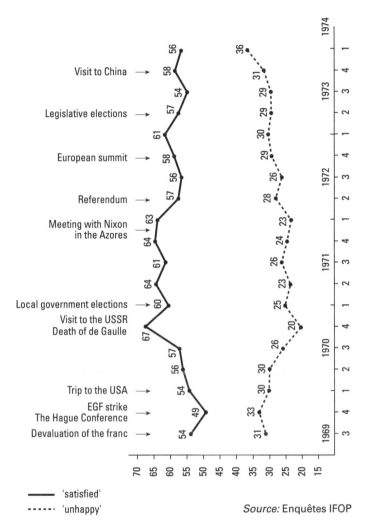

Figure 1 The popularity rating of Georges Pompidou
(quarterly average)

——— 'satisfied'
------ 'unhappy'

Source: Enquêtes IFOP

(55 per cent as against 22 per cent), on the defence of the franc (52 per cent as against 21 per cent), on European policy (49 per cent as against 35 per cent: the narrowest gap), or on regional policy (48 per cent as against 29 per cent). The public tended to welcome the changes that it did note, considering Pompidou more liberal (52 per cent as against 22 per cent), more European (56 per cent as against 17 per cent), and more aware of social issues than his predecessor. Moreover, in October 1970, the French had stated their satisfaction with the balance of power within the executive, a majority expressing the wish that in the future the president of the republic (57 per cent) and the prime minister (55 per cent) should play a role identical to their current one. Indeed, the popularity of Chaban-Delmas did not lag behind that of Pompidou: quite the reverse. Ringed by the halo of his liberal and socially inclusive policies and viewed as the great architect of the 'New Society', Chaban-Delmas was the most popular prime minister since the founding of the Fifth Republic, his approval rating outstripping even that of the president on two occasions, in February 1970 and in March 1971.[35]

This popularity was soon translated into electoral success for the parliamentary majority. In October 1969, six former ministers stood in by-elections in an attempt to win back their seats. Five were re-elected without any difficulty, but Maurice Couve de Murville was defeated in the Yvelines by Michel Rocard, general secretary of the PSU – a result which, we may reasonably suppose, can hardly have saddened the president. The district elections held on 8 and 15 March 1970, normally easy pickings for moderate, socialist and radical notables, saw an upsurge in the Gaullist vote, with a 22.5 per cent first-round score. In the local government elections of 14 and 21 March 1971, the majority coalition, which in 1965 had increased its support in the larger towns and cities, now consolidated its base in medium-sized and small towns. The overall outcome of the 1970–1 local elections was that Gaullism, which was now able to rely on its own well-established local notables, had made deep new inroads into French society and local government: the majority coalition could interpret its success as a promise of longevity. The elections to the Senate, giving the majority alliance ten new seats, provided further confirmation of this.

The popularity of the government was demonstrated in the Bordeaux by-election in September 1970. Following the death of Chaban-Delmas' substitute for the Bordeaux constituency, the prime minister had decided to recontest his old seat. Running against him was Jean-Jacques Servan-Schreiber who in June had snatched the deputy's seat in Nancy from a Gaullist who had incautiously resigned in protest at the planned route for the 'Autoroute de l'Est', which placed Metz at an advantage over Nancy. The 'deputy for the Lorraine', as Servan-Schreiber now styled himself, set out to make the Bordeaux by-election a national test, providing people with an opportunity to reject the government. His rebuff was crushing: Chaban-Delmas was re-elected deputy for Bordeaux in the first round with 63.55 per cent of votes cast.[36]

All in all, until the end of 1971, the weakness of the opposition and the depth of its splits, combined with the success of the government's policies and the broad support of the French people, made the first phase of George Pompidou's presidency a happy period in French history. It was hard to see who could question the authority of the president or the strength of the majority. In fact the challenge was to come from within the majority itself, as rifts already visible in the early months of Pompidou's presidency steadily deepened. This was to lead to the failure of the promises that the 'New Society' had held out and to sow the seeds of the government's eventual decline.

3　The government in crisis, 1971–1972

Tensions at the heart of government

By the autumn of 1969, it was clear that there were tensions at the heart of the executive between the Elysée and Matignon. Although the president and his prime minister did everything they could to conceal them from the public gaze and, as the polls showed, generally succeeded in doing so, insiders were aware of the strains and some of those who disapproved of the prime minister's policies set out to widen the gulf that they sensed existed between the two men. This presented something of a paradox. While the government had nothing to fear from an opposition that had collapsed first at the legislative elections in 1968 and then in the 1969 battle for the presidency, and while not only opinion polls but also by-elections bore witness to the popularity of both president and prime minister, it was within the majority itself that dissent now emerged to undermine it.

Yet the nature of the disagreement between Georges Pompidou and Jacques Chaban-Delmas was not immediately apparent. There was no constitutional controversy. They agreed on the need to restore to parliament a more important role while avoiding any return to government by assembly. Both accepted the division of power within the executive that, in the tradition inaugurated by de Gaulle, granted the president the upper hand. Indeed, Chaban-Delmas missed no opportunity to underline the fundamental importance of this principle. When François Mitterrand raised the issue in October 1970, asking him what would happen if the president of the republic requested him to resign and if, confident of the support of his majority in the National Assembly, he refused to do so, the prime minister replied: 'What sort of prime minister would cling on? That, Monsieur Mitterrand, would indeed be an unsavoury individual!' And in May 1972, on seeking a vote of confidence before the National Assembly, the prime minister clarified matters further: 'Need I remind you that the president of the republic, who alone selects and appoints the prime minister, may at any moment remove him from office?'[1]

This subordination of the prime minister to the president was further accentuated by the fact that Pompidou, having himself served for several years as prime minister under de Gaulle, possessed a thorough knowledge of every area of government and took a close interest in the fine detail of ministerial issues, increasingly playing a prime-ministerial role, even to the point of intervening directly to settle specific problems with the relevant ministers. This clearly belied the impression that Pompidou had given in the early days of his presidency that he would grant his prime minister considerable freedom of initiative. In fact, as Jean-René Bernard, former secretary general to the Elysée, told Eric Roussel, Pompidou's biographer: 'Georges Pompidou respected the scope of action of his ministers, though not necessarily that of his prime minister.'[2] Evidence of the president's will to intervene in every area was provided by the way that councils of ministers were conducted, often giving the impression that the prime minister was treated as totally insignificant. Equally telling was the frequency with which inter-ministerial councils were held at the Elysée to review all the issues facing the government, be they economic, social, international or cultural. There was no longer any prime-ministerial *domaine réservé*: every field of policy was now a matter for the president, with the prime minister seemingly reduced to an executive role and not always a leading one at that.[3] Yet it appears that the prime minister never complained about this state of affairs.

The disagreement between the two men lay in their conception of society. To oversimplify somewhat, one might say that the prime minister, influenced by Simon Nora and Jacques Delors, had developed a view close to that of the reformist left. What was needed was to change society and to transform social practices and behaviours so that all French people and especially the most disadvantaged could benefit from society's progress. This in itself would help to strengthen social cohesion and cut the ground from under the feet of leftist agitators, who would wither and fade until such time as public opinion found their violent denunciations credible. But, as we have already seen, this project carried a political implication: 'opening' (*ouverture*) to the non-communist left.

The head of state had a distinctly more conservative approach to the issue. Though determined to bring about tangible improvements in people's lives, as demonstrated by the scheme for wages to be paid on a monthly basis, he rejected any notion of a transformation in the structures of society, considering this both pointless and risky. In this attitude he was supported – and often outdistanced – by the diehard

wing of the UDR, which considered the 1968 crisis to be the result of a
political plot to which the only solution was vigorous repression. Put
another way, Chaban-Delmas did not have the majority backing he
needed for the policies that he wished to implement and, by personal
temperament, was disinclined to pursue the policies dear to the majority
that supported him. While it would be an overstatement to say that
Pompidou saw eye to eye with a hard right that had been swept to power
in 1968 in a spasm of conservatism, it was undoubtedly true for his
political advisers, Pierre Juillet and Marie-France Garaud, who were to
play a central role in undermining the prime minister. Drawing on the
authority conferred upon them by their access to the president, Juillet
and Garaud acted as organizers of a rumbling insurrection among the
majority against Chaban-Delmas.

As long as the policies of the prime minister elicited from public
opinion an echo of approval in which his popularity was blurred with
that of the president, Pompidou, however irritated, refrained from
intervening, and indeed urged the majority to give the prime minister
their support. But when, in the second half of 1971 and the beginning of
1972, cracks began to appear within the government, the president
began to listen more carefully to those who argued that the divisions
within the majority, combined with the reorganization of the opposition
parties, threatened to have disastrous consequences in the elections
scheduled for spring 1973 and might even lead to a government crisis.
The tensions that affected the government thus originated within the
majority itself, and primarily within the Gaullist movement, which was
still distraught by the resignation and the death of General de Gaulle.

Tensions within the majority: the Gaullists

Georges Pompidou's presidency had begun in a political context dominated by memories of May 1968. Above all, the government had to
reckon with the deeply conservative Chamber of Deputies that had been
elected in June 1968 by a country appalled by the danger of revolution.
Within this Chamber, the UDR occupied the strongest position, though
it was now quite clear that it was a party criss-crossed by different
currents and which, with de Gaulle's departure from the political scene,
had lost its main rallying-point.

So the first challenge for Pompidou was to bind together the scattered
fragments of what Gaullism had been under de Gaulle. Things were not
as straightforward as they might now appear. There is little doubt that
General de Gaulle saw Pompidou as his best possible successor, though
certainly not as his natural heir. The coldness of the messages of support

and congratulations that de Gaulle despatched to Pompidou, the care the General took to avoid any contact with the new head of state, and his trip to Ireland and his public silence throughout the presidential election all spoke volumes. Even though Pompidou took every opportunity to restate his loyalty to the General's legacy, he remained, as it were, on probation, constantly fearing that some action of his might reawaken the sleeping giant, eliciting a crushing judgement that would devastate his credibility. The publication of the first volume of the General's *Mémoires d'espoir*, which narrated events up until 1962, contained nothing to embarrass the president. Then, on 9 November 1970, before the second volume could appear, the General died. This provided the cue for a bout of skirmishing with de Gaulle's family, who arranged the General's funeral in such a way that they could not possibly attend the official mass held in Paris at Notre-Dame cathedral. Moreover, when the president and the prime minister arrived in Colombey, on 11 November, the General's coffin had already been sealed on the order of Madame de Gaulle. The final act in this drama was posthumous. When the General's heirs published the second, incomplete volume of *Mémoires d'espoir*, Pompidou found a portrait of himself which, while it contained nothing insulting, depicted him less as a statesman than as a brilliant underling whom de Gaulle's support alone had plucked from political obscurity.[4]

The ostensible coldness of the General and those close to him was bound to fuel the suspicion that Pompidou had in some way betrayed the Gaullist ideal. There was in any case within the UDR a wing of 'Gaullist fundamentalists' who either shared this analysis or feared that the president might engage in a process of political bridge-building (*ouverture*) that would lead him away from authentic Gaullism. To ward off such a danger, this wing organized a variety of different groups to keep the new government under surveillance. Immediately after the defeat of the 27 April 1969 referendum, Pierre Messmer, Michel Debré and Louis Joxe founded the Présence du gaullisme association. Then, on 2 July 1969, following the election of Pompidou, the General's brother-in-law, Jacques Vendroux and the deputies Hubert Germain and Michel de Grailly founded the parliamentary club, Présence et action du gaullisme, which by September had a membership of about forty. The two groups merged in December 1969 under the chairmanship of Hubert Germain, though the real force behind this current of thought was Messmer. Within the government, Michel Debré represented this Gaullist diehard tendency. In the country, their work was taken up by the Association nationale d'action pour la fidélité au général de Gaulle, chaired by Pierre Lefranc. This current, though it approved of the 'continuity' proclaimed by Pompidou, was alarmed by his policy of 'openness'. Given the prestige of its leaders, it clearly acted as a ginger group within the UDR. This became obvious when the UDR group met for the first time after Pompidou's election. The supporters of Michel Debré launched a violent attack on the policy of *ouverture* and the deputy, Gabriel de Poulpiquet, gave credence to the notion of a betrayal by the *Pompidoliens* by stating: 'those who shoved the General's car off the road are here among us'.[5]

Just how far the diehard Gaullists were prepared to go in denouncing the aims of the new government is unclear. Whether or not they ever envisaged the creation of a Gaullist opposition to Pompidou, certainly none materialized. Indeed, the president was assisted by the excesses that his critics committed. In October 1969, Louis Vallon, one of the leaders of left-wing Gaullism who, like his colleague René Capitant, was highly critical of the president, published a fiercely worded pamphlet entitled *L'Anti-de Gaulle*. This accused Pompidou of usurping power and provoking the General's downfall, motivated by personal ambition and hostility to de Gaulle's policy of 'participation'. The reaction of Présence et action du gaullisme was unambiguous: Louis Vallon was expelled first from the club, then from the UDR parliamentary group, and finally from the party itself. This resulted in a split within the ranks of left-wing Gaullism, with the opponents of the president forming in 1971 a Union travailliste chaired by Gilbert Grandval, while the supporters of the new government, joined by Philippe Dechartre, Léo Hamon and Yvon Morandat, formed the Mouvement pour le socialisme par la participation. This episode had the effect of rallying to the president such men as Pierre Messmer and Hubert Germain, who from this point on focused their worried attention on the prime minister whom they considered to be much more dangerous, given the policies that he was implementing, than the head of state, who after all made no secret of his reservations about those policies.

From the autumn of 1969 onwards, these Gaullist diehards managed to draw the UDR into an attitude of creeping opposition. Chaban-Delmas was criticized both for his behaviour towards the majority party, and for the content of his policies. The main reproach that the UDR laid at his door was that he neglected the party. Though he had been chosen as a man of dialogue, Chaban-Delmas felt scant kinship with the conservative backbone of the UDR and paid the parliamentary grouping little heed, preferring to concentrate his powers of exposition on the Independent Republicans and the centrists. This did nothing to alleviate UDR distrust for Chaban-Delmas' political designs. The Gaullists had no sympathy for the policies that the government was pursuing, roundly condemning the liberalization of the ORTF, which became a constant bone of contention between the prime minister and the majority. As for the 'New Society' project, the Gaullists increasingly saw it as an attempt to woo the left, a move they utterly rejected. They saw confirmation of these fears in statements first by Roger Frey, the minister for relations with parliament, and then by Chaban-Delmas himself who, looking forward to the 1971 municipal elections, argued for a strategy of alliances with the opposition centrists or even the moderate left. Such 'openness' was condemned by Robert Poujade, general secretary of the UDR, who declared that he would not see his party turned into a 'Spanish hotel'. Messmer and Debré's supporters made similar noises, while Jacques Vendroux and Christian Fouchet (who had served as a minister under de Gaulle) left the Gaullist movement. Without going to such extremes, many deputies accused the prime minister of implementing the policies of the enemies of Gaullism, from whom he could expect nothing in return, while neglecting the UDR's constituency, which was rather keener on law and order than on reform.[6]

This distrust towards the prime minister was given a public airing at the party's June 1970 Conseil national in Versailles. Pierre Messmer complained about the position within government occupied by parties allied to the UDR, declaring that Gaullists had no intention of merging with them, any more than with the government. René Tomasini, a spokesman for Gaullism's conservative grass roots, criticized the prime minister's liberalism, especially as regards the ORTF, while Robert Poujade condemned the policy of 'openness' towards the centre left which, in his view, threatened to water down the Gaullist movement. The cheering that greeted Michel Debré, contrasting starkly with the cold reception given the prime minister, bore eloquent witness to the feelings of the Gaullists.[7]

The disaffection of the UDR was encouraged by the feeling, shared by many deputies, that their open hostility to the prime minister in fact chimed with the president's wishes. Pompidou naturally took great care to avoid saying anything that might be interpreted as disowning the prime minister. However, no such constraints applied to the president's political advisers, Pierre Juillet and Marie-France Garaud, both of whom displayed an obsessional hatred for Chaban-Delmas, egging on his critics within the majority. A startling demonstration of this was provided in July 1971 when five UDR chairmen of National Assembly committees (Jean Charbonnel, Jean Foyer, Maurice Lemaire, Alain Peyrefitte and Alexandre Sanguinetti), joined by Hubert Germain, the chairman of the Présence et action du gaullisme club, submitted first to their fellow deputies, and then to the prime minister, a paper highly

critical of the government's record. Going beyond the standard complaints about the state of relations between parliament and the government, the report criticized the policy of social and industrial dialogue
pursued by the prime minister which, it was argued, had the effect of
disproportionately increasing the hearing given the leaders of the
various socio-professional organizations at the expense of the nation's
elected representatives.[8]

Although the president remained discreet, the January 1971 reshuffle
prompted by the death of two ministers, Edmond Michelet and
Raymond Mondon, and the poor health of Jacques Duhamel, could be
interpreted as evidence of a willingness to appease the conservative wing
of the UDR. Some of the appointments were of a purely technical
nature, even if they enabled the president to allocate ministerial posts to
men he could trust rather than to associates of the prime minister. As
well as appointing Jacques Duhamel as minister for cultural affairs, the
president gave Michel Cointat, a UDR member, the agriculture port-
folio and Jean Chamant, an Independent Republican, the transport
brief. Three other reshuffle decisions, however, were of clear political
significance, illustrating the shift in the government's centre of gravity.
The first was the transfer of Roger Frey, a friend of the prime minister,
from the ministry for relations with parliament to administrative
reforms, enabling Pompidou to promote the young junior budget minister, Jacques Chirac, a man whom the president regarded as his protégé,
placing him in charge of relations with the majority, in the position that
Frey had vacated. The second decision was to appoint Robert Poujade,
hitherto the general secretary of the UDR, to head the ministry for the
environment. The real significance of this move was that it made it
possible to put René Tomasini, a representative of the movement's
conservative grass roots and a passionate critic of the policies of Chaban-
Delmas, in charge of the UDR. And indeed the party's new general
secretary wasted no time in showing his mettle by launching, as soon as
he had taken up his new position, a series of fierce broadsides against the
'cowardice' of the magistrates, thereby eliciting a sharp rebuke from the
minister of justice, René Pleven. At the beginning of February,
Pompidou completed the government team – and presumably compounded the prime minister's isolation – by appointing Messmer to the
cabinet. Messmer, the political leader of orthodox Gaullism, became
minister for French overseas departments and territories.[9] In 1971, an
alliance between the president and the UDR began to take shape, with
Chaban-Delmas the clear loser, even though the popularity of the
policies he had pursued – and in which the head of state also basked –
helped to postpone the break which now seemed inevitable.

The strains within the majority party could not fail to satisfy the allies-cum-rivals of the UDR within the majority alliance and above all Valéry Giscard d'Estaing and his Independent Republicans.

Tensions within the majority: the Independent Republicans

After backing Georges Pompidou's candidacy – he could hardly have done otherwise – and having returned to government as minister for the economy and for finances, Valéry Giscard d'Estaing switched his attention once again to his long-term aim. This involved transforming his party, the Independent Republicans, who were still mere auxiliaries to the Gaullists, into their eventual successors as the majority party of government, while making himself the future president of the republic. A question hung over this strategy: how could the Independent Republicans, a part of the majority, persuade electors to vote for them unless they differentiated themselves clearly from the UDR, which they could not do without breaking up the majority alliance? This was the principal dilemma that Valéry Giscard d'Estaing needed to solve, and he tackled it in three ways: through the work of the party itself, through his strategy within the majority, and by attempting to elaborate a specific identity.[10]

Founded in 1966, the Fédération nationale des républicains indépendants had gradually purged its ranks of most of the moderate notables, replacing them with men devoted to Valéry Giscard d'Estaing. While the party still contained men who were close to the UDR and to Pompidou, for example the minister for the interior, Raymond Marcellin, they were outnumbered by the *giscardiens* who now dominated the party apparatus. These included Michel Poniatowski, the party's general secretary, Roger Chinaud, the national political secretary, and Michel d'Ornano and Jean-Pierre Soisson, assistant general secretaries. The party was developing a new political staff, far removed from the small industrialists and shop-keepers, farmers or professionals who until 1962 had formed the backbone of the old mainstream right. Valéry Giscard d'Estaing was now attracting considerable backing from private sector executive staff (engineers and managers) and high-ranking civil servants.

Thanks to his party, Giscard d'Estaing was able to keep two irons in the fire. As a member of the government, he had to display total loyalty to the president, the prime minister and his ministerial colleagues and this he did quite assiduously. But as leader of the Independent Republican party he could allow his lieutenants, and especially Michel Poniatowski – who was a past master in this game – to issue a stream of 'little phrases' designed for the ears of the UDR, or to propose a strategy by which the party might reach its objectives. By October 1970, the *giscardiens* had thus made known their ambition to see 120 of their members elected to parliament in the 1973 elections, that is, to double the size of their parliamentary group. In order to achieve this breakthrough, Poniatowski repeatedly argued that the parties that belonged to the majority should hold 'primaries'. Clearly, competition with the UDR was not always pursued according to the best rules of sportsmanship. Indeed, the UDR could not help wondering whether the zeal that the finance minister's team employed in uncovering financial scandals implicating Gaullists or, for that matter, the leaks from the same team that just happened to damage UDR members, were truly mere accidents.

As part of their overall strategy to shift the balance within the majority, the Independent Republicans hoped to assemble a broad, liberal and centrist party able to provide an even match for the Gaullists. It was with this goal in mind that during the summer of 1970 Michel Ponia-towski held talks with the Centre national des indépendants et paysans and in June 1971 held a meeting with Jean Lecanuet, chairman of the Centre démocrate. Although the plans bore no fruit, they did succeed in laying bare the intentions of the *giscardiens*.

Finally, the Independent Republicans resolved to clarify the ideolo-gical differences that set them apart from their allies within the majority, asserting their credentials as 'liberals, centrists and Europeans', thus shunting the UDR into the camp of the 'nationalist, reactionary right'. In fact, while the Independent Republicans' pro-European stance did place them closer to the centrists, the most significant differences between them and the UDR related to constitutional issues and to matters of economic and social policy. On the constitution, Valéry Giscard d'Estaing and his associates never questioned the constitutional balance introduced by de Gaulle and maintained by Pompidou. But they did argue that in practice parliament ought to be accorded a wider initiating role, and that relations between government and opposition should be less strained. On the economy, they saw themselves as stronger supporters of the free market than the Gaullists, advocating a slowdown in the rate of growth, which was less likely to generate distortions than Pompidou's ambitious targets, and a social policy focusing on changes in mores rather than on the kind of overhauling of structures and behaviour that Chaban-Delmas was attempting to achieve.

The attempt to give the Independent Republicans their own unmis-takeable identity was facilitated by the level of dissent within the government, which had the effect of broadening the finance minister's room for manoeuvre.

The ambiguities of centrism

In the strategies that both Georges Pompidou and Chaban-Delmas pursued to open politics up and to broaden support for the majority, centrism was seen as the key. Yet there was competition for the support of the centrists. The Independent Republicans made no secret of their ambition to draw the centrists into a pact, to create a counterweight to the UDR.

The difficulty was that centrism was less a true political current, with its own philosophy, than an area defined by political geometry where a hotchpotch of movements overlapped. All claimed to stand for a democracy based on participation and dialogue, an international vision embracing both the Atlantic Alliance and European integration, and with a leaning towards supranationalism; and all championed a brand of social reformism that emphasized the defence, through state intervention, of the most disadvantaged by efficient planning to correct inequalities. Beyond such shared positions, which on many points placed them in opposition to both Gaullism and the communist left, the centrists sprang from different traditions, some belonging to the radical family while others were heirs to the Christian Democratic tradition that until 1966 had been embodied by the MRP. The old fault-lines between secular politicians and Catholics had certainly blurred, though not altogether disappeared. Nor indeed had the differences in the ways centrists responded to socialism: while it did not frighten at least some sections of radicalism, it was rejected outright by the former Christian Democrats. Indeed, this had been at the root of the failure in 1965 of Gaston Defferre's *grande fédération*.[11] Pompidou's candidacy had opened up new cracks within each of centrism's two main currents. The radicals split between those who favoured opposition to the former prime minister and, led by the party chairman René Billères, wished to remain in opposition with the socialists, and those who, with Félix Gaillard, were tempted to throw their weight behind the Gaullists. Similarly, while the former Christian Democrats in Jean Lecanuet and Pierre Abelin's Centre démocrate rejected any alliance with Gaullism, the managerial wing of the parliamentary group Progrès et démocratie moderne (PDM), to which deputies adhering to this current belonged, followed the lead given by their chairman, Jacques Duhamel, and backed Pompidou. This had the result that centrism, having fragmented, now presented a challenge for both the majority and the opposition.

At first, it was the majority that made all the running. The appointment to government positions of Jacques Duhamel, René Pleven and Joseph Fontanet, followed by the founding of the Centre Démocratie et Progrès (CDP), giving the majority its third pillar, appeared to be the first stage in a longer process – all the more so since CDP deputies continued to take their seats in the PDM group alongside the opposition members of Centre démocrate. Moreover, the CDP was able reasonably to point out that the Chaban-Delmas government was implementing the European, reformist, free-market and regionalization policies that the centrists had called for. The CDP thus became the prime minister's most stalwart defender against attacks launched from within the majority: 'We are all reformers', Jacques Duhamel wrote in 1971, 'unanimously resolved to back a reforming prime minister.'[12] Indeed, Duhamel was able to argue that Centre démocrate should support the government, pointing out to Jean Lecanuet that the only choice remaining was between a majority from whom nothing serious any longer separated him and an opposition that saw him aligned with a communist-dominated left.[13]

Shaken by Pompidou's victory, both Jean Lecanuet's Centre démocrate and the Parti radical, which in autumn 1969 had elected Maurice Faure as chairman, were searching for a centrist rallying-point that would enable them to avoid being swallowed up by the majority and also help them to preserve their identity. For, as Jean Lecanuet had proclaimed at the beginning of 1970, 'for one party to rally behind another is abdication'. It was against this background that in November 1970 the Association pour un Mouvement réformateur was set up, under the leadership of Pierre Abelin (Centre démocrate), and with the inclusion of the radical Michel Soulier, the socialist André Chandernagor and the former minister of General de Gaulle, Edgard Pisani. The real solution, however, came from the Parti radical.

Maurice Faure, the radicals' newly elected party chairman, was determined to push through a process of party renewal with a clearly centrist agenda and, in order to do so, in October 1969 he brought Jean-Jacques Servan-Schreiber in as the party's general secretary. By January 1970, Servan-Schreiber, the brilliant founder of L'Express magazine and a former supporter of Mendès France, had given the Parti radical a strikingly modern programme: to bring up to date and liberalize the French economy with a policy for growth, to make society more equal by thorough-going reform to the education system, to shake up business by tackling the 'private, hereditary power of capital', and to redistribute political power through devolution to the regions and the creation of a 'United States of Europe'. Riding a wave of interest in both intellectual and business circles, in June 1970 the radicals' new general secretary conquered the parliamentary seat of Nancy without encountering any real opposition. Even if he failed in his attempt later the same year to prevent Chaban-Delmas from regaining his seat as deputy for Bordeaux, this did not seem to stall his triumphant progress. In autumn 1971, Servan-Schreiber supplanted Maurice Faure as party chairman, where-upon Faure suddenly discovered that he was in favour of a *union des gauches* ('left-wing alliance'). Servan-Schreiber's next move was to found a Mouvement réformateur to bring together the opposition centrists. This new grouping, which saw the light of day on 3 November 1971 in Saint-Germain-en-Laye, involved the Parti radical, the Centre démocrate, André Maurice's Centre républicain and the small Démo-cratie socialiste party led by the mayor of Mulhouse, Emile Muller.

Yet this pulling together of the strands of centrism did not resolve its ambiguities, first because the Mouvement réformateur fell far short of securing the support of all centrists. Not only did the CDP remain loyal to the majority, but Servan-Schreiber's braying denunciation of the 'UDR state' upset many PDM deputies who approved of Chaban-Delmas' policies. Moreover, within the Parti radical itself, Maurice Faure and Robert Fabre had started a Groupe d'études et d'action radicale-socialiste which was working to create a left-wing alliance, which in 1972 broke away from the radicals to found the 'Mouvement de la gauche radicale-socialiste'. Though given a fillip by Jean-Marcel Jeanneney, a minister under de Gaulle, who in 1972 joined the Mouve-ment réformateur, it nonetheless remained incapable of bringing to-gether all the different centrist currents. Moreover, the Mouvement réformateur was weakened by its two-headed leadership. Jean Lecanuet and Jean-Jacques Servan-Schreiber, men of profoundly differing tem-peraments, did not get on at all well and Lecanuet was often irritated by Servan-Schreiber's attention-grabbing initiatives and sensational state-ments. Worse, their strategies appeared to be at loggerheads. In Servan-Schreiber's view, the main enemy was 'the UDR state' and, to bring it down, he was ready to enter into an alliance with the left. Jean Lecanuet, however, saw communism as the principal enemy and made no secret of the fact that if forced to chose he would not hesitate to throw in his lot with the majority. With the 1973 elections now looming – to be held on a first-past-the-post system – the Mouvement réformateur was forced to drop its rhetoric and make a hard-headed choice. Yet it had succeeded in raising the biggest single issue that faced centrism: was it or was it not capable of independent existence? After all, any setback raised the question of which way the adherents of centrism would lean – to the left or to the right.[14]

In 1971–2, the renewal of the left, which so worried the majority, made this a burning issue.

The opposition: the Epinay congress and the foundation of the new Parti socialiste

Until 1971 the political climate appeared highly favourable to the majority. Centrism, tempted to support the government, was tearing itself apart. The communist party remained powerful but, given the distrust it aroused and its isolation, it was not a real danger. The non-communist left, which in 1968, with the creation of the Fédération de la gauche démocrate et socialiste, had seemed ready to unite around François Mitterrand, was now in tatters, shattered by the crisis of 1968, the rivalries between its leading figures and its consequent loss of influence and credibility. Its principal component, the Parti socialiste (SFIO), seemed to have touched rock bottom with Gaston Defferre's 5 per cent share of the vote in the 1969 presidential election. French socialism was still split between many different wings. Apart from SFIO, itself anything but united – Guy Mollet's grudging support for Defferre's candidature had been typical – there were socialists in the PSU who were attracted by leftism, and SFIO dissidents in many of the clubs that had formed two rival groupings, the Union des clubs pour le renouveau de la gauche (UCRG), led by Alain Savary, and the Union des groupes et clubs socialistes (UGCS), led by Jean Poperen. To complicate matters further, a number of socialists or at least people with socialist leanings were active, alongside radicals and republicans, in the Convention des institutions républicaines. This was led by François Mitterrand, still basking in the glory that he had won in 1965 as the candidate of the united left, supplemented by the prestige earnt through the Convention's efforts between 1965 and 1968 to forge a left-wing alliance with the Fédération de la gauche démocrate et socialiste.

The government had nothing to fear from a left that was so divided, even if, since the end of 1968, talks had been taking place with a view to drawing together the socialist current around the SFIO and the clubs. A first small step had been taken in May 1969, just prior to the presidential elections, with the merger at the Alfortville congress of the SFIO and Alain Savary's UCRG. But the decisive moves came after the elections. In July 1969, at Issy-les-Moulineaux, Jean Poperen and his UGCS joined the groups that had merged in May to produce a new formation, the Parti socialiste, dropping its old name of SFIO. This transformation was more than skin deep: Guy Mollet, a permanent fixture as SFIO general secretary since 1946, now abandoned his post. His replacement was Alain Savary who narrowly defeated a challenge from Pierre Mauroy, who had argued for a broad left-wing alliance with the communist party. Having got this far, the issue was whether or not François Mitterrand, an independent deputy, would agree to join the PS, bringing with him his Convention des institutions républicaines: after all, the socialism of this organization was far from apparent.

It was at the Epinay-sur-Seine congress in June 1971 that this process reached its conclusion. Addressing the leadership of the PS, whose move to unite the left he approved of, though he deemed the method both naive and timid, Mitterrand proposed to make the party more dynamic, to shift the balance within the left and make the PS at least an equal partner with the communists within the 'union of the left'. His vision was not so much, as Jean Poperen wished, to maintain the Marxist purity of the organization, but rather to win power. To achieve this, he set out to create a party that would open its doors to radicals, republicans and Christians, something that SFIO had always rejected. Moreover, if he thought that in order to gain power it was essential to form an alliance with the communists and their electorate, he viewed this as a purely tactical matter, appearing indifferent to any merger with the 'brothers' from whom they had divided at the Tours congress in 1920. Indeed, according to the analysis proposed by Alain Bergounioux and Gérard Grunberg, it was the fact that Mitterrand had no background within the socialist movement that enabled him to bypass the contradictions that had paralysed the party from birth.[15] Mitterrand's vision was of a modern party, embodying a political culture in tune with the times and free of the kind of theological squabbles around Marxism that had so far dominated its history. Be that as it may, the goals that he set the party entailed a strong anchoring on the left, and this was clearly stated in a speech he delivered that promised a break with the logic of capitalism and the pursuit of a humanist socialism.

But to achieve his ambition by turning the Parti socialiste into an instrument for conquering power, Mitterrand still had to take over its leadership, ousting its principal leader, Alain Savary, who enjoyed the backing of both Guy Mollet and Jean Poperen. To pull this off, François Mitterrand, who at the Epinay congress could count on only the 15 per cent of the vote delivered by his Convention des institutions républicaines, was forced to enter into an alliance with two groups holding almost opposite views: on the one hand, the left wing of the Parti socialiste, CERES (Centre d'études, de recherche et d'éducation socialistes), led by Jean-Pierre Chevènement, which was seduced by Mitterrand's united-left strategy; and, on the other hand, the heirs to the old SFIO, Gaston Defferre and Pierre Mauroy, who were able to deliver the two most powerful regional party federations, the Bouches-du-Rhône and the Nord. This they did out of hostility to Guy Mollet and his protégé Alain Savary, and despite their distrust, even hostility, for the communist party – but then, after all, François Mitterrand had pledged to reduce its relative weight on the left. These then were the circumstances under which François Mitterrand, on 16 June 1971, became first secretary of the PS with 43,926 votes, against 41,757 for Alain Savary and 3,925 abstentions.[16]

The left now possessed a credible and modern political organization, led by a prestigious politician, which was ready to enter an alliance with the communists in order to achieve power, yet which was quite distinct from them. For a deeply divided majority that found it hard to attract centrist support, and with the 1973 legislative elections less than two years away, this represented real danger.

The opposition: leftism and communism

As may be imagined, François Mitterrand's socialist project did not arouse the enthusiasm of the communist party. For several years, the communists had advocated a *programme commun* based on a united-left alliance. This was designed to help the party emerge from its political isolation. The communists could see that the PS had no intention of taking up the invitation until it had consolidated its own position, i.e. until it was able to balance their power. While waiting for the opportunity to negotiate its 'common programme', which Mitterrand had accepted in principle, the communists set out to strengthen their position.

This they attempted to effect in three ways: first, by restating their principles and, especially, their ideological unity around Marxist dogmas. The philosopher Roger Garaudy who, in the atmosphere of general re-evalution inaugurated in May 1968, had attempted to bring party doctrine up to date and had suggested that dialogue should be initiatied with the Christians, paid the price. Accused of 'revisionism', he lost his place on the Central Committee, and was expelled from the party in May 1970. The party's second step was to sort out its leadership problems. Waldeck-Rochet, the party's titular general secretary was unwell, and his worsening health made it impossible for him to run his party. The succession was settled at the nineteenth party congress in 1970 with the appointment of Georges Marchais as assistant general secretary. Third, prior to any talks with the socialists, the party made known its own programme – the basis of its negotiating position. Published in October 1971, it was entitled *Changer de cap. Programme pour un gouvernement démocratique d'union populaire*.[17]

There was a further worry that nagged at the communist party: the fear that it might be outflanked on its left by the groups of *gauchistes*, heirs of the May '68 crisis, who were now determined to seize a monopoly of revolutionary spirit, denouncing the PCF as Stalinist and bureaucratic. Though influential among university and school students, and providing a source of inspiration for certain currents within trade unionism (particularly in the CFDT), leftism enjoyed only limited influence in the country at large. The main cause of its weakness was its division into many separate streams, split by doctrinal or strategic rivalries that led each sect to fulminate and denounce all the others. In the overall leftist haze, battle was joined by Trotskyists from the Front communiste révolutionnaire and from Lutte ouvrière, anarchists from the Fédération anarchiste française and the Organisation révolutionnaire anarchiste, Maoists from the Parti communiste révolutionnaire marxiste-léniniste and the Gauche révolutionnaire marxiste-léniniste, not to mention the innumerable regional or feminist groupings, such as the Mouvement de libération des femmes. In this galaxy of *groupuscules*, where the main means of expression was violent protest, one star, the PSU, outshone all the others. Championing a socialism based on joint worker–management control (*autogestion*), the PSU was a crossroads at which the spirit of May intersected with the real world of political action. Yet the PSU had no immunity against leftism's congenital sickness: division. Split between different factions, each constantly excommunicating the others, the PSU was more a laboratory of ideas for denouncing the electoralism of the constitutional left and the power of the capitalist bourgeoisie than a party serious about playing the game of parliamentary democracy. The public support that the PSU enjoyed relied to a large extent on the personality of its national secretary, Michel Rocard, who stood for a forward-looking and broad-minded left. Indeed, having achieved an honourable score in the 1969 presidential election, garnering over 800,000 votes, Rocard succeeded in entering the National Assembly, beating the former prime minister, Maurice Couve de Murville, in the Yvelines constituency. Though at loggerheads on every other issue, the *gauchistes* were in full agreement on one point: their condemnation of the communist party.

For the communists the danger was real. To hold on to the electoral support on which their strength was based, they had to demonstrate that by attacking the 'party of the working class' the leftists were just indulging in sterile polemics. The communists resolved to fight off the leftists inch by inch wherever they were attempting to supplant them. This was achieved without great difficulty in the workplace, where the strength of the CGT enabled it to limit the influence of the CFDT's leftist tendencies, of interest mostly to intellectuals and managers. In student circles things were more difficult. To prevent UNEF (Union nationale des étudiants de France), the large students' grouping, from falling into the hands of leftists, the communists did not shrink from provoking a split which produced UNEF-Renouveau, which they were able to dominate. Likewise, they strove to infiltrate the comités d'action lycéens (CALs), eventually gaining the upper hand. But the main weapon in the communists' armoury remained their image as a great party, not only able to negotiate with those in power but seriously aspiring, as part of a left-wing alliance, to take power themselves. They used this image to isolate the leftist *groupuscules*, labelling them 'irresponsible'. Naturally, the communists found socialist procrastinations over the drawing-up of a 'common programme for government' highly irritating.

It was not until the first half of 1972 that the communists finally got what they were looking for. In March, a PS national convention adopted a programme for government entitled *Changer la vie*. When the Parti radical split in June 1972, Jean-Jacques Servan-Schreiber lost the left wing of his party which, that autumn, under the leadership of Maurice Faure, Robert Fabre and René Billères, would found the Mouvement des radicaux de gauche, a natural ally for the PS. Meanwhile, on 26 June, the communist and socialist parties signed the *Programme commun de gouvernement*, a platform on which the left, now united, would offer the French voters at the 1973 legislative elections a clear alternative to the right-wing majority that had governed France for fifteen years.[18]

The rebirth of a combative and effective opposition provided a stark contrast with a government that appeared worn out and a majority that was riven by splits. Worried by these developments, the president launched a spate of initiatives designed to regain control of a situation that was slipping from his grip.

The government runs out of steam and into scandals

Government policies, despite attacks from the UDR, enjoyed real public popularity until the summer of 1971. From that point on, however, the tide began to turn, with the prime minister rapidly becoming the target of a clearly orchestrated campaign. The first manifestation of this was the Senate's decision in December 1970 to open a parliamentary enquiry into serious irregularities relating to major construction work at the La Villette slaughterhouses. Even more serious for the majority was the revelation on 19 July 1971 that André Rives-Henry, UDR deputy for the nineteenth *arrondissement* in Paris and former chairman of Garantie foncière, a property company that had been the subject of a judicial enquiry since the beginning of the year, had now been charged with fraud, breach of trust and collusion in the misappropriation of council assets. It was a case that touched the party in power all the closer owing to the fact that André Roulland, a former assistant general secretary of the UDR, had been Garantie foncière's manager until June 1971. Rives-Henry refused to give up his seat or to resign from the UDR with the result that his conviction in May 1972 did considerable damage to his party, which failed to expel him until the following November.

A campaign was launched in autumn 1971, which some believed to be orchestrated by the ministry of finance for the benefit of Valéry Giscard d'Estaing, and took explicit aim at the prime minister. In November 1971, a tax inspector, Edouard Dega, was charged with tax fraud. His brother, Georges Dega, was a former member of Chaban-Delmas' office at the National Assembly. The finance minister lost no time in emphasizing that the fight against tax fraud had the backing of the prime minister, but in January 1972 Chaban-Delmas himself became the focus of a new revelation. On the basis of a leak that could not have originated anywhere except the ministry of finance, the satirical weekly *Le Canard enchaîné* published the prime minister's tax declaration, showing that he had paid no income tax from 1966 to 1969. Although his exemptions were the result of a series of perfectly legal practices – on the one hand, a tax credit, on the other, the partial exemption of his parliamentary salary and the total exemption of his prime-ministerial salary – Chaban-Delmas' reputation was damaged. The press spun out these revelations by looking into the prime minister's links with the Hachette publishing group and highlighting the under-payment of tax by several prominent members of the government, some of whom were close colleagues of the prime minister. Having bought himself a castle in the Corrèze department which, shortly after purchase was reclassified as a 'historic monument', with the result that its restoration could be undertaken at state expense, Jacques Chirac, the minister responsible for relations with parliament, was likewise unable to evade searching questions into what Servan-Schreiber had dubbed the 'UDR state'.[19]

Neither the opposition nor the UDR's allies-cum-rivals within the majority could fail to make political capital from these scandals. In December 1971, François Mitterrand succeeded in gaining the approval of the National Assembly for the creation of a commission of enquiry into property investment companies. Meanwhile, Michel Poniatowski, tasked with saying out loud what Valéry Giscard d'Estaing, who was bound by collective ministerial responsibility, could only think, roundly denounced what he called the 'cronies and rogues', clearly a further swipe at the overweening state power of the Gaullist party.

Just when the left had finally succeeded in organizing itself, the deterioration in the government's image prompted Pompidou to take an initiative designed to win back public support.

The April 1972 referendum

Three years into his presidency and with scandals and allegations lapping at his government, the challenge facing the head of state was to discover a means to reassert legitimacy. Showing himself to be the true heir to General de Gaulle, on 16 March 1972 Pompidou called a press conference to announce his decision to hold a referendum. Rather more surprising was the referendum issue that he had selected. Pompidou had resolved to seek the electorate's approval for the enlargement of the Common Market to include the four states scheduled to join on 1 January 1973. While it is easy to grasp the international kudos to be gained by securing the French nation's approval for an enlargement of which he had been the principal architect, the appropriateness of such a dramatic procedure as a referendum on an issue on which there was scarcely any opposition (except among the communists and a section of the Gaullists) was questionable. Indeed, it seemed like a political exercise for domestic consumption. After all, there was little doubt that not only would all the factions of the majority come out in support of a 'yes' vote (centrists and Independent Republicans from conviction, and the UDR out of loyalty to the president), but that the Mouvement réformateur, the left radicals and the socialists could not fail to give it their approval either, while the communists would find themselves isolated once again in the 'no' camp. The outcome would both shore up the government and deal a fatal blow to the recent 'union of the left', which was forced to face the fact that their members were at loggerheads over such a vital political issue as European policy. Though the idea of a referendum was backed by the prime minister, it was strongly opposed by Pompidou's close advisers Pierre Juillet and Michel Jobert, as well as by Maurice Schumann, the minister for foreign affairs, all of whom feared that it threatened to unite the opposition and the majority malcontents on an issue that otherwise aroused little voter interest. However, the referendum idea was carried and the date set for 23 April 1972.[20]

As things turned out, the trap laid for the opposition snapped shut on the person who had set it. Denouncing the president for seeking to rule by plebiscite, the PS decided to campaign for abstention, while the PSU

Table 3. *The Referendum of 21 April 1972 on EEC enlargement*

		Percentage of electorate	Percentage of vote
Electorate	29,071,070	100.0	
Votes	17,581,840		
Abstentions	11,489,230	39.5	
Spoilt papers	2,070,615	7.1	
Yes	10,502,756	36.1	67.7
No	5,008,469	17.2	32.2

called for a boycott and the communists for a 'no' vote. Under these circumstances the 'yes' campaign, which was backed by the majority and by the Mouvement réformateur (despite the reservations of Servan-Schreiber), could never produce the massive endorsement that the head of state had wished. On top of this, since the victory for the 'yes' camp seemed a foregone conclusion, the campaign was totally devoid of passion, despite two interventions by the president on 11 and 21 April.

Though a mild success in terms of its result, the 23 April referendum on European enlargement was a considerable setback for Pompidou, whose strategy had proved to be flawed. Although the 'yes' camp had won, scoring nearly 68 per cent of the votes cast, as against 32 per cent for the 'nos' (see table 3), what really impressed observers were the numbers of voters who had abstained (39 per cent of all registered electors, to whom should be added the 7.1 per cent of spoiled ballot papers). Almost half the French electorate had failed to express an opinion either way, making the total 'yes' vote equivalent to just 32 per cent of all registered electors.

The president had of course won a clear victory, making it easy for his advisers to argue that the socialists' cries of triumph were misplaced, and that the high abstention rate probably had more to do with the French people's lack of interest in Europe than with any response to François Mitterrand's promptings. Pompidou nonetheless saw his failure to bring the French out to vote as something of a personal setback, even if Pierre Juillet preferred to blame the prime minister, once again demanding his head. Pompidou continued to resist such a move, despite information reaching him to the effect that Gaullist supporters had taken little part in the referendum. Indeed, it was not until Chaban-Delmas sought to achieve the upturn in government fortunes that the president had just failed to secure that he precipitated his own downfall.

The dismissal of Chaban-Delmas

There is no doubt at all that the relative failure of the April 1972 referendum exacerbated latent tensions between the Elysée and Matignon. Conclusive evidence of this was provided when the issue of ORTF reform resurfaced. The publication of a Senate report detailing the organization's financial muddle and rife corruption made its reform essential. However, broadcasting policy remained a major bone of contention between the prime minister on the one hand and the UDR and the president on the other. The job of preparing the reforming legislation was thus entrusted, not to the prime minister, but to the junior civil service minister, Philippe Malaud, a member of the arch-conservative Centre national des indépendants et paysans (CNIP). The implementation of the reform prompted the resignations of the director general of the ORTF and the chairman of its board of directors, both of whom had been appointed by Chaban-Delmas. Further evidence of the distrust in which the prime minister was now held came on 15 May with the replacement of the government's spokesman, the left-wing Gaullist Léo Hamon, by one of the president's own men, Jean-Philippe Lecat.

Thus threatened and, as it were, placed under surveillance, Chaban-Delmas sought a way out of the blind alley, suggesting to Pompidou a move that he believed would make up for the relative failure of the referendum and demonstrate the cohesiveness of the majority. On 17 May, the prime minister proposed to the council of ministers that the government should seek a vote of confidence from the National Assembly, following a general policy debate. Pompidou, sensing that Chaban-Delmas was trying to force his hand by pitting the parliament against his presidential authority, warned the prime minister: 'From now on you are encroaching on my constitutional powers.'[21] Pompidou's misgivings were also apparent in the communiqué that followed the council of ministers' meeting, which stated that the prime minister had been authorized 'if he deemed it useful' to seek a vote of confidence in the government. Despite the president's reservations, Chaban-Delmas pursued his plan. On 23 May 1972, the National Assembly accordingly expressed its confidence in the government by a massive majority of 368 votes to 96, with six abstentions.[22] The contrast between the triumph achieved in parliament and the relative failure of the referendum in the country at large sealed the prime minister's fate. The president could not allow the National Assembly to oblige him to maintain a government which, under the logic of the Fifth Republic, depended for its existence on him alone. To do so would be to risk a split in authority, introducing a diarchy. To avoid this, de Gaulle had forced Pompidou to step down after the 1968 elections, and de Gaulle's successor now proved no less cautious. At the president's request, Chaban-Delmas handed in his resignation at the end of the council of ministers' meeting on 5 July 1972.

The departure of the prime minister, whose differences with the president and a section of the majority had supplied news editors with a steady stream of stories for the past three years, left the president free to manage the run-up to the 1973 elections and to conduct government policy as he saw fit. It also meant that after three years of procrastination, Pompidou now had to choose between the left-leaning social policy of his first prime minister and the tough line embodied by the UDR and its conservative majority in the National Assembly: he came down at last on the side of the latter. By doing so, the president gave the government a much more consistent line, but at the same time he deprived it of the social approach that had contributed greatly to his popularity with the public, and which Chaban-Delmas had embodied. A new chapter thus opened in the history of Pompidou's republic, a sharp departure from the dynamism of previous years. Conservatism now gained the upper hand at the very moment when the economic situation made it impossible to achieve the goals that Pompidou had set the country. The end of economic expansion was to coincide with his death.

4   Endgame, 1972–1974

The Messmer government

For the general public, the removal from office of Jacques Chaban-Delmas came as a complete surprise. Immediately prior to his departure, according to a SOFRES poll, the majority of French people (54 per cent) believed that the president and his prime minister saw eye to eye on practically every issue.[1] In political circles, on the other hand, where this turn of events had long been expected, the only surprise lay in the choice of Chaban-Delmas' successor. Instead of Olivier Guichard, who everyone had predicted would be the next prime minister, Pompidou turned to Pierre Messmer who nobody had thought would get the job.

It was not until well after the event that attempts were made to account for this appointment. Pompidou was said to have wished to rid himself of the stifling tutelage exercised by Gaullist 'barons', of whom Olivier Guichard was one of the most prominent, and this reading of events seemed to be corroborated by Roger Frey's removal from government. Pompidou, it was thought, had not approved of the cautious approach taken by Olivier Guichard as minister for education during the wave of student unrest, believing like most of the UDR that he had been far too soft. The president had made no secret of his preference for a crackdown and, indeed, Guichard now lost his post at education.

Yet the main explanation of Messmer's appointment was that Pompidou was now determined to ensure that the policies of the French government should henceforth be exactly as he decided, down to the last detail. This is why he appointed as prime minister a man who, he correctly thought, would not be tempted to pursue any personal political agenda, would be indifferent to popularity, and would not dream of one day becoming head of state. Messmer, a former administrator in France's overseas territories, a man of discipline, authority, and complete integrity, had served from 1960 to 1969 as minister for the armed forces under de Gaulle. Indeed, it was as if the responsibilities of office

had somehow rubbed off on Messmer's personal conduct: the face that
he presented to the public was that of a military man with a feel for
hierarchy and order, tinged with a certain stiffness in both his physical
movements and his speech. Also, Messmer provided Pompidou with a
double shield against his critics. First, as a former member of the
Resistance, with a record for valour gained at Bir Hakeim, Messmer
protected Pompidou from the wrath of former Resistance fighters,
indignant about the pardon that the president had granted Paul Touvier,
the former chief of the Lyon Milice, as well as about the attendance at
the Elysée, among the president's advisers, of such former collaborators
as Jacques Benoist-Méchin and Georges Albertini. Second, the crucial
role that Messmer had played in the Présence et action du gaullisme
association appeared to provide tangible evidence of the president's
loyalty to the General at the very moment when he was busy margin-
alizing the Gaullist barons.[2]

The composition of the new government was the outcome of direct
intervention by the president and his political adviser, Pierre Juillet.[3] At
first sight, the political balance was unchanged, with Debré remaining
minister for the armed forces, Maurice Schumann still at foreign affairs,
René Pleven at justice, Valéry Giscard d'Estaing still finance minister
and Raymond Marcellin retaining his post at the ministry of the interior.
But it was the changes and new ministerial appointments that gave the
new team its real significance. Replaced by Joseph Fontanet at education, Guichard was put in charge of the huge and prestigious ministry
for national and regional development, though in fact this was a post
without any real political weight. Even more telling was the decision to
bring into government Jean Charbonnel, Jean Foyer and Hubert
Germain: these three had been among the signatories of the critical
manifesto produced by the parliamentary committee chairmen in July
1971, and had subsequently spearheaded UDR opposition to Chaban-
Delmas. Of equal note was the promotion of 'president's men' like
Jacques Chirac, who became minister for agriculture, and André Bettencourt whose appointment as a minister-delegate at foreign affairs raised
the question as to whether his role was to support Maurice Schumann
or to keep an eye on him on behalf of the president. The only real
exception to the general 'Pompidolisation' of the government was the
arrival at the ministry for social affairs of the skilled and unflagging
Edgar Faure whose brief appeared to be to reassure public opinion that
the sacking of Chaban-Delmas did not spell the end of social policies,
even if the 'New Society' was certainly off the agenda.

The first steps taken by the new government underlined the message
that its composition had already sent to the world of politics and, above

all, to parliament. Appointed in July during the parliamentary recess, Messmer waited until the parliament reassembled to present his general policy statement to the National Assembly, judging there to be no need to convene a special session. Moreover, he let it be known that he had no intention of submitting his statement to a vote of confidence as Chaban-Delmas had done in 1969. This prompted the opposition to introduce a censure motion demanding a confidence vote, which of course was voted down. The message in any case was unmistakeable: government emanated from the president, not from the National Assembly.

The measures taken on broadcasting were no less significant, marking the end of the liberalizing 'New Society' project. On 12 July, the ORTF was given a new director general in the shape of Arthur Conte, a UDR deputy for the Pyrénées-Orientales (previously a socialist constituency), and a friend of the president. The independence of information units was removed and a ministry for information was recreated, entrusted to the arch-conservative Philippe Malaud.[4]

Under the enhanced authority of the president of the republic, the clear task of the new government was to prepare the ground for elections in 1973, with Messmer cast in the role of chief-of-staff rather than generalissimo.

Preparing for the 1973 elections: the opposition

The 1973 elections presented government with a considerable challenge. It was obvious that the majority could not hope for a repeat of the huge victory it had won in 1968, when fear of revolution had stalked the country. It was more a matter of making sure that its expected loss of support did not amount to a rout that would strip it of power and unleash a government crisis. Yet things were not looking good: pre-election polls gave the majority only 38 per cent of voting intentions and it therefore ran the risk of being forced into talks with the reformers who, it seemed, had the support of 15 per cent of the electorate. Yet while Jean Lecanuet was known to be willing to reach an agreement in order to avert the risk of a socialist–communist majority, the same could not be said for Servan-Schreiber. The prospect of a left-wing victory could not be ruled out.

The polls attributed 46 per cent of first-round voting intentions to the three left-wing groupings – communists, socialists and left radicals. These three groupings had now reached an agreement covering polling tactics as well as the eventuality of their electoral triumph. For the first round, communists would stand separately from socialists and left radicals, the two latter groups having agreed to 'share out' constituencies. For the second round, agreement had been reached between the three groups, with the participation of the PSU, on a system of reciprocal withdrawals designed to maximize the chances of the best-placed left-wing candidate in each constituency. For the first time since 1946 the 'left alliance' had reformed.

Moreover, the left was now able to offer the French its *programme commun de gouvernement*, signed in June 1972. This outlined a genuine democratic alternative, articulated in four chapters – 'Living better, changing life', 'Democratizing the economy', 'Democratizing the constitution' and 'Contributing to peace'. There were a lot of catchphrases, statements of principle, vague slogans and declarations of intent. When it came to European policy, an issue on which communists on one side and socialists and radicals on the other were keen to hide their fundamental differences, the slogans grew particularly fuzzy. Also, some of the declarations of intent were tinged with populism: there was no indication as to where the money was to come from to finance, for example, the promise of across-the-board pay increases combined with shorter working hours. But in constitutional and economic policy areas the *programme commun* offered a real alternative. In terms of the conduct of government itself, the left wanted to do away with 'personal power', which they considered to be characteristic of the Fifth Republic, and to shift the balance of power in the direction of parliament. The desire to return to a 'rationalized' parliamentary rule, rather than Fourth Republic-style government by assembly, was at the root of proposals to repeal article 16, to limit recourse to referendums and to reduce the presidential term from seven to five years – though the election of the president would still be by universal suffrage. These measures would be supplemented by a reinforcement of the powers of parliament and the institution of a legislative contract on the British pattern (an old idea dear to Mendès France) between the government and the Assembly.[5] Lastly, the *programme commun*, pandering to public opinion, demanded that regional assemblies be directly elected by universal suffrage.

On the economy, the left radicals' attachment to free enterprise and the fear of alienating the electorate by an over-collectivist programme accounted for a certain woolliness in the way policy was formulated and the reliance on such vague terms as *autogestion*. Yet those who had signed up to the *programme commun* were in fact agreed on a broad package of nationalizations affecting a dozen major companies and on the increased 'participation' of employees in the administration and management of public companies, as well as on the need for the state to acquire shares in a range of other companies. The underlying aim of the *programme commun*, to establish a managed economy, was in sharp contrast with the economic liberalism of the right.

Whatever the uncertainties and flaws of the *programme commun*, the left was now seriously asserting its wish to run the country and demonstrating that it possessed a set of detailed policies. This created a real political dynamic, all the more so since the election campaign propelled into the news once again the socialists' new leader, François Mitterrand who, as in 1965, embodied the left's refound unity.

Enfeebled by its internal squabbling and shaken by scandal, the majority had good reason to fear the forthcoming elections. It was with this in mind that Pompidou had decided to take control of the situation by changing prime ministers.

Preparing for the 1973 elections: the majority

The immediate risk facing Georges Pompidou was that the majority might arrive at the elections in disarray and that the first-round competition between its three strands might leave scars that would then compromise its success in the second round. This fear was not just theoretical. With Michel Poniatowski as their mouthpiece, the Independent Republicans had made no mystery of their intention to hold 'primaries' in order to shift the balance within the majority in their direction, taking some seats from the UDR, whose crushing domination they found hard to put up with.[6] For its part, the UDR, while aware that it could not avert some decline in its support, was worried about the intentions of Chaban-Delmas, who seemed willing to sacrifice Gaullist seats for the sake of a gesture of 'openness' towards the centre. The apparently relaxed attitude of the president towards such a prospect only deepened UDR concern.[7]

Fearing that over-vigorous competition might have catastrophic results, Pompidou decided to set out some clear ground rules. As early as February 1971 he entrusted Jacques Chirac, at that time minister-delegate for relations with parliament, with the task of bringing together the general secretaries of the various parties of the majority to find a way of sharing out first-round constituency nominations. When the Messmer government was formed, it was Jacques Chirac's successor as minister for relations with parliament who inherited this challenge. In the end, after the Independent Republicans rejected the prime minister's attempt at arbitration in November 1972,[8] the president himself was forced to intervene to sort out the rash of conflicts triggered by the prospect of elections.

The president turned his attentions first to the UDR. René Tomasini, who represented the UDR grass-roots 'troops', a man not known for either his shrewdness or his diplomatic skills and, to make matters worse, whose name had been mentioned in connection with a variety of scandals, was replaced as general secretary by the brilliant Alain Peyrefitte. Although this was the president's express wish, it was not easy to achieve, given that the Gaullist barons and the growing band of Chaban-Delmas supporters fielded their own candidates for the job: André Fanton (a friend of Michel Debré) and Alexandre Sanguinetti. Indeed, Alain Peyrefitte did not clinch the job until the second round of voting, when he beat Sanguinetti by sixty-one votes to fifty.[9]

As for the Independent Republicans, it was essential to go some way towards meeting their desire to increase their party's influence within the majority. Yet at the same time care had to be taken to avoid rubbing salt into the wounds of the UDR, which was already smarting from the harsh attacks launched by Michel Poniatowski, and by the political strategy pursued by Valéry Giscard d'Estaing, who in October 1972 had spread commotion in the ranks of the UDR by stating: 'France wishes to be governed from the centre.'[10]

After endless haggling, the president eventually got his way. The Union des républicains de progrès pour le soutien au président de la République, the ticket on which the candidates of the majority would run, put forward 422 agreed 'Union' candidates to contest the 473 constituencies of metropolitan France. Of these, the UDR accounted for 359.[11] The president thus accepted from the start that the Gaullist party would not enjoy an absolute majority in the next Assembly. Indeed, it was now clear that he favoured an albeit composite presidential majority that gave him its full support, over a Gaullist party whose sectarian approach to politics failed to inspire him with any confidence. The decisions taken immediately after the elections supported his analysis.

The candidates, however, still had to be provided with a programme capable of holding its own against the left's *programme commun de gouvernement*. This job fell to the prime minister who, in a speech delivered to the UDR national conference at Provins on 7 January 1973, listed thirty-three proposals, each on a specific issue, amounting to a complete programme of government to run for a full parliament.

There remained one key question that was of decisive importance for the outcome of the forthcoming election: to what extent was the president prepared to make a personal issue of the election result? After all, General de Gaulle had frequently used the various elections held during his term of office as plebiscites. Under Pompidou, nothing similar was attempted. Yet the president did allow a degree of uncertainty to hover over how he intended to proceed if the opposition won.

76   The republic of Georges Pompidou

Table 4. *Legislative elections of 4 March 1973: first round*

		Percentage of electorate	Percentage of valid votes
Electorate	29,883,748	100.00	
Votes	24,288,585		
Abstentions	5,595,163	18.72	
Spoilt papers	537,161	1.79	
Valid votes	23,751,424	79.47	100.00
PSU and extreme left	778,183	2.60	3.27
PCF	5,084,824	17.01	21.40
Socialists and left radicals	4,919,426	16.46	20.71
Other left	241,388	0.80	1.01
Reformers	3,048,520	10.20	12.88
URP	8,224,447	27.52	34.02
Other pro-majority candidates	784,985	2.62	3.30
Other right	669,651	2.24	2.81

While stating that he would abide by the constitution and brandishing the threat of a dissolution of parliament, he intervened energetically both at press conferences and during radio and TV discussions to denounce the *programme commun* and to reaffirm his determination to defend the powers invested in him by the French people. He vowed to stand firm against the attempt, which he thought he could detect in the schemes of the left, to create a totalitarian society on the communist pattern. He accordingly appealed to electors to back 'all the other parties' against the parties of the *programme commun*.[12]

The 1973 elections

Roughly in line with opinion poll predictions, the results of the first round of the 1973 legislative elections held little surprise. Indeed, they were so similar to the 1967 first-round results that they seemed to represent a balance of political strength that, except in periods of crisis, was a permanent feature throughout these years. Voter turn-out was exceptionally high, with over 80 per cent of registered electors going to the polling station (see table 4).

As the results of the first round became known, the main feeling was that nothing much had been settled. While the majority, with 37.9 per cent of the vote, found itself in possession of a solid bedrock of support (indeed, a slight improvement on the 37.8 score achieved in 1967), it had clearly failed to earn any electoral dividends from the support of the CDP (see maps 1 and 2). Moreover, its support both south of the Loire and in its traditional heartlands in the east and west had been eroded.

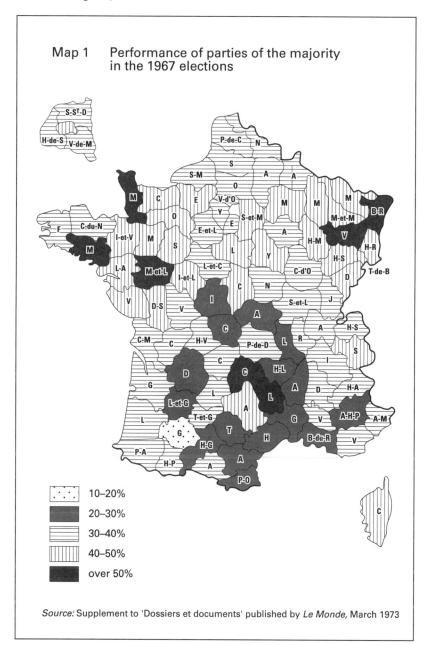

Map 1   Performance of parties of the majority
         in the 1967 elections

10–20%
20–30%
30–40%
40–50%
over 50%

Source: Supplement to 'Dossiers et documents' published by *Le Monde,* March 1973

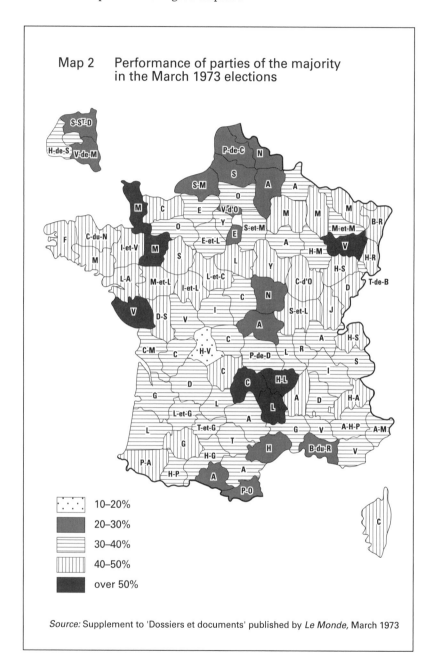

Map 2   Performance of parties of the majority
in the March 1973 elections

Legend:
- 10–20%
- 20–30%
- 30–40%
- 40–50%
- over 50%

Source: Supplement to 'Dossiers et documents' published by *Le Monde,* March 1973

The left now consisted almost exclusively of parties who had signed up to the *programme commun*: as compared to the presidential elections of 1969, support for the leftists had slumped. With 21.4 per cent of the vote, the communist party remained – though only just – the largest single political grouping, scoring slightly less well than in 1967 (22.5 per cent), owing to declining support in its strongholds, the Nord and the Paris suburbs, though this was offset by gains in the Midi (see maps 3 and 4). The socialists and their radical left allies, though they failed to achieve the spectacular breakthrough that the PS had been hoping for, had two grounds for satisfaction: first, their 20.71 per cent share of valid votes was an improvement on the 18.7 per cent achieved by the FGDS in the 1967 elections; and, second, they had very nearly drawn level with the PCF. The shift in the balance of the left that François Mitterrand had made his goal at the Epinay congress was within reach.[13]

It was obvious, however, that the key to the second round lay in the stance that the reformers now chose to adopt. For them, the first round had been a real disappointment. With under 13 per cent of the valid votes cast, they could see that once again the actual votes they had managed to win at the polling stations had failed to reach the level predicted by the polls. A bitter pill, it was sweetened somewhat by the realization that the fate of the majority now rested in their hands and that their strategic position, while it turned their electors into bargaining counters, enabled them to exert pressure on both camps. In particular, the precedent set in 1967, when the second-round centrist vote in favour of the left had almost placed the Assembly under left-wing control, concentrated the minds of the majority wonderfully.

For the presidential majority it was thus essential to secure the support of the opposition centrists. Matters were made easier by the contacts that Chaban-Delmas had initiated between the government and the reformers through the intermediary of General de Bénouville, and which Pierre Messmer had continued.[14] Immediately after the first round of voting, Pierre Messmer received Jean Lecanuet with whom he proceeded to negotiate a series of candidate withdrawals. Servan-Schreiber also came for talks, though he proved much more reluctant to enter into any pact. The two leaders of the Mouvement réformateur did at least agree on one point – that it was essential that they should end up with at least thirty deputies in the National Assembly so that they could retain their status as an independent grouping. Holding the electoral balance in their hands, the centrists came down in favour of the right, rejecting the *programme commun* parties. This choice appeared to set the scene for the bulk of the opposition centrists (or at least the Centre démocrate) to declare for the majority.[15]

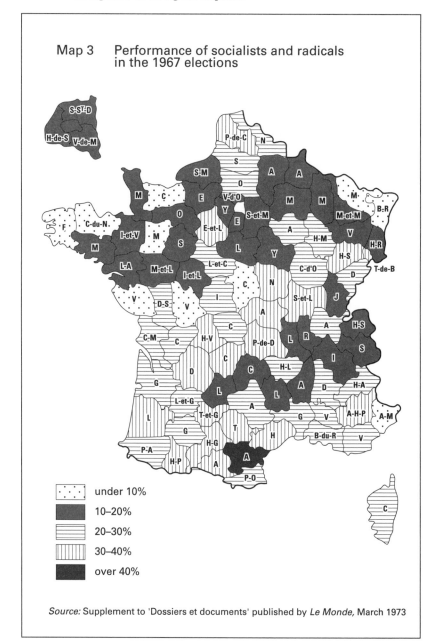

Map 3   Performance of socialists and radicals
in the 1967 elections

under 10%
10–20%
20–30%
30–40%
over 40%

Source: Supplement to 'Dossiers et documents' published by *Le Monde,* March 1973

Map 4   Performance of socialists and radicals
in the March 1973 elections

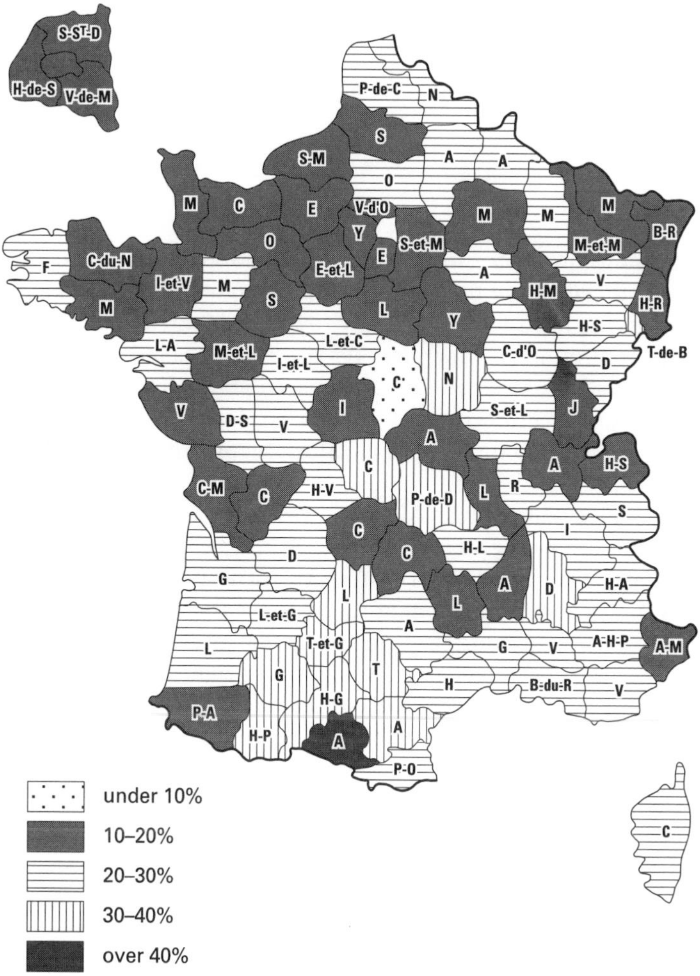

under 10%

10–20%

20–30%

30–40%

over 40%

Source: Supplement to 'Dossiers et documents' published by *Le Monde,* March 1973

Table 5. *Legislative elections of 4 and 11 March 1973: outcome in seats*

Opposition		
PCF	73	
PS and left radicals	102	(including 2 allied)
Social-democratic reformers	34	(including 4 allied)
Majority		
Centrist Union	30	
UDR	183	(including 24 allied)
Independent Republicans	55	(including 4 allied)
Independents	13	

Source: (17), vol. I, p. 488; (182).

Pompidou, however, made a last-minute appeal to voters, broadcast after the official end of the electoral campaign on 10 March. He stressed once again the need for the country to make common cause against the threat of communism 'which ignores or suppresses individual freedoms, political liberty, the right to own property, and submits the life of each individual to the authority of a totalitarian party and administration'.[16] But by now, the outcome of the elections seemed in any case a foregone conclusion.

By the late evening of 11 March it was indeed clear that the majority had won a convincing victory even if, as had been expected, it had lost many seats. There had been a massive turn-out, with only 18.72 per cent of the electorate abstaining (even fewer than in the first round) in these head-to-head contests. Indeed, in the overwhelming majority of constituencies, there had been straight left–right run-offs. The results showed how evenly balanced the parties were, with the majority and the left opposition achieving almost equal scores, each with approximately 47 per cent of the votes, leaving the reformers (many of whom had stood down in favour of the majority) with about 6 per cent. It was evident that opposition centrism now constituted a 'reserve tank' of votes on which the right could draw and it was this that accounted for the improvement in the fortunes of the right between the first and second rounds.[17]

With 268 of the 490 seats, the majority had won a clear victory, with almost a hundred seats more than the left opposition (see table 5). It would not even have to seek the support of the thirty-four reformers, almost all of whom belonged to Centre démocrate, Servan-Schreiber's radicals having won just four seats. Moreover, at the heart of this consolidated majority, the UDR itself with its 183 seats continued to occupy the strongest position. Not only had the Independent Republicans failed to attain their goal of electing 120 deputies, thereby forming a counterweight to the UDR, they had even lost a few seats. As for Jacques Duhamel's CDP, it only managed to reach the threshold of thirty seats required for it to retain its status as a parliamentary grouping thanks to the 'loan' of some deputies from other sections within the majority.[18]

Following the elections, which had clearly freed the hands of the president of the republic, it was expected that a policy of political 'openness' would be pursued, bringing Jean Lecanuet's centrists into the majority and implementing the package of reformist policies at which Pompidou had hinted both during the election campaign and in private conversations shortly after the results were declared.[19]

A conservative crackdown

To put it mildly, the shape of the new government caused deep disappointment both within the UDR and among centrists. The decision to keep Messmer on as prime minister did not come as a surprise to anyone, after he had acquitted himself so perfectly in the role assigned to him by the president, acting throughout as a loyal instrument of presidential policy. More surprising was the fact that the new government, rather than opting as expected for *ouverture*, moved to boost the president's personal control over the government.

Some of the departures from the government were due to circumstances beyond the president's control. Ill health forced Jacques Duhamel to step down: indeed, he died shortly afterwards. René Pleven and Maurice Schumann had lost their seats in the elections and, unlike General de Gaulle, who after the 1967 elections had decided to retain as ministers men who had been beaten at the polls,[20] Pompidou accepted their resignations, thereby following a course of action that could be read as a demonstration of his resolve to respect the wishes of the electorate. However, it was a matter of clear presidential will when it came to the departure from government of Michel Debré, a man who ever since the General's death had served as a walking reminder of the Gaullist legacy, and who moreover had set his sights on the ministry of finance. The only 'Gaullist baron' now left in government was Olivier Guichard, minister for public works. UDR members of course remained in a majority within the government though many now felt that the president had eliminated the UDR's leaders in order to make room for younger men with views closer to his own. These included Robert Galley, minister for the armed forces; Alain Peyrefitte, who was rewarded for his work as UDR general secretary, a job he retained, by being placed in charge of the ministry for administrative reforms; and Jean Taittinger, deputy mayor of Rheims, who became minister for justice. It was again thanks to the president's personal influence that Michel Jobert was appointed minister for foreign affairs. As the secretary general at the Elysée, a post at which he was succeeded by Edouard Balladur, Jobert had been Pompidou's closest collaborator and his move to the foreign ministry was seen as evidence that the president intended to strengthen his grip on the nation's foreign policy. Pompidou's increasingly apparent concern to oversee a return to morality in French life was demonstrated by the inclusion in the new government of two crusaders for moral values, the deputy mayor of Tours, Jean Royer, appointed minister for small business and commerce, and Maurice Druon, member of the French Academy who was brought in to fill the post vacated by Jacques Duhamel at the ministry for cultural affairs.

Lastly, while the liberal-minded Valéry Giscard d'Estaing remained at the ministry of finance, his party colleagues all blended well with the conservative tones of the new government: Raymond Marcellin, a strong advocate of repressive policies to deal with social and industrial agitation, stayed on as minister of the interior, while Michel Poniatowski became minister for health.

The first steps taken by the new government, and the political decisions prompted by the president, all served to underline this con-servative outlook, which was further confirmed by the failure of talks with Jean Lecanuet and the reformers. Thus, Chaban-Delmas, who had expected to stand for the post of National Assembly chairman, watched as Pompidou imposed the candidacy of Edgar Faure, who was duly elected on 2 April 1973 by the 274 votes on which the majority could count once a number of independent deputies had been won over. This inevitably appeared as a further gesture of defiance directed at the promoter of the 'New Society'.

Meanwhile, Maurice Druon, the new minister for cultural affairs, made a name for himself with some tough language aimed at cultural representatives who, he alleged, asked for subsidies while holding 'a begging bowl in one hand and a Molotov cocktail in the other'.

In June 1973 the determination to crack down on extremists led to the forced disbandment, on the orders of Raymond Marcellin, of the Ligue communiste, a Trotskyist organization, though admittedly this was balanced by meting out the same fate to the small extreme right-wing group, Ordre nouveau.

In the autumn, the process of retaking control of the ORTF was completed with the dismissal of Arthur Conte, whose directorship was deemed to have failed to produce the desired results; he was replaced by a high-ranking civil servant, Marceau Long. Meanwhile, a presidential protégé, Jean-Philippe Lecat, was placed at the head of the ministry for information.[21]

Though unmistakeable in terms of political appointments, this shift to the right was not unqualified. Although conservatism now imbued the statements made and the stances adopted by government members, it was not allowed to get in the way of contractual policy and indeed entailed no retreat from the progressive social measures that had been introduced at the start of Pompidou's presidency.

Yet the way the political shift was interpreted suggested that the goals set during the early years of Pompidou's term in office were now effectively shelved. A further consequence of the shift was to deepen the rift separating the president and the main party within the majority, the UDR.

Discontent within the UDR and the issue of the presidential succession

One of the immediate effects of the formation of the new government was to irritate the UDR. During the election campaign the Gaullists had expressed concern with the offhand attitude that the president had displayed towards the fate of the party. But this was the last straw. The departure from government of Michel Debré and the arrival of Michel Poniatowski, whom the UDR viewed as a sworn enemy; the removal of most of its leaders from positions of power; the selection as president of the National Assembly of a radical, Edgar Faure, instead of Chaban-Delmas: everything reinforced the UDR's feeling that Pompidou was perfectly happy to sacrifice party interests. The removal from the presidency of SOFIRAD of Pierre Lefranc, chairman of the Association pour la fidélité au général de Gaulle, further exacerbated their bitterness.

But worse was to come. The moment the elections were over, rumours began to circulate about a deterioration in the president's health. Having suffered for several years from a serious blood condition, Waldenström's disease, for which he had failed to obtain regular treatment, Georges Pompidou knew that he had little time left, though he did not know just how little. This may help to explain his fear of any upheaval that he might not have sufficient time to steer and bring under control, and also his desire to be flanked by loyal underlings rather than by strong personalities with whom he would be forced to negotiate or whom he would have to confront. If the deterioration in his health aggravated his long apparent conservative tendencies, it also created alarm in the UDR. The Gaullists feared that were the president to die they would lose a lot of ground, above all since Pompidou did nothing to discourage the ambitions of Valéry Giscard d'Estaing, who was now talked about in veiled terms as a future prime minister, which under the circumstances was tantamount to ensconcing him as presidential heir apparent.

Annoyance with overtures made towards its rivals, combined with apprehension about the future, help to explain why the UDR was becoming restive. As soon as the government had been formed, Alexandre Sanguinetti, the party's assistant general secretary, sounded a warning: '*ouverture* must not mean the obliteration of Gaullism to the advantage of those it has defeated'.[22] Such Gaullist ill humour was to become an enduring feature of French political life. When parliament reassembled, it was on display again as the UDR group elected as its chairman Roger Frey, a former minister and one of the so-called barons of Gaullism, who was known to be close to Chaban-Delmas. It was the same tetchiness that prompted protests at Alain Peyrefitte's accumulation of jobs, after he added to his ministerial responsibilities his duties as UDR general secretary. Peyrefitte's resignation from the latter position paved the way for a succession in which the Elysée now seemed incapable of intervening. In October 1973, in the third round of voting, Alexandre Sanguinetti, whose misgivings regarding the president were common knowledge, was elected UDR general secretary by fifty-eight votes to André Fanton's fifty-six. But above all it was at the party conference in Nantes on 17 and 18 November 1973 that the near split between Pompidou and the UDR appeared in full view. The conference rewarded Michel Debré, who had presented himself as the spiritual heir to the General, with a standing ovation, whereas the appeals made by Jacques Chirac and Pierre Messmer for Gaullists to unite behind the president were met with polite indifference. However, the most significant development at the Nantes conference was the UDR's enthronement of Chaban-Delmas as their potential candidate for the presidency. Having announced in an interview to the weekly magazine *Le Point* that he was preparing himself for whatever role circumstances might thrust upon him, the former prime minister used his speech to the Nantes conference as an opportunity to present his 'New Society' project as the natural sequel to de Gaulle's policy of 'participation'. Though it had frequently attacked him in the past, the UDR gave him an enthusiastic reception now that he seemed to be the only presidential candidate available who might just enable the Gaullists to retain their hold on the Elysée. From this point on, the Gaullist party intended to ensure a political succession that would protect the interests of the UDR which

Pompidou had so neglected. In December, when the party's executive committee came up for renewal, several serving ministers were defeated – clear evidence that the UDR no longer saw itself as the president's party.[23]

Yet seething UDR discontent made little real impact on political decision-making. When it came to a confidence vote, the Gaullists lined up four square behind the Messmer government. However, it was symptomatic that in December 1973 the reluctance of the UDR to back the government forced the referral back to committee stage of a draft bill on abortion. Yet the main victim of this state of affairs was the government's constitutional reform package, including the president's plan to shorten the presidential mandate from seven to five years.

The failure to introduce five-year presidential terms

It was during his speech to parliament on 3 April 1973 that Pompidou announced a constitutional reform bill that he wished to see enacted quickly, by the end of the year. To win over the support of deputies and senators, he stated his intention to adopt the procedure set out in article 89 of the constitution and which in effect gave parliament the whip hand: both chambers had to approve the same bill by the same deadline. In practice this entailed a joint session of parliament, which then needed to approve the revision of the constitution by a three-fifths majority.

There were many reasons for the reform that was envisaged. Some were narrowly constitutional, like the basic unsuitability of a long seven-year mandate to the broad new powers that the Fifth Republic conferred on the head of state. The most serious risk was that legislative elections might produce a parliamentary majority unable or unwilling to work with the president, now elected, it should not be forgotten, by universal suffrage. Indeed, this could have happened in March 1973. Such a scenario would unleash a constitutional crisis, given that the president would occupy a morally inferior position *vis-à-vis* an assembly able to claim that its popular mandate was more recent. This danger would be reduced if the president had to face the electorate as frequently as the deputies, even if not necessarily at the same time. But this was probably not the only reason for attempting reform. Pompidou may well have wished to regain public support by promoting a reform that enjoyed the backing of the main parties of the left as well as a sizeable section of the majority. Agreement on the measure might also provide an opportunity to achieve the longed-for *ouverture* to the centrists, having failed to gain their support in March 1973. But nor can the personal dimension of this issue be ignored: the precarious health of the president. In view of his worsening condition, Pompidou wished perhaps to shorten his own mandate. Or perhaps, unaware of its gravity, he may have hoped that by shortening his term to five years he could try to achieve a second term.

While these calculations may have played some part, it quickly became apparent that, as with the April 1972 referendum, the president's strategic analysis was mistaken and that, opposed on all sides as it was, the bill stood little chance of success. While the centrists, at least at the outset, gave it their support, the Independent Republicans let it be known that they would rather see the introduction of a genuinely presidential system of government. The left, for its part, having loudly demanded precisely this reform in the past, now announced that they would be opposing it, on the grounds that it did not go far enough. In their view, the revision to the constitution provided an opportunity to rein in the powers of the president. The government, however, had already stated that it would oppose any amendment that sought to broaden the scope of the reform. Most importantly, the challenge to de Gaulle's constitutional legacy aroused deep unease within the UDR. Maurice Couve de Murville and Michel Debré, both of whom had served as prime minister under the General, mounted fierce opposition to the reform, as did Christian Fouchet, a former minister.

The National Assembly debates on the constitutional reform bill in October 1973 brought all these diverging views into the open. The centrists performed a U-turn, making their support for the bill conditional on the inclusion of a limitation of any presidential mandate to two terms. Since the government refused to go along with this, in the end the bill was approved by only 270 votes, with 211 votes against. Three-quarters of the reformers and three UDR members, including Maurice Couve de Murville, had joined the left in opposing the bill, and Michel Debré had taken refuge in abstention. The bill met a similar fate in the Senate, where it was approved by just 162 votes to 112, with seven abstentions. The required three-fifths majority of parliament as a whole was clearly beyond reach.[24]

Not wishing either to be defeated before a joint session of parliament, or to lose face by jettisoning his reform, Pompidou decided to postpone it. The rapidly deteriorating international situation and resulting economic upheavals, combined with severe social tensions at home, in any case pushed constitutional reform off the immediate agenda.

With an ailing president, enfeebled by a two-year run of setbacks and no longer in full control of the majority party, France was entering stormy waters.

A skipperless ship?

At the very moment when Pompidou was confronted with major difficulties in internal affairs, a sharp deterioration in every area of the economy left the government looking powerless.

It was on the international horizon that the first warning signs appeared. It was in this area too that the president focused his dwindling strength, supported by Michel Jobert, the sharpness of whose tongue did little to enhance diplomatic relations. The president's overriding fear was that the United States might reach an accommodation with the Soviet Union, abandoning the European continent to its fate. In January 1973, Henry Kissinger, American secretary of state, had signed the Vietnam peace accord, and in June the American president received the Soviet leader, Leonid Brezhnev, in Washington. Pompidou was also concerned by Chancellor Brandt's *Ostpolitik* and the risks that it posed of a German–Soviet *entente*, threatening to detach the Federal Republic from the West. Lastly, he had to confront the determination of the United States to impose its vision of world trade at the GATT negotiations in Tokyo, and the impact of the second devaluation of the dollar in February 1973. These issues combined to revive the Franco-American tensions that had marked de Gaulle's period. Pompidou's trip to Minsk in February 1973 and Brezhnev's visit to Rambouillet in June had convinced him that the two superpowers were intending to reach an agreement: a return of the 'Yalta syndrome'.[25] In April, he saw his fears confirmed when Henry Kissinger proposed a new Atlantic Charter which, if accepted, would reduce France to the rank of a regional power under the American protectorate. Fearing that de Gaulle's historic ambition to turn France into a major world power might be challenged, Pompidou went to Reykjavik to meet President Nixon on 31 May and 1 June 1973. The talks were frank but produced nothing very positive, apart from a restatement of Pompidou's determination to oppose the main planks of American policy as he saw it take shape on trade, Europe, the currency, and so on. It was in this same spirit of resisting an attempt by the two superpowers to create a world 'directory' that Pompidou went to China in September 1973, where he was heartened by Mao Zedong's resolve also to oppose 'dual hegemony'.

Nonetheless, this traditional approach to foreign policy with its authentically Gaullist firmness began to give way in October 1973 to a much fuzzier approach, with the outbreak of the Yom Kippur War, after the Egyptian offensive against Israeli-occupied Sinai. In line with the policy that de Gaulle had pursued following the Israeli occupation of Sinai in 1967, and with the pro-Arab policy that he had himself overseen since arriving at the Elysée in 1969, Pompidou once again came down clearly on the Egyptian side. Commenting on the Egyptian offensive, Michel Jobert expressed this stance in his own way: 'Does attempting to set foot again in one's home have to constitute an act of unforeseen aggression?' As always, the government's pro-Arab policy encountered a great many reservations, both among the public and in the political parties where there was strong sympathy for Israel. France's policy in this area even led to the failure of the December 1973 EEC summit in Copenhagen where France's partners expressed views very different from her own, as well as strong disapproval of Michel Jobert's policy and acid irony.[26]

Whereas in foreign policy, although not all of his ventures were crowned with success, Pompidou appeared to hold his own, the same could not be said of domestic policies where, rightly or wrongly, the French people took the view that the mounting tide of troubles was being met at the apex of the state with an absolute vacuum.

This feeling was particularly acute as regards economic and social affairs. From the very start of his term of office, Pompidou had opted for vigorous growth regardless of the inflationary pressures that this was bound to unleash. In 1973, when both growth and inflation seemed set to soar, no reaction was forthcoming from the head of state, who was accordingly delivered a severe reprimand by Michel Debré in the Gaullist newspaper *La Nation*. Moreover, the Yom Kippur War had persuaded the Arab oil-producing states to attempt to influence the decisions of the major industrialized countries, most of which supported Israel, by shipping oil less frequently and by introducing big increases in the price per barrel. In a matter of months crude oil prices quadrupled. This struck a severe blow at one of the foundations of Western prosperity, raising questions about economic expansion itself which, for almost thirty years, had constituted the constant backdrop to world history. According to Eric Roussel, Pompidou's biographer, the world economic downturn came as no surprise to the president. Indeed, Roussel quotes many statements from 1972 in which Pompidou spoke of the problems that would be posed by the end of growth – which he judged to be approaching.[27] Such clear-sightedness, however, was not translated into any coherent set of policies. Indeed, government reactions to the economic and monetary turmoil were astonishingly feeble: energy-saving measures were introduced that consisted of pleas to consumers to turn down their heating systems during the 1973–4 winter to help reduce the cost of oil imports; and in November 1973 the suggestion of alterations to the tax system as part of an attempt to combat inflation, though this was shelved after the small businesses represented by Gérard Nicoud's CID–UNATI brought pressure to bear on the minister of commerce, Jean Royer. The consequences of the policy vacuum soon made themselves felt. By early 1974 France had entered the era of 'stagflation': on the one hand, stagnation in manufacturing due to the loss of markets caused by the increase in oil prices and the energy-saving policies; on the other, inflation, with the rise in the oil bill accentuating long-running trends, and further exacerbating the rigidities of the policy of indexing wages to rising prices, with the result that earnings remained high despite plummeting production. Moreover, rising unemployment, which was worrying even in 1972, was the end result of these imbalances. The currency too was severely affected. On 19 January 1974, the council of ministers decided to float the franc, following the example set by a number of other currencies since the devaluation of the dollar. The franc was taken out of the 'European monetary snake', which had been set up in April 1972 with the specific aim of limiting European currency fluctuations.[28]

The government's social and industrial policies were equally tentative. As far back as 1962, Pompidou had called for the structural modernization of the French economy. Yet in 1973 the conservative tendencies that were gaining the upper hand caused him to abandon this goal. For example, on the issue of retailing, he bowed to protests from small outlets and allowed the minister for commerce Jean Royer to bring forward in the National Assembly a bill to place restrictions on the creation of large specialist outlets (*grandes surfaces*). Clearly he was still determined to maintain order by doing battle with militancy of any type. Indeed, strikes by blue-collar workers in Le Mans and in Fos-sur-Mer were met with tough repressive measures. A similar response greeted the fresh round of student agitation that followed the implementation in 1973 of the 1970 'Debré law' limiting the length of time that students could postpone their military service, along with the reform of the first and second year of higher education.[29] But the event that proved most significant and revealed the tensions at the heart of government was the 'Lip affair'. In June 1973, this major watch-making company was forced into liquidation. The workforce, threatened with dismissal, occupied the factory under the leadership of Charles Piaget, the head of the local CFDT branch. Having seized and begun to market the firm's stock, the workers then resolved to run the company themselves. The highly symbolic character of their struggle brought the workers at Lip broad support among the public at large, the parties of the left and the church. When police moved in to clear the factory on 14 August, positions hardened still further, with the workers deciding to pursue a battle that now resonated nationwide. It was at this point that Jean Charbonnel, minister for industrial and scientific development, intervened in the conflict. In December 1973 he entrusted a young left-wing proprietor, Claude Neuschwander, with the task of getting the company back on its feet, a job that he resumed in January 1974. Yet although the government appeared determined to find a solution to the crisis, the prime minister, Pierre Messmer, declared on several occasions: 'Lip, c'est fini!' This then was yet another area in which the government appeared divided and its policy incoherent. As France slid further into crisis, the French felt that there was no longer anybody in charge.[30]

The death of Georges Pompidou

After May 1973, the president's illness, which previously only insiders had known about, became an open secret despite attempts by the Elysée to maintain confidentiality. The television pictures of the president in Reykjavik had shocked the country: Pompidou seemed to have put on weight, to walk unsteadily, to be overwhelmed by weariness, wrapped in a heavy overcoat, his hat pulled down over his eyes. From then on all his journeys, whether in France or abroad, were judged newsworthy and the public was able to chart the deterioration in his health and his increasing exhaustion. Nobody gave any credence to the frequent communiqués from the Elysée citing bouts of flu or flare-ups of haemorrhoids to account for the cancellation of receptions or the president's frequent absences.

Furthermore, illness made him irritable and abrupt and his isolation deepened, in particular cutting him off from the UDR, which now seemed reinvigorated. After autumn 1973 an end-of-reign atmosphere appeared to descend on the country. With the majority party now under the control of Alexandre Sanguinetti, the Gaullist 'barons' prepared the ground for a Chaban-Delmas candidacy. Meanwhile, Valéry Giscard d'Estaing took a series of initiatives designed to maintain his image as a man of youth and dynamism, a modern man of the future.

If a majority of the French public still had a favourable view of the head of state – at the end of 1973, between 54 and 56 per cent of French people declared themselves satisfied[31] – 63 per cent of those polled in November considered that the overall situation was deteriorating.[32] The government was further weakened by the revelation in Le Canard enchaîné that a group of men posing as plumbers had attempted to bug their premises. Although the true facts of the matter never emerged, similarities with the Watergate affair, the repercussions of which were then buffeting the Nixon administration, were not lost on the French. But above all opposition politicians like François Mitterrand and

Georges Marchais, and weeklies like *L'Express* and *Le Point*, were now saying in public what many leaders of the majority were thinking in private: France had been left without a government. On all sides calls were now heard for Messmer to stand down and Valéry Giscard d'Estaing was expected to replace him. *L'Express* and *Le Monde* openly questioned whether Georges Pompidou could remain in power and mooted his possible resignation.

The president made one last attempt to stop this all too evident slide. On 28 February 1974, he accepted the resignation of Pierre Messmer, only to call on him on 1 March to form a new government. It was not clear quite what the point of this manoeuvre might have been: neither the reduction in the number of ministerial portfolios nor the promotion of three junior ministers (Valéry Giscard d'Estaing, Olivier Guichard and Jean Taittinger) appeared likely to administer the shock to public opinion that was needed. The only really significant change was the appointment to the ministry of the interior of the outgoing minister for agriculture, Jacques Chirac, who thus swapped portfolios with a rather disconcerted Raymond Marcellin. The appointment of a Pompidou loyalist to this post was widely interpreted as an attempt to gain control over forthcoming elections.[33]

Events were to support this interpretation. On 2 April 1974, a terse statement from the Elysée announced that the second president of the Fifth Republic had passed away at 9 p.m.

Georges Pompidou had seen himself as rightful heir to Charles de Gaulle and had sought to adapt France to the new structures and changes in behaviour ushered in by growth. His death, occurring at the moment when France was plunging into the crisis that was to mark the last decades of the twentieth century, brought to an end a chapter in the nation's history.

Conclusion to part 1

How are we to assess the impact of Georges Pompidou's five years in office? The fact that no clear dividing line between his achievements as prime minister (1962–8) and as president (1969–74) can consistently be traced makes the task all the harder. Moreover, since it is impossible to evaluate structural changes over the short term, we are often forced to study intentions rather than measure results.

To step into the shoes of Charles de Gaulle was no easy matter. At the start of his presidency, Pompidou had first to grapple with the huge shadow that the General cast, then later with de Gaulle's more or less self-proclaimed followers, each of whom, as the repository of a fragment of the true cross, measured every action of his successor against what they deemed to be the spirit of the great man. Confronted with Gaullist diehards, Pompidou, even though he never missed an opportunity to acknowledge that he lacked the charisma of the Fifth Republic's founding father, was on permanent trial.

Allowing then for circumstances, how are we to judge Pompidou's achievements? It is probably in the constitutional field that he adminis-tered de Gaulle's legacy most effectively. It is worth recalling that after the General's retirement it was by no means inevitable that the system of government he had founded would survive. Yet not only did the new president confound all the predictions, he even managed to safeguard the pre-eminence of the presidency. Lacking the charisma that had enabled the General to trade on his historical stature, Pompidou achieved this through a constant and painstaking intervention in every field of governmental activity. The presidential *domaine réservé* had disappeared or, rather, it had been extended to every aspect of the nation's politics. If the Fifth Republic, owing to the General's excep-tional personality, was an elective and temporary monarchy at the time of Charles de Gaulle, it was Pompidou who made the regime permanent through his use of the institutions of power. It is no exaggeration to regard Pompidou as the Fifth Republic's second founding father, inau-gurating a tradition that all his successors would later pursue. Yet, by the same token, Pompidou highlighted a number of dysfunctions previously attributed to de Gaulle's personality but which turned out to be consequences of the pre-eminent position occupied by the president within the constitution. One such problem concerned the criteria for selecting prime ministers: it was essential that they possessed neither a strong personality nor their own political views. In Pompidou's reading of the constitution, the most suitable prime minister was not Chaban-Delmas, under whom the ghost of dyarchy that had so haunted all previous presidents breathed again, but Messmer, the loyal and obedient underling. In other words, the conviction spread during Pompidou's presidency that whatever article 20 of the constitution stated on the matter, the government might be said to 'conduct' the nation's politics, but it certainly didn't 'determine' them. Another obvious dysfunction related to the rights that parliament enjoyed. Despite the parliamentary nature of the system, parliament continued under Pompidou to play a subordinate role and, like the General before him, Pompidou strove to confine its powers to the enactment of laws and the approval of the budget, believing that any greater involvement in government affairs might, through the use of confidence votes, strengthen the position of the prime minister who would thus achieve a measure of genuine independence *vis-à-vis* the president. In short, it was during Pompidou's term of office that the institutions of the Fifth Republic took root and its system of government assumed its final shape.

There was another area in which Pompidou revealed himself to be a loyal trustee of de Gaulle's legacy: foreign and defence policy. Wedded to a haughty conception of national independence and wishing to see France play a major international role, Pompidou demonstrated the same distrust regarding the domination of the planet by a directory of the two superpowers, considering, as de Gaulle had done, that Europe, conceived as a federation of sovereign states intent on reconciling their policies in order to escape from domination by the opposing power blocks, was the right instrument for the intended objective. In this area, the real contrast between de Gaulle and Pompidou was one of tone. To grand visions and rousing challenges, Pompidou preferred diplomacy, negotiation and appeals to common sense. It has to be said, however, that Pompidou's achievements failed to live up to his ambitions, just as de Gaulle's had failed to measure up to his. If Pompidou's deliberately measured words found less of an echo than those of de Gaulle, he was in any case powerless to turn France into the world power she had long ceased to be. As for European policy, it was no fault of Pompidou's, as it had been no fault of de Gaulle's, if France's European partners proved more attached to the Atlantic Alliance than to the prospect of organizing a body of states independent of the two superpowers, or if national interests (which France took great care never to neglect) inclined the other European nations to envisage their futures in terms rather different from those mapped out in Paris.

It is probably in the field of economic and above all in social policy that Pompidou's record was most distinctive and where the contradictory motivations that drove the president were most visible. On the one hand, Pompidou was a modernist firmly believing in the country's industrialization at the hands of concentrated and competitive corporations, an enlightened follower of contemporary art, and a man fascinated by urban planning – and, in this connection, eager to transform the nation's capital. But at the same time he was an authentic product of the Third Republic, attached to his peasant roots, imbued with the morality and values of the pre-war years, based on a sense of measure, a belief in social advancement through work, competitive effort and thrift, and horrified by the liberalization of mores and the permissive society that the 1968 crisis had ushered in. Both sides of his personality left their mark on his record, making it hard to assess. But it is safe to say that his modernizing and forward-looking side prevailed during the initial period of his term in office, whereas from 1972 onwards illness seemed to bring to the fore the other, distinctly conservative, side to his character. Looked at in this way, Pompidou certainly wished his presidency to stand out for the spectacular development of large-scale industry, enabling France to compete on world markets. Also, to a greater extent than de Gaulle, Pompidou had sought to adapt the structures of French society to the new phenomenon of growth, thereby offering one possible way out of the 1968 crisis. This record obviously bears the strong imprint of Pompidou's first-serving prime minister – to the point where the very expression 'New Society' became Chaban-Delmas' property. Yet the president, however irritated by what he considered to be the over-intellectual form in which his prime minister couched his social policy, was nonetheless far from hostile to the actual measures that it comprised.

In contrast, the last few years of Pompidou's presidency were overshadowed by illness, which inclined him towards conservatism. And there is no doubt that he managed neither really to foresee the crisis, nor to respond to it once it had arrived, nor indeed to mitigate its effects. Equally, he felt no need for reforms designed to bring legislation into line with changing mores – a field in which Giscard d'Estaing, his successor, was to excel. Bearing in mind the president's illness and the downturn in the economy, it is tempting to take the view that the really significant period in Pompidou's mandate was over by the summer of

1972. It was under Pompidou that France saw both the high point and the end of the boom that had started in the mid-1950s and at whose heart had stood the presidency of de Gaulle. With the death of Pompidou, the major wave of expansion that twentieth-century France had enjoyed came to an end.

Part 2

France under Georges Pompidou

5   The growth-rate society

Whatever the rebels and strikers of 1968, shouting that no one could 'fall in love with a growth rate', might think, France in 1974 had just lived through the golden age of what Jean Fourastié would later celebrate as France's 'thirty glorious years'.[1] This country, which had so often been described as 'chronically Malthusian', mired in statist 'Colbertism', economically fallow, and which Pompidou himself feared had never learned to love its industry, had not only sunk its teeth into the fruits of the global economic boom on which every Western country had grown rich, it had clasped growth to its heart, making it the very touchstone of a new social order.

With GDP swelling between 1960 and 1973 at an unprecedented annual rate of 5.8 per cent, with prosperity now so visible and its human and cultural effects so tangible, the French could hardly fail to experience the euphoric buzz of such expansion. De Gaulle first,[2] and then Pompidou had insisted repeatedly that there could be no national grandeur without economic power, no wealth or even comfort without effort, no way of constantly 'aiming high and standing tall', casting off mediocrity and dependency, than through production. Emerging triumphant from the struggle throughout the 1950s to rebuild and modernize their country, for the last fifteen years the French had responded with alacrity to their leaders' enlightened *dirigisme*. Between 1968 and 1973, France doubled its exports, increased its output by a third, and achieved an annual industrial growth rate of 6.3 per cent, the highest in Europe. With living standards up by 25 per cent, France had almost caught up with Japan, had left Great Britain trailing and was now neck and neck with Germany. France was the front-runner at last and some futurologists, gazing towards 1985, predicted even more staggering triumphs.[3] And then came slump.

The industrial imperative

'Our prime economic objective is to make France a truly industrial nation . . . to give the French economy an international dimension': this was how Georges Pompidou, addressing his first press conference as president on 10 July 1969, identified the challenge facing the new government. And, as we have already seen, this twin priority shaped a strategy linking industrial development, the spread of prosperity, and France's position in Europe and the world.[4] While filing down some of Gaullism's economic rough edges, with a shift towards economic liberalism, policy under Pompidou started by backing industrial dynamism. Indeed, the president wanted even social activities to be run on this industrial pattern, founded on the drive for productivity that the state would use as a spur to achievement, on the increased market responsiveness generated by global competition, and the promise of social harmony through greater economic prosperity.[5] Some of those who subscribed to this 'neo-Saint-Simonian' faith even dreamt of France's industrial capacity doubling in the space of ten years (see table 6).

The relevant data were so unanimous that there seems little point in drawing up a detailed table of the industrial triumphs on which such ambitions were founded: almost every branch of industry was swept along with the force of the tide. One need only observe the predominant trends,[6] following the lists and inventories drawn up by INSEE statisticians whose job was, as it were, to monitor the spaceship's instrument panel and tweek the commands with a view to the country's bottom line and forward planning. The ship was, however, plentifully provided with energy, given that in the space of twenty years its supplies had quadrupled in size and almost tripled in value in francs. Faced with the increasingly acute shortfall of French-produced energy (76 per cent of primary energy had to be imported in 1973, up from 50 per cent ten years earlier), the choice had been clear and the switchover from French-mined coal to reliance on imported oil dramatic. Primary electricity remained a small proportion of total energy production (7.5 per cent in 1950, 7.4 per cent in 1973): hydro-electric generation could not be expanded any further, geothermal sources were ageing, and nuclear energy only just coming on stream. EDF had for a long time hesitated to promote gas-graphite reactors, a technology favoured by the CEA and strongly supported by de Gaulle, using a model similar to the controversial Chinon reactor that had been in operation since 1963. Pompidou's decision in December 1969 to adopt the American Westinghouse enriched-uranium system, which as well as being cheaper meant that France would no longer be technologically isolated, was greeted

Table 6. *Structure of the French economy, 1959 and 1973*

	Percentage contribution of each branch to GDP			Percentage of working population employed in each sector	
	1959	1973		1959	1973
Agriculture	9.7	6.4	Primary sector	22.1	10.9
Food industries	4.0	4.4			
Energy	4.0	5.0	Secondary sector	35.2	37.8
Intermediary industries	7.4	9.6			
Plant and machinery	6.2	9.5	Tertiary sector	42.7	51.3
Consumer goods	5.6	6.1			
Construction and public works	7.8	7.2			
Transport and telecommunications	5.3	6.0			
Commerce	11.3	11.0			
Other services	38.7	34.8			

with relief.[7] Declining output at the Lacq natural gas field and the inflated cost of Algerian gas (20 per cent above world prices, in line with the Evian accords revised in 1965) were more than offset by cheaper petroleum imports, with the result that the overall share of energy consumption accounted for by gas production rose from 0.5 per cent in 1950 to 8.6 per cent in 1973.[8] The collieries, whose shrinkage had been orchestrated by the 1960 Jeanneney plan, now represented a mere 17 per cent of total energy (down from the 1950 level of 74 per cent), severely weakening entire regions in the centre, south and even in the north and north-west of France. Responding to the fall in oil prices prior to 1973, there was such a dash for oil that its share in total energy consumption rose from 18 per cent to 67 per cent, flooding industry with heating oil, the production of which had quadrupled since 1958, and feeding motor-car euphoria. CFP (Compagnie française des pétroles) and ELF-ERAP (Entreprise de recherches et d'activités pétrolières), based principally in African oilfields, supplied about half of the total, while the rest was bought from the major global oil companies and came principally from the Middle East.

   The production of plant and machinery for both industrial and household use was enjoying a boom period, as was metals processing and the manufacturing of mechanical, electrical and electronic goods. Achieving high levels of productivity, outstanding growth rates and excellent profits in 1971–3, while at the same time creating a lot of jobs, these sectors aroused lively interest in both the private and public sectors (especially via research). They also generated more real surpluses than

Table 7. *Development and ranking of industrial sectors, 1952–1972*

	Annual growth (%)	Growth index (1952=100)	Value added per person (annual growth %)	Employment growth (000s)
Food and agriculture	4.2	229	4.4	+2
Energy	7.2	403	8.8	−74
Intermediary industries	6.9	379	6.7	+131
Plant and machinery	7.4	416	5.7	+811
Consumer goods	4.7	248	6.2	−415
Construction and public works	6.5	355	3.8	+815

other branches of industry, yet retained the ability to self-finance practically 90 per cent of their further development. The most prominent industries in this field were electronics, shipbuilding and weapons production (with France's nuclear strike force as well as foreign arms sales), all of which areas were dominated by Dassault.[9] Equally important fields were aeronautics – where the widely predicted success of the Airbus jumbo trialled in 1972 went some way to make up for disappointing returns on investments in Concorde – and above all the automobile industry, riding high on the exceptional dynamism of both domestic and export markets. Indeed, between 1965 and 1973, the annual growth rate in this flagship sector touched 10 per cent, equal to that achieved by the Japanese. In 1973, Régie Renault manufactured 40 per cent of a total output of approximately three million vehicles, trailed by Peugeot with 21 per cent of production and Citroën, who had been bought out by Michelin, on 20 per cent. The Peugeot and Citroën groups, both privately owned, were merged in 1974.

The dynamism apparent in the field of intermediary goods (transformable products used in iron and steel making, chemicals or construction) was, however, uneven, with a widening gulf between a sector that relied on state aid and a sector energized by demand alone. Iron and steel making in particular were still staggering from the effects of the downturn in the world market since 1964 and the increasing substitution of aluminium, plastics and concrete in many fields. Deep in debt and yet forced to invest larger and larger sums to fight off European and Japanese competition, the industry was poor at marketing its products, dominated by firms that had started out as family concerns and were only just waking up to modern realities, and haunted by fears of nationalization. Iron and steel making had had to be cajoled by the authorities into a drive to modernize, to shift investments abroad, and to think big, rather than sticking to the typically French 1966 'professional plan', under which the state loaned the industry 27 per cent of the capital. Usinor immediately took over Lorraine-Escaut, while Vallourec, De Wendel and Sidelor merged in 1967 and Creusot-Loire was founded in 1970. But restructuring had not gone far enough and forward integration in particular was inadequate. One should not be misled by the rosy figures – seventeen million tonnes of steel in 1960, rising to twenty-seven in 1974: the industry as a whole was lop-sided. On the one hand, there was the Lorraine, scratching for limonite, breaking all known records for the production of hard-to-sell 'long products', and providing 70 per cent of French steel; on the other, there was the coastal industry, placing all its trust in pure oxygen steels and automation, with Usinor installed at Dunkirk since 1963 and Somer, a subsidiary of Sollac, planning to start production at Fos in 1975, using Mauritanian ore but with no guarantees for the future.[10]

In contrast, the chemical industry had managed to invest in research and development, diversify and increase the sales of its products: rubber, synthetic fibres, plastics of all kinds, fertilizers, detergents, solvents, insecticides, drugs, glues, colourants and paints – everything that directly fuelled mass consumption. It had also geared up its process of concentration in order to confront German and British competition. Since 1970, the French chemical industry had been dominated by three rival groups: Péchiney-Ugine-Kuhlmann, Rhône-Poulenc and Saint-Gobain-Pont-à-Mousson,[11] whereas Michelin was now concentrating more on automobiles. With an annual growth rate of 9.3 per cent from 1962 to 1973 and unparalleled capitalist intensity, the chemical industry remained the beacon for the *trente glorieuses*. Such success provided a yardstick for measuring the relative backwardness of other sectors: consumer goods (textiles, clothing, paper, printing and publishing); food and agriculture; and building and public works. These industries expanded less strongly, alternating between the break-up of family firms and extreme concentration: in cement manufacturing three groups, including Lafarge, controlled 90 per cent of production; in textiles, Agache-Willot, Dollfus-Mieg and Prouvost completely dominated the jumble of technologically backward and uninventive small producers and retailers, who were subject to wild fluctuations in demand, slower to secure a return on productivity drives and, apart from the building industry, untempting to investors.

On the whole, this overview of industry presents a radiant picture and one is immediately tempted to search for endogenous causes for such prosperity. In the following chapter, we shall examine the major role that domestic demand played in this process. But the effort at accumulation was so intense and the determination to substitute labour for capital so strong – rooted as it was on technological progress – that one has first of all to recall the eagerness and success with which investment was sought to compensate for the sharp downturn since 1966–8 in capital profitability and in productivity. By 1974 the French investment rate was the highest of any OECD country, reaching 24 per cent of GNP (as compared to 21 per cent in West Germany and 18 per cent in the USA), even if the annual rate of directly productive investment plummeted from 13 per cent in 1969 to 5 per cent in 1974. An effort was made to encourage personal and household savings (with the proportion of income saved rising from 12.7 per cent in 1959 to 17.7 per cent in 1973). These funds were tapped rather more effectively than in the past by SIVACs (variable capital investment companies), which had been set up in 1964. Savers were encouraged by tax exemptions (tax credits had been introduced for shareholders in 1965 and lump-sum deductions became available in 1966 for holders of debenture loans), while better orchestrated appeals were addressed to the banks, which by 1973 in fact provided two-thirds of business credits as compared with 49 per cent in 1962. This development helped to offset the steady decline in the ability of firms to finance themselves, down from 91 per cent in 1959 to 79 per cent in 1973. Overall, firms were well financed and prosperous:[12] an investigation into 1,000 companies in 1974 revealed that their profits were higher than those of their German counterparts. But, highly significantly, they were only passing on to their shareholders 18 per cent of their profits: they had become prudent and were accumulating their own funds, knowing only too well that they would be unable to grow further without going into debt. For the current glorious economic climate automatically drew companies into debt and, already, some company owners were neglecting investment in production and were taking out loans in the knowledge that the capital thus acquired would effortlessly bring in more than it cost to purchase. The result was a relentless pursuit of discounted profit rather than acquired profit that ended by placing companies even more at the mercy of competition, eroding their profitability or forcing them to beg for state support.

Similarly, changing structures in industry, and above all the spate of company groupings and mergers, were strongly encouraged by the July 1965 law that Pompidou had promoted and which enabled firms to revalue their assets during the process of concentration. The examples we have already mentioned in the fields of iron and steel making, and in textiles and the automobile industry, were preceded in banking and insurance[13] and later spread to retailing and even agriculture. However, such mergers often entailed a straightforward clustering of similar activities, without any particular industrial logic and tended actually to benefit those sectors that were already the most concentrated. Even so, few European-class 'national champions' were created in this way. Yet the results certainly looked impressive: by 1974, companies with over 500 employees (4.2 per cent of all firms) employed 60 per cent of the entire labour force, accounted for two-thirds of turnover and attracted 77 per cent of investment. Companies with 1,000 employees and over employed 96 per cent of the total workforce in the power industry, 58 per cent of workers in intermediary commodities, 52 per cent in plant and machinery, and just 15 per cent in consumer goods. 'Technological concentration' along German lines, INSEE observed, had increased considerably. Yet despite the massacre of very small firms, small and medium-sized firms with under 200 employees survived: they still employed over a third of the country's total workforce and Léon Gingembre's CGPME (Confédération générale des petites et moyennes entreprises) had formed these companies into a pressure group that the authorities could not afford to ignore, as was demonstrated at the time of Gabriel Kaspereit and the Royer law in 1973.[14] Indeed, their survival clearly shows that this incomplete process of restructuring could not be regarded as a decisive factor. A further sign of underlying hesitancy was that the public had little understanding and still less enthusiasm for merger fever.

In fact the motor for 'industrializing growth' remained exogenous: it was the opening of the French economy to the industrialized world that proved decisive. Once the war with Algeria had been brought to an end – putting the lid back on what de Gaulle had called a *boîte à chagrin* – France, relieved of its imperial burden, and buoyed up by a policy of cooperation or aid to under-developed countries, had nonetheless begun to trade heavily first and foremost with other equally affluent countries. Indeed, between 1959 and 1973, trade with the franc zone – essentially Africa – slumped, with an 87 per cent drop in imports and an 84 per cent drop in exports; meanwhile, trade with the EEC countries roared ahead, with imports rising by 77 per cent and exports by 70 per cent. This headlong plunge into international free competition was quite deliberate:[15] the franc had been a convertible currency since 1961, trading quotas had been abolished in 1960 and customs tariffs had fallen 50 per cent between 1968 and 1972 in line with GATT agreements, while the Common Market and the European Free Trade Area (EFTA) had created a vast market-place on France's doorstep. Exposure to such competition benefited the most competitive sectors of the economy such as food and agriculture, transport equipment, aeronautics, and the queen of exports, the motor-car. At the same time, this immersion in the market prompted a search for goods that could be imported at a better rate than those produced at home, for example Italian white goods or German machine tools.

Apart from straightforward trading, the French economy was by this time plugged into the best international circuits for supplies and finance. This was how most of France's oil and foreign capital were now sourced, and they flowed in much more abundantly and eagerly with Pompidou installed in the Elysée. In 1973, foreign capital, above all American, dominated share-holdings in 1,029 companies, together employing 14 per cent of the country's workforce, accounting for 19 per cent of industrial investment and 20 per cent of sales. This ongoing 'colonization' certainly caused some concern: the country's export drive was still far too weak and not enough French firms were able to compete with their European counterparts. Furthermore, dependence on imports deepened the trade deficit and stoked inflation, bringing French products into line with foreign prices. Nonetheless, the trade balance moved into surplus in 1971–3 for the first time and this was proof of a vigour that could now be felt throughout the economy. Equally, the employers' mindset had altered and in 1965 the CNPF had adopted an economically very liberal charter that resisted the old temptation to retreat into protectionism. Sectors as diverse as agriculture and metallurgy had been forced to face the challenge of world trade, with competition ruthlessly obliging them to modernize and specialize. The opening up of the economy gave it an undeniable impetus and, in the opinion of the real economic and political decision-makers, this was the decisive factor.

The strength of Pompidou's economic policy lay in its determination to confront French state interventionism with this international climate and the stimulus it afforded. As at the time of de Gaulle, though now with a broader horizon and a vigorous free-market philosophy, public authorities maintained their ability to steer firmly and to intervene. The state could still control about half of the country's investments through a variety of levers that had become ever more flexible. Examples included treasury disengagements, the Fonds de développement économique et social, in existence since 1955, or the Caisse des dépôts et consignations. Another important factor was the decision not to make such great demands on the wealth of the nation (the proportion of the state budget to GDP fell from 24.4 per cent in 1969 to 19.6 per cent in 1974), the regulation of prices and the development of a pricing policy, tax breaks to encourage saving and investment, and the sketch of an incomes policy. In addition, the public authorities knew how to influence and lead the nationalized sector. They encouraged the concentration of the chemical industry around Houillères, and the petroleum industry around ERAP. They also speeded up mergers in the automobile industry and aeronautics (for example, SNIAS in 1970) and forced EDF, as we have seen, to go for the more profitable nuclear option. By sticking to the 1967 Nora report, they even undertook a thorough-going reorganization of the way public enterprises were managed, signing *contrats de programme* with a number of them, like SNCF and EDF, the purpose of which was to keep an eye on profitability, make their prices and tariffs conform more closely to reality and at last give them a taste of competition.

The public authorities also proposed development patterns, though they took the risk of making these less binding. The 'Plan', for example, since the departure of Pierre Massé in January 1966, was no longer the *obligation ardente* of the Gaullist age. It could no longer claim to hit its former, purely quantitative, targets: the Fifth Plan (1966–70) was knocked off course by the overheating of the economy, the May 1968 explosion and the 1969 devaluation; the Sixth Plan (1971–5), which had dared to predict growth of 7.5 per cent a year, was punctured by slump from 1973 onwards. Moreover, with the development of more direct relations between the state and the world of business, and with decision-making now scattered among different ministries all under the watchful gaze of the finance ministry, planning found itself adrift. No longer a direct tool of government, it became instead a huge research outfit providing analyses and projections to local bodies and enterprise, albeit with scarcely any ability to affect their eventual decisions. Its committees swelled in an effort to register the aspirations of every social group while its theoretical models grew ever more sophisticated.[16]

There is no evidence, however, that the Plan loosened its hold. But it was no longer the core of a system of state intervention and it was no longer in a position to put forward balanced patterns of growth, even if approximately 60 per cent of businesses stated that they complied with its guidelines when deciding on investments and overall strategy. When it came to research in high-tech areas, state action appeared rather more hesitant than before.[17] In information technology, the costly 'Computer Plan' launched in 1967 proved extremely disappointing, failing to prevent incursions by American and European capital and technologies, including Honeywell (1970) and Unidata (1972). This forced the French companies Bull and above all CH, which the state created and propped up until 1972, to enter into humiliating agreements on market share. While it is true that the European Space Agency forged ahead with the Ariane project, that atomic research made steady progress at the CEA, and that the Délégation générale à la recherche scientifique et technique (DGRST), attached to the prime minister's office, was functioning perfectly honourably, national expenditure on R&D which had peaked at 2.2 per cent of GDP in 1967 (as against 1.1 per cent in 1959) had fallen to 1.6 per cent for 1973. *Grands programmes* were now deemed too costly and their technological spin-offs too uncertain. Even if state aid still helped indirectly to finance 60 per cent of private research projects, the state was clearly backing away from research with industrial applications, preferring to place more emphasis on 'socio-economic' goals that tended to favour the biological and social sciences. As a result, France was left exposed in a key area, a prey to all the dangers of the globalized research trade, and subject to American supremacy. It was here that industrial Pompidolism revealed a limit and a contradiction which, though scarcely visible in the euphoria of the moment, boded ill for the future.

Yet the impression that prevailed in 1974 was that the drive to industrialize was a gamble that had paid off, given that, as we shall see, its social consequences were so tangible. Public intervention took some well-deserved credit from this. An early bout of inflation following the May 1968 crisis had been throttled by a price freeze, credit squeeze and, above all, by the shock devaluation of August 1969. The new inflationary surge, in the aftermath of the international monetary crisis triggered in 1971 when the Americans took the dollar off gold, was brought under control by a rise in interest rates and further restrictions on credit, which certainly had the effect of attracting floating capital but which also revealed and helped to consolidate the budgetary balance achieved since 1969. This was enough to buttress the illusion of progress. Yet short-term economic policy was already caught in a dilemma: how could one protect, on grounds of national interest, what was now a highly industrialized economy when the process of opening it up to world competition was the prime factor in its dynamism?

This uncertainty was heightened when lone voices began to question the sense of the worldwide growth in which France was sharing: for although no one yet knew that its glorious cycle was coming to an end, many people were already feeling disillusioned.[18] Published in spring 1972, the Meadows report, which the highly elitist Club of Rome had commissioned from experts at MIT, rang the ecological alarm bells. It described humankind as being in danger of suffocating on its own growth, and in a plea for the rights of the sovereign individual pointed to the gulf that was opening up between destructive industrialization and a modern industrial society which, it had been gambled, would deliver harmony and justice, and which Pompidou had been so intent on inaugurating in France.[19] What if growth-rate worship were to become unacceptable? This misgiving, shouted from the rooftops in May 1968, was now whispered among certain elites who were increasingly alarmed by the experts. If it failed to bother the vast majority of French people, its circulation was greatly assisted by the turn now taken by industrial strikes and service sector disputes. Not only had they dragged on ever since 1968 – with 2,900 disputes settled in 1970 and 3,700 in 1973, and the number of days lost in strike action doubling, from two to roughly four million – but the agitation now cut across all former divides, with no regard to company size, degree of unionization, salary levels or the employer's willingness to negotiate. Above all, it was the manufacturing system itself with its cult of machinery, its hierarchical relations and petty authoritarianism that were rejected. What was demanded in their place were more interesting tasks, greater variation in working hours, more independence for work teams, and the maintenance of regional industrial identities. The Lip strike in Besançon in summer 1973 appeared to open up a prospect of workers' control (*autogestion*), strongly encouraged by the CFDT. And many other conflicts seemed to confirm that the time was now ripe to tear up industrial society's new rulebook.[20]

The rise of the *groupe central*

Whatever doubt was cast upon it in its later stages, the deliberate application of the industrialization model had major social repercussions.[21] In particular, the changing structure of the working population revealed the extent of the upheaval that economic growth had triggered. Whereas in 1954 agriculture, industry and services each employed about a third of all workers (31.4 per cent, 33.6 per cent and 33.8 per cent respectively), twenty years later the effects of industrialization were spectacular. Between 1962 and 1974, the primary sector had dwindled to half its size, dropping from 20.6 per cent to 10.1 per cent of the workforce, the secondary sector had swollen from 38.7 per cent to 39.1 per cent, and the tertiary sector, now the largest and still expanding rapidly, had risen from 40.7 per cent to 50.8 per cent. It is possible to observe the same process at work by looking at the pattern of jobs, whether in absolute terms or as percentages, over the period 1968–74: jobs in agriculture fell from 3,100,000 to 2,200,000 (from 15.6 per cent to 10.6 per cent), jobs in industry rose from 7,500,000 to 8,200,000 (from 37.4 per cent to 38.5 per cent), and tertiary sector jobs rose from 9,500,000 to 10,100,000 (from 47 per cent to 50.9 per cent).

Moreover, this new structure went hand in hand with the faster turnover in employment that resulted from natural population trends.

Indeed, the raising of the school-leaving age, on the one hand, which between 1962 and 1975 reduced the employment rate of fifteen- to twenty-four-year-olds from 66 per cent to 55 per cent and, on the other, an ageing population which swelled the ranks of the retired from 120 to 130 per thousand, meant that a roughly equal number of French people were in work, though turnover was much more intense. Never before had there been so few adults of working age as at the time of the 1968 census. In 1974, there were 22.2 million people in work, that is to say 42.5 per cent of the total population, a proportion comparable with that of other Western countries but which had not seen much growth for a long time: the corresponding figures and percentages for 1968 and 1962 are, respectively, 20.8 million and 41.9 per cent, and 19.9 million and 42.9 per cent. However, it has always been at times when the employment rate is at a historic low that output and productivity have soared.[22] It was therefore essential to set to work any new arrivals on the jobs market, who could then bring youth and dynamism to employment as well as greater fluidity. Immigrants entered the secondary sector *en masse* and the last influx from rural areas was channelled into either manufacturing or services, with women became increasingly numerous in the tertiary sector.[23] It was equally vital to insist on steady improvements in labour productivity, which had increased 5 per cent a year on average since 1949, and which Chaban-Delmas' contractual policy had tied in more closely to rises in salary. Indeed the size of such increases in productivity offset the reduction in the working week which had stabilized since 1954 at −0.3 per cent each year, though the French were still working longer hours than any other Western European nation.[24] If one adds that there was still practically full employment (the ministry of labour registered only 113,000 unemployed persons in 1964, 254,000 in 1968 and 394,000 in 1973, who were well provided with benefits and tended to find work in under nine months or were granted early retirement), everything points to an optimistic conclusion: the *trente glorieuses* had expanded work and the Pompidou years in particular had been spectacular in this regard.[25]

Caught between the relentless decline of France's agricultural base, once the country's mainstay, which was brutally exposed by the negligible proportion of the workforce now employed on the land and, on the other hand, the development of the tertiary sector in response to the increasingly pressing consumer needs of a population that was itself growing (46.5 million in 1962, 49.7 in 1968, 52.6 in 1975), the moderate growth of employment in manufacturing industry (51,600 a year between 1968 and 1973) seemed to betray a degree of uncertainty. Indeed it underlined the fact that industrialization in France was more than ever a top–down voluntarism that relied on a combination of enterprise spirit, intense exploitation of the workforce, and state assistance. Yet the drive to industrialize had little control over its most positive social consequence. The impression was gaining ground that a 'post-industrial society' was dawning, the complexity and worrying implications of which flew in the face of official discourse, while the hopes that it awakened had found vigorous voice in May–June 1968. Everything conspired to erode the old myth of a single working class, stationed at the heart of productive society, and to foster the awareness that the very structure of society was now splintering. Trade unionists and sociologists, employers and top civil servants now vied with one another to proclaim that the world of labour was being torn apart in the tension created between different working patterns, while some people, especially in the CFDT, thought they could discern in this tension the stirrings of a revolution through workers' control (*autogestion*).[26]

On the one hand, in heavy industries like metallurgy, car production (for example, Citroën in Choisy, Renault in Flins, and Peugeot in Montbéliard),[27] chemicals or even textiles, one could observe the spread of 'shift work', combining the old Taylorist breaking-down of movements performed at the production line with the new continuous rotation of mixed teams whose job it was to keep the line supplied at its required pace. Such shift work devastated the skills base, required minimal on-the-job training lasting a couple of days, and compounded all the ills of monotony, vacuousness and deskilling. It led to nervous rather than physical fatigue, given that heavy handling work, now either automated or assigned to subordinates, was no longer entrusted to the 'skill-free' worker, who confined himself to regulating the use of his body in a very limited space. On the other hand, the reskilling of a 'new working class' was advancing apace, often in the very same industries (one could cite Renault's automation systems in Sandouville or Le Mans). Here, what was being created was an avant-garde of workers representing about 5 per cent of the total workforce.[28] The model companies, frequently the subject of research, were Neyrpic in Grenoble, Thomson-Houston, Bull, Caltex and Sollac. They were manned by highly skilled specialists in white overalls, regulating machines and production units that they themselves installed, monitoring the smooth running of the automated systems, and performing abstract finetuning tasks without really dirtying their hands. The production process and the material nature of the industrial product had become almost invisible to these attentive operators, who were capable of making instant decisions, and were allocated to homogeneous teams whose knowhow and work was to monitor, as it were, by remote control.[29] On this basis, certain observers ventured to announce an imminent 'automation' revolution.

Competition between these two patterns was naturally very strong in the most profitable sectors of industry but still weak in the vast majority of small and medium-sized businesses. The three stages of industry that Alain Touraine had identified – multi-skilled labour, specialized mechanized labour and automated labour – were often telescoped within the same corporation or even on a single shopfloor. Mining, boiler-making, glass-making and a large section of the textiles industry held out against modernization and still valued genuine knowhow, whereas automation and high-grade skills took the oil and chemical industries, electronics and aeronautics by storm. Yet the changes in employment highlighted the hierarchical structures attendant on the old and new working patterns. Between 1963 and 1972, industries producing intermediary goods held almost level, their share of the total workforce slipping only from 28 per cent to 27 per cent, plant and machinery expanded from 33 per cent to 38 per cent, while consumer goods manufacturing, which was more fully modernized, fell from 39 per cent to 35 per cent. The frontiers of the working class had become blurred at the very moment when it was better integrated than ever before into society as a whole – at least in terms of consumption and improved standards of living. Its numbers had swollen from 6 to 8.2 million between 1954 and 1974. However, within this overall number, the proportion of workers, narrowly defined, was in constant decline. In 1974, 32 per cent of all industrial jobs were in unskilled production, 47 per cent in skilled work, and engineers and office staff already accounted for 21 per cent. In the building industry, the respective percentages were 24.3, 61.1 and 14.6; in general mechanical engineering, they were 43.7, 36.1 and 20.2; but in the oil industry they were 10, 46.3 and 43.7.

Managerial staff, supervisors and technicians had thus increased in numbers in line with the modernization of work and the increasing profitability of invested capital. Skilled workers (now referred to as 'professionals' and ranked in a three-level hierarchy as P1s, P2s or P3s) also multiplied (from 2.6 million in 1968 to 3 million in 1975), given that their work, now modelled on the more technical content of the next rung up, was more productive than previously. By contrast, there were still large and stable numbers of so-called 'specialized workers' (known as 'OS' – *ouvriers spécialisés* – but in fact low-skilled) as well as unskilled labourers (a total of 4,100,000 in 1968 and 4,600,000 in 1975). These workers, however, were increasingly at the mercy of their employers' and supervisors' whims and very uncertain about the future. Unsurprisingly, it was above all these insecure jobs that attracted fresh young recruits, especially women and immigrants. Indeed, whereas in 1968 one worker in every five was a woman, this had risen to one in four by 1974. Of these women workers 80 per cent were low-skilled ('OS') or unskilled. Indeed, 28 per cent of unskilled jobs were filled by women in 1975 as compared to 26 per cent in 1962. As for immigrants, in 1974 roughly one worker in ten was an immigrant but 27 per cent of workers in the building trade and 17 per cent of those in the metallurgical industry were immigrants, and in the car industry they accounted for one third of all low-skilled 'OS'. Overall, immigrants filled 11 per cent of unqualified jobs in 1962 and 17 per cent by 1975. Wages, the range of which had narrowed since 1968, widened still further the gaps that changes in working patterns had brought about. Whereas the purchasing power of workers as a whole rose steadily by 4.5 per cent a year from 1960 to 1973, that of low-skilled 'OS' and women remained a third lower than the average and the ratio of the wages of an unskilled worker to those of a foreman was still 1 to 2.2. It was only the overtime available to workers that to some extent compensated for this in-built inequality.

Yet all these classifications and hierarchies had become much less rigid. There were factory inspectors who reported that low-skilled workers ('OS') were doing skilled work or that so-called professional workers (*ouvriers professionels*, 'OP') were in fact sweeping floors or doing security work. There were companies that chose to 'rotate' their entire staff faster by giving each person a new job every three months. And there were sociologists who stressed the role of the worker's personal aims, to which a company might respond by offering much better adapted and more suitable forms of promotion than previously imagined.[30] Encouraged by the growth in labour sub-contracting, indefinite contracts and the recruitment of staff via manpower agencies, which by 1974 affected 5 per cent of employees in industry, increased labour fluidity or, alternatively, confusion. The working class, once united around a particular mode of production and the promise of a better tomorrow, had thus lost a sizeable chunk of its social distinctiveness. It had not dissolved completely into the broader mass of wage-earners and it still retained a portion of its cultural heritage, an amalgam of alienation and pride, but it was certainly now so scattered that even Marxists were beginning to doubt its proletarian virtues, given that it was no longer 'the most advanced product of social evolution'. Other observers, on the other hand, rejoiced to see that the 'embourgeoisement' of the working class was now well under way, thanks to the new forms of knowledge that it had acquired, plus its taste for social climbing.[31]

Industry had left its mark on the whole body of society by imposing wage-earning, which it had pioneered and continued to champion: 95

per cent of industrial workers were wage-earners and increasingly they were paid on a monthly basis. A host of factors contributed to the expansion of wage-earning: the disappearance of jobs in agriculture at the rate of 6 per cent a year since 1968; the numerical erosion of the so-called 'independent professions in industry and commerce', a hold-all category into which INSEE lumped small industrialists, small shop-keepers and artisans, who were all victims of company concentration (the group shrank from 10.6 per cent to 7.9 per cent of the active population between 1962 and 1975); the arrival on the labour market of greater numbers of women and immigrants; the changing patterns of low-skilled work just described; and the general rise in educational levels and qualifications. However, this expansion in waged work proved much stronger in middle and higher ranking positions: indeed, it was rising salaries that signalled the coming-of-age of industrial society and sketched the blurred outlines of the middle classes that Valéry Giscard d'Estaing in 1976 labelled 'the immense central group with ill-defined boundaries' to which 'two out of every three French people' belonged.[32]

First and foremost, the *groupe central* included white-collar workers, who were hard to fit into any 'new working class' and whose numbers had risen from 2,900,000 to 4,600,000 between 1962 and 1975. Representing just 14.7 per cent of the total working population in 1962, this share increased by 4 per cent a year until, in 1975, white-collar workers accounted for 21.2 per cent of the entire active population. This spectacular development had more to do with the rapid growth in office jobs, two-thirds of which were filled by women (especially typists and early computer operators) than with the rather sluggish increase in the numbers of employees in sales and commerce. Advantage was often taken of opportunities for upward social mobility, with the families of workers and small farmers often steering their children towards work of this kind. As for middle managers, technicians or the future 'inter-mediary professions', as they were classified by INSEE, 45 per cent of whom were women, this group had expanded even faster than white-collar workers and was now very nearly as large.[33] In this category, the old professions of teaching (primary school teachers and administrative staff), technicians and industrial draughtsmen rubbed shoulders not only with the newer 'social' professions – whose numbers increased fivefold between 1968 and 1975 (physio- or speech therapists, social workers, special-needs teachers, psychologists, counsellors, etc.) – but also with equally fast-growing and even more go-ahead professions in the arts, culture, media and public relations (journalists or press spokes-people), and design and publicity (which employed 5,000 people in 1968 but 12,000 by 1975). But senior management and the liberal professions were the groups that had grown fastest since 1968. Yet this growth had not been even: while the numbers of secondary school teachers and members of the literary or scientific professions grew by 8.5 per cent a year between 1968 and 1975, the numbers of engineers, members of the liberal professions and upper administrative staff grew more slowly. This highly complex pattern of expansion among middle-ranking wage-earners was related to the development of the welfare state: by 1975, local government officials, health and social security staff, etc., half of whom were women, accounted for 15.8 per cent of the active population and 31 per cent of the tertiary sector, as against 11.5 per cent and 25 per cent in 1967.[34]

In economic bottom-line terms, this flowering of the tertiary sector – what the statisticians called 'services to enterprise' – still had the wind in their sails, thanks to their role in industrialization. Yet they were in danger of being surpassed by 'indirect services' – connected with administration, management and consumption – given that this sector was more dynamic and better attuned to short-term social demand. Adding together these various sub-groups, one arrives at an impressive sum: white-collar workers, managers and members of the liberal professions, who now formed the bulk of the 'middle classes', numbered 5,200,000 people in 1962, 6,700,000 in 1968 and 8,900,000 in 1975, that is, at the said dates, 26.2 per cent, 32.4 per cent and 40.6 per cent of the working population. On above-average salaries, employed mainly in the tertiary sector, generally town or city based, equipped with college qualifications, and increasingly female, they performed the work of the future, were eager consumers, and showed a concern for personal freedom and the arts: in short, they set the tone, the rhythm and the taste for social mobility for the whole of industrial society.

And over the medium term there was undoubtedly very considerable social mobility. This could be observed not only in family strategies but in the changing employment patterns from one generation to the next, as illustrated in figures 2 and 3 and table 8, which are based on a series of investigations conducted by INSEE between 1953 and 1977. Not only had economic expansion shaken society to its roots, it had elicited in people a propensity to look for different kinds of work and had thus even, on occasion, encouraged social advancement. As much a cultural as an economic matter, such advancement was the outcome not only of the way that the structures of the working population responded to growth (structural mobility), but also of geographical and social 'churning' (net mobility). All the evidence shows that growth had brought enhanced structural mobility, with the result that those who managed to move up the social ladder far outweighed the immobile or

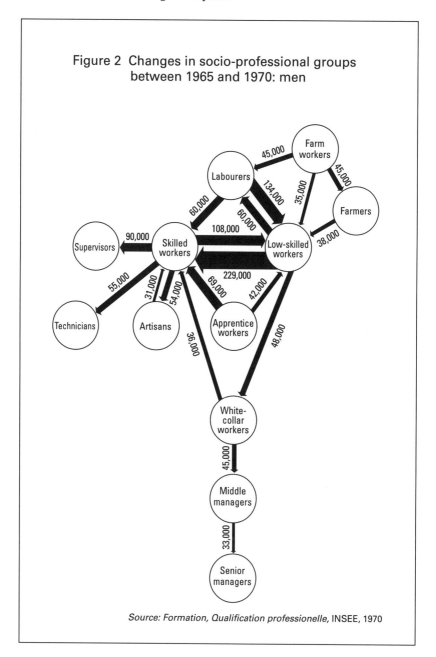

Figure 2 Changes in socio-professional groups between 1965 and 1970: men

Source: Formation, Qualification professionelle, INSEE, 1970

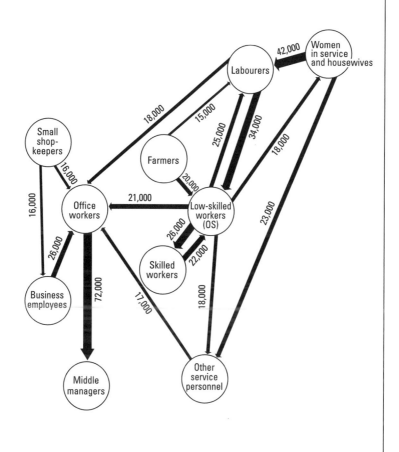

Figure 3 Changes in socio-professional groups
between 1965 and 1970: women

Source: Formation, Qualification professionelle, INSEE, 1970

Table 8. *Increase in social mobility, 1953–1977: men in work between the ages of 40 and 59*

Father's socio-professional group	Son's socio-professional group								Total
	1	2	3	4	5	6	7	8	9
1. Farmers									
1953	59.72	6.04	7.82	0.95	0.71	2.13	5.09	17.54	100.00
1977	37.79	3.52	6.14	1.48	3.00	3.71	8.92	35.44	100.00
2. Farm workers									
1953	13.46	25.77	12.69	–	0.38	0.38	7.31	40.00	100.00
1977	3.57	13.22	5.91	0.94	1.36	4.10	9.58	61.32	100.00
3. Small business people, shop-keepers									
1953	3.98	1.49	47.76	2.99	3.23	6.22	8.46	25.87	100.00
1977	2.64	1.05	21.42	6.42	12.51	9.85	13.89	32.22	100.00
4. Industrialists, large commercial operators, members of liberal professions									
1953	2.86	1.43	10.00	42.86	11.43	7.14	7.14	17.14	100.00
1977	1.38	–	13.99	20.92	26.04	11.90	9.71	16.05	100.00
5. Secondary-school teachers, senior managers									
1953	3.92	–	15.69	5.88	41.18	17.65	13.73	1.96	100.00
1977	2.21	–	4.25	10.10	42.44	21.28	9.62	10.91	100.00
6. Primary-school teachers, middle managers									
1953	–	–	16.28	11.63	16.28	16.28	18.60	20.93	100.00
1977	0.51	0.27	4.09	5.73	30.17	30.03	11.38	17.83	100.00
7. White-collar workers, service personnel, other groups									
1953	5.14	–	10.29	4.00	12.00	13.71	17.14	37.71	100.00
1977	1.40	0.68	6.98	2.38	15.63	20.69	16.83	35.41	100.00
8. Blue-collar workers									
1953	3.13	2.14	11.54	0.57	1.42	8.55	10.83	61.82	100.00
1977	1.15	1.01	6.71	1.99	6.30	10.66	13.80	58.37	100.00

Source: R. Pohl *et al*, *Formation, Mobilité sociale, Salaires*, INSEE, 1983.

downwardly mobile. Around 1970 many children were certainly still going into the same kinds of jobs as their parents and this level of 'self-recruitment' bore witness to the powers of resistance of the previous social structure. Indeed, socio-professional self-recruitment applied to 64 per cent of workers' sons, 42 per cent of the sons of senior managers and members of the liberal professions, 38 per cent of farmers' sons, between 31 per cent and 35 per cent of sons of middle managers, and 25 per cent of sons of artisans and small employers. Yet mobility had nonetheless increased, with a strong influx from agriculture into industry or from industry into white-collar work and middle management. And in the choppy waters of the 'central group' mobility was particularly strong. Industrial society was on the move, shaking itself out, though as yet there was no perceptible reduction in economic inequalities or in the social and cultural gulf between groups.[35]

Urban dynamism

In 1954, 58.6 per cent of the French population lived in urban or suburban areas. By 1975, this had risen to 72.8 per cent, an increase of over 14 per cent, that is, of almost 2 per cent per year. At these dates, the respective percentages accounted for twenty-five and thirty-eight million French people. This human explosion was focused almost exclusively on cities and towns with over 5,000 inhabitants which, having struggled to house six million newcomers between 1911 and 1954, had then sucked in a further thirteen million in the space of twenty years. Yet the Pompidou era was confronted, as it were, more with blast damage than with the blaze itself, since by this time the annual urban growth rate was declining, slipping from 1.9 per cent for 1954–62 to 1.8 per cent for 1962–8, and then falling more sharply to 1.1 per cent for 1968–75. Essentially, this decline was the result of a generalized drop in migration – the drift from the land was now just a trickle and the influx of immigrants had also slowed – combined with a downturn in the rate of natural population growth throughout metropolitan France. Urban growth, a central feature of the *trente glorieuses*, now became a broader and steadier phenomenon, with softened edges and a new sense of order: in the Pompidou years, the urban menu was more of an after-dinner liqueur than an apéritif.

Naturally, towns did not all expand at the same rate. For example, since 1968, Bruay-en-Artois had lost 11 per cent of its population whereas Montpellier's had grown by 65 per cent. The Paris conurbation, as usual, exceeded all national trends, its demographic moderation astonishing the experts with a growth rate of only 0.5 per cent between

1968 and 1975. Indeed, its expansion was now wholly fuelled by a natural rate of increase that since 1962 had stabilized at 0.8 per cent, whereas the conurbation's balance between inward and outward migration was now negative (−0.2 per cent). The population of Paris was 9,800,000, just one quarter of the country's total urban population, down from 29 per cent in 1962. Other major conurbations with over 200,000 inhabitants had also seen falling growth, with an annual rate of 1.2 per cent, a third of which was accounted for by a positive migratory balance.[36] In contrast, medium-sized towns of between 50,000 and 200,000 inhabitants continued to grow very fast, at rates that swung between 1.5 per cent and 1.6 per cent, and here the positive migratory balance accounted for 40 per cent of growth. Small towns with fewer than 50,000 inhabitants were still swelling at between 1.2 per cent and 1.4 per cent a year, drawing people in from the surrounding countryside: indeed the drift from the land often represented half of such towns' increase in population. In other words, the era of vast population movements was coming to an end and towns were adopting a more balanced pattern of growth, relying increasingly on their own resources and taking greater steps to manage community relations. It was now the fertility of their inhabitants that was the main component in their growth. Whereas between 1962 and 1968 the role played by fertility had been well down the list of factors contributing to urban growth – territorial extension (35 per cent), positive migratory balance (31 per cent), natural increase (29 per cent) and the drift into town from neighbouring districts (5 per cent) – from 1968 to 1975 natural increase far outstripped all other factors (56 per cent), as against 19 per cent for territorial expansion, 18 per cent for positive migration and 7 per cent for influx from neighbouring districts.

However, it was the penetrating force of industrialization that drove urban expansion, throwing up new hierarchies and ensuring the national spread of the phenomenon. By 1975, statistical and geographical investigations had revealed that since 1954 this process had split in a way that was to prove beneficial. Small towns with 50,000 inhabitants or fewer owed their growth mainly to industry: they either caught up, after a historically slow start, or became markedly over-industrialized. Both medium-sized towns and large conurbations harnessed the surge in the services sector: again, it was a matter either of catching up or of over-tertiarization. The old contrast thus persisted, across an imaginary line bisecting the country from Caen to Montpellier, between an urban western France reliant on farming and the services and an eastern France of industry and government. But tertiary activities, however ubiquitous, were hardly decisive, except for the Mediterranean coastal

towns.[37] It was much more common for industrial activity to bring
about concentrations in population or indeed shortfalls, unevenness in
development or lasting successes and, moreover, major industrial companies tended to accentuate the concentration of jobs in technology and
the services within urban areas. Similarly, if one looked at the numbers
of workers, France still remained divided, with the towns of the north
and east effectively homogenized by the presence of 40 to 50 per cent of
workers, while the west of the country had under 40 per cent workers
and over 60 per cent middle managers, white-collar workers, shop-
keepers and so on. Urban development did not therefore erase such
long-standing divisions.

The same investigations, however, also revealed that the outstanding
feature of the Pompidou years was the emergence of a modern
economy that blurred once-important traditional distinctions and
transformed the 'brand images' of towns, injecting greater dynamism
into centres of development and putting each region's technological
and human resources to more imaginative use. The industrial under-
pinning of urban growth remained of fundamental and tangible importance, even in terms of jobs and wages: given that the overall
proportion of industrial workers in the working population of towns
had only decreased from 45 per cent to 41 per cent between 1954 and
1975, the urbanized 'post-industrial society' that some people were
already announcing was still a long way off. Yet it is true that towns
were now able to maintain their momentum and their position within
regional and inter-regional competition by drawing above all on their
technological base, their service industries and their social capital. In
the meantime, the combination of economic growth, greater social
mobility and an improved supply of urban housing had boosted
geographical mobility, especially among the youngest and most fully
employed section of the population. This was a great source of strength
to every type of town: by 1975 one French person out of every two was
no longer living in the same apartment as in 1968, one in three no
longer in the same district council area (commune), and one in ten no
longer in the same region.[38]

If the housing logjam had not been broken, the results of these trends
would have been quite spectacular. In fact, around 1970 economists and
geographers invented the expression 'urbanizing urbanization', and
indeed it was now obvious that the new supply of housing was less a
product than a catalyst of, and even stimulant to, urban growth. There
were of course some extreme illustrations of this: the leisure industry,
for example, created from almost nothing several towns on the Côte
d'Azur, the coast of Languedoc and in high Alpine valleys in order to

attract seasonal residents. Perhaps more surprising, the Paris conurbation, despite a downturn in construction, was still being developed faster than anywhere else in the country, and continued to attract newcomers by supplying new accommodation at a speed that now outstripped its population growth. Between 1968 and 1975, the housing stock increased by 12 per cent (14.8 per cent in urban areas and 5.4 per cent in the countryside), as compared to a 6 per cent increase in its population. Yet the increased supply of homes did nothing to slow down the contraction of some towns, for example in the Nord region and in the Lorraine. Better coordinated through policy initiatives at local and national level, house-building managed to get one step ahead of population growth, becoming a decisive factor in the increase of housing supply, reinforcing the solid and typically French network of small and medium-sized housing estates, and contributing at least temporarily to an improvement in the management of living conditions in the larger ones. Some spectacular figures provide some idea of its impact on society: by 1974 the construction industry, which had itself undergone modernization and concentration, was still developing at almost 6 per cent a year, a rate it had maintained for two decades; the industry employed 12 per cent of the workforce and generated 10 per cent of the value added of the whole economy; between 1971 and 1975, at an average production rate of 500,000 new housing units a year, France built more homes than between the two world wars.[39]

This building frenzy followed a dual logic firmly rooted in the Fifth Republic's ideological commitment to industrialization. The challenge was, on the one hand, to improve and modernize town and city centres, adapt them to burgeoning road traffic and improve their links with the surrounding urban area, while helping them through the increasing tertiarization of local employment by providing them with offices and functional service units. On the other hand, it was to confront the most urgent issue head-on by reining in the anarchic proliferation of outer urban districts, neighbouring suburbs and small country towns engulfed by urban sprawl, and to promote large-scale housing projects without being too particular about setting up industrial plant and commercial outlets on the edges and in the interstices of what was still a very loose urban fabric. To make old urban areas pay their way by bending them to the industrial imperative, while stemming the flow of people to the suburbs, which were already swollen due to changes in working patterns and their disproportionate share in demographic growth: this was the approach adopted by banking investors in both the private and public sectors (in particular Crédit foncier and La Caisse des dépôts), by property developers, public–private partnerships, council housing ('HLMs') departments, and local government. Indeed, it was also the approach taken by the state which, having reached a quick assessment of the true extent of the challenge, set about tackling it with a mix (very reminiscent of de Gaulle) of planning measures and top–down technocracy.

From 1958 and 1959 onwards, new rules and orders speeded up the process of compulsory purchasing, made it easier to raise capital, set up procedures for redeveloping urban centres and earmarked areas for fast-track development, the so-called ZUPs, where public investment would henceforth be concentrated. In 1962 a further category was created: future development zones (ZADs), where the plots to be developed had already been purchased. Great care, however, was taken to differentiate between the master plans – the real blueprints for urban development – and what was in effect town planning by special dispensation, whereby private initiative had a free hand once it had been given authorization.[40] All these measures were strengthened and rationalized in 1963, under pressure from DATAR which wanted to consolidate the country's network of towns and cities by developing eight *métropoles d'équilibre*.[41] The new Direction de l'équipement set up in 1966 by the ministry of the same name had dispatched its top technocrats and engineers to the four corners of the country. Meanwhile in the Paris region, thanks to the commitment of Paul Delouvrier, with the direct backing of General de Gaulle, a master plan was given the go-ahead in 1965 – despite opposition from local government – envisaging the emergence of *pôles restructurateurs*, 'growth axes' and a network of communications projected to produce five 'new towns', of original architectural design, on the capital's outskirts.[42] Following a *loi d'orientation* on land ownership use, enacted on 30 December 1967, urban development plans (SDAUs) and land use plans (POS) had been drawn up throughout the entire country, while a Towns Commission had painstakingly drafted the Sixth Plan.[43]

Once it was clear that this authoritarian policy had not achieved the success that had been so confidently expected, and after the sharp fall in the housing market in 1968, a change of policy was introduced in 1969.[44] Paul Delouvrier was sidelined and the ZUPs were replaced by more 'concerted' development zones (ZACs). In practice, 'concertation' entailed 'debudgeting', i.e. the transfer of responsibility for financing particular operations away from state-run bodies, an increasing effort to attract private capital to finance public amenities such as motorways and, in practice, town planning by negotiation, grant and special dispensation. Albin Chalandon, the minister for housing and amenities (*équipement*)s took the view that it was necessary to 'liberate town planning' by reincorporating it in the market economy – just when a housing shortage had become apparent and the prices of building land were soaring. It was deemed equally vital to review nit-picking rules and regulations in order to respond to the increasingly individualistic aspirations of French people, many of whom now dreamed of owning their own homes.[45] In 1969–70 he launched an own-your-own-home scheme under which 70,000 so-called Chalandonettes were erected to showcase the new policy (many of them, hurriedly built, soon collapsed amid scandal), while he also injected fresh energy into the home buyers' savings scheme. In 1970 *contrats de plan* over several years were introduced in an attempt to ease relations between the state and urban communities. In 1971, the 'Construction Plan' set out to develop technical and social experimentation in housing, with 'flexible' homes, building components chosen from catalogues, terraces and flower beds, while illustrious architects were employed to wax lyrical over housing developments and new towns. In 1973 development contracts were introduced to improve medium-sized towns and, with Olivier Guichard at the ministry for regional development, the agenda now shifted to a new 'local' emphasis for planning policy, the slimming-down of ZACs, a reduction in the proportion of tenant-occupied HLMs and a ban on all future housing schemes of over 500 homes. The age of Pompidou moved away from planning as an end in itself, wishing instead to focus on the urgent need for homes that was now being articulated. At the same time, attention began to be paid to issues relating to the environment and urban pollution, laid bare in May 1968, though certainly blown out of proportion by early ecologists, without neglecting the need to ensure that town centres paid for themselves. The individualism and huge recourse to private investment typical of housing policy under Pompidou were a sharp departure from the state-led modernist logic of the de Gaulle years.

Be that as it may, by 1974, after twenty years of sustained effort that had seen the housing stock rise from 16 million units in 1962 to 18 million in 1968 and reach 21 million in 1975 (by which time a quarter of all homes were new), the era of the vast housing project-cum-town was at its height. These homes had been built quickly, cheaply, and uniformly, in the knowledge that within fifteen or twenty years they would have to be demolished. The architects involved, including many holders of the Prix de Rome, had nonetheless been strongly influenced by standard international practice, modelled on Le Corbusier or de Mies van der Rohe: they failed to avoid the general state of sclerosis then overtaking their profession, in thrall to a post-Bauhaus aesthetic of the poor, while the training of new architects remained in a state of crisis predating 1968. Hostile both to the unrestricted sprawl of detached houses, and to standard rented property, they believed – as did the property developers, civil servants and elected representatives who all conspired to turn the architects' scale models into buildings – in ambitious schemes for mass use, in abstract designs plonked down on a surrounding landscape, in the flatness of façades with neither cornices nor pilasters which, they postulated, would just shrug off any bad weather, in the monotonous regularity of the structural pattern, in the rough concrete prefabricated unit, and in decent but standardized interior fittings. What they often neglected, through lack of time and money, was the provision of public transport or indeed the essential ingredients of any real local community life. Schools, social services and sports or cultural amenities tended to appear later while, in the mean-time, the inevitable supermarket tapped into any semblance of socia-bility. The architects, planners and others contented themselves with producing a rationale for their developments, citing the imperative of the *plan-masse* and the shortage of construction land as a pretext for building huge and high.

Tower blocks and *barres* (long unbroken lines of medium-rise flats) thus came into being as clear symbols of the shift from an age-old society of muddle to a new world which was both bright and trans-parent. Some of the *barres*, for example the one at Haut-du-Lièvre near Nancy, were over 400 metres long. Furthermore, the long walls of flats and high towers were combined – though sometimes it was the width of the cranes available during construction that directed the precise mix – with lower-rise but equally cold and box-like buildings, and interspersed with patches of grass and car parks. The result was the vast outer-district estates or ZACs that provided, on schedule and seemingly out of the blue, anything from 5,000 to 10,000 new homes, sometimes more. About a third of the newly housed, who tended to arrive all at once, came from shanty towns and shacks built at the time of the Liberation or from city centre slums. Most of them were young couples with small children, but with few aged relatives: at Viry-Châtillon, for example, the average age of the adults was thirty-three, and 95 per cent of all residents were under forty. In many cases they felt dazzled and grateful for such bright surroundings, comfort and cleanliness and this did not wear off at once. Yet they also immediately fell victim to the effects of 'zoned' planning, being forced to commute back and forth, morning and evening, between home and a distant workplace. Indeed, in 1974, 30 per cent of those who lived in conurbations of over 200,000 people and 55 per cent of those who lived in the Paris suburbs faced a daily journey to work and back of over an hour and a half.

One hundred and fifty-three developments of this type had been built since 1954 in the Paris region alone, including a number of estates on a truly gigantic scale, for example the Cité des Quatre Milles at La Courneuve and the Grande Borne at Grigny. But other cities and regions were not to be outdone, as was demonstrated by Les Biscottes in Lille, La Fontaine-d'Ouche in Dijon, the 'Muraille de Chine' in Clermont-Ferrand, the vast towers in Vaulx-en-Velin, les Minguettes near Lyon, the Echirolles ZUP just outside Grenoble, the estates around Fos, and the 'ZUP no. 1' in Marseille. It did not take long, however, for any managers or clerks in temporary transit in such estates to find their way to the better sort of apartment of which, given their social rank, they could legitimately dream. It was for them that the property developer Balkany in 1966 completed a total of 5,000 new apartments at Parly II, near Versailles, with lawns, tennis courts, an up-market shopping centre and housing units on a more generous scale. Under Pompidou, this kind of development really took off with the result that many suburbs now became a patchwork of large estates that tended to age quickly, attracting social problems and vegetating as dormitory housing, alternating with more luxurious and livelier *résidences* earmarked for the 'central group'. In the meantime, the parcelling out of land for detached houses on the pseudo-American village pattern, as at 'Bouygues' or 'Phénix', built at a yearly rate that rose from 195,000 in 1969 to 273,000 by 1976, began to eat into agricultural land, accentuating the moth-eaten appearance of the suburban fabric. In other words, the 'sarcellitis'[46] so often in the news at this time, and the *métro–boulot–dodo* (tube–work–sleep) treadmill, so vociferously denounced first by the protesters in May 1968 and thereafter by those engaged in 'urban struggles',[47] had both assumed a much subtler social character than could have been hoped for ten years earlier, given the brutality of planning and architecture in the outlying districts. Once again, a breakaway social grouping was in the process of coming to terms with economic and technological developments. Acute problems were certainly being stored up for the future, with the formation of hard pockets of socially isolated drop-outs, overcrowding, and the raising of an entire new generation in such soulless surroundings. The dressing-up of high-rise façades, the unusual layouts, the studied irregularities and the efforts to encourage social mingling – all of which initiatives were introduced around 1970 by those designing the latest estates (Aillaud in Pantin or Renaudie in Ivry, for example) – had failed to erase from people's memory the unbending white walls of the first great wave of 'rabbit hutches', which though initially welcome were quick to disappoint.

The renovation of town centres, on the other hand, was highly spectacular and, by and large, more meticulous as well as much more controversial. The scheme that demolished the run-down Mériadeck district of central Bordeaux was typical of the social, functional and symbolic thinking behind town centre renewal. The idea was to trigger improvements in neighbouring areas, in this particular case the district surrounding the city hall and the cathedral, while conspicuously installing in the heart of the city an architecturally complex centre providing space for previously cramped local government, a mass of offices for the tertiary sector,[48] renovated businesses, hotels, cultural amenities, and blocks of apartments for well-off executives. In 1974, in the Tonkin area of Villeurbanne, which abuts on the Part-Dieu district of Lyon, where renovation work had been proceeding since 1964, the social thinking behind the scheme was even more obvious, indeed almost a caricature. Seventy-two per cent of the inhabitants of the now demolished area had been blue-collar workers of various sorts, 21 per cent had been craftsmen, small business people, and pensioners, and just 4 per cent executives. By contrast, 65 per cent of the inhabitants of the new Tonkin were executives, 18 per cent white-collar workers and only 7 per cent blue-collar workers.[49] In many small and medium-sized towns, megalomaniac property developers and local officials hacked brutally at once lively areas (for example, the Place du Théâtre shopping centre in Châlons-sur-Marne or Tulle's administrative quarter).[50]

But, as so often, the challenge and symbolism of these schemes were focused on Paris. Using the pretext, boldly asserted by none other than President Pompidou, that 'modern great city architecture boils down to tower blocks' and arguing that, since Paris was neither 'a dead city' nor 'a museum in need of upkeep', it had to 'adapt itself' to the motor-car, public and private schemes mushroomed. Not only was large-scale housing development, in a tidied-up and posher version, introduced into the Place des Fêtes on the embankment of the Seine, and in the capital's 'Italie' district, but the frenzy for building office space and areas of tertiary development took hold of the Maine-Montparnasse project, with its 210-metre-high tower crushing the city with its 110,000 square metres of offices. Another example was provided by the rise of the vast business district at La Défense, whose forest of towers, it was realized in 1970, completely dominated the view between Concorde and the Arc de Triomphe. The completion in 1973 not only of an express way along the Right Bank but also of the Boulevard Périphérique, started seventeen years earlier, proved that the cult of the motor-car was no empty phrase. Meanwhile the Palais des Congrès at the Porte Maillot (with, inevitably, its 120-metre-high tower), which was opened in March 1974, summed up the efficiency of 'Fifth

Republic style', and exemplified its opulent ambition.[51] Moreover, the highly questionable and controversial affair surrounding the demolition of the Baltard pavilions in 1971, following the transfer of Les Halles to Rungis in March 1969, and the launch, at the instigation of the president, of the plan to build a new exhibition space on the neighbouring Beaubourg site worried not just Parisians but many friends of Paris throughout the entire world. Some spoke of a 'massacre of Paris', but were unable to make themselves heard.[52]

Bearing in mind all these controversies, the urban policy record of the Pompidou administration is necessarily very mixed, and many of the people directly involved at the time were quick to admit their misgivings. There was no doubting the economic and geographical dynamism of towns and cities, which continued to shake the country forcefully, but the human problems raised by their development and organization had now become topics of confused but vehement public debate. And, after fifteen years of Gaullist power, state intervention in town planning and regional development was unavoidably at the heart of any discussion. Yet the discussion itself remained lop-sided: not only could no one differentiate precisely between the respective roles of the private and public sectors in the benefits reaped and difficulties raised, but nor could anyone gauge the extent to which Pompidou had broken with or carried forward the policies he had inherited from de Gaulle.

Policy under Pompidou was profoundly influenced by two firm convictions that had survived since the early 1960s: first, that town-planning issues had to be managed within the framework of regional development and national planning; and second, that in all tasks calling for drive and hard work, commando units of civil servants and Parisian experts should always override local authorities and notables, and those placed in charge of the project in question and public–private partnerships should then impose modernity on 'outlying authorities'.[53] This legacy had not been squandered, as we have seen in connection with the development of new towns around Paris, which got off the ground only after hard-fought battles. For its part, industrial logic tended to follow the lead given by regional development, though it is hard to say which met with greater success. Nonetheless, the desire to slow down the industrialization of the Paris region, and to switch attention to that part of France lying to the west of the Caen–Montpellier axis, including Lower Normandy, the Loire region, Brittany and the south-west (regions which together secured 70 per cent of the jobs in industry created prior to 1970), while assisting the fragile areas in the Nord and Lorraine regions, had tangible effects on migration, the training and skills of the working population, the concentration and diversification of business and, consequently, helped to ensure that towns grew in a more balanced and ordered way.

However, this underlying voluntarism was offset by two strong trends. The free-market philosophy that informed Pompidou's presidency prompted it constantly to shed state influence in favour of the private sector, whether in the field of property development, inward investments or even the zoning of industrial plant for major corporation subsidiaries. The fragility of his majority and the abandonment of Chaban-Delmas' 'New Society' policies forced Pompidou to make concessions to locally elected centrist and Independent Republican representatives, to professional bodies and to financial pressure groups, all of whom had found ways of using local interests and corporatist networks to promote or to hamstring the planners' 'blueprints'. And above all, haunted by the memory of May 1968 and by the failure of the 1969 referendum, Pompidou thought it shrewd to play for time, first by urging Chaban-Delmas to postpone any experimentation, and subsequently by diluting the town-planning challenge by setting it within the broader context of regional policy. This was in fact designed both to give reassurance at a time when the opposition was loudly raising the 'regional question' and talking in terms of people's 'right to the city', and to provide a cautious response to the notion of a 'Europe of the regions' that was beginning to agitate the Nine. The law enacted on 5 July 1972 conferred on regions the rather curious status of 'public establishments' and set up a regional council and an economic and social council, both of which were charged with a consultative role on questions of development and planning. It also gave the go-ahead for the regional elaboration of a policy on investments, drawing on transferred resources and above all on tax revenue from applications for building permission. Yet this did not represent any loosening in the state's Jacobin grip: having beaten a retreat following the ill-fated referendum, the law on regional reform was in fact based on a highly centralist notion of decentralization and on a highly nationalist view of regionalization. Moreover, the purse strings remained very tight: in the first few years after the law came into force, total fiscal receipts and additional taxes earmarked for the regions never exceeded 0.5 per cent of the state's resources. Besides, the human and economic imbalances between different regions, if not actually worsening, were not addressed adequately (see map 5).

The result was a sort of prudent watering-down of public intervention, ratified by the creation under the Messmer government of a huge and prestigious ministry, headed by the highly respected Olivier Guichard, with overarching responsibility for regional planning and

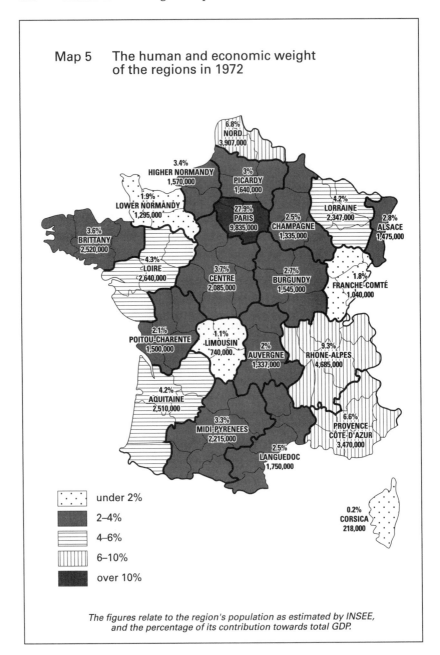

Map 5   The human and economic weight
of the regions in 1972

under 2%

2–4%

4–6%

6–10%

over 10%

0.2%
CORSICA
218,000

*The figures relate to the region's population as estimated by INSEE,
and the percentage of its contribution towards total GDP.*

development, housing and tourism, but which in fact had little real political clout. In July 1971, the thinking behind regional development produced a 'tendential scenario' – actually the work of SESAME, a small forecasting think-tank set up by DATAR. This painted a vivid and rather apocalyptic picture of France in the year 2000, in which highly polarized and partitioned areas (the Paris region, border areas, the Rhine–Rhône axis, and some coastal strips), plus a handful of urban conurbations (with very little to offer in terms of 'balance'), would monopolize all economic activity, while turning their back on the economic desert covering the bulk of the country. This nightmare scenario was deemed unacceptable even by those who wrote the report, yet it was clearly a caricature of the conclusion to which the voluntarist line of policy which was so confusedly espoused first by de Gaulle and then by Pompidou seemed to be leading.[54] The free marketeers, back in power after 1969, could not help but rebel against such a schematic approach that ignored the market and played down the European imperative. Yet economic liberalism itself had at the same time to address the increasing impatience in the regions, rooted as much in economic issues as in issues of identity, that militant minorities were busy channelling and shaping into a highly subversive struggle by the *pays* against the state.[55] Another intractable issue with implications far exceeding any regionalism was posed by rural France and its fallen civilization.

The reprieve of rural France

The 1960s had at one and the same time proclaimed the 'end of the peasantry'[56] and striven to turn peasants into entrepreneurs by harnessing the threefold momentum of the launch of the Common Market and the explosion of world trade, the determination of the farming profession itself, and government policies that since 1960 had been urging modernization while courting what was a 'safe' rural electorate. By 1974, if peasants appeared indeed to have been turned into entrepreneurs, their 'end' was not in sight. Twenty years earlier, 41 per cent of the French population had been country-dwellers and 21 per cent were actually farmers, but by 1974 the figures had declined to 27 per cent and 8 per cent respectively. Whereas in 1954 agriculture (defined broadly to cover farmers, family helpers and full-time workers) employed approximately five million people (27 per cent of the working population), by 1975 this had dropped to 2 million (9.5 per cent). Worse still, rural areas had emptied, losing their population to towns, industrial developments, sprawling suburbs or areas of rapidly shifting population. After 2,500,000 people had moved from country to town between 1946 and 1968, the rural exodus slowed down, though it now devastated the countryside's liveliest resource, agriculture itself.[57] Fertility was on the decline: between 1952 and 1972, the number of births to farmers' families plummeted by 58 per cent. Shop-keepers and young people were leaving in droves: of every two people who began their working lives on the land, only one remained; in the case of young women, only one in three remained. Meanwhile, the remaining rural population was ageing, schools and presbyteries were closing, and the postal service deteriorated: by 1969 only 38 per cent of rural communes still had a post office. Local railway lines had also closed down and parish fêtes were Americanized with the introduction of majorettes and early 1960s pop music. It was a world in headlong decomposition, anaemic, glued to the TV sets that now lit up 75 per cent of homes, and reliant on the motor-car (often old and second-hand but now owned by over 80 per cent of households), and the telephone (fitted in 15 per cent of homes) which, along with domestic gadgetry, came in for heavy use as country-dwellers struggled against isolation.

Yet the French countryside could point to a string of impressive figures. After being ranked fourth in 1963 among the world's exporters of agricultural produce, in 1974 France moved into second place behind the United States, and these sales, which accounted for 17 per cent of total output, made a significant contribution – roughly seventeen billion francs a year – to the trade surpluses that France had achieved since 1969. Output of every major item of produce was expanding. Between 1954 and 1974, corn production rose from 105 to 180 million quintals, beef production from 1 to 1.5 million tonnes while the production of dairy produce and fruit more than doubled. This had the effect of boosting overall agricultural output on average by 3 per cent a year since 1959. From a baseline of 100 in 1961–5, agricultural output had risen to 126 by 1973, making France self-sufficient and indeed creating surpluses that could then be placed on the world market, thus achieving an average annual increase of 4 per cent in gross agricultural income. Given that the surface area under cultivation had remained practically unchanged, while the number of concerns had declined sharply (1,600,000 in 1970 as against 2,300,000 in 1955), as had the farming workforce, these gains were the result of an unprecedented rise in the productivity of agricultural labour (5.9 per cent a year until 1969 and 4.7 per cent thereafter). This had been brought about by intensive motorization – there were 628,000 tractors in use in 1959 but 1,330,000 in 1973 – combined with the unbridled use first of fertilizers then of chemical weed-killers and industrial foodstuffs, which had increased fivefold since 1950. The increased monetarization of the process of production testified to a firm embrace of the capitalist logic, as was noted by all the experts in national accounting. Intermediary consumption – the outlays that farmers made in order to secure the year's output – amounted to 43 per cent of the value of this output in 1974 as against 26 per cent in 1959. At the same time, owing to the need to pay suppliers and make the necessary investments, the personal indebtedness of farmers with Crédit agricole (which in 1966 had become financially independent of the public authorities and whose banking success was envied throughout the world) had risen from 12 to 132 billion francs. Furthermore, after 1969, the food processing industry, which by 1974 employed 647,000 people (15 per cent of whom were employed in cooperatives), increasingly operated as an intermediary between producer and consumer. It thus played a role at both ends of the production chain by supplying fertilizers and animal foodstuffs, and then by buying the end produce: altogether, it now absorbed over half of agricultural output, the remainder being consumed in the producers' homes.

This development, however, had undermined stability and accentuated inequalities in the rural world, despite the corrective efforts of the authorities. In 1970, 50 per cent of gross agricultural output came from 27 per cent of farming concerns and there were wide regional imbalances between, for example, the index of 50 for the Lozère and that of 543 for the Brie area. In the same year, the average net disposable income for people engaged in farming remained low (8,340 francs, as compared with 7,931 for blue-collar workers and 10,277 for white-collar workers), even if the average income of farming households was 50 per cent higher than the average income of all households taken together. After all, farmers had first to pay off their debts and invest in order to secure or safeguard the property that was the tool of their trade. Indeed, in 1970, unlike anywhere else in Europe, French farmers still owned two-thirds of total agricultural land and property. And they had scarcely any other means left of securing it than by tightening their belts and consuming less. In 1972, for a baseline of 100 for consumption levels across all socio-economic groups, farmers came in at 79, agricultural wage-earners at 71, as against 86 for blue-collar workers, 109 for white-collar workers, 127 for middle management, and 172 for senior management. This figure of 79 was the most worrying, since it revealed the partial exclusion of farmers from consumer society and seriously called into question the modernizing creed of the 1960s.[58]

The situation appears even more complex if one looks more closely at the much-lauded wealth of variations of the French farming regions. For three unequal social groups lived here side by side with ever increasing difficulty – to the point where militant minorities could speak of a revival of class struggle in rural areas.[59] On the edges of society, the poor subsisted on a million or so outdated and unprofitable concerns, embittered and reliant on state assistance. In the main, they were agricultural labourers, retired farmers rescued from outright hardship by the minimum pension they received from the Fonds national de solidarité and, above all, small peasants with less than twenty hectares of cultivable land, always looking forward to receiving their benefit cheques, consuming little, seldom going out and living without any real comfort. Increasingly, they remained unmarried or were left behind after their children had all left for the town. Often elderly, they were prime candidates for the state incentive to retire (IVD: *indemnité viagère de départ*), and they clustered in regions given over to very small-scale farms or isolated from the rest of the country, especially in the Alps and the Massif Central. In sharp contrast with the poor, the million or so farmers working on family concerns of between thirty and one hundred hectares remained the focus of hopes for modernization. Typically, since the 1950s these farmers had managed to extend their land and property, while railing against soaring land prices, which had indeed tripled over the intervening years; or they had secured a good deal on the rental they paid as tenant farmers, built several more functional buildings for their livestock, and purchased machinery, specializing in particular lines of produce depending on their profitability or in response to directives from European authorities. By this time, they had grasped the new roles of investment and accountancy, often entrusting them to their wives. They had taken on large debts and entered into agreements to sell their produce to cooperatives or food processing companies, though they jealously defended their status as free artisans of the land who had now become modern farmers. Often unionized and sometimes former members of the Centre national des jeunes agriculteurs or of an association linked to Action catholique, these medium-sized farmers were keen to form business partnerships, enjoyed a certain social standing within their local communities, had equipped their homes with the latest durables, and in general put their families first. They now aspired to consume at the same rate as town and city-dwellers. One might easily encounter this identikit in the livestock-rearing areas of western France or in the south-west maize and fruit growing belts. Contrasting with these small-scale updated market farmers were the large capitalist farmers in possession of 100 hectares or more, very often located in the Paris basin. In 1970 this group owned about 15 per cent of all agriculturally cultivable land and specialized in just a few profitable cereal crops. These farmers were frequently in a position to bring effective pressure to bear on the public authorities through the association of specialized producers. Certainly their lifestyle was in no way inferior to that of well-off city-dwellers.

Disparities such as these might vary considerably from one region to another, but generally farmers felt that their chances of fitting into the new society that was taking shape were severely undermined by the fact that, while their primary income and the property they owned positioned them among the self-employed middle classes, their level of consumption, access to the comforts of modern living and to the arts, or, for example, their ability to go away on holiday, left them clinging to the lowest rung of national statistics, far behind the vast bulk of white-collar workers. Indeed, as regards holidays, only 14 per cent of farmers, almost all among the well-off, were able to leave their farms and livestock during the summer. Besides, modernization did not come cheap and it brought financial dependency and unremitting labour. French agriculture had certainly achieved a feat unprecedented in Europe: it had opened itself up to trade and embraced the market while at the same time strengthening the family-based farm and transforming it into a small yet fully fledged business, sustained by the grinding labour of medium-sized farmers. What it had failed to do was to allocate them a better place within modern society and culture. And, in the process, the risk had been run of destroying the fabric of tradition without persuading the rural world of the guaranteed benefits of growth and progress. Here too the crisis, when it came, shone a bright light.

There were, however, several new developments that offset this impression of a process left half-finished. By 1970, 45 per cent of farmers were only actually working on the land part-time. Mostly these were 'worker-peasants', but there were also 'clerical-worker-peasants' (for example, post office workers and social security staff), artisans, those who had taken early retirement from other types of work, wage-earning husbands and wives of all sorts keeping their small-holdings afloat by leading a double life. Alongside them were ranged thousands of 'neo-rural' incomers – young well-educated people, combining energy and idealism, who, moved by the spirit of 1968, had rejected urban life. Unwilling, however, to confine themselves to producing goat's cheese, it did not take them long to mark themselves out from the declining communities of hippies. They became involved in real issues affecting the countryside, even if its inhabitants remained hostile to them. Eventually, they did find their place and in fact brought much-needed new life to innumerable rural communities. Many of these incomers, particularly in western France and south of the Loire, quickly became the main representatives of a mounting cult of the peasantry (*paysannisme*), arguing for a return to ancestral values, culture and language. Increasingly tinged with ecological activism and militant regionalism, they would denounce the misdeeds of standardizing modernization and the disastrous pursuit of profitability, lament the loss of 'roots', and attempt to defend a natural and human legacy that they felt was under threat. They launched associations, took social and cultural initiatives, revived age-old practices and festivities, fought for their children to be taught in Occitan, Breton or Basque and thus participated fully in the fashion phenomenon known as *rétro* which gathered strength throughout the 1970s and was given a huge airing in the media but which, thanks to them, was not wholly devoid of a social basis.

There is one other essential feature that distinguishes the world of agriculture within French society: its relative militancy and the disproportionate interest with which the state follows its development. The long-standing propensity for peasant farmers to pool their strength, to press their demands forcefully, and to seek constant dialogue with the authorities – if need be in the name of an allegedly united countryside – was further strengthened. Farmers grasped at activism as a way of maintaining their legitimacy and they discovered a national audience that their declining numbers and deep economic divisions tended to undermine. Farmers were ringed, as it were, with the prestige that derived from having once represented the very essence of the French nation: as Pompidou, a deputy for rural Cantal, had declared on 22 May 1969, during the presidential election campaign, peasants provided 'a guarantee of stability and good sense'. Indeed, the state and the political parties were delighted to find in this socio-economic grouping people with whom they could really do business and whose strong roots, moreover, made it a much more loyal electorate than could be found in towns or cities.

The Jeunesse agricole chrétienne (JAC) had provided the basis for this convergence. It was at the height of its strength in 1961 when it was relaunched as the Mouvement rural de la jeunesse chrétienne (MRJC), though it later became a focus of turbulence and then after 1972 of open crisis, torn apart by clashes with the Catholic hierarchy and by the left-wing commitment of many of its wage-earning members, who were linked to the PSU, the CFDT above all, and even to the 'worker-peasants' movement. Yet it succeeded in bringing forward rural elites to topple the former notables, and after 1957 it served as a source of ideas for the Centre national des jeunes agriculteurs (CNJA). Significantly, it produced two contrasting yet representative personalities in Bernard

Lambert, a socialist apostle declaiming from his base in the Loire-Atlantique region the demands of struggling 'worker-peasants', and in Michel Debatisse, prophet of the 'silent revolution'[60] and the unity of the peasantry, chairman of the Fédération nationale des syndicats d'exploitants agricoles (FNSEA) and future minister for agriculture under Giscard d'Estaing. With its 700,000 members, though torn between the associations of livestock farmers and cereal producers, and between large and medium-sized farmers, and weakened on its right by a split in 1969, the FNSEA retained its dominant position, persisted in its quest for unity and stood its ground in negotiations with the public authorities. At its side, the Assemblée permanente des chambres d'agriculture withstood the pressure while the powerful Confédération des unions de la mutualité, de l'assurance, de la coopération et du crédit agricole brought its economic and financial clout to bear. Pitted against this organization, the communist-led Mouvement de défense des exploitants familiaux (MODEF) and the Comité de Guéret or the Comité de liaison des paysans-travailleurs were of little consequence. Everything was thus in place for a bold agricultural policy to be negotiated with the FNSEA as chief interlocutor.

In 1960 and 1962, Edgard Pisani promoted two far-reaching *lois d'orientation* that subjected agriculture to competition throughout the Common Market on prices (not indexed since 1959), on trading terms, and on productivity, in an attempt to place it on an equal footing with other economic activities. At the same time, however, farming was granted substantial aid and, with the full agreement of the CNJA, priority was given to family-type medium-scale concerns. The same laws encouraged land development through SAFERs (Sociétés d'aménagement foncier et d'établissement rural) and the grouping together of producers into GAECs (Groupements agricoles d'exploitation en commun), while helping to convince public opinion that 'Green Europe', brought into being in 1962, represented an opportunity for French farming. In 1968, however, a report by Sicco Mansholt, vice-chairman of the European Community Commission, stated bluntly that chronic over-production could only be tackled by losing five million farmers, and that the survivors would have to raise their profitability. In other words, he relaunched the scramble for productivity and cut-throat competition between producers, while strongly hinting that henceforth French agricultural policy would increasingly be made in Brussels. This brutal revelation, confirmed in 1969 by the Vedel report, that what the future held in store was fallow land and falling prices, inevitably soured the compensation-driven relationship between the welfare state and the farming community, provoked demonstrations that were then cleverly orchestrated – sometimes by the forces of the left – and sowed grave misgivings in the minds of all concerned.

The agricultural policies of Pompidou, efficiently implemented by the ministry of agriculture, first under Jacques Duhamel and then under Jacques Chirac, clearly foresaw this emerging scenario. Setting out his plans for farming in a speech on 25 June 1971 in Saint-Flour, Pompidou stressed the importance of balance and complementarity, still in the name of growth but with a new emphasis on the environment. For the first time, the future of agriculture was linked to regional reform, the stated aim being to safeguard 'a natural environment that [was] both farmed and inhabited' and in which farmers were to act as the 'custodians of the countryside'. It was also a matter of protecting from the Mansholt plan family concerns in livestock-rearing areas, enclosed meadowland areas, and the mountains. Above all, the search was on for a 'farmer's compromise' capable of calming the political agitation aroused by the new challenges facing the industry. On the whole, these policies proved beneficial. Even if structural questions remained unresolved, above all the issue of pricing and European farm surpluses, the alliance forged between a forward-looking farming industry and the Fifth Republic majority was confirmed in 1974: in the presidential elections, seven out of ten farmers voted for Giscard d'Estaing.[61]

6   The outbreak of prosperity

'First, the eye would slip along the grey carpet of a long corridor . . .':
thus begins Georges Perec's *Les Choses* (1965), a meticulous tracking
shot of the sense of wonder experienced by a yuppy couple as they set
out in search of all the things promised to them, and learn how to
negotiate the new order: for between the modern world and happiness,
between objects and dreams, there was a point of passage that could not
be avoided and was preferably 'carpeted' in grey. The de Gaulle and
Pompidou years were crammed full of things and the desire for things,
as well as ageing desires that had at last become tangible, all joined in
the same rush to consume. Society, rejuvenated and energized by
economic growth, had somehow retained the spiritual innocence of
large appetites. Crisis had been consigned to the past, and the 1971 and
1973 shocks had scarcely registered: the age of plenty had arrived. It was
time to enjoy life without remorse, to work hard but to seize one's
pleasures, whatever the constraints.

Even a puritanical state-owned company like EDF had understood
this. In 1963, after an intense advertising campaign, it launched its 'blue
metre' which, as well as being the colour of happiness, was powerful
enough to drive a whole host of household electrical gadgetry. Within
seven years, the electricity consumption of the average household had
doubled, as had the country's total number of electrical goods. Between
1971 and 1973, EDF struck again, this time offering every household a
central heating system. By the time a further seven years had elapsed,
two out of every three new homes had indeed been fitted with one.[1] Yet
the good life was not founded on economic and commercial factors
alone. Economists themselves were forced to admit that the advertising
people were right. By 1974, lifestyle strategies had grown complex and
varied, the relation between society and mass production was no longer
one of straightforward causality, and comfort had become a cultural
phenomenon. The blue metre was a sign of the times.

The pursuit of small pleasures naturally irritated the constitutionally
morose. Sociologists and semiologists denounced what they saw as a

diabolical *rupture*, hunted down every symptom of 'alienation', and protested against the standardization of everyday life, utilitarian morality and herd-like gratifications. In 1970, Jean Baudrillard, for example, moaned: 'Just as medieval society was balanced on God and the Devil, so ours is balanced on consumption and its denunciation. Though at least around the Devil heresies and black magic sects could organize. Our magic is white. No heresy is possible any longer in a state of affluence. It is the prophylactic whiteness of a saturated society, a society with no history and no dizzying heights, a society with no other myth than itself.' And, to underline his point, he brandished a grim remark by Dostoevsky as his epigraph: 'Plunge him into happiness up to the roots of his hair and little bubbles will burst on the surface of this happiness, as if on water.'[2]

Rising incomes and widening disparities

With or without added bubbles but to the constant alarm of its thinkers, France went on consuming, regardless. On occasion it also gave itself a good shaking but without feeling eternally alienated. It savoured its cocktail of new words, which the first edition of the *Petit Robert* dictionary had respectfully welcomed in 1967: *shetland, minijupe, collant, self, convivialité, show-bizz, jeans, pilule, phallocrate, audit, mailing, co-ordonnées, mixer, computer, hot-dog, look, drague* and *rock*. Everything was there to be consumed, and as a way of addressing this craze the 'franglais' debate now seems rather dated. In a state of confusion, riven by inequality but without looking back, the French threw themselves into a frenzy of consumption amid a swirl of messages.

Before sifting through the statisticians' numbers, it is worth putting a couple of faces on this brand-new age: those of two perfectly average consumers questioned at the beginning of the 1980s. Marie-Louise D. was a housewife in Paris, the daughter of a grocer from Noisy-le-Sec and the mother of a sensible girl to whom she had passed on her taste for keeping precise and up-to-date accounts covering everything from the cost per metre of extra-strong ribbon to the price of powder puffs. Richard S., for his part, was the son of a miner and himself a skilled worker. He came from the Moselle region, was married and had two children.[3] At fifty-two, after a lifetime of struggle to make ends meet, Marie-Louise was willing to admit her fondness for the shopping trolley: supermarkets sold goods cheaper retail than her father could buy them wholesale. But, as a shrewd consumer, she never turned her nose up at the corner shop or market stall: in Paris, after all, 'I've always paid less, because in Paris there is competition.' She had seen for herself the huge

shift in spending habits. Up until 1965 her budgeting had been dominated by food, the month's rent and seasonal essentials: she 'clothed her
daughters' and made sure her family had two square meals a day. Then,
after 1965, the *petit beurre* biscuit crumbled into eighteen different
varieties, beans began to grow in winter time too and the old winter
trinity of potato, carrot and chicory was abandoned. Nescafé remained
reasonable but the price of Galettes des Rois soared. Eggs, on the other
hand, got cheaper, provided you bought them in a box. Overall,
expenditure on food fell as Marie-Louise's family spent more on equip-
ping their home. The family's clothing bill doubled, and expenditure on
electricity, the phone bill, household appliances, medicines, instalments
on loans, transport and holidays also rose. With the figures at her
fingertips, Marie-Louise would jot down the essentials, from socks that
no one any longer darned to the rainbow-coloured choice of school
exercise books, from the suddenly ubiquitous aspirin to the durability of
nylon shirts. Between 1954 and 1975, the proportion of expenditure
that went on subsistence essentials fell from a half to a quarter. What
was left over went on health, creature comforts, communications and
leisure. Madame D., who was nobody's fool, was quick to see that
industrialization did not necessarily save housewives money. With
anarchy overtaking retailing, shopping done at a sprint and the tendency
to splash out on a treat for one or other of the family, any economies
were soon gobbled up. Yet she had saved time, spruced up the family
home as never before and given herself a bit of a break. In the
economists' jargon, spending on consumption had taken over from
spending on investment: the way one lived had gained the upper hand
over mere survival.

Richard S., born in 1933, had married in 1954. At that time, thanks
to his qualification (CAP) as a locksmith, he could earn 35,000 old
francs a month. He ran a Solex moped long and hard and never turned
down an odd job, 'cash in hand'. In 1958, his daughter was born and his
wife went out to work. This was essential to earn the couple that little bit
extra, so that they could afford a home of their own, and the family firm
that employed Richard found them a flat at a very reasonable rent. By
1960, their dream was no longer beyond reach. Richard had his first car,
a second-hand 2CV, purchased for 3,000 francs on credit, even though
he earned only 743 francs a month. Other judiciously staggered loan
repayments equipped the flat with a television and a refrigerator. By
1965, Richard was driving his family around in a new car, a sparkling
3CV that, on his monthly salary of 1,286 francs, cost him half a year's
earnings. It was a fair reward for a good worker who could turn his hand
to anything – cutting, welding, fitting or cabling – and who had just

gained his 'OQ3' qualification and so was now officially a skilled worker. The firm he worked for was now moving into small-scale industrial systems and beginning to export a fair amount. In 1970, the S. family invested the equivalent of seven months of Richard's salary in a Citroën GS costing 14,000 francs. In 1975, they treated themselves to the new model GS Pallas with tinted glass and metallized paintwork. At 35,000 francs, this was an extravagance that the coming slump in the Lorraine would soon make them regret. The following year, the entire family – Dad, Mum, Martine, now eighteen, and Sandrine, twelve – headed off triumphantly with a superb 14,000 franc caravan in tow for their first far-flung summer holiday. They stayed at the municipal campsite in Narbonne, 'without skimping on anything', but they still stole envious glances at the millions of other holiday-makers rushing to flake out on the Costa Brava. Richard had certainly been lucky to find a flat without too much trouble, and to have had the basic primary-school skills of reading, writing and arithmetic that sufficed to turn the young lock-smith's apprentice into a skilled boilermaker, able to follow a plan and draw up an invoice. He had also been fortunate both in his employers and in his home life. Every Sunday morning he worshipped his well-furbished cars with an eager shammy. Yet he never turned down the opportunity to work overtime, even if it ate into his free time. He managed his affairs with care, taking his first holiday when he was forty. Yet round the corner the slump was lying in wait. Looking back, he felt that those fifteen years from 1960 to 1975 had been the best. This worker, who had bitten so appreciatively into the fruits of growth, had an important lesson to impart about these happy times: consumption was well deserved and just.

The figures were unambiguous, inebriating even for the econometricians watching them take off from their observation towers at INSEE, CERC or CREDOC. GDP had increased on average by 5.5 per cent a year from 1960 to 1975 – and by a full 5.7 per cent a year between 1969 and 1974. Meanwhile, GNP had increased over the same period by an average of 5.6 per cent a year, rising from 413 to 852 billion constant (i.e. inflation-adjusted) francs at 1970 values and from 269 to 1,298 current francs, while average per capita income had risen by 4.6 per cent. As a result, the primary income of households (the destination of roughly 80 per cent of wealth produced) rose by 4.7 per cent a year between 1960 and 1975, and between 1970 and 1975 in current (i.e. unadjusted) francs actually doubled (from 584 to 1,129 billion francs, while GDP rose from 783 to 1,452 billion); meanwhile the purchasing power of households expanded on average by 5.9 per cent a year between 1969 and 1973.[4] In volume after euphoric volume of the popular *Que sais-je?* collection, the economic forecaster, Jean Fourastié, reported in glowing terms the happy effects of productivity and growth. A blessed era indeed when the sturdy bicycle made by Manufrance, which had cost 135 francs in 1910, 'that is to say 420 hours' work', by 1967 cost a trifling 240 francs, 'that is, sixty-four hours' work'; moreover – what heights of luxury and safety! – it was fitted with 'reflector equipment'![5] The living was now easy in France, where bottled gas had reached isolated farmhouses and delapidated flats at prices even lower than those demanded by Gaz de France for their piped supplies, and where the domestic kilowatt hour now cost one tenth of its 1927 price. To everyone's satisfaction, the slashing of prices soon took in haircuts, hotel rooms, hospitalization charges, private tutoring and dentistry! *Machinisme* and *bien-être*: these were the buzzwords.[6]

But, as we have seen, these goods and services were not obtained without effort. The number of people in work grew slowly and given that the workforce still included large cohorts of young and old workers, work was arduous and hours were long. Yet hard graft was rewarded by rising wages and, with a growth rate of 4.3 per cent a year, pay levels kept pace with economic development. This resulted in the only round figure that mattered: in the space of twenty years, between 1958 and 1978, both per capita and household income doubled and the de Gaulle and Pompidou years saw it rise by at least 80 per cent. Not everyone benefited equally from this. Between 1954 and 1974 the spread of incomes – better understood following the publication in 1977 of the first and quite sensational CERC report[7] – had broadened out as a result of the partial rediscovery of free-enterprise economics. This development was most marked between 1954 and 1963, and there was a levelling-off from 1963 to 1967. Then, in 1968, there was a substantial narrowing of the incomes range due to the social measures introduced by the Grenelle agreements, though this was followed by a further widening-out from 1969 to 1974. More than ever before, inequality in incomes was rooted in skills disparities, gender, variations between industrial sectors and between regions. On average a senior manager earned four times more than a worker and a middle manager twice as much;[8] men were paid one and a half times more than women; pay in the tertiary sector was consistently higher than elsewhere; and, indexing Paris at 100, comparable work in other towns and cities scored 75 to 80 and in rural areas 68. For instance, in 1971 on average a man employed as a senior manager earned 62,200 francs while a woman in the same job earned only 40,400; in middle management, the figures for average men's and women's pay were 30,700 and 22,000 francs respectively; in white-collar work, 18,000 francs and 15,000; and, in blue-collar ('OS') work, 13,500 or 10,000 francs.[9]

A serious attempt was, however, made to ensure that low wages made up some of the ground lost between 1955 and 1967 and indeed the gap was narrowed substantially. Between 1963 and 1970, while salaries increased overall by an average of 85 per cent, blue-collar workers' wages and senior managers' salaries both rose by 83 per cent, while white-collar workers' pay went up by 81 per cent and middle managers' earnings increased by 74 per cent. Meanwhile, women's earnings in all these occupations increased by an extra 5 per cent. Between 1959 and 1975, the proportion of primary income originating as wages and salaries rose from 60 per cent to 70 per cent, while the proportion of wage-earners within the overall working population climbed from 67 per cent to 82 per cent. This consolidation of the position of wage-earners within the economy, added to the fact that they were increasingly paid on a monthly basis – by 1973 this applied to 75 per cent of blue-collar workers – helped to smooth out some of the sharper contrasts. Whatever the ups and downs of the economy, the SMIC, rechristened SMIC in 1970, had closed the gap between average wages and their related purchasing power. Set at 700 francs a month in 1969, 4.4 per cent of wage-earners were 'on the SMIG'. By 1973 the SMIC had risen to 980 francs a month, but now covered just 2.7 per cent of wage-earners. By July 1974, however, this had risen to 5.8 per cent. Only state employees (*fonctionnaires*), as poorly paid as ever, lagged behind this general trend, with the purchasing power of their salaries rising at an annual rate of scarcely 3.6 per cent between 1962 and 1968 and at 2.4 per cent between 1968 and 1974.

To this state-led voluntarism was added the new and massive effect of redistribution, which also benefited the least well-off. For these years saw a barely perceptible yet far-reaching revolution with the establishment of a constantly intervening welfare state. Of course, recent studies assure us that the long-held and widespread view that the state exerted a positive economic and social effect was a mere illusion, despite de Gaulle's talk of the 'ardent obligation' of the Plan. It even seems that the state's initiating role has been overstated as has its ability to steer the course of events during critical periods, in tricky international circumstances or when under assault from pressure groups.[10] But, even if less commanding and more experimental than previously allowed, the state nonetheless managed and redistributed a growing amount of ready cash, channelling it back into the economy and consumption. The Fifth Republic had inherited the impressive machinery of social welfare put in place since 1945, from a national health system to family allowances and unemployment benefits. Increased government and local authority expenditure, as well as general consumption, had the effect of boosting trade and, if direct and above all indirect taxation remained as unjust as ever, social benefits and pensions were now steadily redistributing income. From 1959 to 1974, tax and social security contributions rose from 33 per cent to 36 per cent of GDP, while their share of GNP rose from 20 per cent to 25 per cent.

Whereas welfare contributions grew slowly from 1965 to 1975, rising from 19 per cent to 23 per cent of gross income, social benefits grew more rapidly (from 22 per cent to 27 per cent), redistributing the income available: indeed, they grew 8.4 per cent a year between 1959 and 1969 and 6.2 per cent a year from 1969 to 1974.[11] Meanwhile, the purchasing power of old-age and retirement pensions had increased on average by 6.7 per cent a year since 1959 and by 6.6 per cent since 1970. As a whole, therefore, 'social incomes' served to offset inequality in 'economic incomes', thus reintroducing a measure of equality and narrowing the incomes range while systematically favouring the jobless, agricultural workers, blue-collar workers and large families, in that order. Care was taken to avoid penalizing farmers or the self-employed, but middle and senior managers were forced to tighten their belts. Indeed, senior managers' 'transfer income' was negative between 1962 and 1970, standing at −3.3 per cent, whereas that of farmers was positive, representing 14.5 per cent of their overall disposable income. As for the jobless, their transfer income accounted for 61 per cent of overall disposable income. Put another way, in 1973 disposable income after deductions and transfers represented 98 per cent of the gross income of the jobless, 96 per cent of the gross income of farmers, and 80 per cent of the gross income of blue-collar workers, but only 70 per cent of the gross income of senior managers. These transfers, selectively allocated to top up primary incomes, boosted consumption among precisely those broad social groups that had worked up the keenest appetites. However, given that the average tax rate rose only slightly between 1959 and 1974 so that higher earners continued to pay income tax according to a scale that penalized them, direct taxation could have been integrated into this redistributive machinery. The fact that this did not happen reveals a weakness compared to France's European neighbours. As before, the taxation system helped finance the state, local authorities and investment, and was weighted in favour of the unwaged and the out of work, yet the failure to modernize the system meant that its overall social effect was slight. Since nobody dared attempt to reform it, income tax stagnated at 3.3 per cent of GDP in 1965 and had only reached 4 per cent ten years later, while VAT rose from 7 per cent to 9.5

per cent. The entire tax take, in any case, accounted for only a small proportion of compulsory deductions. Indeed, it even fell a little, from 4.7 per cent in 1965 to 4 per cent in 1975.

The combined effect of redistribution and increased collective consumption (amenities and services relating to public health, education and training, transport and social work, for example) demonstrated that the authorities had at last addressed the underlying, long-term needs of the French people. The preambles to the Fourth and Fifth Plans, covering the 1960s, welcomed the improved standard of living but deplored the *civilisation du gadget*, the artificial hyping of short-term needs, and the illusions manufactured by advertising. Against a background of alarmist remarks on the social contradictions inherent in American-style growth, they urged individuals to save and to act responsibly. The experts, in the meantime, anxiously hunted down all social and regional inequalities, calculated imbalances and identified 'pockets' of poverty. The issue of 'La France pauvre', which was raised very effectively in 1965 by Paul-Marie de La Gorce's book of that title, was soon a hot topic, focusing variously on the 'distress' of the peasantry, the 'anguish' of small shop-keepers, the 'destitution' of the elderly, or the 'enslavement' of immigrants paid less than the SMIG. These themes were then taken up by Occitan and Breton movements which, as we have seen, had lost faith in regional development and denounced 'centralizing Jacobinism' and *Paris-vampire*: their reaction to the Evian accords was to demand 'internal decolonization'.

The statistical evidence on property and wealth, however imprecise, appeared to confirm this grim picture. An investigation undertaken in 1975 by CREP[12] revealed that the total wealth of the French amounted to 3,800 billion francs (an average of 222,000 francs per household), but that the 125,000 households (0.7 per cent of all households) that owned two million francs or over accounted for 70 per cent of all wealth, that is, as much as the 60 per cent of households that owned less than 120,000 francs. This sharp pyramidal ratio of 0.7 to 60 highlighted the persistent disparities between the social classes and was a reminder of the extreme concentration of wealth, regardless of the emergence of the 'central group'.

Other investigations, however, based on tax data, showed that ever since 1949 the rich had been amassing property while the disadvantaged sank further into poverty. This gulf was at its widest in 1973 when members of the liberal professions possessed on average 370,000 francs, senior managers 218,000 francs and blue-collar workers 46,000 francs. However unequal the process had been, the overall enrichment of society had been dramatic: the total value of property owned by households had risen in constant (inflation-adjusted) francs from 2,236 billion in 1970 to 4,116 billion in 1975. Above all, its composition had developed in the right direction, emphasizing durable goods, and especially homes. Between 1970 and 1975, the proportion of total household property accounted for by bricks and mortar rose from 40 per cent to 45 per cent, whereas the proportion accounted for by financial investments excepting securities grew from 19 per cent to 24 per cent, while land stagnated at 14 per cent and the ownership of securities, in the absence of any initiatives on the part of the stock exchange or the banks, dropped from 10 per cent to 8 per cent. Between the same dates, the amount of debt taken on by households in order to purchase consumer goods rose from 8 per cent to 10 per cent of the estimated value of the properties.[13] It is thus reasonable to think that the social logic of engineering high levels of consumption for all, thereby maintaining real assets as against financial assets and savings at a ratio of 70 to 30 in the composition of wealth, probably helped to dampen the pressures towards increasing inequalities at work throughout the 1970s. With the arrival of *l'argent facile* in the 1980s, however, this would all change.

Consumption takes off

Official warnings and statistics lost a good deal of their force amid the rising tide of wealth, goods and services now on increasingly effective display. If the cake was unfairly divided, at least it was growing fast enough for everyone's slice to get a little larger (see table 9). Studiously attentive to customer needs, retailing outfits had been quick to adapt, with supermarkets and mail order firms now well established,[14] and hypermarkets making their first appearance. In January 1963, Michel Fournier had opened in Sainte-Geneviève-des-Bois the very first hypermarket, covering 4,000 square metres, and self-service throughout. The Carrefour chain, with its gigantic car parks and out-of-town siting, was better suited to the motor-car and to city life: people could stock up fast on everything they needed. By 1970, the company's turnover per square metre was 14,000 francs, as compared to the 8,000 francs of a typical department store or *supérette*. This pattern of gigantic marketing operations had been imitated but was not yet the rule: the typically French desire to cultivate a wide range of retail outlets was not to be lightly swept aside. Edouard Leclerc, a Breton, very successfully launched a chain of stores that slashed prices while cutting in-store clutter to a minimum. Yet small shopkeepers in the vicinity of a Leclerc store always managed to survive perfectly well.[15]

Banks and companies were also skilled at enticing consumers with

Table 9. *Household consumption 1960–1975 (as percentages of total)*

	1960	1965	1970	1975
Food	33.5	30.0	27.0	23.9
Clothes	8.7	9.0	8.6	7.8
Housing	12.0	13.1	14.5	14.8
Home equipment	10.1	10.3	10.0	10.6
Health	7.2	8.8	9.8	11.8
Transport and telecommunications	9.1	10.5	11.6	11.6
Leisure and the arts	5.5	6.0	6.2	6.8
Various	13.6	11.4	12.2	12.5
Total in billions of francs at 1970 values	275.0	368.0	469.0	594.0

Source: INSEE.

startling credit facilities on household goods and hire purchase schemes: 'enjoy now, pay later' offers quickly flooded the market. Households were quick to respond, without going mad but with a lot of calculated hope. They sucked in a steadily increasing share of the credit that was now being injected into the economy: 12 per cent in 1960, 15 per cent in 1965, 20 per cent in 1970 and 24 per cent by 1975. They made shrewd use of inflation to wipe out their debts and finetuned family strategies, planning their loans over the medium or long term in order to buy durable goods, their home, the car and the major home appliances. The 1970s saw this trend broaden still further, so that even holidays and major shopping sprees could be put on credit. The cake had got rounder and easier to reach: the main thing now was to get a slice. The French no longer paid much heed to prophets of doom or to those who counselled caution. Since their money was of such 'interest', they would demand money and the freedom to enjoy it. Consumer society was leaving those in authority trailing, while the act of consuming imparted a new form of independence, that of social actors.

From here it was but a small step to the caricature world of Jacques Tati, as in *Mon Oncle* (1958), *Playtime* (1967) and *Trafic* (1971). But the comedians and the enemies of gadgetry were wrong. There was nothing frivolous about this consumption. It was certainly much less 'manipu-lated' – a vogue word at that time – than was claimed by intellectuals who anyway were not too proud to equip themselves with the latest products. The basic trends were clear: between 1960 and 1975, the share of total household consumption that went on durable goods rose from 20 per cent to 25 per cent while expenditure on non-durable goods (food, clothes, etc.) dropped from 44 per cent to 39 per cent. Meanwhile, spending on services remained at a high and stable level: 35–6 per cent. 'Things' were arguably less sturdy than 'before the war', as the elderly in their wisdom recounted, but for French people who had come through crises, wars and privations, and who in actual fact loathed nothing more than 'American-type' wastefulness, their acquisition represented a rational investment in a better standard of living.

The figures confirm this overall trend. The consumption of food and clothing increased in both volume and value, yet as a proportion of overall spending it fell. Whatever social variations remained in people's eating habits and whatever specific family or regional traditions were internalized and handed down by the women, everyday sustenance was no longer either a source of obsessive terror or a compensatory pleasure, except on the great festive occasions or on a gastronomic outing to a restaurant. These would be rounded off with a bout of cultural-cum-venal shopping, the future of which was mapped out from 1969 onwards in the pages of Gault and Millau's magazine. Thanks to bulk selling, standardization and a more rapid consumption of food produce, it was now possible to eat one's fill more cheaply, while remaining resolutely modern. Starchy and fatty foods, meats in sauces, the family loaf of bread and the bottle of red wine all retreated, in good order, but with no hope of staging a comeback, before the advancing cavalry of grilled meats, green vegetables and dairy produce – the sales of yoghurt, from 1967 onwards retailed in plastic containers rather than glass bottles, rose from 110,000 tons in 1962 to 330,000 tons by 1972 – while fruit and non-alcoholic drinks, in ever greater variety, steadily gained ground on urban and eventually even rural tables. The kind of physical figure associated with a breakfast rusk–French bean–mineral water diet – the one and a half litre family-size bottle was introduced in 1970 – gradually became fixed in the collective mindset, since to be modern and free was to be beautiful, young and therefore slim. Old, insufficiently 'dietetic', myths crumbled one by one. The Sunday chicken, now rather less carefully reared than before, commenced its long hormonal decline, becoming ever more tasteless, fit now only for end-of-month cash crises or as canteen fare. *Vin ordinaire* bought from 'Félix Potin' or 'Nicolas' suddenly seemed short on fizz, and its consumption plummeted between 1962 and 1972 from 121 to 95 litres on average per person per year, while contempt for Coca-Cola evaporated. As for mutton ragout and calf's head, they were enough to make the 'with-it' and willowy retch. *Steak-frites* alone was left to keep the proud Gallic flag aflutter. However, in 1972 the first McDonald's opened in Créteil and – on a decidedly more elitist plane – in October 1973 the Guide Gault et Millau launched the gastronomic fashion for *nouvelle cuisine*.[16]

Surprisingly perhaps, the share of the family budget now spent on clothing decreased. Despite the endless blether about Parisian *haute couture* just for the 'jet set', about bullish adverts and a younger generation of alleged wasters, the revolution of the 1960s in fact brought a degree of standardization that boosted demand while lowering costs and extending freedom with *prêt-à-porter*. There was a froth of fashion-wear for instant consumption by teenagers or hip young women – from the young thing's twin-set to the 'gypsy look' achieved by dipping into supposedly American army surplus stores, from the felted 'Shetland' pullover for dancing the twist to rags reeking of patchouli, from the mini-skirt to bermuda shorts – yet neither can this conceal the advance of cheap and convenient everyday wear or the way that people's bodies were being freed, affording a foretaste of all the thrills of the coming decade. In women's clothing, stays disappeared, panty girdles were replaced by panties *tout court*, old-fashioned suspenders gave way to tights promoted with slogans that spoke of the liberation of legs, and blouses reappeared around 1961, freer fitting than before and signed Cacharel. In 1963, Denise Fayolle saw to it that the claws of the major fashion designers were sunk into the popular Prisunic stores, in 1965 the Courrèges house detonated its geometrical 'bomb', and this was followed by a whole series of weird metal creations by Paco Rabanne and by 'Pop Art' for the masses, which finally called time on austere ladies' suits and hard-wearing overcoats guaranteed to last ten winters. Chanel consoled itself by launching a range of perfumes. Then, in 1971 for the first time, the number of dresses and skirts produced – including the short-lived 'maxis', which were unable to hold out against a hem-line that had been rising relentlessly for ten years – fell by three million, while the number of pairs of trousers rose in precise proportion. For men, with their slower reflexes in matters of liberation, blouson-style jackets and suits-and-ties remained in use. Younger men did, however, increasingly prefer open-necked shirts, rejecting vests, eagerly adopting colourful hipster briefs,[17] and swearing by the all-purpose pullover and suede 'desert boots'.

Only the elderly, attached to their combinations and to their smocks and overalls and buttoned up tight to conceal their poverty, stood up to the most powerful invasion the country had ever known: blue-jeans. Fashionable, designer styled and a 'unisex' symbol of general exhilaration, the number of jeans manufactured in France quadrupled between 1970 and 1976. After lengthy resistance, May 1968 clinched their victory. Faded now and flared, denim crashed through every social barrier, reconciling utilitarianism and the counter-culture, work and leisure, plumbers and girlfriends, students and horny-handed sons of toil, in a hommage to a less stuffy but still slim-hipped way of living. In 1965, barely one French person in twenty wore jeans; by 1975, it was one in five.[18] From jeans to blousons, it was young people who launched and sustained most of the clothing crazes and revolts. If the fifteen to twenty-four age-group were the prime customers for this industry, their juniors did not lag that far behind: after 1969, children's fashion took off spectacularly.[19] Youthful whims, combining functionality and provocation, set the general tone for a form of consumption whose social codes first jostled and jarred but eventually blurred.[20]

Expenditure on all other items, however, was on the increase, as part of a dual cult of the individual and the nuclear family, entailing massive investment in private life. Increasing emphasis was placed on improvements to the home and to one's health, with over a third of all consumption concentrated in these areas. As we have seen, the number of new homes started each year rose from 300,000 to 550,000, with a marked acceleration in the early 1970s. With the 1948 housing law still protecting millions of households from spiralling rents and an increase in the number of homes purchased under co-ownership,[21] many households found they had enough money left over to furnish and equip their homes decently. Between 1968 and 1975, the number of first homes with running water rose from 91 per cent to 97 per cent, those with an indoor toilet from 55 per cent to 74 per cent, those with a bath or shower from 47 per cent to 70 per cent, and those with central heating from 35 per cent to 53 per cent. By 1973, more than six out of ten homes had every single one of these modern conveniences. Nor was living space as cramped as before, and this quantitative advance was to have a considerable impact on the art of home living. The average home in 1973 consisted of 3.5 rooms with an average of eighteen square metres per person.[22] It was no accident if the mistress of the house no longer shrank from letting the guests get a peep at the kitchen and bathroom, for these two rooms, following the trail blazed by the 'living-room', were now gaining social acceptability: indeed they were the rooms that any prospective flat-buyer would inspect first.

For it was here that the domestic sciences were on display. The refrigerator, which in 1960 had found its way into only one in four French kitchens, was by 1972 ensconced in 85 per cent of them. The washing machine was only a little slower to catch on, in 24 per cent and 64 per cent of households at the same dates. However, the dish-washer (in 8 per cent of households by 1972) and the deep-freeze (in 5 per cent), did not really 'arrive' until the Giscard years. But now change was unstoppable. Oilcloths and wooden tables were abandoned to one's needy grandparents, while kitchen layout became a standardized craft, comprising 'units', 'storage space', 'worktops' and 'tiling'. Formica and gleaming steel were tended by the 'white tornadoes' of Ajax 'plus ammonia' or 'with added lemon freshness'. Scandinavian-style cutlery and crockery, trays and plumbing fixtures were taken down-market by the Uniprix chainstores; Bauhaus style ended up in teapots, and Italian modernism in pendant lamps or door knobs. Not to be outdone, French designs, for example by Roger Tallon, adorned Peugeot's coffee-grinder, Frigidaire's refrigerator, Téléavia's television set, and SNCF's 'Corail' trains. Every kitchen had its mixer, pressure cookers saved time, and there were even 'pingers' to tell you that the milk was about to boil over – were it not for the fact that the spread of pasteurized packs had removed any need to sterilize it.

Progress in the bathroom had kept pace. It is true that in 1973 only 60 per cent of all homes had baths (58 per cent of blue-collar homes and 93 per cent of senior managers' homes), but at least wash basins now had hot running water. Soaps became softer, shampoos diversified, and the Obao bubble bath arrived, trailing creams and after-shaves, manicure kits and bathroom scales. Here again, design triumphed, from the streamlined hair-dryer to the lively competition between Braun's grilles and Philips' floating heads, in this the golden age of the electric shaver. And as for the living room! Sofa-beds became an essential feature, lampshades blossomed and bloomed, following the seductively 'natural' Laura Ashley style, while the 'set' in the corner served as a focus of attention. By 1973, 85 per cent of households had television, and 8 per cent of them had colour – by 1975 this had risen to 20 per cent. There were often two radios, a mains one for Papa and a portable transistor version for Madame and the kids, often flanked by a record player and even, after 1966, by a cassette recorder. The telephone alone lagged behind, having made a very sluggish start in the 1950s and 1960s. Indeed, even by 1973 only 28 per cent of all households had been connected (10 per cent of blue-collar workers' homes, as against 75 per cent of those of senior managers). But demand was so strong that in 1969 the rigid administrative link between telecommunications and the post office was at last broken and a rapid catching-up operation was launched. By 1970 there were four million telephone subscribers and by 1975 this had risen to seven million. Yet you still had to wait sixteen months to get a phone line installed.[23]

It is right to round off this inventory of 'things' with the motor-car, a multi-dimensional symbol of social standing, individualistic comfort and the longing for power shared as a family that far outweighed its utilitarian function, given that traffic jams, the snail's pace of motorway construction and the figures for road deaths were already causing concern. In 1962 there were 250 kilometres of motorway, but by 1972 this had risen to 2,041. But it was not until 1966 that one could drive along a motorway non-stop for 200 kilometres, from Paris to Avallon, and not until 1974 that Paris and Marseille were at last linked. As for road accident deaths, the numbers rose from 9,900 in 1962 to 15,100 in 1970. Despite this, it took until 1972 for a speed limit of 90 kilometres per hour to be introduced on major roads with a 130 kilometre per hour limit enforced on motorways two years later. Safety belts were not made compulsory until 1973. Also, apart from a few instances of destructive anti-car fury in the Latin Quarter in May 1968, which had the effect of stunning the broad mass of French people who saw it on television, the motor-car remained rooted at the heart of consumer society. It invaded towns, cities and holiday resorts, sparked conversations, spawned a vast and profitable market in accessories and a network of service stations: indeed, it was the motor-car age. By 1973, 70 per cent of households had a car and there was now a total of fifteen million vehicles on the roads, separated by only minor social gradations, thus emphasizing the car's majestic position as the supreme commodity: it quickly lost any cachet of exclusivity, whether economic or symbolic. Car ownership in the higher socio-professional groupings ranged between 79 per cent and 96 per cent; two-thirds of blue-collar 'OS' and unskilled workers already owned one, as did 70 per cent of country dwellers. The exception were the elderly jobless, with just one household in three owning a car. The 4L, launched by Régie Renault in 1961, and its R5 unveiled in 1972, took over from the 4CV of blessed memory, underscoring the twofold success of French-manufactured cars and front-wheel drive models, while the R16 was aimed at the better-off. Citroën, with its range of 2CV, Ami 6, DS 21 and then the GS, provided continuity to suit all pockets. Peugeot's 404, 204 and 504 were well positioned in the middle-of-the-range, 'sensible' bracket, while the Simca 1000 and 1300, manu-factured in Poissy, retained their popular appeal. But the Italians with their Fiats and the Germans with their Volkswagens, not to mention German-manufactured Fords, had already fired the opening shots in a European war of competition.

The general rule set out earlier in relation to incomes also applied to these purchases: those who were initially the least well-off gradually closed the gap. Thus, in the case of the car–fridge–TV trinity, by 1967 workers had outstripped national purchasing averages. The singer–song-writer Léo Ferré could well sing *Le Temps du plastique* with all the vengeful verve that an old anarchist could muster, yet the French seemed quite content to wallow in their vinyl armchairs. Consumption also extended its beneficial effects to health, now a major mass-market commodity that accounted for 9.4 per cent of overall household expenditure in 1970, as against 6.5 per cent in 1960. Between 1970 and 1975, the per capita consumption of medicines and health care increased by a further 6.7 per cent a year, rising from 6 per cent to 7 per cent of GDP. Individual spending on health was more and more fully reimbursed by the national health system (Sécurité Sociale), following a process of contracting-in of doctors started in 1960, and the spread of private add-on health insurance schemes (Mutuelles), whose coverage of individuals' health expenses rose from 60 per cent to 70 per cent between 1960 and 1970. By 1965, there was a total of 3,000 products available for the treatment of 500 recognized medical conditions. Run-of-the-mill ailments were treated at home, while the average stay in hospital fell from twenty-five days in 1958 to eighteen by 1970. Consumption provided the clearest category for the mass of 'signs' that were suddenly turning social life upside down. It was all very well for the film director Marco Ferreri to jeer at La Grande Bouffe, but this just demonstrated all the more clearly that consumption also fed into people's fantasy and cultural lives.

The social and economic sciences found themselves confronted with a question imported from the United States: why was income becoming, in the jargon, so 'discretionary', so free of any drive to invest? The creation and fulfilment of needs had given birth to a new dynamic, as was demonstrated by the first investigations into women's work. Though initially viewed as a source of extra money, enabling a household to climb out of hardship, it turned out to be the source of cascading desires. Whether 'absolute', 'relative' or 'conspicuous', consumption had indisputably become significant. Statistically, it was now known that white-collar workers in the service industries were leading the dance. Indeed one suspected that it was managers who supplied the pattern for a pervading way of living to which the blurred mass of the middle classes aspired and whose messages they then relayed to the farthest reaches of society. One discovered – under electric shock treatment if necessary, in May 1968 or with the rise of feminism – that young people and women had achieved a highly effective degree of social autonomy rooted in their improved standard of living, as if consumption, whether for survival or for fun, had become the engine of a new society.

Much of this satisfaction was displayed in the whirlwind or bulimic frenzy of signs, messages and distractions with which daily life now bristled. By 1970, advertising and publicity, a new force frequently accused of debauching a country steeled to withstand its depredations, accounted for almost 1 per cent of GNP.[24] Investments in la pub – this idiomatic abbreviation of publicité made its entry into the Dictionnaire

Robert in 1969 – doubled between 1957 and 1967, rising a further 30
per cent between 1967 and 1972 (from 324 to 422 billion francs),
transforming it from a commercial toolkit into a social institution. It
brought into being the language of mass, constructing its highest-
number and hugest-impact semiology on the back of tautologies (*Omo,
ça c'est de la lessive!*: 'Omo, now that's washing powder!'), of minuscule
details able to clinch a decision (so that, for instance, a car might be
bought for its convenient cigarette-lighter), or of shock statements
containing patently absurd 'information' (*A 140 km/h on roule plus vite en
R16*: 'At 140 km an hour, you go faster in an R16').[25] Ad-men and
women, hiding behind their hoardings, or tucked away in their slots on
such radio stations as Europe 1, no longer conveyed information – they
manufactured messages, with a degree of supple creativity and ingenuity
that broke through every barrier and stormed every stronghold. Even
politics, though for a long time more stubborn than soapflakes, eventually joined the dance.[26] The long march to the promised land of
generalized contentment had begun, with its promoters attentively
listening to the poundings of desire in the breasts of consumers, who no
longer refused their love. For there could be neither hearty consumption
nor tranquil pleasure without a strategy for desire. Hidden persuasion
was no longer enough. Motivation and marketing studies, fresh from the
United States, had revealed that people purchased and savoured
symbols just as much as products: all-year-round oranges meant health,
the dull thud of the shutting car door signified class. Having failed to
make itself sufficiently lovable, Leroux chicory-coffee slumped into
obsolescence, while Rosy bras were forced to decorate themselves with a
rose. Swept along by this new art form, French society took *la pub* to its
heart, with a typically Latin energy. The French consumer rights movement remained feeble, despite the success of *Que choisir?*, or the
strategies for profitable austerity introduced by the Leclerc and Darty
stores. Set up in 1968 with public funding, the Institut National de la
Consommation, for example, denounced mendacious adverts yet never
succeeded in building a consumers' movement as combative as its
American counterpart. French consumers somehow refrained from
consumerism.

It was other media, especially the latest and brashest newcomer,
television, that imposed a degree of social regulation on popular appetites. Yet *la pub* did not appear on television until 1969, and even in
1974 film and television still only accounted for one quarter of total
advertising spend, as compared with the 60 per cent that went on the
written press and 12 per cent on hoardings. But *la télé* was already a
hugely powerful disseminator of patterns and signs, as well as being a

mass manufacturer of fashions and behaviour. As a corollary – or perhaps a consequence – of the decline of other media, standardization crept into day-to-day attitudes, a process of homogenization overcame the spirit of the age, while the right to pursue happiness through the arts and leisure was proclaimed on all sides. Sociologists and moralists promptly turned out a stream of incisive observations on 'mass culture', the bulk of which, it was already suspected, would turn out to be an American import. The fact that young people were emancipating themselves and emerging as a specific category of consumers with their own lifestyle reinforced the notion of dislocation, the idea of successive *nouvelles vagues*, the vision of devastating cacophonies poised to lay waste to everything inherited from the past. Yet it was not quite like that. Any such assessment, whether constructed on the *yé-yé* craze or on Beatlemania, ignored two major phenomena: the proliferation of disparate practices fuelling the merry-go-round of consumption, and the countless social and cultural behaviours serving to reinforce it.

One example from the arts will suffice to illustrate this state of confusion and to temper the trite lament about the dictatorship of fashion or the perversity of sales people. The secret of the record industry's success at that time had less to do with the accelerated churning out of 'hits', driven by hit-parades that were fixed in advance, than with the cumulative effect of an unprecedented musical output. Young people, of course, were sold Johnny Hallyday and Claude François hits, followed by the Beatles and the Rolling Stones. But there was no neglecting the Vivaldi lovers, the Charles Trenet fans, the Jacques Brel enthusiasts or the accordion nostalgics. Some of the major labels may have aspired to launch new styles: more emphatically French, in the case of Polydor, with their signing of Serge Reggiani and Georges Moustaki; more 'Anglo-Saxon' in the case of CBS and RCA. For their part, the younger generation exploited the new music for all it was worth, using it as the basis for a strong albeit elusive cultural identity. As for the recording industry professionals, they could see the wisdom of engaging artistic directors with broad tastes and turning their back catalogues to good account: they had realized that in order to sell they had to produce something for everybody, from bagpipe fanatics to lovers of Purcell.[27] To shift goods and to maintain a flow of alluring products, you had to acknowledge a multiplicity of different audiences, and cater for their eclectic tastes. Even a cursory glance at the statistics confirms that the record sellers were right. The case of the music industry demonstrates just how far the homogenization of cultural practices still had to go before it would be complete. Age was perhaps still less of a constraint than membership of a social class, let alone the old heritage of

Table 10. *Cultural and leisure activities in 1973 (percentages according to head of household's socio-professional group)*

	Overall	Out-of-work and over-60s	Farmers	Blue-collar workers	Blue-collar supervisors	White-collar workers	Senior managers and professionals
Telephone	28	23	29	10	12	32	75
Colour television	8	10	3	6	8	8	18
Books	73	56	61	66	78	86	97
Records	62	26	54	65	71	75	93
Stereo system	7	1	0	5	8	7	33
Electric drill, DIY	37	17	38	32	47	40	53
Fishing kit	35	23	25	38	51	38	30
Sports kit	36	9	21	33	44	52	74
Watch TV every day	65	75	71	68	66	63	44
Go out in the evenings	31	10	24	32	31	38	55
Museum-goers	27	16	16	21	30	34	55
Go to football matches	24	9	26	27	30	24	27
Go to pop concerts	6	1	1	5	6	9	17
Go to election meetings	9	7	18	5	6	11	20

Source: (233).

family, district or region. At least in 1974, any rant that bewailed the process of levelling-down to which France was doomed through mass culture and consumption had to be greeted with scepticism.

Leisure and private life

There was, however, one value that did tend to rally the market behind mass hedonism: leisure (see table 10). To heap praise on the new *civilisation du loisir* even briefly represented a sociological talking-point.[28] But a measure of relativism is again in order. While it is perfectly true that in 1973 67 per cent of French people went on holiday, 50 per cent in the summer and 17 per cent for winter skiing, as compared with a total of only 51 per cent in 1969 (44 per cent summer and 7 per cent winter), and a mere 44 per cent in 1964 (only 1 per cent of whom went skiing), social divisions still ran deep. Of senior managers and members of the liberal professions 88 per cent had gone on holiday, taking an average of forty days off work, 78 per cent of middle managers had been away with thirty-one days off, and 60 per cent of white-collar workers had holidayed with twenty-eight days off work. By contrast, only 44 per cent of blue-collar workers and just 15 per cent of farmers had had a holiday and on average these had lasted, respectively, twenty-five and sixteen days.[29] Also in 1973, the French on average spent more on the year's leisure than they earnt in a month. In 1970, however, only 15 per cent of French people, mainly senior managers and members of the liberal professions, enjoyed the luxury of a second home. The healthy balance-sheets that tourism now boasted had not yet turned the heads of the statisticians, even if they already came in useful when arguing for regional development schemes, like the Grande Motte and Port-Leucate resorts in Languedoc-Roussillon, or for the pursuit of 'white gold' in the Alpine snow at Arcs or La Plagne. The Club Méditerranée, founded in 1955, had of course increased its membership tenfold in the space of fifteen years (from 45,000 members spread over ten villages in 1960 to 432,700 members and a profit of forty million francs by 1975), largely thanks to the savoir-faire of Gilbert Trigano. The success of 'Club Med' was taken as the very pattern of liberation by all those who joined the social cult of the *les trois 's'*, 'sea, sun and sex'.[30] But for every fine jaunt under a faraway sun, in shell-necklace and grass skirt, the social and other possibilities of which titillated the *groupe central* on the constant look-out for something new, how many summer breaks were spent in an echoing tower block, how many all too restful stays with that aunt in the country? And once past the Paris traffic jams around the St Cloud tunnel or the Autoroute du Sud, for every tragic weekend of the type caricatured by Godard in *Week-end*, how many short and sensible strolls 'au Bois', how many games of *boules* in some car park, how many siestas in one's own bed, to the accompanying strains of an electric drill?[31]

Some of the old French passions, however, were still going strong, in particular sport and gambling. And some retained their popular flavour, like *tiercé* betting, which was launched under state control in 1954. This really took off in 1962 with the introduction of the three-franc three-horse bet, quickly becoming a feature of everyday life with its weekly or even daily male ritual of heated betting commentary in the local *café-tabac*. What is more, it became the most successful public enterprise in France. Indeed, between 1962 and 1974, *tiercé* turnover rose from one to six billion francs, that is, eight times higher than total cinema takings. In 1968, there were 8,000 lucky winners who, thanks to a winning 'ratio', became (French franc) millionaires, and this figure reached 19,000 in 1973: no section of society was left untouched. A *France du tiercé*, impassioned yet home-loving, had taken shape, making the old Loterie Nationale seem merely a chancy flutter. Only *pétanque*, now taking the country by storm, both as a competitive and as a family game, could compare with the *tiercé's* exceptional geographical and social spread.[32] Overwhelmingly, it was men who took part in or were spectators at mass-appeal sports, their passion fuelled by the televised broadcasting of such major national and international events as Five Nations Rugby (France's grand slam in 1968 made a national hero of the commentator Roger Couderc), the French football championship (dominated from 1964 to 1974 by Nantes, Marseille and five-time winner St Etienne), and the ever-popular Tour de France, won by Eddy Merckx every year from 1969 to 1974. This enthusiasm may have had more to do with a search for identity or some sense of community than with any pursuit of leisure, let alone physical exercise. The gregariousness of the fans, their shared language, the edifying early-morning ritual of reading *L'Equipe*, the re-living of highlights and the gigantic sums of money tied up in advertising and TV broadcasting revenue that were above all targeted at young people, the considerable economic clout that sport had already acquired (0.5 per cent of GDP and 0.8 per cent of household expenditure by 1971): all these aspects nudged sport into developing in a social direction rather than as pure leisure activity.

Backing for this view is supplied by the fact that the numbers of sports practitioners and loyal supporters varied very little. While in 1958, 5 per cent of French people belonged to sports clubs, by 1976 this had risen to just 15 per cent. Similarly, average attendance at first-division football matches rose only slowly from 8,000 in 1969 to 11,000 by 1975. Yet rapid expansion had occurred in sports amenities, from 12,000 sports stadiums and pitches in 1965 to 16,000 by 1973. With the spread of gyms and the arrival from America of jogging, participation in sports was becoming more a matter for the individual, less heavily supervised, and often minimal. Martial arts, judo and karate, as well as skiing, were all the rage. It was no accident that after 1968 the only sport to be really democratized, thanks to the patronage of the rising middle classes, was the highly individualistic game of tennis: the number of regular players had quadrupled since 1960 and as the sun rose on the era of Björn Borg, the winner of Roland-Garros in 1974,[33] the number of tennis-club members in France reached 200,000.

The emerging culture was thus impelling people towards leisure, which was in fact a decisive part of a new 'quality of life', yet no standard rule was issued as to its uses. And it would be wrong to place the blame for the leisure frenzy of the late 1970s on the preceding decade. From three- or even four-day weekends to the discovery of the first charter flights, from reverence for historic monuments or for great works of art displayed in museums to the proliferation of slides recording one's exploits of the previous summer, the French plunged willingly into a whole range of after-work activities. Yet there was no evidence to show that they had as yet made leisure their overriding concern. Indeed, between 1959 and 1973 opinion polls on the subject of happiness, the verdicts of which have been collated by IFOP, paint a very different picture: every single poll established a trinity of key values – work–family–leisure – in which the first two components vastly outweighed the third. Money was scarcely mentioned, though it underpinned everything, while beliefs and public-spiritedness were both clearly on the decline. But day-to-day work and the delights of the home got everybody's vote. Even after a long detour into the value of collective entertainment, one ends up facing the same set of preferences revealed by the statistics on refrigerator sales and the number of hours worked, though now with a shift of emphasis that became more distinct with each passing year. As early as 1966, the anonymous authors of *Partage des bénéfices* had noted laconically: 'Amenities and collective knowhow have a social usefulness that is in proportion to people's ability to make use of them.'[34]

This imbalance, rooted in social inequality and following a strongly individual or family logic, touching all areas however material or cultural, embraced the most promising developments of the decade, and helps to explain many of the features of the May 1968 explosion. Consumer society had perhaps shaken France less by virtue of the profusion of goods with which it had showered the country than with the mounting worry as to their use value and the division of power that they implied. Increases in knowledge across every age-group and generally expanding horizons indicted the consumption that had made them possible. The confused promise of consumption for all thus revealed its ultimate trickery. There was a suspicion abroad that plenty, albeit relative and still unequally distributed, would not necessarily engender satisfaction. This crack in the edifice was room enough for every imaginable negative argument to thrive. Some immediately raised regional and social imbalances. Others were constructed by aping arguments from abroad or perspectives from the social sciences, heralding the arrival of 'one-dimensional Man',[35] dispossessed by the objects with which he surrounded himself. From Abraham Moles to Jean Baudrillard, nothing was heard but complaints about artificial needs, pernicious egalitarianism, and the 'technocratization' of attitudes. From the

Nouveau Roman to triumphant structuralism, French high culture, as we shall see, also strove to destroy the autonomy of the human subject. Yet this obscured not only the formidable catching-up accomplished during the Pompidou years, which had made France a rival for Japan and Germany, but also the secret and worrying gaps that yawned in 1965 when, with troubling symmetry, the figures for births, employment, inflation and fixed capital productivity all began to plummet.[36] With the oil crisis virus already incubating and the chasm between the well-off and the excluded persisting, the realm of ideas failed to register the material changes taking place.

The French consumed without either disdain or regret, though not, it seems, without worrying about it. CERC surveys showed that 70 per cent of senior managers and 73 per cent of members of the liberal professions felt their standard of living was improving, though their satisfaction was shared by only 61 per cent of middle managers, 53 per cent of white-collar workers and 48 per cent of blue-collar workers. The polls hint at a question whispered with growing insistency: 'can it really be true?' Against all the evidence, in survey after survey from 1956 to 1969, a sizeable majority of those interviewed maintained that neither their standard of living nor their purchasing power had risen. At most, they were willing to concede that they had not fallen. But they refused to credit either the de Gaulle years or the Pompidou years with any positive impact on their daily lives. Even as late as 1977, 47 per cent of French people still expressed the wish that the next ten years would be better than the previous![37] To consume without quite believing it: this was the attitude that the majority seemed to adopt. This reiterated denial of the evidence on consumption levels stated what the strikers in May 1968 had expressed piecemeal with their refusal to fall in love with a 'growth rate', while yelling for more money (*'Charlot, des sous!'*). The rejection of privilege was intimately linked to the fear that one might not oneself manage to accede to it: an authoritarian chanting of words amid the sweet tranquillity of things.

Above all, this hesitancy betrayed a deeper concern stirring in the hearts of the winners of the 'consumer society': how to make the transition from 'things' (i.e. 'having') to 'being'? The improvement in day-to-day living and the free time snatched from work fuelled the longing for a life of greater personal ambition. The evident developments in the economy and in leisure upset social rituals, codes and institutions, and amplified the demand for a modern private life and for personal fulfilment. Society was relaxing, humour gaining a foothold, relationships growing both more intense and more direct, not only in the enjoyment of consumable commodities but also in all that ensued logically from the outburst of liberating insolence that was May 1968. The history of the family provides quite a good overview of these general trends as they rippled through the body of society, each at its own pace. More often than not, the family was now pared right down to the couple and their children, the culmination of a well-known contemporary trend. It was now acknowledged socially that the joining together of two people should be founded on love rather than on 'bourgeois' convenience, though the institution of marriage retained its appeal while managing to make room for this conviction.[38] Another indication of enhanced social fluidity was that an increasing number of people, especially among white-collar workers, were marrying outside their social class. In 1953, 45 per cent of couples consisted of spouses from the same social background but by 1977 this figure had fallen to 34 per cent. From 1964 to 1972, the marriage rate – the number of weddings in any year as a proportion of the population – rose steadily from 7.2 per cent to 8.1 per cent but then in 1973, at 7.7 per cent, it began to dip. With 347,000 couples marrying in 1964, 416,000 in 1972, but just 400,000 in 1973, it was clearly in the early 1970s that marriage peaked as a civil and religious institution, though many of those taking their vows no doubt felt increasingly that it was just a formality, and that people were no longer really obliged to get married in order to gain independence from their parents.

Evidence of this was provided by the rapid spread of what sociologists would later label *cohabitation juvénile*, a cross between a trial marriage and the inevitable expression of an individual right. In 1969, 17 per cent of couples had already lived together before they got married. By 1974, this had risen to 37 per cent, 85 per cent of whom lived in towns, comprising students and above all children of blue-collar or white-collar workers; and 60 per cent of these couples had been together for between one and three years. Between 1969 and 1974, the rate of premarital conception rose from one child in five to one in four. In January 1972, this trend was ratified by a reform of the civil law code on filiation, which accorded the same rights to illegitimate children as to those conceived within wedlock but vested sole parental authority in the mother. Between 1969 and 1973 the average age at marriage fell from 25.3 to 24.3 years for men and from 22.7 to 22.3 for women though it rose slightly thereafter, as long-cohabiting couples married out of a sense of duty to their children or under family pressure. There was a parallel increase in the number of divorces, occurring at an ever earlier stage in couples' conjugal lives. Having ranged between 40,000 and 50,000 since 1950, the number of divorces in 1974 exceeded 50,000 and, taking 1970 for a baseline of 100, 1974 already represented 130.

The institution of marriage was clearly at its zenith, even if it was undergoing rapid privatization.[39]

This propensity went hand in hand with people's desire to have fewer children. While the number of births remained at post-war baby-boom levels (874,000 in 1964, 875,000 in 1972, though only 854,000 in the following year, that is, birth rates, respectively, of 18.1, 16.9 and 16.4 per thousand), the drop in fertility levels mysteriously steepened in the mid-1960s, falling from 8.1 in 1964 to 7.0 by 1973: whereas for every 100 women of reproductive age in 1961–5 there were 134 births, by 1971–5 there were only 110 births. Moreover, the *groupe central*, always the most Malthusian of classes, blazed a trail that the other more hesitant sections of society then followed. A battery of polls and investigations with very similar findings revealed that it was not that the French were rejecting children – there was no increase in the number of childless couples – it was just that they were concerned to stagger births so that they could care for and raise their offspring all the better. The social strategy at work here was quite clear: in the opinion of 35 per cent of those polled in 1965, the ideal family consisted of one or at most two children; and by 1976 this view was shared by 42 per cent; the three-child family retained its popularity but approval for families with four or more children collapsed. This urge to curb family size seemed set to erase not only the age-old regional disparities that had made northern France markedly more fertile than the south, but also strong social and family pressures to conform, and it even chipped away at religious teachings. Yet, given that all the factors are so entangled and so socially and geographically contradictory, it is hard to present a clear account of this. How is one to assess the relative weight of women's increasingly frequent refusal to give up work in order to bring up a small child, the hectic pace of urban life, the fact that most homes were poorly designed for large families, the distance from grandparents, or simply the temptation for couples more fully to savour the selfish pleasures of life by seeking fulfilment through procreation rather less often than before.

Besides, how else is one to comprehend the strength of the campaign at that time for the right to limit births, if not in terms of this demand for individualism, whether solitary or à deux? Couples, as is well known, had not been content just to wait and, despite the harshness of the 1920 law prohibiting abortion, they had for the best part of a century learnt by hook or by crook how to limit their families to a maximum of two children. What was new was that birth control was now regarded as a right, and first and foremost of course as the right of women, who wanted at last to have control over their own bodies and futures and who were no longer willing to be confined to a 'biological destiny' as mothers and housewives. Thanks to the press,[40] there had long been a broad awareness of just how widespread the often inevitable recourse to backstreet abortions had become: they were estimated to number between 250,000 and 350,000 each year from 1962 to 1973. The Planning Familial association had campaigned since 1956 for the contraceptive pill, invented in 1953, and the intra-uterine device (IUD), developed in 1963, to be made available for use. In 1965, François Mitterrand, while running for president, called for the repeal of the 1920 law. Then, after fierce debate, on 28 December 1967, the Neuwirth law was enacted, making contraception legal, though restrictions were placed on birth control publicity. The provisions of the new law, however, were not made public until 1972, whereupon contraceptive products, legally authorized since 1969, at last went on general sale in pharmacies.

With a little help from May 1968 and the birth in 1970 of the Mouvement de libération des femmes (MLF),[41] the press soon embarked on a campaign to liberalize abortion. The magazine *Elle* took the first step, but the crucial blow was struck with the publication in the 5 April 1971 number of *Le Nouvel Observateur* of a manifesto signed by 343 women, many of them famous, stating that they had all had abortions and demanding this freedom as a right. This was followed in July by the creation by Gisèle Halimi and Simone de Beauvoir of the association 'Choisir'. In October 1972, the court of Bobigny acquitted a seventeen-year-old girl accused of having had an abortion, after a trial conducted under the full glare of the media. Then, in 1973, the campaign turned into a free-for-all involving doctors and politicians, and was an issue in the run-up to the legislative elections. It was at this time that MLAC came into being, performing terminations using the new Karman method, and encouraging women seeking abortions to travel to Great Britain or the Netherlands (12,000 made the journey in 1971 and 36,000 in 1974). At the opposite end of the spectrum, the supporters of the Laissez-les-vivre campaign, most of whom were extremist Catholics, denounced abortion as a 'crime' and warned that Europe was committing 'demographic suicide'.[42] By the time Jacques Chaban-Delmas stood down as prime minister, a draft bill had secured Pompidou's approval. But it was not until December 1974, under Valéry Giscard d'Estaing, that the Veil law legalizing the deliberate termination of pregnancy was enacted, after a debate, the scope and passion of which demonstrated the extent to which society was still exercised by issues of contraception and the control over one's body. By this time, 67 per cent of French people regarded abortion as a basic right and 82 per cent, including 93 per cent of women, were in favour of contraceptive methods. This acquiescence quickly became part of common mores: the percentage of women who took the pill rose from 6 per cent in 1972 to 12 per cent in 1973, and by 1975 had reached 24 per cent.[43]

This victorious campaign highlighted, in passing, two other major shifts in family relationships and private life: a new concern with the body, and with sexuality. We have seen how growing consumption fostered the ambition to own a well-honed body that was better nourished, thanks to an approach to dieting that *Elle* magazine in 1972 dignified with the term *nouvelle morale* ('new morality'), kept in trim by regular exercise, narcissistically pampered and preened – between 1966 and 1976, the average amount of time that people spent washing and dressing rose by a third – and identified as the core of one's being. To complete one's sentimental education, certain conspicuous forms of sexual liberation were necessary. This was less a matter of the much remarked upon appearance on French beaches of the *monokini* (topless swimsuit) or the opening of the first thirty-four sex shops in Paris in 1970, or indeed the erotic success of the first *Emmanuelle* movie in 1974; it had more to do with the emergence of a media-backed social conformism that sneered at the notion of girls retaining their virginity until they married, heaped praise on experiences thought to be individually fulfilling, asserted a right to pleasure and, above all, lazily conceded to young people the exclusive responsibility of mapping out the only possible modern path to emancipation, that is, via the full expression of one's sexuality.[44] This ostentation of the body had now become compulsory, sometimes with disastrous consequences for couples and families. It was this that altered gender roles, undermined the *phallocrates*, went to the heads of 'subjugated women', tormented teenagers and, in the form of glossy magazines, cluttered the coffee tables of the nation's living rooms.

Within families, the transition accelerated from what was already a post-authoritarian age to a more liberal one, forming the cornerstone of a cellular, associative and consensual democracy, under which individuals, including children, would affirm themselves above all as private persons, where affection was the test and sole pledge of consistency, and where the personality of each person could rock the established play of appointed roles. It was fathers who bore the brunt of this metamorphosis: mothers, after all, were buoyed up by the promising mood in favour of women's emancipation. Although they had more leisure time than before and were now better integrated into the family grouping, fathers had lost some of their former authority. Also, owing to the increasing demands placed on them outside the home, they were very aware of the general tide of uncertainties. Yet they had somehow to be caring and watchful, concerned with household matters and the children's upbringing, partners to their wives and daddies to their children, yet vested with a flagging authority: equals and fathers, tugged at and torn in a way that many found hard to come to terms with.[45] This was compounded within the home by the skill that many young people displayed in exercising their egocentric right to happiness, inflating family consumption and expenditure, demanding freedom to go out or to adopt a particular lifestyle, and making fast-changing emotional demands, as well as through the gregarious behaviour that the so-called *bof!* ('so what!') generation cultivated right through the 1970s. Youthful questioning of the adult world could not fail to trouble the many parents who were now looking for a more up-to-date way of bringing up their children. Evidence of this quest is provided by the higher profile achieved by parents' associations in schools and by the success of magazines such as *Parents*, founded in 1969, the circulation of which rose from 400,000 to 700,000 copies between 1970 and 1973.

However, by 1974 it was a cliché of almost ten years standing to point to what had self-evidently turned the social order upside down: the collective emergence of young people and, indeed, of a youth culture, along the lines traced by other Western societies, and to the accompaniment of 'the world-wide youth insurrection' of 1968.[46] Not all young people were deeply affected by the *temps des copains* – far from it – but its media-hyped effects forced the pace of change in contemporary mores, most markedly in the realm of material and cultural consumption, but also in terms of attitudes towards personal and community life. Youthfulness, this high-profile and much-hyped new social force, was experienced by an entire generation as the most obvious and authentic guarantee of personal fulfilment. On occasion, youthfulness was even held up as an example for all age groups, since youth itself was now defined as a microcosm of the social order, while the youthful promotion of new values promised society an inexhaustible adolescence. Yet this conclusion was not very widely held in 1974. For, given that individualism and standardization increasingly went hand in hand, social pressures to conform retained a vast potential to mould each individual, whether young or not so young. If the family sometimes appeared to falter, mass culture could step into the breach. And, when it came to asserting the least contestable of social imperatives, schools could not be outdone.

The supply and demand of teaching

The scale of economic growth and social change inevitably shook to its foundations the schooling apparatus inherited from the Third and

Fourth Republics and which, since 1966, had become known under the
rather more ambitious, albeit imprecise, label of *système éducatif*.[47]
Schools were thought ripe for the introduction of detailed policies which
Georges Pompidou hoped would not clash too strongly with the old
classical humanities approach. Schools were subjected to statistics and
forecasting, integrated into planning objectives and summoned to
respond to the imperatives of the modern age.[48] Above all, they were
overloaded with a vast social demand for education that was fuelled by
families. Parents viewed their children's success at school as not only
their due – given that the state proclaimed equality of opportunities –
but also as a gamble justified by the euphoria generated by economic
growth, and an investment in a future that no one had yet imagined
might include crisis. But, at the same time, parents increasingly off-
loaded on to the teaching profession those educational tasks that changing mores and the proliferation of intermediary agencies made them
less inclined or less well equipped to discharge themselves – for
example, sex education, which was introduced into the classroom in
1974 as part of the natural sciences curriculum.

This strong and wide-ranging demand for schooling, heightened still
further by vigorous demographic growth, was met with vastly expanded
public provision, which required and in fact secured prompt and excep-
tional commitment, above all in financial terms. The budget of the
education ministry, calculated in constant francs and taking 1952 as
baseline 100, rose to 213 in 1959, leapt to 469 in 1967 and reached 568
in 1970. Between 1958 and 1966, the proportion of total state spending
earmarked for education increased from 10 per cent to 17 per cent,
before stabilizing by 1975 at around 17 per cent.[49] Yet the fundamental
question bedevilling all developed societies had not been successfully
addressed: what should the rising generations be taught and, amid the
overwhelming profusion of rapidly evolving new subjects and methods,
what value should be attached to tradition and heritage?

In 1974, higher education was still making news, with a mixture of
still spectacular post-1968 agitation – over which the media pored in
puzzlement – and worrying lethargy. The protests had expanded into a
sort of *Mai rampant* ('creeping 1968'), infecting each wave of fresh
intakes. At every possible opportunity, but most notably in opposition to
the April 1970 *anti-casseurs* ('anti-rioter') law or the February 1973
Debré law limiting the deferral of military service, the militant, mainly
Trotskyist or Maoist and mutually excoriating *groupuscules* – alongside
which the Young Communists and Young Socialists made a rather better
showing than in 1968 – would emerge from their workaday routine of
handing out tracts, fly-posting, slogan spraying, heckling at lectures and

hawking at the tops of their voices their glowingly red press, to launch demonstrations that now attracted a growing band of school students, who by this time had been effectively inducted into the *comités d'action*: it was not rare for these events to culminate in a clash with the police.

In the Paris region, the experimental Vincennes university, open to students who had no baccalauréat, and with a high proportion of foreign students, let all the flowers of the various varieties of leftism bloom, while Nanterre and the Sorbonne, still shuddering, struggled to pick themselves up, and Assas fell into the lap of the extreme right. The resulting highly politicized, verbose and violent tension, stoked up by minorities germinated under hothouse conditions and nursing the 'revolutionary' illusion that they could turn the universities into 'red bases' for every other form of social protest, was fuelled above all by the students' refusal to countenance any re-establishment of order in their course studies and by clashes within the university institution itself, as well as by the students' own anxiety.

The *loi d'orientation* enacted on 12 November 1968 had proved hard to implement. Though adopted unanimously by the National Assembly following wide-ranging and active consultations initiated by Edgar Faure, Pompidou had never given it his support.[50] It proved impossible for universities to consolidate the three main pillars of the law: institutional autonomy, participation and multi-disciplinarity. The old faculties were dismantled and granted a new legal status as 'public establishments of scientific and cultural character' (EPCSC) – a move that introduced greater flexibility into the rules governing their financial administration – and they were reorganized as 'teaching and research units' (UERs) (which could also assume EPCSC status), and entrusted with the provision of shared services. What emerged at the end of a complex reshaping process lasting from 1971 to 1973, painstakingly overseen by Faure's successors at the ministry of education, Olivier Guichard and then Joseph Fontanet, were sixty universities and nine *centres universitaires* (university conglomerations). Each of these was autonomous and had its own powerful vice-chancellor, elected by its own joint committee, as well as directors and councils (at UER level). From 1971–2 onwards, this pyramidal structure was placed under the umbrella of several outspoken national bodies: the 'National Council for Higher Education and Research' (CNESER), the 'university vice-chancellors' conference' (CPU), and the 'university consultative committee' (CCU) which made recommendations on teaching staff recruitment and careers.

This blend of autonomy and centralism ushered in a process of institutional 'normalization', which was vigorously denounced by teachers' and students' unions, 'action committees', and by militant *groupuscules*, yet it in fact failed to harmonize teaching methods, degree course structure or course content. Many dispensations were granted. Medicine, for example, retained the special status it had been accorded under the 1959 Debré law, and in 1971 intake to the second year was made selective. In 1973, however, a standard course structure was imposed, setting up a first – normally two-year – 'cycle' leading to the *diplôme d'études universitaires générales* (DEUG), quite separate from the vocational training courses run by the 'university institutes of tech-nology' (IUT) that had been created in 1966. Following the DEUG, the 'second cycle' of studies culminated in the *licence* (normally one year after the DEUG) and the *maîtrise* (normally two years after the DEUG). In 1974, a 'third cycle' was introduced, access to which was via a *diplôme des études approfondies* (DEA) or a *diplôme d'études specialisées* (DESS) – advanced or specialized study certificates respectively – and culminating in the completion of a thesis. This effort at harmonization did not succeed in ironing out the educational inconsistencies created by the jumble of course credits that a student would accumulate over the course of their studies, or the often sloppy process of continuous assessment. Nor did it put a stop to internal rivalry over funding and positions between UERs and even between individual lecturers, a phenomenon that severely undermined interdisciplinarity. Nor indeed was there any breakthrough in addressing the absurdly uneven geogra-phical distribution of universities, which was the outcome of multiple political and economic pressures from regions all demanding 'their own' university close at hand. Confronted with such instability, many people felt discouraged and disillusioned: the average participation of students in the university elections instituted under the 1968 law fell from 52 per cent in 1969 to under 20 per cent in 1973. The 1976 campus distur-bances were viewed as the implosion of a system that had been merely muddling through, had failed to implement its own rules and in general responded too unevenly to young people's aspirations.[51]

In part, it was the demographic expansion that had occurred in teaching that made these issues insoluble. From a baseline of 100 in 1959, by 1977 student numbers had shot up to 430, with annual rates of growth in the student population swinging between 10 per cent and 15 per cent. Numbers had risen from 214,000 in 1960 to 625,000 in 1970, and then to 751,000 in 1974.[52] In 1960, there were barely 8,000 teachers in higher education, including fewer than 2,000 full professors. By 1974, there were 40,500 higher education teaching staff, including 4,700 professors, 5,500 senior lecturers, and a further 30,000 assistant lecturers supervising the student influx as best they could. For it was the universities, on their own, that had to cater for the new demand for higher education qualifications, given that the *grandes écoles* – as well as the *classes préparatoires* designed for students wishing to sit their competitive entrance examinations – had, in both academic and social terms, bolted their doors ever more firmly: the children of blue-collar workers now represented only 1 to 2 per cent of intake, whereas senior managers, members of the liberal professions and large employers steadily furnished between two-thirds and three-quarters of matriculating students. As for the great national scientific colleges and institutes, they were determined to steer well clear of all upheavals.[53]

There persisted, in fact, a state of skewed competition, disguised by a welcome opening-up of higher education to a mass population. At one end of the spectrum, a 'closed' sector, selective both at intake and during the course of studies, had survived and even expanded slightly, maintaining its social prestige intact. This included all the *grandes écoles* and their 'preparatory classes', a handful of scientific UERs, some IUTs, and all the medical and paramedical degree courses. This sector, which accounted for 30 per cent of higher education students in 1970, and 39 per cent in 1975, selected the country's future elites. At the other end of the spectrum stood an 'open' sector of run-of-the-mill universities. Drawing in the vast bulk of new baccalauréat holders, it was overcrowded, long on trouble and short on regulations, but it did at least turn out two-thirds of all those with university qualifications, though without guaranteeing them a job that in any way matched their ambitions – in 1974, 8.7 per cent of university graduates experienced a spell of unemployment as compared with 3.9 per cent in 1971 – and without providing any assurance that their work qualification would not be downgraded. It was this open-access sector that pumped up the student figures, anxiously pored over and triumphantly proclaimed as evidence that higher education in its entirety was undergoing democratization. After all, the ratio of probability for obtaining a higher education qualification, as between the child of a blue-collar worker and the child of a senior manager or member of a liberal profession, was moving in the right direction: from 1:41 in 1962 to 1:25 in 1968 to 1:15 in 1975. Yet taking all branches of higher education together, huge energies were squandered through this process of selection by individual failure, and through the frequent dashing of the social hopes that people pinned on securing a degree. While student numbers at intake climbed relentlessly, 'at the other end' a mere 192,000 qualifications were awarded in 1973, and this figure had changed little by the end of the decade. The typically 'New Society' measures designed to encourage firms to release their employees to attend training courses, usually held at the university, proved a relative success, with 90,000 people enrolled in 1974. Yet this could do little to correct the generalized dysfunctioning of the country's educational system against a European and international background of increasingly tough training and selection of degree-holding elites.[54]

While less spectacular and less controversial – and also less exposed to public or media criticism – the reforms introduced into other parts of the education system were of equal importance for the future. One has to go back to 6 January 1959, when an order signed by General de Gaulle and his minister for education, Jean Berthoin, raised the school-leaving age from fourteen to sixteen for all children born in or after 1953. This measure, which was fully operational by 1967 and supplemented by an 'implementation decree' that set out a detailed plan for the overhauling of the educational system, laid emphasis on the most crucial issue, which had first been raised more than fifty years previously: how might the mass education of a modernized nation narrow the gap between primary schooling for all, and secondary education, which alone provided access to higher education and to more advanced forms of technical training via the baccalauréat? Attended by students of intermediate age and positioned socially at the point where this issue generated the greatest tension, the *collège* (middle school) thus found itself at the core of what was emerging as an hierarchically structured apparatus: it registered the progress of democratization that was apparent even before 1960, while advocating, in the name of equality, a redistribution of educational opportunities for the good of both the country and its individual citizens.

Primary schools, which now admitted all children between the ages of six and eleven – lycées had lost their few remaining junior classes – had not undergone any orchestrated upheavals. No longer overcrowded, their rolls even began slowly to decline: from a total of five million pupils in 1960 to 4,700,000 in 1975, with average class sizes shrinking from 30 in 1958 to 23.5 by 1976. With the collapse of rural life came the closure of many classes with dwindling numbers, a process that prompted the introduction of an efficient system of bussing children often over considerable distances. In 1959 there had been 73,000 state-run 'country' schools but this number fell to 64,000 in 1963, and to 48,000 in 1976. In 1962, a policy was unveiled to turn what had been separate boys' and girls' schools into mixed schools, divided into several classes or forms, and by 1974 this change had been implemented everywhere except in the most remote areas. From 1965 onwards, all new school developments, especially those sited on large suburban housing estates, were obliged by law to have five separate classes, one for each age-group. In a complete turn-around from Jules Ferry's time, the genders were now mixed while the age-groups were separated out. As a result of economic growth and urbanization, schools were getting larger: in 1958 there was an average of 2.2 classes per year, and this rose to 3.4 in 1975.

With the baby-boom bulge of the post-Liberation years now tapering off, primary schools, relieved of the task of preparing children for the rest of their lives, had become just one stage in a process. The Berthoin reform of 1959 defined their main task as that of steering children without mishap into the *sixième* (the first year of the secondary school). As a result, primary 'school-leavers' classes had emptied, plummeting from a total of 730,000 pupils in 1958 to 6,600 by 1973: almost the entirety of each successive age-group now 'went up': in 1958 primary schools had a total of 781,000 pupils over eleven, but by 1973 just 85,000, most of whom were repeating their 'CM2' (final year of primary school). On the other hand, pre-school classes became overcrowded, reflecting an increased demand for schooling, linked to galloping urbanization, and the increasing numbers of working women: 56 per cent of married women between twenty-five and twenty-nine had jobs in 1975, compared with 35 per cent in 1962. By 1975, there was a total of 2,600,000 children in the pre-school classes that catered for ages two to five, accounting for 26 per cent of all two-year-olds, 80 per cent of three-year-olds and almost all four- and five-year-olds – the figures for 1958 had been 8 per cent, 32 per cent and 72 per cent respectively. Thronged and buzzing, French kindergartens and nursery schools gained an excellent reputation that was much envied abroad. They drew children into educational play while seeking to bring out their 'themes of interest', implementing an innovative approach to teaching that stressed confidence-building and spontaneity. Blessed with quite remarkable teaching staff, pre-school education became a happy experience – a haven of active freedom, where educational planners might dream of correcting social inequalities before launching the children into the assault course that was the schools 'system'.

For the move to the 'big school' left many families and pupils bewildered. Primary schools had failed to keep their curriculums and teaching methods in step with changing times.[55] Under pressure from those who promoted 'educational science', they had experimented with a threefold division of the teaching timetable (a core of French and arithmetic; 'early-learning' activities; and physical education). This approach succeeded in stimulating the active interest of pupils, and was therefore adopted by the 1969 reform, along with the reduction in the school week from thirty to twenty-seven hours, conveniently freeing Saturday afternoons for family weekends away. The reform also urged schools to abandon rote-learning, marks, grading, homework and tradi-

tional arms-crossed-on-desks discipline, which was now deemed trau-
matizing. After 1970, however, modern maths was rather too quick to
displace multiplication tables and the square on the hypotenuse, while a
supposedly 'linguistics-based' scheme designed to modernize the
teaching of French laid emphasis on 'free expression' at the expense of
spelling, the 'global method' for teaching children how to read did little
to prepare them for the study of grammar, and 'awareness-based'
teaching neglected dates in history and place names in geography. The
upshot was puzzled teachers, worried families and children deprived of
the basic knowledge and skills they required if they were to make a
successful start to their first year of secondary school. In 1975, the
disappointing performance of primary schools led to a policy U-turn,
though any sense of balance has since remained elusive.

At the other end of the schooling process, lycées had not been subject
to any overarching reform, apart from the one introduced by Christian
Fouchet to reshape the baccalauréat. Under this, a distinction was
introduced between 'technical' baccalauréats (subdivided into two
types: 'F' geared towards industry and 'G' towards the service sector)
and 'general education' baccalauréats, in reality ranked in terms of a
single criterion: success at mathematics. Pupils who were no good at
maths were corralled into the 'A' series of baccalauréats (previously
known as *philo*: philosophy), not all of which included Latin. Others,
whose mathematical talents were considered average, were steered into
the 'D' series (previously known as *Sciences ex*) or into the new 'B'
'economic and social' series. The best pupils, however, whatever their
vocational outlook, were forced to struggle – special coaching at the
family's expense had become virtually obligatory if a student was going
to 'keep up' in maths – in the coveted 'C' series (previously known as
Maths élem), which was believed to contain the country's future elite.[56]
Demand for higher education, however, was so strong that even this
excessively pyramidal structure did little to curb expansion in the
numbers passing their *bacs*: from 9.7 per cent of young people in 1959,
to 16.2 per cent in 1969 and 24.2 per cent in 1975.

What was actually taught, however, changed slowly, despite the
vigorous challenges issued in 1968. Modern maths, though too abstract
and complex for the majority of students, had been raised to the status
of tablets of stone in 1969 by the Lichnerowicz commission which
admired its 'objectivity', and it had thus replaced Latin and Greek as a
means for selecting students. A similar trend towards formalization had
taken over the study of combined physics and chemistry, as well as the
natural sciences, while literary subjects had entered a period of crisis.
Philosophy tended to adopt a critical stance – and itself came in for

much criticism – while history emphasized work from documents of all sorts, and on an issue-based global perspective, at the expense of national identity. Under pressure from active minorities – the newly founded Association française des enseignants de français, for example, launched a campaign against the venerable *Franco-Ancienne* in 1969 – French teaching gradually broke with classical studies and with literary history, focusing instead on the critical study of selected extracts, preferring the summarize-and-discuss format to the more traditional essay form. French teaching had, however, been spared the brunt of militant linguistics and structuralism by the introduction in 1970 of a pre-baccalauréat exam, sat in the penultimate year at secondary school. Teaching methods developed very unevenly, with frequent recourse to pupil presentations, group work, and whole-class interaction (*cours dialogué*).

In fact, it was in the *collège* (middle school) that the future was taking shape. The Berthoin reform had created a *cycle d'observation* (monitoring period) covering the first two years of secondary school, with a limited common-core syllabus that made no distinction between traditional and modern teaching methods. It had also merged some of the 'observation classes' in what had been the final year of primary school, relabelling them *collèges d'enseignement général* (CEGs), with teaching provided by former primary-school teachers (*instituteurs*) whose status had, for this purpose, been elevated in 1960 to that of secondary-school teachers (*professeurs*). The CEGs were quick to attract new pupils, demonstrating that the standardization and democratization of the educational system hinged on the eleven-to-sixteen age group, at the watershed between primary and secondary schooling, now focused on the *collège*. The 1963 Fouchet law, in which the Elysée had taken a direct interest, had launched a 'first cycle' in *collèges d'enseignement secondaire* (CESs: 'middle schools'), which offered both the standard and the CEG syllabus, while postponing the moment at which students had to opt either for the 'long' lycée-type route to the baccalauréat or for the 'short' and more vocational path. It was on entering the *seconde* (roughly 'year 11'), that students now had to decide on their future direction, after a two-year *cycle d'orientation*, intended to focus their aptitudes.

The policy choice was now clear and it meant using the CESs as an instrument to achieve mass standardized provision. What then ensued was a construction programme, the like of which had never been seen in the history of school education. Between 1965 and 1975, 2,354 *collèges*, each designed to accommodate 900, 1,200 or even 1,600 pupils, were built: almost one for every working day![57] Following Edgar Faure's decision in 1968 to postpone the start of Latin studies until the *quatrième* ('year 9'), the new CESs brought together and strove to mix three separate strands: one aiming to provide the 'long' lycée-type route, typically culminating in the baccalauréat, and taught by qualified secondary-school teachers (*professeurs*); a second that offered a range of shorter and more vocational CEG-type courses, and was taught by former primary-school teachers; and the third strand that brought together 'transitional' or 'practical' final-year classes, and attempted to provide remedial help for those students excluded from the other strands by the selection process.[58] This third, stragglers' strand was dropped in 1974, and a year later the Haby reform abolished all distinction between CEGs and CESs, merging the two structures to produce the *collège unique*.

It is questionable whether this process of mass standardization in education, with CESs designed to act as regulators, had the effect of equalizing opportunities. As Antoine Prost has shown in his investigation into secondary schools in Orléans,[59] a lot of progress in democratization had already been achieved by 1960, but the mass provision of education foundered on the failure carefully to think through the inevitable differentiation in the types of course content that needed to be delivered. Moreover, differences in professional status between primary-school and secondary-school teachers (*instituteurs* and *professeurs*), which were jealously defended by their respective trades unions – SNI and SNES,[60] which acted as rivals within the overarching FEN – made it impossible to nurture any avant-garde ideas among primary teaching staff, either in terms of course content or teaching methods. The *collèges* thus remained unable to tackle the widespread failure of schools, which first became apparent within their own walls: in 1973, 41 per cent of the entire year's age-group left the educational system without any qualification, 13 per cent with a general 'BEPC' (*brevet d'études du premier cycle*), 18 per cent with a CAP or a BEP, just 16 per cent with a baccalauréat, and 12 per cent with a higher education diploma. In spite of transitional classes, the *collèges* operated a system of selection through failure, thus undermining the effects of the democratization in its intake.

Moreover, the authoritarian inflexibility of the school-list system that allocated children to secondary schools in their family's immediate district was regularly circumvented by better-off, more sophisticated or just better-informed parents who would simply enter their children for a course that included a less usual second language (e.g. German), which was available only in prestigious, often city-centre, schools.[61] Above all, the veneer of educational uniformity that sought to manage mass schooling on the pattern of traditional 'all-round' general education – and which in 1972 applied to three-quarters of all young school-attenders[62] – gave free rein to the whole panoply of sociological bias which, through the process of repeating years and poor school results, held up or indeed rejected many children of blue-collar workers, white-collar workers or small employers, who failed to learn quickly enough to 'play' what was for them an over-traditional 'game'. The proportion of children from such backgrounds entering a *classe de seconde* (roughly a 'year 11') hardly varied at all between 1973 and 1980, and after 1974 children of senior managers had a 17:1 advantage over them when it came to getting a place in a *seconde 'C'*. In addition, technical and vocational training, which had undergone reform in 1959, remained something of a poor relation, charged with picking up and dusting down those whom the general-education approach applied during the early secondary-school years had failed. This helps to explain the growth of this sector: technical courses, whether 'short' or 'long', swelled from 509,000 students in 1958–9 to 830,000 in 1968–9 and to 928,000 in 1973–4.

Given this state of affairs, a great many families found that the best way of alleviating or short-circuiting the inegalitarian effects of state education on their children was to turn to private schools which, after the 1959 Debré law urging the private sector to accept all the goals and targets of state sector provision, generally operated under a partnership agreement (*contrat d'association*): by 1970, in the west, the north, the Massif Central and the Rhône-Alpes regions, private schools were educating over 20 per cent of children. Whereas debates over the principle of non-religious education had now died down, most French people remained keen, for reasons that had less and less to do with any confessional or ideological convictions, to retain this 'free space', which was seen variously as an option of last resort, an environment where discipline survived intact, a haven of restrained initiative, or of un-abashed elitism. In 1971, private primary schools were educating about one million children and private secondary schools about 900,000. Of this total of 1,900,000, about 1,700,00 were taught in the 8,900 Catholic schools, which employed roughly 90,000 teachers. Since 1959, the private sector had grown by about 12 per cent, as compared with the public sector's 26 per cent. From 1958 to 1974, all the opinion polls confirmed that about 60 per cent of French people (and 64 per cent of French women) felt that the existence of 'free' educational institutions alongside state schools was right, useful and provided a stimulus, above all because it meant freedom of choice should their children run into difficulties within the state system.

Overall, the French educational system had changed size without sufficiently changing shape. There is no doubt that the reforms introduced – with the country's eager support – first under de Gaulle and then under Pompidou, had certainly made access to schooling more democratic. Yet the complexity and over-centralization of the system, the excessively hierarchical structure of courses, the inadequately diversified and old-fashioned content of curricula, and the inadequacy of careers guidance given to each individual student, left too much free rein to social inequalities, which all too often fatally undermined sincere efforts to promote equality of opportunity. Teachers, though now more numerous,[63] suffered from a declining social status, and tended to be immured in their sectional and disciplinary concerns. Dispossessed, often by the media, of their monopoly of knowledge, and prone to feel misunderstood at just the moment when the challenges facing them were becoming so arduous, they struggled to keep abreast of the inevitable changes under way, after having split so openly in May 1968. Many teachers were enraged or discouraged when they read the preliminary conclusions of educational sociologists who displayed summary contempt for the curriculum being delivered, and who set out to pick apart the mechanisms of social 'reproduction' at work within the various classes, proceeding in strident Marxist-Leninist terms to denounce 'capitalist schooling'.[64]

Yet, despite all its shortcomings and bottlenecks, despite its persistent failure to grasp the demands of economic and professional life, this system, however imperfect, played its part in raising the general level of education of the French people and thereby contributed to the country's growth – even if, it is fair to say, the issue of jobs for school-leavers and youth unemployment was not yet a major worry.[65] The proportion of the population that had no educational qualifications fell from 75 per cent to 67 per cent between 1968 and 1975, while over the same period the proportion of French people possessing either a higher education qualification or the baccalauréat rose from 11.6 per cent to 17.2 per cent. In its 1972 report, a review committee set up by Pompidou and chaired by Louis Joxe concluded that much work remained to be done to adjust the inherited educational system to its social environment, even if inequalities in opportunities to gain access to the 'system' were being tackled. For, as the crisis of the mid-1970s loomed, everyone had realized that, as the report put it, 'nowadays, it is within the school itself that the future of each individual is shaped . . . What was a haven of culture has become a field of competitive combat upon which the social situation of each student is decided.'[66]

7   A splintered culture

In the early 1960s, once the issue of decolonization had been settled, the emergence of a new France, a prosperous nation of consumers, provided a constant stimulus to thinkers and artists alike.[1] The challenge now was to decipher the new age, to gain some purchase on the teeming mass of signs that it placed on display, and to find a critical way of thinking about such brash modernity. These questions were framed in such unapologetically French terms that, in retrospect, it is possible to see the 1960s as a proud decade of 'traditional' French thinking. Yet the framework was simultaneously extended to address matters of global proportions, thanks to the impact of intellectual and artistic influences and fashions from abroad, especially the United States. This was underscored by the way that a 'mass culture', which soaked up anything American, took spectacular hold – though less rigidly than its detractors thought – at the very moment when *la culture cultivée* (high or 'cultured' culture) was lurching between deconstruction and protest, the beliefs of the past were fraying fast, and there was no *culture publique* (low or 'public' culture) that had any hope of bridging the social and cultural divides.

The deconstruction of *culture cultivée*

'The alert and uneasy awareness of modern knowledge', of which Michel Foucault would later speak, was at that time embodied by structuralism. For it was in structuralism that thinkers from quite different backgrounds believed they had discovered not only a new method of investigation and an effective way of applying the rapidly expanding social sciences, but even an anti- or non-ideological programme capable of carrying the work of Marxism and liberalism forward into the age of technocracy. In one field after another, the Other displaced the Same, and the Static saw off the developmental, as everything became liable to reduction to the rank of a linguistic code. The rules by which an object operated were deemed more significant than

180

the object itself, universalism was deconstructed, history placed on ice and Man summarily dismissed. What therefore emerged to dominate these years was a systematic anti-humanism, a throng of disparate discourses each claiming to have mastered the Real and to have sent the human Subject packing.

It was Claude Lévi-Strauss's hour of glory. Anthropology, as he understood the discipline, had been the first of the human sciences to turn to linguistics, and had drunk of its best sap. This had enabled Lévi-Strauss to demonstrate that, in every society, the elementary structures of kinship, the see-saw of gift and counter-gift, and the ordering of founding myths operated without regard to empirical reality; that language had become the sole link between the system and its signification; that the sign always outweighed the concept; and that nothing in the real world was intelligible apart from its structure. This almost neo-positivist vision of the world, with its claim to scientific status, which reduced all signification to an effect created by a signifier, was snapped up and generalized, debated and hyped.[2] The active pessimism of this outlook blossomed in 1962 with the huge sales of *La Pensée sauvage*, came into full bloom between 1964 and 1971 with the *Mythologiques* tetralogy, attracting a vast array of disciples, and then triumphed in 1973 with the publication of the second volume of *Anthropologie structurale* and the election of its author to the French Academy.[3]

This closing-down of History, this confinement of Man within a totality on which he has no hold, seemed to be confirmed by the latest scientific thinking, which rejected evolution and set out to dismantle the architecture of the universe. New physics now talked in terms of repetitive discontinuities, and molecular biology in particular asserted that living beings fulfilled no final purpose, indeed that every organism was merely a point of transition between a hereditary system and reproduction, encapsulating both its origin and its end. François Jacob and Jacques Monod (who in 1965, with Etienne Lwoff, had been awarded the Nobel prize for physiology and medicine) popularized this brand of universal indifference in, respectively, *La Logique du vivant* and *Le Hasard et la Nécessité*, both of which sold very well in 1970.[4] Yet 'difficult' sciences and technologies had too slight an impact on popular culture for structuralism to be able to dispense with contributions from the more 'human' sciences. This source, indeed, proved particularly fertile in 1966 – a year that some observers regarded as an *année lumière*[5] – with the much-acclaimed publication of Foucault's *Les Mots et les Choses* (which by 1967 had sold over 100,000 copies), Jacques Lacan's *Ecrits*, Tzvetan Todorov's *Théorie de la littérature*, Emile Benveniste's *Problèmes de linguistique générale*, A. J. Greimas' *Sémantique structurale*,

Pierre Bourdieu's *L'Amour de l'art* and G. Dumézil's *La Religion romaine archaïque*, as well as a new edition of Fernand Braudel's *La Méditerranée*. Meanwhile, such journals as *Communications*, *Esprit* and *Les Temps modernes* devoted sizzling special numbers to this outpouring of structuralism.

But it was Michel Foucault who most successfully focused attention on emerging trends, even if he was quick to deny any strict adherence to the structuralist credo.[6] His vigorous prose style, his appetite for knowledge, his tireless agility at gleaning fresh ideas, the barbed comments he directed at historians and the runaway success of *Les Mots et les Choses* made Foucault the outstanding example of the new intellectual, keenly exploring every front. His research into madness in classical times and the birth of the clinic uncovered signs of the human subject's disappearance from Western consciousness, while his investigations into forms of knowledge disclosed the irresponsibility of humankind in the construction of their own history since the Renaissance. 'The fact that philosophy has always been and is still coming to an end and the fact that within philosophy perhaps but even more outside of and against philosophy, in literature as much as in formal thinking, the question of language arises, proves without a doubt that man is in the process of disappearing', wrote Foucault in *L'Archéologie du savoir*, in 1969.

Yet linguists, even if access to their work was often arduous, also played a role as explorers and unifiers. Semiology, which as early as 1957 in *Mythologies* Roland Barthes had brought to bear on a whole range of consumer goods and institutions, became the founding science of signs, furnishing all the social sciences with a common language. Barthes' structuralist 'discourse on method' even took on literature and criticism. In 1965, a heated debate over Racine pitted Raymond Picard, the Sorbonne's foremost Racinian scholar, against Barthes, who advocated a 'new criticism' that renounced the author-as-individual approach, and focused instead on the operation of a pure 'play of figures', before rehabilitating the authentic pleasure of the text, shorn of context.[7] For its part, the *nouveau roman*, which Nathalie Sarraute and Michel Butor had promoted during the 1950s, was now entrenched in its publishing redoubt at Les Editions de Minuit, while also managing to seduce Gallimard. Given a theoretical grounding in 1963 by Alain Robbe-Grillet in his *Pour un nouveau roman*, the 'new novel' pursued its goal of refuting the bourgeois novel by obliterating character, narrative and plot, while scrutinizing the strangeness of a world that is watched by Man, yet which 'does not return his gaze', while making an attempt at an art for art's sake that 'can only create for nothing'.[8] By diluting meaning, decentring the human subject, granting writing a primacy over meaning, resolutely spelling out a discontinuous universe, and disengaging as writers, young novelists like Philippe Sollers (*H* was published in 1973) and Jean-Marie Le Clézio (from *Procès-verbal* in 1963 to *La Guerre* in 1970), along with such journals as *Tel Quel* (at least until it went over to Maoism after May 1968),[9] took over where their elders had left off, convinced they were bleeding the novel to death. In the process, they put off a great many readers – who seemed, on the other hand, only too happy to pounce on such old-fashioned well-made 'novels' as Michel Déon's *Les Poneys sauvages* and Robert Sabatier's *Trois Sucettes à la menthe*, big hits in 1970 and 1972 respectively.[10] Yet the very same 'new' novelists did not shrink from pursuing success and respectability along paths more congenial to the media, thus taking to the cinema their struggle against the illusion of realism.[11] The psychoanalyst Jacques Lacan was another figure who, following the considerable worldly success of the seminar he gave at the Ecole normale supérieure, aroused great interest in the media, who flatteringly echoed his ideas and granted him enigmatic interviews in the best weekly papers: indeed, he became the guru of the moment. Anxious to carry forward Freud's work, Lacan explained by dint of metaphorical formulae which he presented to rapt lecture halls that the sub-conscious was structured like a language and that it conformed to laws 'that are those revealed by the study of positive languages' since Saussure, and which 'decentre' the subject. Taking issue with all non-Lacanian Freudians, whom he deemed too full of psychology, Lacan argued that analysis was exclusively a matter of listening to the language of the patient, since the key to the structure of a mind could be grasped in the chaotic outpouring of speech.[12]

Yet it would be rash to reduce the heights of intellectual activity to the flourishes of these musketeers of many-headed structuralism, to the enterprise of their imitators, to their clout with the media or to their university conquests after 1968, most notably at Vincennes. The fact that the intellectual 'field' had changed shape created an opportunity for rival ways of thinking.[13] One example of this, at the end of the 1960s, was 'Teilhardism', based largely on the success of R. P. Teilhard de Chardin's *Phénomène humain*, published in 1955, which had sold over 250,000 copies. Condemned once again by the Holy Office in 1962, Teilhard de Chardin's work had argued the need for a reconciliation between science and faith, blending cosmic evolutionism and Christian eschatology to concoct a distinctly sulphurous and ahistorical convergence of the world at the 'Omega point'. This managed briefly to seduce so many elites that it came to be denounced as a convenient ideology for technocrats desperate for a long-term vision.[14]

More significantly, Marxism was by no means ready to abandon the field to the onslaught of the structuralists. The existential interpretation of Marx was still making good headway, after being relaunched in 1960 by Sartre's massive *Critique de la raison dialectique*. Having previously stated that Marxism remained the 'unsurpassable horizon of our times', Sartre now admitted that it 'had come to a halt' with Stalin's ice-age, though he claimed that his philosophy of praxis, founded on the action of the free individual *en situation* who refused to become mired in the *pratico-inerte* (i.e. the nitty-gritty) of everyday life, could breathe new life into Marxist thinking. Sartre also maintained that his own theory of the *groupe en fusion* was particularly well suited to the new and violent forms that class struggle was assuming, whether in its anti-imperialist, Third-World or leftist manifestations, and that the meaning of history was far from lost.[15] Sartre's teachings were still listened to avidly, imbued as he was with the prestige of the century's foremost moral philosopher, who bade a first farewell to literature with an autobiographical gem in *Les Mots* (1963), followed by a *portrait-fleuve* of Flaubert in *L'Idiot de la famille* (1971). Despite the vehement commitments that Sartre, true to the spirit of 1968, continued to undertake, he could still mount a highly classical defence of intellectuals.[16]

Yet it was above all the work of Louis Althusser that strove to rescue Marxism, and to clear it of the crimes committed in its name, by uncovering a scholarly and philosophical Marx who had nothing whatsoever of the ideologist about him. From *Pour Marx*, published in 1967, to his *Réponse à John Lewis* in 1973, Althusser championed historical materialism as an 'unassailable and unavoidable' science, as expounded in the only book that still demanded to be read, *Das Kapital*, the logic of which had marked an 'epistemological break' from the Hegelian writings of the young Marx. This truly revolutionary liquidation of the idealist, humanist and bourgeois avatars of 'universal thought' granted Marxism everlasting protection against revisionism: all one needed to do was refer back constantly to its authentic theory. This self-evident fact, hammered home in insistent detail in a lively seminar that Althusser delivered at the Ecole normale, and strongly backed by a tiny band of fervent disciples, made it conveniently possible to dismiss as false, by Althusserian edict, all that was deemed 'ideological' in the implementation of Marx's thinking). Viewed in this light, 'socialist humanism' as advocated in the Soviet Union, along with the 'cult of the personality' denounced in 1956 at the CPSU's twentieth party congress, were pitiful concepts of the 'dubious superstructure' variety.[17] If Althusser's obsessional loyalty to Marx's science rehabilitated the original purity of Marxism in the teeth of history's trickery, the only contribution that it made to the analysis of contemporary society was the convenient and valued though short-lived assistance of an all-purpose talk about the force of 'state ideological apparatuses', printed in *La Pensée* in 1971. Although curiously disconnected from developments in the real world, this gloss nonetheless left a strong impression on many people. Finally, however, in spite of its best efforts, Althusserian thinking became trapped in the partitioning-off and closing-down of the intellectual field that structuralism had ushered in.

There came a time, however, after May 1968, when structuralism appeared dated, overtaken by the renewed march of history and thus obsolete, when Nietzsche's tragedy took revenge on the savage mind. Such disloyalty came chiefly from the linguists, literary critics and philosophers who had once been the foremost propagandists of structuralist thought. Thus it was that Roland Barthes in *S/Z* (1970) took his conceptual vision of literature to pieces, and argued for a return to intuition. In *La Dissémination* (1972), Julia Kristeva and Jacques Derrida pursued the task of deconstructing the metaphysical implications of structuralism, while breaking down the partitions between philosophy and fiction, seeking the disseminated polysemy of texts prior to their meaning, and attempting to found a grammatology. Michel Foucault admitted that he was 'simply Nietzschean', and then, in *L'Archéologie du savoir* (1969), engaged in a more historically based form of research intended to demonstrate, in opposition to the main paradigm of structuralism, that 'discursive relations are not internal to discourse' but that they proceed from dated social logics. In 1972 *L'Anti-Œdipe* by Gilles Deleuze and Félix Guattari exploded like a bomb, with its violent criticism of psychoanalysis, psychiatry and Lacan, its affirmation of an unconscious that was not structural but 'machinic', its blend of Freudo-Marxism and Nietzscheanism, and its exposition of a political philosophy of desire that came to haunt many a veteran of 1968.[18] Finally, the Althusserian cohort imploded. Althusser penned a self-criticism in which he confessed that in *Lire le Capital* he had flirted more than he ought to have done with structuralism. Jacques Rancière abandoned Althusserianism altogether, opining that it had 'died on the May barricades with many other ideas of the past', while his young comrades at the Ecole normale sank into an imported Maoism already in an advanced state of decomposition.[19]

Analyses of industrial, urban and material aspects of contemporary society, which had been elaborated since the end of the 1950s, gained fresh force under the impact of the May events, which were perceived as the revenge of the active, revolutionary and desiring subject over the structuralist ice-age and in particular over the alienation of the 'one-dimensional' man by consumer society that had been denounced by the philosopher Herbert Marcuse, a simplistic Freudo-Marxist whom students engaged in the world-wide 'movement' had handed a moment of fleeting triumph. The pamphlets produced by the situationists Raoul Vaneigem and Guy Debord, brimming with student-type illustrations, castigated the 'society of the spectacle', and their utopian appeals for *jouissance de soi* (self-pleasure) as against *l'usage des choses* (the use of things) induced feverish excitement in their many readers, though the movement itself disbanded in 1972.[20] The Marxist critique of towns and town life enjoyed a strong revival with the updating of Henri Lefebvre's analyses,[21] while Jean Baudrillard's critique of consumer society took on a more active complexion. Sociologists, many of whom had been at the forefront of the May movement,[22] now dominated the critical analysis of French society: Michel Crozier's *La Société bloquée* (1970) made a huge impact, building upon his ruthless description of the *Phénomène bureaucratique* (1963). Pierre Bourdieu and Jean-Claude Passeron in *La Reproduction* (1970) and, following in their wake, Christian Baudelot and Roger Establet in *L'Ecole capitaliste en France* (1971), launched an extremely mechanical denunciation of the French school system which, they alleged, aided and abetted the wealthy in their domination, while cynically cultivating inequality. Alain Touraine, in the meantime, identified the emergence of 'new social movements', while Edgar Morin examined the broad rifts that the May events had gouged through French society.[23]

A number of less focused analyses provided ideological justification for various forms of post-'68 militancy. A combative regionalism, inveighing against the 'interior colonialism' and 'regional alienation' perpetrated by Parisian centralism, relied on linguistic demands in an attempt to 'rethink France' and to shore up ethnic and cultural minorities. This movement took succour from the 'anti-colonialist' arguments that the deeply Occitan Robert Laffont advanced in *La Révolution régionaliste* (1967). Building on this rejection of the standardization and uniformity of industrial society, and following the example of struggles such as those surrounding Larzac in 1971, there emerged from 1970 onwards a *rétro* movement, entailing a return to one's personal 'roots' or heritage and an appeal to ecology.[24] At the same time, pre-'68 anti-imperialist militancy had now been converted, at least in part, into a Third-Worldism that the Maspero publishers and the *Combats* series, launched by Claude Durand at Seuil, took great pains to foster.

All of these efforts failed, yet a strong trace of deconstructionist uncertainty lingered, with May '68 serving as a link between structuralism and the activism of negation.[25] Conclusive proof of this is to be found in the arts, where Pierre Boulez in music and Mondrian in painting joined forces with the novels of Michel Butor and the complicated grammar of Derrida to erect a highly eccentric structure as a testament to modernity. It was not that artists had abandoned their effort to grasp and subvert reality, or to play a social role. Quite the reverse: an art whose works were 'open' could embrace technical progress, experiment with new materials (the scrap metal, plastics or foam rubber that artists such as César compressed) or criticize mass consumption. The 1951 law that made it compulsory to earmark 1 per cent of all spending on the construction of public developments or buildings for decorative art or monumental display was strictly enforced from 1965 onwards, resulting in a rush of commissions that provided modern art with a broader and more appreciative audience. Often the boundaries were blurred between fine and applied arts, and between painters, architects, sculptors, fashion designers, and advertising artists. Thus it was that the Malassis cooperative produced *L'Appartemensonge* (a made-up compound word, suggesting 'apartment–dream–lie'), Gropius applied his polychromic effects to a housing development in Créteil, and in 1971 Pignon-Ernest covered Paris with 2,000 screen prints commemorating the hundredth anniversary of the Paris Commune. It was in the same spirit that Varsely decorated the university of Montpellier, while in 1974 works by Soto, Arman and Dubuffet appeared at Renault's new headquarters in Billancourt. In fact it was the various avant-gardes, especially in painting, that were now losing their grip on reality, their work shorn of meaning, as the artists themselves declared war on art. The Paris *Ecole* was no more, its cosmopolitan influences had collapsed into one another, the art market was scattering, while the public grew weary of provocative exhibitions, even if Paris still bubbled with creativity. The methodical project launched in 1961 by the Groupe de recherche d'art visuel gradually petered out, without succeeding in its attempt to reconcile kinetic art with op art. The provocative *Nouveau Réalisme* group, which the critic Pierre Restany had supported since 1960,[26] abandoned its efforts to draw together the ambition of *affichistes* (literally 'poster designers') such as Hains and Villeglé, Tinguely's *dada-barbare* machinery, the suicidal asceticism of Klein, and Bryen's 'ready made' art. The mid-1960s' return to figurative art, obsessed as it was with the strip cartoon and descending at times into extreme kitsch, recruited only Courmes, Aillaud, Adami and Arroyo. Hyperrealism, despite the huge media interest it aroused, remained too American an import. After just two years in existence, from 1970 to 1972, the young members of the Supports-Surfaces group gave up their collective attempt to relaunch abstract art: roped rigging suspended in the middle of the countryside and the daubing of empty frame-stretchers had quickly palled. By 1974, painting was showing signs of acute aphasia.

All this portentous posturing and intellectual and artistic drift was offset, or balanced, by a revival of historical studies which, amid all the surrounding hubbub, grabbed hold of a sizeable slice of intellectual terrain, and then succeeded in disseminating throughout the 1970s its multi-disciplinary and unifying concerns. Influenced by structuralism and linguistics, which *Annales* initially greeted very favourably,[27] political history continued to be regarded as excessively *événementielle* (bound by events) and was accordingly despised, although ammunition for its future fightback was already being stockpiled at the university of Nanterre and at the Fondation nationale des sciences politiques, especially around René Rémond. On 30 November 1973, Emmanuel Le Roy Ladurie began teaching at the Collège de France, with a first lecture on *L'histoire immobile*, with its stationary sense of time, reposing on the patient computing of statistical series, fed through the latest software, leaving no blot at all on the surrounding structuralist landscape, supposedly already under deconstruction. Clearly influenced by Foucault, Paul Veyne, on the other hand, in *Comment on écrit l'histoire* (1971), argued that all that was left were 'partial histories', arising from the midst of disorder and chance. Historical studies, therefore, caught between freezing solid and shattering, made the very best of what was to hand, sweeping up the crumbs of the various deconstructions, entering into pacts with the other social sciences, and clinging to the economic and social fields that Ernest Labrousse, Pierre Vilar and Jean Bouvier had researched. Meanwhile, Philippe Ariès and Robert Mandrou successfully introduced the concept of *mentalités*, while Georges Duby explored Dumézil's notion of trifunctionality. Throughout these years, history jealously defended its disciplinary turf by means of major doctoral theses such as those by Pierre Chaunu on Seville and by Pierre Goubert on the Beauvaisis area of north-west France. More than this, history launched a major publishing and media offensive, whose first sign of success was the production in 1975 of a bestseller: Emmanuel Le Roy Ladurie's *Montaillou, village occitan*.[28] In 1974, this 'history in pieces, eclectic, expanding to embrace oddities that indeed one ought not to neglect', far removed from the 'total history' of which Marc Bloch and Fernand Braudel had dreamed, provided itself with passport and guide-book in the shape of the three-volume *Faire de l'histoire*, by Jacques Le Goff and Pierre Nora.[29] Well attuned to the intellectual mood of the times, though without entirely capitulating to it, this work turned the tables on the years of structural immobilism, the debris from which, however, had shored up what later came to be known in the media as 'Nouvelle Histoire'. It was also a good example – indeed, perhaps the only one – of a promising transition between a *culture cultivée* in tatters and a flourishing 'mass culture' that was achieved by virtue of a widespread and fierce thirst for communication.

The advent of mass culture

In 1962, in *L'Esprit du temps*, Edgar Morin had noted the advent of a new culture, the forms of which were being imported from the United States.[30] A child of the burgeoning mass media, its dynamism unsettled and marginalized the high or 'cultivated' culture of the intellectuals and elites, poured scorn on national heritage, and overwhelmingly seduced young people. This multi-form culture with its global reach was, in Morin's view, not only designed on an industrial scale but was 'manufactured for mass distribution'. It was 'addressed to a human mass, that is to say, to an agglomeration of individuals considered in isolation from their professional or social status',[31] and it promised them hitherto untried yet perfectly accessible forms of pleasurable consumption. It was disseminated by means of events which, though disparate, were all given huge media coverage.[32] These included the promotion in 1960 of the singer Johnny Hallyday who for a time became a teen idol, or the launching in 1965 of a radio 'Pop Club' hosted by José Artur on France-Inter. Another example was the live television broadcast on 21 July 1969 of man's first steps on the moon, a mix of live footage, news and entertainment that made it 'the model modern event':[33] 10 million TV sets remained switched on and EDF had to obtain emergency back-up power. Each of these 'launches' focused on a very specific cultural genre, while mobilizing familiar feelings and fantasies, yet all depended on the combined deployment of different media forms, and only achieved their success through the consumption of their brilliance and warmth. Each displayed and held out the latest kind of pleasure, a surge of well-being, and a confidence in progress: what was on offer to each individual was playful happiness, the very basis of mass culture. Yet mass culture was no fleeting fad, no chain of random events, no mere eclectic rummaging around among those cultural artefacts and practices assumed to guarantee the best 'lift'. After all, mass culture was governed by rules that structured its output and identified channels for the publicity stunts that it then turned into events: a mass audience to ensure profit, a selective use of the media, and orchestrated consumption.

Should one therefore conclude that mass culture was choosy about the media it used? To judge by the evidence from France in the 1960s and early 1970s, the answer is tautological but clear: individual media prospered in exact proportion to their ability to formulate and spread mass culture. For proof of this, one need look no further than the fate of the medium that until the mid-1950s had propelled to such heights popular culture's 'imaginary man', as Edgar Morin expressed it in 1956:[34] cinema. Its inexorable slide down the hierarchy of mass cultural practices is charted in French ticket sales: from 411 million in 1957, to 328 million in 1960, 259 million in 1965, 184 million in 1970, and just 170 million in 1975. Between 1958 and 1976, cinema had thus lost 58 per cent of its lifeblood. The number of cinemas also fell: from 5,700 in 1962 to 4,300 in 1970, with the gradual death of the 'local' cinema. In 1973, an investigation by the ministry of culture's research unit[35] showed that cinemas still provided the most popular 'evening out': in the previous year almost 52 per cent of French people had gone to the movies at least once, as compared to 24 per cent who had been to a football match, 12 per cent to the theatre, 11 per cent to a variety show (*music hall*) and 6.5 per cent to a jazz or pop concert. However, cinema audiences had become lopsided: 87 per cent of fifteen- to nineteen-year-olds went to the cinema, but this percentage decreased sharply with age. Cinema had also become intellectual, only really appealing now to those in senior management or the liberal professions, with the emergence of enthusiastic film buffs. Lastly, cinema-going was now concentrated in Paris and the major cities, at the expense of the towns and villages of rural France. This withering of cinema's social and geographical base was to prove irreversible. Cinema had lost not only its monopoly as a great modern art form with mass appeal, but also any hope of reversing the trend by recapturing a popular audience that had now deserted it in favour of television – which in 1973, after all, screened a total of 460 films.[36]

Yet the economic climate could hardly have been more favourable to the film industry. Film distributors and cinema owners had faced the crisis head-on and had even managed to boost box-office takings, raising their turnover between 1957 and 1976 by a factor of 3.2. This they had achieved by making more intensive use of each film, cutting showing times, and dropping short features, while raising ticket prices. It was a high-risk strategy that relied on rapid returns, and therefore fostered films that, by banking on the appeal of the director or star actors, were surefire instant hits. Ten-year records for ticket sales and takings were broken by a series of films which sold between 17 and 7 million tickets each – in descending order: *La Grande Vadrouille* by Gérard Oury, with Bourvil and Louis de Funès (1966), Sergio Leone's spaghetti western *Once upon a Time in the West* (1969), Darryl Zanuck's

The Longest Day (1962), *Le Corniaud* (1965), another huge hit for the Bourvil–de Funès duo, Walt Disney's *The 101 Dalmatians* (1961), *Doctor Zhivago* (1965), with Julie Christie and Omar Sharif, *The Great Escape* (1963), with Steve McQueen, *Le Gendarme de Saint-Tropez* (1964), a typical vehicle for 1960s French comedy, yet again starring Louis de Funès, and Claude Zidi's *Les Bidasses en folie* (1971) with Les Charlots starring in the first post-1968 farce. Of these nine films, four were French, though they bore no relation to the New Wave so celebrated among intellectuals, four were standard American productions, and one was a brilliant Italian parody. The eclecticism of this list shows that the French public remained attached to the popular artistic canons of traditional cinema, rooted in real-life adventure and violence, humour and storybook narrative. But it also demonstrates that distributors, in their eagerness to hold this audience, had aimed solely at people's wallets, concentrating on guaranteed successes and had, in the process, impoverished their industry by narrowing its range of genres, and in particular by neglecting *le cinéma d'auteur* (directors' films). Indeed, in 1963, 2 per cent of such films reaching the screens, well packaged and boasting major names, succeeded on the basis of only 14 per cent of annual ticket sales; in 1973, just 3.3 per cent of films accounted for 62 per cent of tickets sold.

Yet the restrictive logic of market forces could have been applied differently, by enabling cinema-goers to enjoy the full creative daring of French directors, cultivating – in the true sense of the word – the cinema-going audience, explaining, for example, that in *Le Mépris* (1963) Godard had killed off both the star and the film producer. Advantage might have been taken of Hollywood's relatively lean years to explore in greater depth the cinema of Eastern Europe, Latin America, Africa or India, or to sample the offerings of the 'underground'. Above all, more could have been made of what was, after all, a unique situation in the history of cinema – the overlapping in France of three generations of talented film-makers, ranging from Jean Renoir (*Le Caporal épinglé*, 1962) to such dazzling thirty-somethings as Chabrol, Truffaut, Godard, Demy, Rivette, Rohmer, Rozier, Eustache and Garrel, by way of masters of the 1940s like Tati (*Playtime*, 1967). Yet this was not to be. As long as the critics at *Cahiers du cinéma* and *Positif* and the ageing *ciné-clubs* pandered solely to that slice of the public that was wedded to the militant pleasure of frequent movie-going, and as long as the New Wave filmed its own era with acuteness and sensitivity[37] while chasing in vain after commercial success, Louis de Funès would resolutely wave the flag for an ailing industry that had failed to grasp the fact that mass culture, far from entailing banal standardization, thrived not only on conventional fantasies but equally well on versatility, daring eclecticism, playful distancing and even, after 1968, on the coopting of mass protest.[38]

Light entertainment for everyone: it was now television's job to purvey this to the French. In the space of a few years, TV had become the mass-cultural equivalent of 'running water and piped gas on every floor': the sovereign medium of the new age, the one that aimed straight for the bullseye, the broad 'popular' audience, i.e. a socially indistinct mass seeking happiness in the simple things of life. Here again, the figures are eloquent. Based on the numbers of people paying the very reasonable television licence fee, the proportion of households with television sets rose from 13 per cent in 1960 to 45 per cent in 1965, exceeded 70 per cent in 1970, and by 1974 had reached 80 per cent. The number of televisions in use leapt from seven to fourteen million between 1966 and 1974. When the market appeared to be nearing saturation point, the medium found a way of reviving its appeal by launching a new channel in January 1964, and then a third regional network in December 1972. Thanks to the French SECAM procedure, from 1968 onwards colour gradually pushed out the black-and-white sets of the pioneering age, thus launching a whole new generation of sets. *La télé* – the term had entered everyday speech in 1965 – wove itself into the social fabric, and into the leisure and cultural activities of the vast majority of French people.

The ministry of culture's 1973 survey revealed in fact that only 6.7 per cent of French people never or almost never watched television (down from 24 per cent in 1967). It also found that the average number of hours spent each week in front of a set – 15.7 hours on average, though other surveys put the number at 22 even as early as 1965 – increased with age (20 hours for the over-sixties) and fell with rising educational qualifications and social status (those without educational qualifications watched for 18 hours, whereas senior managers and members of the liberal professions watched just 8.7). The television set was already an immovable household presence: indeed, in 28 per cent of all homes – but in 40 per cent of blue-collar households – its blue-grey screen was now left flickering all day long, even when no one was watching it, or only absent-mindedly out of the corner of their eye while doing chores. In 1964 it was calculated that on average each individual saw 57 minutes of television a day, and by 1970 this had risen to 115 minutes. Its biggest audience was among the lower social classes, especially young people under twenty and pensioners, farmers, country-dwellers, blue-collar workers, white-collar workers, shop-keepers and junior managers. It was these groups who were the least choosy about the programmes they watched (the 4,000 hours of programming laid on

in 1964 had soared to 7,400 by 1974), sticking to their favourite channel
and demanding above all to be entertained.

According to the viewers questioned in the survey, every hundred
hours spent watching television comprised forty-six hours of 'relaxation'
(films, light entertainment, and animal and nature programmes were
particularly popular), twenty-eight hours of 'culture' and twenty-six
hours of 'boredom', which increasingly meant ballet, opera and classical
music. Viewers showed strong preferences: one out of five wanted
television to carry predominantly cultural programming, two out of five
favoured a balanced diet of culture and entertainment, while the
remaining two out of five craved straight undiluted entertainment.
Other surveys reported that 80 per cent of respondents favoured
'relaxing' television. This ambivalence is rather telling. Viewers were at
one and the same time disloyal and herd-like, proud of the individual
logic that drove their choices and yet more attached than they cared to
admit to the family appeal of long sessions in front of the box. Television's approval rating slipped from 90 per cent to 70 per cent between
1956 and 1974, with twenty- to twenty-four-year-olds increasingly
switching off and intellectuals sniffing in disapproval. Yet the fact is that
the state-run television of the 1950s, with its aim of dispensing culture
to the great viewing public, had now given way to the entertainment
industry of the 1960s – and most viewers welcomed the change.

Until 1964, under the directorship of first Jean d'Arcy and then
Albert Olivier, the public-service approach, jealously protecting its
monopoly, had provided an amalgam of news, entertainment and
education, in an atmosphere of good-natured virtue.[39] This golden age
had been shaped by the all-powerful first generation of often left-wing
producers of the 'Buttes-Chaumont school', who had opened television
up to the whole world while vying among themselves to deliver popular
educational programming in the style of the 1930s or 1940s. But 1964
ushered in a decade that for television, shaken by its own rapid growth,
brought great upheavals and conflict. A string of directors either threw
in the towel or were unceremoniously dismissed, while major alterations
were made to the corporation's statutes. In 1959, RTF became a
government-owned corporation (*établissement public*); in June 1964 the
renamed ORTF was granted state-owned-company status (*entreprise
nationale*); then, after a tumultuous bout of protests in May–June 1968,
the corporation was broken up into seven separate companies in July
1974:[40] all this against a background of repeated staff strikes and
simmering union discontent.

The authorities of state, through the minister for information, continued to monitor television news extremely closely and occasionally

stepped in to condemn or even suppress a programme they deemed subversive: for example, Stellio Lorenzi*'s La Caméra explore le temps*, in February 1965, and *Le Chagrin et la Pitié*, which was banned in 1971. The government adopted this line of action for two main reasons: firstly because, faced with a press that was generally hostile towards the founders of the Fifth Republic, it took the view that television was the only powerful means of information over which it could exercise supreme control with impunity; and secondly, because it increasingly sensed that the televised image was effecting far-reaching changes in the exercise of power and the functioning of democracy. The glimpse of General de Gaulle as a highly telegenic star during his televised press conferences, combined with the lessons of the 1965 presidential election when television may have played an important role in producing the second-round run-off between de Gaulle and Mitterrand, provided a timely warning.[41] Jean Ferran and Igor Barrère's *Face à Face* programme, which went on the air in January 1966, was an early version of the personalized political head-to-head sparring match. The 1968 upheavals did the rest, with fear foregrounding demonstrators who dreamed of bringing the walls of the new Jericho crashing down. In the aftermath, once repression had been meted out to the television mutineers, it fell to Pierre Desgraupes, appointed by Chaban-Delmas, to find a way of defusing tensions.[42] In September 1972, President Pompidou could still opine that 'television is regarded as the voice of France', though the newly appointed director general at ORTF, the booming Arthur Conte, was already looking for a way round the issue: his plan was to give the small screen over to an outpouring of 'the forces of joy'.

There were therefore some weighty political reasons for taking the view after 1968 that television's first duty was to 'entertain'. Yet those in charge of the medium allowed themselves to be talked round extremely easily, much to the displeasure of those who still yearned for popular culture, or who advocated a 'quality' television that catered for the eclectic tastes of viewers. By 1969, one-strand programming for all audiences had had its day. From 1970 onwards, 1,600 people were polled daily to determine programme popularity and ORTF managers kept a very close eye on ratings, eager to tap into the new phenomenon of advertising revenue: the first television advert – for Boursin cheese – was screened on 1 October 1968. Thus armed, the ORTF moved cautiously to ratify a clear separation between 'big audience' TV, screened prime-time, and 'intellectual' TV, carefully slotted into the schedule. They gambled on decentralization and encouraged competition between channels broadcasting similar programmes in the same time-slots, pitting a games show against other games shows, or an American soap against a French one. This mainstream/highbrow split produced highly inflexible programming, opened the door to foreign imports and increased the disaffection of a viewing public that was growing impatient. From 1971 ORTF increasingly surrendered to the laws of unchallenging consumerism.

Yet the path followed had at least possessed originality, the demands of mass culture had been well met, and the resulting picture album was impressive. Whereas TV news, fronted by American-style anchormen from 1971 onwards, appeared dozy and sometimes went in for self-censorship, current affairs programmes, from the trend-setting *Cinq Colonnes à la une* (1959–68), hosted by the 'three Pierres' (Desgraupes, Dumayet and Lazareff), through to the second channel's fast-moving *Zoom* (1966–8), demonstrated an outstanding feel for the mood and aspirations of the moment. This was equally true of Harris and Sédouy's *Seize Millions de jeunes* (1964), Eliane Victor's *Les Femmes aussi* (1964) and *Dim Dam Dom* (1965–71), launched by Daisy de Galard, which targeted a slightly more sophisticated audience while making good use of *caméra-vérité* techniques. Reporting resources naturally remained focused on big events, giving television the chance to display and contemplate its power, going first 'Europe-wide' and then global, to cover everything from major sporting events to such unique world news items as the American moon walkabout.

Such quintessentially French serials as *Le Temps des copains* (1961), *Janique aimée* (1963), *Thierry la Fronde* (1963–6), *Belphégor* and *Les Saintes Chéries* (1965), and *Jacquou le Croquant* (1969) were thus able to hold their own against American imports such as *The Untouchables* (1964). Other very popular programmes included *La Piste aux étoiles* (running since 1954), *La Caméra invisible* (1964), *Au théâtre ce soir* (1966), and *Le Grand Echiquier* (1972), as well as music hit-parades. Games shows spread fast, including *La Tête et les Jambes* (1957), *Des chiffres et des lettres* (1972), *Intervilles* (1962), *Le Mot le plus long* (1965) and finally the all-time ratings champion, *Le Schmilblic* (1970). Children too were wooed and won, starting with *Bonne nuit les petits* (1962), via *Manège enchanté* (1964) and *Titi le canari* (1973), to *L'Ile aux enfants* (1974). Yet the flag of unalloyed and sometimes even cutting intellect was never lowered, with major successes such as Jean Prat's adaptation of Aeschylus' *Les Perses* (1964), *Les Raisins verts* (1963) and Averty's *Ubu roi* (1965), cartoons such as *Shadoks* (1968), and Bernard Pivot's book programme *Ouvrez les guillemets* (1973). For many years Christmas Day and New Year's Day specials celebrated this durable marriage of entertainment and culture, despite pressure for a divorce after 1969.

The 1964 Christmas and New Year specials, produced by Claude Santelli, were of a brilliance never since equalled and soon looked back upon with nostalgia.

Such a feast of images made it self-evident that, when it came to promoting and disseminating mass culture, television reigned supreme. It also demonstrated that *la télé* had never simply copied imported models, or entailed the crass Americanization that so many intellectuals deplored. This is not to deny a degree of imitation and influence, notably in the art of news presentation, in the pairing of rival politicians, or in audience involvement. Yet television went no further than other media, adhering closely to the latest fashions seducing young people. Television was certainly instrumental in introducing jeans, t-shirts, rock music, weekly news magazines, theoretical modelling in social science, the 'peace and love' of anti-Vietnam War protestors and Californian communes, wall posters and shows, all of which helped to spread *franglais*[43] and were certainly taken up with alacrity by certain still rather small sections of the French population, but the effects of this exposure were less devastating than was feared.

Nor would it be hard to demonstrate that even such a vehicle of mass culture as the paperback book – from the 10/18 series launched by Plon in 1962 to the Folio collection introduced by Gallimard in 1972 – fuelled an eclecticism that owed more to the contemporary French appetite for all kinds of books, including social science and politics, than to any rush to clamber aboard an Anglo-Saxon publishing bandwagon. Similarly, French and European *bandes dessinées* (BD) or comic strips held their own very well against their North American counterparts. The Belgian pattern set by *Tintin* and *Spirou* was ageing very gracefully, thanks to the arrival of the 'Schtroumpfs' and the Gaston Lagaffe character. The socially progressive current initiated by *Vaillant* survived in *Pif Gadget* (1969), and in Rahan, its hero. *Pilote*, launched in 1959 and edited by Goscinny, boldly carried forward this torch until 1972, with a brand new panel of heroes: Astérix, Barbe rouge, Michel Tanguy, Achille Talon, Valérian, and finally Le Grand Duduche. The Astérix books, produced by Goscinny and Uderzo, were hugely successful, extolling the eternal Gaulois' courage and cunning in the face of every invader.[44] New BD authors gradually emerged, including Bretécher, Cabu and Gotlib, and after 1968 a breakthrough was achieved by fanzines and adult-oriented comics (*L'Echo des savanes*, 1972). Publishers of BD thrived and in 1973 the first yearly Angoulême BD Fair was organized to exhibit the finest gems of what was now a flourishing market. Moreover, the brilliance of BD draughtsmanship, its icy humour and violence was soon emulated in the written press. Whereas

Actuel (1970) lost its mass appeal and collapsed, due to its excessive adherence to patterns set by American rock music and underground 'comix', *Charlie-hebdo* – which succeeded from *Hari-Kiri*, banned in 1970 – prospered by adapting to contemporary fashionable insolence what was in fact a venerable anarchistic vein of distinctly French satirical triviality.

Lastly, the detective novel staged a rather remarkable comeback. After slipping from public favour in the early 1960s, at a time when readers had grown weary of the American heroes of the *Série noire* books, and the plots concocted by Boileau-Narcejac, Monteilhet or Exbrayat, the genre struck a rich home-grown French seam, fuelled by the disappointments of May 1968. A whole new generation of authors – including Manchette (*Nada*, 1972), Vautrin and ADG – emerged and launched the *néo-polar* ('neo-whodunnit'), replete with vitriolic social criticism. Léo Malet was eagerly rediscovered, San Antonio's glory reign prolonged and, above all, a new spy novel was developed to cater to a bloody and cynical world. The most notable product of this type was Gérard de Villiers 'SAS' series: launched in 1965, thirty titles had been published by 1974, selling a total of over 50 million copies.[45]

Similar trends could be observed at work in radio broadcasting. Neither public networks nor private radio stations, whether the ORTF, Europe 1 or RTL, hesitated to draw on French traditions of programming, with disc-jockeys like 'President' Rosko gaining recognition on the RTL *Minimax* programme and assailing the position of *Salut les copains* which Europe 1 had launched in 1959, even if Maurice Siégel had introduced a North American mix of music and news to RTL in 1965. Yet the home-grown radio editorializing and debates still flourished, along with agony aunt Ménie Grégoire's kind counsel from 1967 onwards, Madame Soleil's clairvoyant predictions from 1970, and, after 1971, discussions chaired by Anne Gaillard. Some programmes had a considerable track-record: Saint-Granier's wholesome *La Minute du bon sens* had first been broadcast in 1935 and survived until 1974; the soap *Hélène et son destin* lasted from 1965 to 1969 on Europe 1; Pierre Bonte's *Bonjour Monsieur le Maire*, also on Europe 1, ran from 1959 to 1974; while the evergreen *Le Masque et La Plume* had had its first airing on France Inter in 1954. These were all very popular examples of radio's loyalty to a style of programming that was indigenous in both its use of the medium and in the kind of subjects treated. Boasting greater flexibility than television and accessible to the entire population, thanks to the spread of the transistor, radio found a way to exploit one of the most fertile resources of mass culture: it set out to conquer the imagination of listeners of all ages by sticking closely to reality, while filling in the gaps apparent in day-to-day life by offering an uninterrupted cocktail of short news items, up-to-the-minute advice and entertainment of all kinds.

Print journalism also demonstrated the importance of achieving a mix. It certainly had to face strong competition from radio and television: between 1960 and 1974, the number of daily papers fell from 111 to 86 (those covering Paris fell from fourteen to nine) and their combined circulation dropped from 12,500,000 to 11,300,000 copies – after a brief upsurge in 1968, when the 'events' sold a lot of papers. Moreover, the press was ill prepared for increased competition and slow to grasp the challenge of the coming revolution in electronic typesetting: it remained subject to the Malthusianism of the all-powerful and persistently strike-prone Fédération CGT du Livre, which controlled manning, and – in terms of distribution – was at the mercy of NMPP, who creamed off 60 per cent of sales proceeds. The concentration of its assets and their carve-up between a handful of groups – Hachette, Prouvost, Amaury, Del Duca and Hersant, together still monopolizing barely 40 per cent of circulation – was not on a scale comparable to other European countries.[46] And the press retained several strong points. Its journalists (8,000 in 1960, 13,000 in 1974) were better trained than before (in 1971, half of them had been through higher education, as compared to 38 per cent in 1964, and, again in 1974, 18 per cent had been to a college for journalism, as against just 6 per cent in 1964). Overall, journalists were now better educated and well aware of social issues.[47] And their audience scarcely faltered, especially outside Paris, and even among young people. Print journalism remained the main vehicle for advertising: including 'free sheets',[48] the press accounted for 43 per cent of total advertising spend in 1959, 45 per cent in 1969 and 42.8 per cent in 1973.[49] Above all, as the ministry for culture's enquiry showed in 1973, French people still saw a clear educational and cultural dividing-line between reading a newspaper, listening to the radio and being entertained by TV, because television was just poised to impose its own formidable competitive synergy.

By 1974 the effects of standardization on daily papers were evident: there were just five titles with a circulation of over 500,000, and seven others with over 300,000. Paris still boasted the four most important papers: two 'popular' or down-market titles, *Le Parisien libéré* which had expanded to cover the entire Paris conurbation (980,000) and *France-Soir* which was in free fall (720,000); and two quality papers, a right-of-centre one, *Le Figaro* (490,000), which had been in continual crisis ever since the death of Pierre Brisson in 1964, when a company formed by the paper's staff was attempting to act as a counterweight to the financial

power of Jean Prouvost, and, both more neutral and further to the left –
indeed, not immune to post-'68 editorial wobbles – *Le Monde*
(540,000), now run by Jacques Fauvet, who in 1970 had stepped into
the shoes of Hubert Beuve-Méry, the paper's founder.[50] But the strongest resistance was mounted by a band of wealthy provincial dailies,
increasingly in a position of near-monopoly in their respective areas.
Indeed, with its circulation of 700,000, *Ouest-France* was now one of the
main players, followed by the larger titles of the various city-baronies: *Le
Progrès de Lyon* (490,000), the Bordeaux-based *Sud-Ouest* (420,000),
Lille's *La Voix du Nord* (420,000), *Le Dauphiné libéré* in Grenoble
(410,000), *Le Provençal* in Marseille (340,000) and *La Dépêche du Midi*,
based in Toulouse (310,000). And *L'Equipe* proved a remarkable
survivor: the only daily paper solely devoted to sport – the single most
popular leisure activity – and read with passionate interest right across
the entire country.

However, it was the periodical press that mirrored developments in
society the most closely. In particular, TV-listings weeklies grew with a
vigour proportionate to that of television itself: by 1974, *Télé 7 Jours*,
launched in 1960 by Hachette and Prouvost, had a circulation of
2,800,000, while *Télé-Poche*, Del Luca's 'me too' response the same
year, sold over 1,550,000. Competition in this promising market,
however, was stiff and *Télé-Succès*, *Télé-Magazine* and *Télé-Gadget* all
collapsed or went out of business, whereas the rickety *Télérama*,
launched in 1972 by the Bayard group, clung to the moral austerity of
its Christian origins. All leisure activities and personal issues were
catered for, from *L'Automobile* and *L'Auto-Journal*, which both sold over
500,000 copies, to *Dimanche-Turf* and *Week-End*, including Alain Aya-
che's *Le Meilleur*, founded in 1971, and devoted to *tiercé* gambling. *Salut
les copains* and *Mademoiselle Age tendre* were both targeted at the early
and mid-teen years, while Daniel Filipacchi's *Lui*, from its launch in
1963, had a monopoly in upmarket (*embourgeoisé*) and expensively
packaged sex, challenging *Playboy*. Meanwhile, from 1969 onwards,
Parents aimed to reassure modern young couples, *Modes et Travaux*
(1,800,000) dispensed tips for sensible housewives, while the *Sélection
du Reader's Digest* (1,400,000) catered to the unquenchable thirst for the
encyclopaedia format, as did André Labarthe's deeply French riposte,
Constellation. The financial titles were now well established, sticking
closely to trends in economic growth, and benefiting from the notion
that economic information was one of the keys to success: *Vie française*
held its own, while *Valeurs actuelles* was relaunched in 1971, and
L'Expansion achieved a circulation of 140,000 following its successful
launch in 1967 by Jean Boissonnat and Jean-Jacques Servan-Schreiber.

By way of contrast, *Paris-Match*, a victim of television, saw its circulation plummet to 800,000 (from 1,800,000 in 1958), and romance and women's magazines stagnated, with *Nous Deux*, *Confidences*, *Marie-Claire* and *Bonne Soirée* all appearing decidedly dog-eared. *Elle* alone continued to prosper, tackling an ever wider range of issues, though without feminizing them *a priori* – even though in 1970 it had famously organized a women's 'states general'.

But it was the success of the general news weeklies, based as they were on a pattern imported from the United States, that provides the best measure of contemporary cultural originality. As the pioneer, ever since its 1964 relaunch, of a French-style news magazine, *L'Express* had adopted an A4 format, systematic sub-editing, in-depth investigations interlarded with factual surveys and eye-catching news stories, and forceful advertising throughout. The success of this formula, especially among managers with considerable purchasing power, was immediately proportionate to its attentive yet light-hearted tracking of contemporary trends. In 1974, under Françoise Giroud, its circulation reached 720,000, though the magazine had struggled since 1968 to follow the political course set by Giroud's co-founder, Servan-Schreiber. After political differences between its editorial staff erupted into crisis, the magazine swerved from left to centre, and ended up calling on its readers to back Giscard d'Estaing's bid for the presidency in 1974.[51] With its smaller circulation (310,000), its left-wing rival, *Le Nouvel Observateur*, had recast itself, also in 1964, after a team from *L'Express* had abandoned the *France-Observateur* title. In 1972, under the influence of Claude Perdriel, who put up the capital, and Jean Daniel, who assembled a brilliant editorial team, the magazine finally adopted the news weekly format. Very alive to movements within society, and politically committed – though with a critical edge that often caused internal strains – the *Nouvel Obs* supported François Mitterrand, and provided a sounding-board for all the twists and turns of the latest thinking. It published all the big names, imposing itself as essential reading for intellectuals, students and 'dynamic' manager types.[52] *Le Point*, founded in September 1972 by Olivier Chevrillon, Claude Imbert and Georges Suffert – defectors from *L'Express* and *Paris-Match* – also enjoyed a following wind: at once more austere, more civilized and more irreverent, *Le Point* had a circulation of 210,000. On the extreme right, *Minute* (200,000), far removed from any American spirit, traded in polemical argument and leaks in order to provide the fiercely 'national' wing of French politics – kept well out of sight during the de Gaulle era – with a modern mouthpiece, for which *Rivarol* was no longer a rival. The continuing variety of the 'weeklies', their caustic audacity, their nose for a story, and their impact on French people's day-to-day lives, bore witness yet again to the eclecticism of mass culture in France.[53]

One final and somewhat paradoxical example of this singular French characteristic is provided by an examination of an area to which the Anglo-Saxon invasion threatened to lay utter waste: music aimed at young people. As we have seen, by the end of the 1950s, the optimistic rock-and-roll of the American great open spaces had well and truly landed in France. From 1963, it had assumed a fresh new form, with the emergence of 'pop' music, highly chaotic and heavily influenced by the British 'underground'. It then went on to embrace all the misgivings and meanderings that closed that decade, and around 1971 found itself torn between the extremes represented by Pink Floyd and Jimi Hendrix. In about 1965, pop music had broadened out with the 'folk rock' revolution of Bob Dylan, Joan Baez and the Byrds, only to then drown itself in the hippy psychedelia of the Doors. Drawing successively on 'country music' and ghetto 'soul', it celebrated its high masses at Newport and Woodstock. The Beatles and the Rolling Stones remained pre-eminent throughout the development of 'rock', which, by 1974, enabled the record industry to achieve a turnover one third higher than that of the film industry. A section of French youth keenly followed each latest trend in the world-wide phenomenon that was 'Beatlemania', while the French media gave it full rein.[54] Yet France put up stiff resistance, by cultivating with all the more brio its own native tradition: the serious high-quality French singer-songwriting produced by such artists as Jacques Brel, Georges Brassens, Barbara, Léo Ferré, Serge Gainsbourg and Charles Trenet. Yet the French also produced a lively hybrid of their own, by marrying the raucous Anglo-Saxon sound with syrupy French sentimental lyrics and the gyrations of the 'twist': the result was *yé-yé* music, hugely successful throughout the 1960s but failing to outlive the decade.[55]

The quality of its output was not consistent. Even Johnny Hallyday sometimes turned in a poor performance, while the cover versions produced by Eddy Mitchell and his Chaussettes noires or by Dick Rivers' Chats sauvages were decidedly strained, and the talents of Richard Anthony and Antoine petered out in *la country*. But, to the resounding applause of an audience thoroughly 'broken in' by television, the decade steadily worked its way through a stream of mediocre new hits doggedly concocted by such varied, endearing and anodyne stars as Sheila, Claude François, Salvatore Adamo, Hugues Aufray, Michel Polnareff, Marie Laforêt, Sylvie Vartan and Hervé Vilard. The monotonous drone of such hypermarket, night-club and TV-variety pap provided a good illustration of the twin-track way that France was entering the new age. While easy-to-digest, one-dimensional songs helped to popularize a mass culture that was top–down, brutal, juvenile and stateless, the same channels were used to preserve and, little by little, to promote a highly diluted national sensibility that the French of whatever age were quite ready to buy.

What thus emerged was a culture of a new type, with an impact and market that was regulated by the media, adolescent in terms of its target audience, yet constantly selective in its outpourings, cosmopolitan and global in its outlook though much more aware of the national context than was at first apparent. It promised a 'happy end' to a history to which economic growth and consumption – likewise mass phenomena – had provided such weighty arguments. But it did not keep all its promises. In 1968, as Edgar Morin would later say, 'cultural rifts' had opened up, strains and conflicts had returned with a vengeance: the mythology of happiness had turned to world-weariness. Around 1974, there were signs that this chameleon culture was winded, that its complicated mosaic was working loose, with a mix of increased prosperity and still bottled-up desires. The French 'sixties' were dead or dying. All that was left was a burgeoning nostalgia.

Fragmented beliefs and values

Such sweeping social and economic change could not fail to have a direct impact on 'the bread of dreams' – that blend of religious faith and secular beliefs that underlies the intelligence, actions and sensibility of the French. A battery of polls, very helpfully reviewed by Jacques Sutter, affords a glimpse of the main trends.[56]

It is no surprise to see that as May 1968 loomed, the values whose scores were rising in one way or another all acknowledged a degree of technological progress and improved social well-being. Roughly three out of every four people questioned spontaneously expressed the opinion that things were getting better in the realms of knowledge (86 per cent), intelligence (71 per cent) and health (74 per cent). On the other hand, the proportion of satisfied respondents was much smaller when the more traditional values were broached: happiness (35 per cent), morality (24 per cent), religion (19 per cent), honesty (12 per cent) and peace of mind (10 per cent). That these values were being constantly undermined by the very way that modern life was now evolving as well as by the 1968 shockwave was confirmed in December 1971 by a survey designed to discover what people felt was the most important factor in a successful life. Two very positive aspirations stood out: 'a happy family life' (26 per cent) and 'sound health' (25 per cent),

and these far outdistanced 'looking on the bright side' (11 per cent),
'setting oneself an ideal' (8 per cent), 'belief in God' (7 per cent),
'having enough money' (5 per cent), 'knowing how to face ordeals' (5
per cent) and 'feeling one is useful to lots of people' (3 per cent).
Withdrawal into the family unit and into creature comforts thus
appeared to be the most widespread response to the sobering realization
that the moral and spiritual legacy was fractured if not indeed obsolete,
overthrown by the shock of the new.

The established religions were obsessed with the need to respond to
and meet the anxious aspirations of modern-day people: their dramatic
predicament lay in their relative powerlessness to deliver the desired
message. Given that France was still an overwhelmingly Catholic
country – at least nominally – these strains were sharpest within the
Church of Rome, which reacted by emphasizing its ongoing *aggiornamento*. Yet it was unable to update and adapt its teachings as quickly as it
would have liked to the massive and socially diverse challenges that now
confronted it. Meanwhile, the sociology of religion, a discipline born of
a growing awareness of the crisis facing the church's 'mission' in a
country undergoing steady dechristianization, presented it with a detailed and discouraging picture of decline, stretching back to the 1940s.

In 1968, for example, polls and investigations – which had replaced
censuses – showed that roughly 85 per cent of French people stated that
they were Catholic and 90 per cent had been baptized. Yet among those
baptized, there was now a clear distinction between 'regular church-
goers' who attended mass every Sunday (23 per cent, though by 1972
this had fallen to 17 per cent); 'festive seasonals' who just went to
church for the grand liturgical occasions (39 per cent); 'seasonal
conformists' who merely observed the grand rites of passage: christen-
ings, weddings and funerals (10 per cent); and, finally, the 'detached',
who no longer attended any church services at all (18 per cent). Three
out of every four people baptized now made a 'profession of faith',
which had replaced the 'solemn' or first communion, got married in
church (77 per cent in 1968, but 73 per cent in 1971) and had a church
burial, whereas barely one in three attended Easter mass, only one in ten
received communion regularly, and just seven out of every hundred
went to confession. In 1972, a SOFRES poll differentiated between: the
'integrated' who had a real feeling of belonging to the church (24 per
cent); 'waverers', disconcerted by the way it was evolving (12 per cent),
'peripheral outsiders', for whom the church was no more than a familiar
and useful part of their cultural and social background (38 per cent),
and, lastly, the 'indifferent', who were oblivious to its message (21 per
cent). Other investigations concluded that at roughly the same date the

'practising fraternity' of 'God's people' comprised 30.7 per cent of the baptized rural population, as against 19.2 per cent of baptized town dwellers, and 5.2 per cent of blue-collar workers as compared to 18.9 per cent of white-collar workers and 31.3 per cent of 'liberal professionals'. Clearly, these sharp social divides, while they bolstered the church's well-established notion that different *milieux* called for different pastoral approaches, also suggested that it was increasingly difficult for the gospel message to get through at all to a society in the throes of change. Accordingly, in the absence of any theology sturdy enough to steer it through these seas, the church was forced to search for signposts in the world around it, and to decipher the modern age, while standing back and attempting to recast an unchanging truth that otherwise ran the risk of no longer being heard at all.

The desire to drag the church into the present-day world had informed the work of the Second Vatican Council, convened in Rome from October 1962 until December 1965, to which bishops and theologians from France made a coherent, influential and very important contribution.[57] Well covered by the media, the event was regarded as bold and decisive by French Catholicism which, though bruised, never forgot the pioneering role it had played since the start of the century. The decision taken by the church, on the initiative of Pope John XXIII, to open itself up to the world by making a clear break with its ancient triumphalism was thus welcomed by both clergy and believers as a 'divine surprise'. In fact, the 'conciliar dynamic' left the doctrinal edifice untouched, though it did promise to provide a pledge of renewal and a point of departure. At a stroke, the autonomy of secular culture and progress was in effect proclaimed, the modern world was cleansed of the many sins stigmatized throughout the nineteenth century, and opinion and communication were accorded legitimacy. This acknowledgement that earthly realities had their own certain autonomy was expected to close the Constantinian era, and to provide the gospel with fresh opportunities within the framework of a newly outward-looking Christianity. This acquiescence to the world, confirmed in the two encyclicals, *Mater et Magistra* (1961) and *Populorum progressio* (1967), called for a concerted development of humanity in its entirety, thereby providing a justification for Third-World theologies of liberation, and urging Christians everywhere to get involved in the thick of things.

Such optimism was soon disappointed, since the implementation of the Council's decisions prompted more discouraged questioning than renewed enthusiasm.[58] The aspiration to seize the essence of the Christian mystery actually led to a dangerous purification of religious practices, and to an adherence to the over-austere opinions and tastes of the most militant clergy and lay members, who were frequently recruited from among the technically trained middle classes. The most spectacular item in the reform package, the celebration of the mass in French with the officiating priest facing the worshippers, would have found broader acceptance if only the customary forms and ornaments of worship had been preserved. The churches might have been rather less deserted if those devotions and superstitions now deemed excessively 'popular' or naive had not been rooted up with contempt. For what was suddenly installed, across the board, was a greyer form of worship, devoid of either pomp or mystery, emphasizing words over gestures and symbols, stripped of its gold and its baubles, abandoning the Virgin, the saints, the angels and even Satan, in the name of the uniqueness of the Son made Man. This was a destructive iconoclasm that had the effect of denuding church naves, ensuring that from 1962 onwards most priests no longer wore cassocks, scrapping the notion of salvation and watering down vespers. While over-intellectual homilies were now very much 'in', much-loved triumphalist hymns, the murmuring of the rosary, and the Friday abstinence from meat were definitely 'out'. The sacraments were now delivered in a manner both dry and mean, while family occasions, like the ancient rite of passage of one's first communion, had been stripped of all significance.[59] Frequently interpreted as an abandonment of the trappings of identity,[60] this ill-assorted accumulation of innovations nonplussed many of those it surprised, shocked 'seasonal' worshippers who could no longer recognize their own religion, and above all disconcerted and repelled believers from modest backgrounds. Meanwhile, a militant elite continued to agitate in all good conscience, pushing sometimes to an extreme the conciliar logic, and invoking the 'renewal' of the church, while grass roots Christianity turned inwards and withered. A number of small minorities reacted quickly, but in ways that conflicted. Coalescing around Monsignor Lefebvre, a counter-revolutionary 'integrism' sprang up and denounced the 'excesses' of the Council, claiming to speak for the 'silent majority', and laying the foundations for a counter-offensive by opening a traditionalist seminary at Ecône in Switzerland in 1971. Meanwhile, at Taizé, a band of younger Christians stocked up on festive ecumenism. Also, the first charismatics, who had been noticeable at parish level since 1973, made a return to the sources of their faith that by-passed the hasty and disconcerting teachings of the Second Council.

The shock delivered by May 1968 threw this already fragmented picture into utter disarray. Thousands of Catholics of all ages had taken part in the 'movement', discovering in it a confirmation of their post-conciliar commitments, and a renewed quest for meaning, as well as a leavening of radical protest against the ecclesiastic establishment. A virulent libertarian anticlericalism was displayed, which condemned the church of the 'mighty', and intoned the old theme of 'Neither God, nor Master'; 'grass-roots groups' blossomed, aiming in all innocence to introduce revolution into the parishes and movements; various unauthorized communions took part in the occupation and highjacking of a number of places of worship; numerous priests, having heard the whisperings of the Spirit, called for the church's 'declergification'; and, meanwhile, Maurice Clavel welcomed a prophetic May which, in his view, heralded a new Pentecost.[61] From this soil, a challenge took root that claimed to spearhead the 'reinvention' of the church.

The number of believers belonging to 'critical' or 'questing' groups and communities appears never to have exceeded 25,000. Yet they could boast a lively press, ranging from *Témoignage chrétien*, which in 1971 still had a circulation of 50,000, to *Lettre*.[62] They held assemblies (in Rennes in 1972, in Dijon in 1974), gathered at 'retreats' where they engaged in group dynamics (the Dominican centre at l'Arbresle or the Benedictine monastery of Boquen), devoured the social sciences, read Freud by way of Lacan and Marx by way of Althusser, bewailed the 'ideological apparatus' of the church, flirted with the theologies of the death of God and of liberation borrowed from Anglican or Protestant circles or imported from Latin America, before sinking back into their internal wrangling and admitting their impotence. Yet at Lourdes in 1972 they did manage to push the bishops into drawing up a critical statement on *Politique, Eglise et Foi*, which railed at the power of money and condemned arms sales and the French nuclear *force de frappe*; in addition, in the summer of 1973, Monsignor Marty, Archbishop of Paris, refused to take up the place reserved for him on the official platform for the traditional 14 July march-past, while Monsignor Riobé, Bishop of Orleans, issued a condemnation of French atomic testing at Mururoa, leading to a temporary chill in relations between church and state. Above all, some became actively engaged in politics, even pronouncing themselves in favour of a form of socialism – as did a number of dwindling groups, like 'La Vie nouvelle',[63] and movements in trouble with the church hierarchy, for example, the ACO (Action catholique ouvrière) and the JEC (Jeunesse étudiante chrétienne). These were the same people who clung to the PSU, manned the 'Rocardien' tendency that emerged in the PS at the end of 1974, and campaigned within the CFDT for a degree of workers' control (*autogestion*).[64]

Taken all together, these varied forms of militancy bewildered the silent majority of believers, yet appealed to only a small wider audience. As early as 1966, Jacques Maritain denounced what he referred to as 'genuflexions before the world',[65] and in 1971, a poll revealed that 59 per cent of French people took the view that by trying too hard to adapt to the modern world 'the church [was] no longer the church'. Indeed, the activities of the militants reinforced many of the trends towards splintering that increasingly threatened a Catholicism whose 'crisis' and straitened circumstances were now clearly visible. The secular clergy, utterly ignored by the Second Vatican Council, was everywhere threatened with extinction. Whereas in 1960 there had been 41,700 diocesan priests, and 40,900 in 1965, by 1975 the number had fallen to 36,000. In 1963, 573 new diocesan clergymen were invested, as compared with just 190 in 1974; meanwhile there was a speeding-up in the rate at which, amid various degrees of scandal, they were deserting the church – generally to get married (485 left between 1956 and 1969, and 972 between 1970 and 1974). This headlong collapse in vocation was combined with demoralization and a material and emotional state that often bordered on poverty, undermining pastoral work in many parishes: the basic framework of a Christian life was often perceived as being a truly empty shell, despite attempts to improve 'collegiality' and teamwork, in particular in urban areas.[66] Moreover, the recruitment and hence the renewal of the elite of the lay clergy declined once the awareness had dawned that it no longer made any sense to focus specialized action on specific milieux. Whereas the handful of town-based JOC worker activists managed to hang on all right,[67] the rural and the self-employed milieux, from which the church for half a century had drawn so much of its strength, were now too heterogeneous for proselytizing to gain a foothold. In addition, confronted with the realities of family planning, abortion and the emergence of a women's 'cause', women in the church found themselves split.

In 1974, with enthusiasm for the Second Vatican Council on the wane, it could be fairly said that Christianity was 'splintered',[68] all the more so since Rome now sought to reassert its authority, against the grain. In 1969, Pope Paul VI proclaimed his opposition to the construction of any 'anthropocentric religion' that sought incautiously to give sociology primacy over theology, and he rejected any type of 'corrosive criticism'. Most important, his encyclical *Humanae vitae*, published in July 1968, which roundly condemned birth control, and stubbornly refused to take into consideration changing public mores, raised a storm of dissent and alienated a great many Christian couples who saw the encyclical as a denial of the church's desire to move with the times (*aggiornamento*). This rebuff, on such a sensitive issue, severely undermined the efforts of ten years, while the attempt at renewal was decidedly feeble. A situation of crisis descended, strongly internalized by the majority of Catholics and tirelessly detailed by the media.[69]

France's religious minorities showed no such signs of difficulty. As yet, the Islam of immigrants from the Maghreb or from black Africa, unassuming and quietly integrated, posed no great issue.[70] The Jewish communities, swollen by the arrival from North Africa of 140,000 Sephardis of all social backgrounds between 1954 and 1962, experienced this influx as an intensely important development, though the Ashkenazis, with their deeper roots, retained for the time being their dominant influence.[71] Yet this demographic upheaval launched a process of renewal that was very apparent among young people, many of whom, after being very active in 1968, had turned to spirituality. Religious teaching in the yeshivots was shaken up and Talmudic studies were enlivened, while various inner city districts and suburbs gained a tinge of Mediterranean exoticism (Sarcelles and Créteil, for example). The main concerns that arose were political or emotional in character, rooted in the memory of the genocide of the Second World War. Another source of worry was provided by the pro-Arab policy that France adopted in 1967, in its firm desire to break with what Maurice Schumann in May 1970 termed the 'Zionist temptation'. Indeed, French Judaism, for the first time in its proudly republican history, organized in 1967 a series of demonstrations in support of Israel. Signs of a resurgence of antisemitism (for example, the 'rumours' of Orléans and Rheims in 1969[72]) were vehemently condemned. Yet despite the enactment on 30 July 1972 of a law that redefined antisemitism as a racist crime and as such severely punishable under the law, it did not disappear.

There remained very broad diversity among Protestants, with the failure in 1968 of renewed attempts to unite the Reformed and the Lutheran churches.[73] And a wide rift had opened up between the 'progressives', in the majority in the early 1970s, and the 'evangelicals', with their strongly 'integrist' or fundamentalist views, who, like their Catholic brothers, longed to 'reach out to the world' and to make a mark on it. On the one side, Pastor Casalis also fell to prophesying in May 1968, thereby running the risk of annoying a lot of different communities. Then, in October 1971, the Fédération protestante drew up a document on *Eglises et Pouvoirs*, signally failing to steer a middle course between reform and revolution,[74] and fuelling further rows with its excesses. Indeed, the theologies of revolution were viewed favourably by such militant teams as La Cimade or the Mission populaire, whereas the influence of Karl Barth declined and specialized movements suffered a recruitment crisis. On the other side, 'joyous' apostacy was denounced for threatening the faith, and hope was placed in a new Awakening.[75] Meanwhile, in all reformed circles, ecumenical initiatives were welcomed and such issues as family planning – the Fédération was in favour of pregnancy terminations 'in extreme cases', and in 1974 came out in support of the Veil law – and development, which it examined with a much greater wealth of proposals and initiatives than was mustered by the Catholics. Yet such bold positions had only marginal effect on a country in which only 4.5 per cent of the population was estimated to be of the Protestant faith.

Overall, while the beliefs of the French people were thus bruised and torn, established religions had failed to retain sufficient strength or coherence to propound any responses to people's concerns or to set forth a new, clearcut and focused hierarchy of values.

The emergence of a public culture

The splintering of the arts, culture and beliefs had been met with a public determination to implement the first fully fledged cultural policy that France had ever seen. In July 1959, when André Malraux, minister of state and friend to General de Gaulle, was placed in charge of creating a ministry for cultural affairs, his task was the modest one of 'making the greatest works of humanity, and primarily of France, accessible to the greatest possible number of French people', and 'to secure the widest possible audience for our cultural heritage, and to promote the creation of such works of art and the spirit as may enrich it'.

Under the new republic, the state wished not only to fulfil its traditional mission of providing patronage to artists and of protecting the nation's heritage, but also to promote the nation's 'cultural development' and to ensure that the right of all French people to a more equal share in culture that was enshrined in the constitution was more effectively guaranteed. As early as 1959, Malraux was boasting of the attempt to 'realize France's dream: to restore to life its past genius, to bring to life its present genius, and to welcome the genius of the world'.[76] Under Pompidou, who took a great personal interest in cultural issues, even to the point of creating a presidential *domaine réservé* on certain matters of town planning and architecture,[77] the centrist Jacques Duhamel, an outstanding minister for cultural affairs and an active supporter of the 'New Society' ideal at the heart of the Chaban-Delmas government, placed his brief within a social context: 'Culture', he said in 1972, 'is an adventure that is proposed to people, it is a communication that is offered for the purpose of a desired communion'. He went on to say that the duty of the state was to offer to each person whatever was needed 'for a day of work to become a true day of life', to combat the indifference of consumer society, the social intolerance and the ideological interventionism that destroys all national communion. In the Pompidou years, culture 'must be the principal response to the disarray of modern man'.[78]

The means fully to implement such a policy were not of course forthcoming. Public intervention remained very patchy: for example, the ministry for foreign affairs retained control over the international dissemination of French culture, and the ministry for national education had no intention whatever of being dispossessed of its ancient prerogatives. Moreover, the frail young minister for culture never had the chance to intervene at the right moment or to make any lasting impact on 'popular education', youth and sports policies, issues surrounding information and communication, town planning, development or the environment. For their part, the treasury accountants were consistently mean and scornful: until 1974, the annual budget earmarked for cultural affairs languished at about 0.4 per cent of total state expenditure; indeed, its accelerated expansion was not even approved in principle until 1972. If to this one adds the fact that the ministry was staffed haphazardly and for a long time assiduously avoided by *énarques* (high-flying civil servants, graduates from the Ecole national d'administration), and that it was not until the appointment of Jacques Duhamel that local and regional authorities were invited to become involved in what was after all a collective enterprise, then one is tempted to conclude that mediocrity persistently dogged the implementation of this quest for democratization.[79] If, indeed, nothing came of it, this is doubtless because, having failed to gain any control over the movement of a society which was so spectacularly installing individually consumed 'popular' culture and leisure, the authorities did discover a way of intervening at the right level to satisfy some of the demands now being made by the French people and, most crucially, to meet the need for cultural amenities and to cater to the appetite for heritage. This was achieved through intervention that did not violate any freedoms and that modernized and rejuvenated culture along the lines followed in other economic and social fields that had received a shake-up since the 1950s.

Initially, the logic of providing amenities was powerful. From 1961, a commission overseeing 'cultural amenities and artistic heritage' was attached to the Plan, chaired after 1969 by the poet Pierre Emmanuel, a member of the French Academy. His very free-ranging and sometimes iconoclastic reflections found their way into the policies pursued from 1962 to 1975.[80] The Fourth, Fifth and Sixth 'social and economic development' Plans thus comprised a short but to-the-point chapter on culture. The planning experts believed that, in order to frame the collective aspiration for prosperity, all they needed to do was apply to the field of arts and culture the modernization methods that had proved so effective in achieving economic expansion, with the creation, therefore, of the appropriate sites and democratic machinery within which cultural policy might be, as it were, distilled. This conception had meshed with Malraux's thinking, and their cooperation led most notably to the opening of nine of the twenty planned *maisons de la culture* (arts centres, often comprising a library, cinema, performance spaces, etc.) – 'twentieth century cathedrals' as the minister had called them, which could be built and staffed in each department 'for the price of twenty-five kilometres of motorway'. Among others towns and cities to gain a *maison de la culture* were Le Havre (1961), Bourges (1963), Amiens (1966) and Grenoble (1968). The regional and municipal councils, especially in the Rhône-Alpes region, were quick to note the contribution that the new amenities – or 'integrated amenities' as they were called after 1968 – could make to the life of the urban areas that the councils, having hastily helped to construct them, now wished to develop and improve. From that point onwards, there were two competing policies, neither of which ever succeeded in completely defeating the other. One approach was to install the new amenities, especially the former *maisons des jeunes et de la culture* ('youth and arts centres'), at the heart of a community environment held together by grass-roots associations and development workers, in an attempt to orchestrate the 'popular' education, leisure pursuits and cultural practices of a population.[81] The other approach was to regard the amenities as the engine for public 'cultural action' rooted in the provision of access for all to masterpieces and to creativity, while turning one's back on any aspirations regarding education or leisure, and run from Paris as part of a regional development scheme rather than in response to local needs.

Malraux's period in office has to its credit a number of spectacular measures, such as the first ever cleaning of Paris building façades, the controversial temporary transfer of the Mona Lisa to New York and of the Venus de Milo to Tokyo, the restoration by Chagall of the ceiling of the Paris Opera House, as well as many extremely well-attended exhibitions. Above all, in 1964 he launched the painstaking job of compiling a general inventory of all the artistic monuments and riches of France under the direction of André Chastel.[82] He also drove forward the decentralization of French theatre, provided support for the film industry, music and painting, and identified urban conservation areas. Although Malraux was not always able to inject as much dynamism as he would have liked into the personnel or working structures of the old established Beaux-Arts, he lacked neither boldness nor grandiose ideals and these, through his strength as an orator, he succeeded in popularizing, in particular at the state funerals of Braque in 1963, Jean Moulin in 1964 and Le Corbusier in 1965, as well as at commemorations such as those for Joan of Arc in 1964. He declared that public culture for everyone signified both 'Notre Dame de France with its church tower buzzing with supernatural birds' and 'all the mysterious answers that a man may find when he looks in the mirror at what his face will be in death'.[83]

However, beneath the flights of lyricism, a weakness in Malraux's record of office soon became apparent. In 1971, the report on the Sixth Plan noted the persistent inadequacy of the resources placed at the disposal of the ministry, and other enquiries revealed that innovative and creative work continued to be underfunded. Cultural activities were worst affected, and it was concluded that arts programming was scarcely reaching the 'non-audience' – those who still never set foot in libraries or went to shows – whereas heritage conservation and old-fashioned 'fine arts' management had gobbled up the budget. In other words, the redistribution of cultural wealth had been sluggish and the process of democratization had stalled. This alarming realization was then capped with all the anti-establishment fervour of May 1968. In January the *Cinémathèque* was thrown into crisis following the dismissal of its founder, Henri Langlois: under pressure from a large section of the country's intelligentsia, who were disgusted by such authoritarian action, Langlois was reinstated. This really set the ball rolling. The Théâtre de l'Odéon was occupied, with scant resistance from Jean-Louis Barrault, its director. A '25 May Charter' was drawn up and signed by angry theatre people whom Roger Planchon rallied to denounce the 'bourgeois' culture that they had been involved in staging. And, to the despair of Jean Vilar, the Avignon summer festival erupted in violent clashes. These events, heavy with symbolism, constituted a repudiation of the ideals, personalities and institutions of the Malraux age. When, along with General de Gaulle, Malraux left office in 1969, the challenge for his successors was to go beyond the vituperation of 1968, to renounce overblown lyricism and, as Pierre Emmanuel put it, 'to reunite Man' through a search for a humanism fit for the 'New Society'.

It was Jacques Duhamel, minister for cultural affairs from 1971 to 1973, following Edmond Michelet in the post and preceding Maurice Druon, who found the best way to respond to this situation. To the 'cultural action' of the previous years, denounced by the protestors of

May '68 for the statism that they felt had perpetuated a fatal wavering between integration and subversion,[84] Duhamel preferred the less attention-grabbing and more reassuring notion of 'cultural development'. Convinced that the arts were an area in which nothing could any longer be decreed, and that freedom had to be paramount, he got rid of censorship, set up DRACs (regional locally based ministerial delegations), forced local councils to become more accountable, assisted creative artists, and supported private theatre companies, while urging state-funded theatres to 'reach out to their audiences' more than before. He also reinforced the music policy that Marcel Landowski had drawn up under Malraux, appealed for private arts patronage, and helped to promote the president's scheme to build a major contemporary arts centre on the Beaubourg site in Paris.[85] On the other hand, one of Georges Pompidou's other initiatives, aimed at demonstrating that Paris could still hold its own in the visual arts against New York by putting on the exhibition 'Twelve years of contemporary art in France' at the Grand Palais in May 1972, proved something of a flop. On the day the show opened, a band of anti-establishment artists from the visual artists' 'Front' clashed with CRS riot police, and then held the exhibits up to ridicule. Questioned in the National Assembly by Michel Poniatowski on the 'twelve years of contemporary hoaxing', Duhamel stoutly defended the freedom of living art.

Theatre provides quite a good overview of the successes scored and the difficulties encountered by the public service outlook that was adopted over fifteen years. Great vitality was in evidence in the mushrooming of original creative spaces, in the supreme powers granted to directors sometimes over the text itself, and in the drive to perform the very best plays from the whole world. While the first companies that were subsidized under the move to decentralize the theatre – and even the Théâtre national populaire, managed in succession by Jean Vilar, then from 1963 by Georges Wilson and after 1972 by Jack Lang – ran out of steam, theatres began to spring up in the suburbs, the *maisons de la culture* made full use of their new resources, and festivals proliferated. With Jean Dasté at Saint-Etienne, René Allio at the Commune d'Aubervilliers theatre, Pierre Debauche at Nanterre's Amandiers, Jack Lang at the Nancy 'world' festival from 1963 to 1972, Jean Mercure at the Théâtre de la Ville de Paris, Jean-Louis Barrault at first the Théâtre des Nations and then the Odéon, Marcel Maréchal at the Cothurne in Lyon, Guy Rétoré at the Théâtre de l'Est Parisien, Ariane Mnouchkine at the Théâtre du Soleil de la Cartoucherie in Vincennes (where *1789* and *1793* were huge hits in 1970 and 1972): the list of resounding successes over this decade could easily be extended. Meanwhile, the Comédie Française, entrusted to Pierre Dux in 1970, was anything but idle. Equally, private theatres ran successful performances of Arrabal, Beckett, Dubillard, Ionesco or Obaldia, and the light comedies of so-called *théâtre de boulevard*, dominated by Françoise Dorin, continued to turn out pure entertainment – vehicles for such stars as Poiret, Maillan, Mondy and Le Poulain. Yet this broad array of talent struggled to reach the audience of which it dreamt, and any consensus on what public authorities could be expected to deliver had now disappeared: worried and penniless theatre companies were left dithering, as Maurice Druon put it in 1973, between 'the begging bowl and the molotov cocktail'. The *maisons de la culture* and the subsidized centres came sorrowfully to realize that blue-collar workers, despite support from works councils, only accounted for about 15 per cent of their audiences and that instead it was the rising middle classes that went wild on 'easy-access Brecht' and the latest inventions of a supposedly 'popular' theatre. As early as 1966, Pierre Bourdieu had shown that in the case of museum attendance democratization was something of a mirage, and that cultural inequality tended to persist – though cultural action did at least have the positive effect of convincing those who promoted it of the legitimacy of their efforts. Bourdieu's analysis set out to identify the 'laws of cultural diffusion': these might then be applied to the art of the theatre, which by this time doubted its own ability to play a role in 'cultural development'.[86]

The French responded to this gamut of more or less effective appeals by reordering their cultural practices. The statistical data available reveals that the vast majority of people were perfectly happy to follow the clear signposting so insistently provided by mass culture and that they readily opted for cultural forms of leisure (see table 11). After 1968 there was a new development, related to the first stirrings of *rétro* fashion and to the 'roots' cult in a country which was now, as it were, stepping backwards into a period of generalized crisis affecting both the economy and society's values: interest in the artistic heritage was on the rise. It is after all remarkable in a society so acutely fearful of 'Americanization' that large-scale museum and art gallery shows drew such crowds, with 400,000 visitors to the Picasso exhibition and 300,000 for Vermeer in 1966, 1,200,000 visitors the following year for the Tutankhamun exhibition, 490,000 for Van Gogh in 1972 and 500,000 for the Centenary of Impressionism in 1973; that the numbers of visits to historical monuments and museums were rising so fast (7,800,000 entrances in 1960 and 11,500,000 in 1970); and that there was at last a desire to preserve and restore the historic hearts of towns that had so frequently been devastated by concrete. It was as if heritage was already a refuge for a nation that was culturally in transit and in doubt.

Table 11. *The main cultural practices of the French in 1973 (percentages of the population)*

Listening to the radio at least every other day	76.9
Watching the television at least every other day	74.4
Reading a newspaper several times a week	62.6
Regularly taking part in a parlour game (cards, etc.)	44.0
Going to the cinema between one and ten times in a year	36.5
Listening to records or cassettes	34.3
Visiting a historical monument	31.8
Going to a theatrical performance	29.6
Visiting a museum	27.4
Reading a women's or family magazine	26.8
Going to a football match	24.3
Hunting for antiques or second-hand bargains	22.7
Going to a visual arts exhibition	18.6
Reading between one and four books in a year	14.3
Going to a performance of folk dancing	12.0
Going to a light entertainment/variety show	11.5
Going to the circus	10.8
Going to a concert of classical music	6.9
Going to a jazz or pop/rock concert	6.5
Playing an instrument or group singing	5.1
Going to the opera	2.6

Source: (233), vol. II, pp. 150–2.

Conclusion to part 2

The analysis that has been presented here, under the three headings of the economy, society and culture, certainly needs to be extended and fleshed out to reflect a more nuanced picture of the French people – forever changing, diverse, and imaginative, as eager to embrace progress as they are concerned to set their destiny within a deeply rooted national culture. Yet our analysis has made it possible, we hope, to identify three new developments at the heart of social activity which had entered into social mores, while jolting both mindsets and institutions, and which – and this was the most outstanding new development of all – advanced together, growing stronger the more closely they meshed.

The first and most important of these developments was the relative fluidity that the careful management of the 'industrial imperative' had introduced into society. As the 'thirty glorious years' drew to a close, many changes were startlingly obvious to contemporaries. The nation's balance-sheets showed consistently strong growth in production, income and redistribution that were sufficient to sustain confidence in the combined virtues of domestic and international competition, broad-based increases in productivity, a real eagerness to work, improved social mobility, and ongoing welfare state intervention. In many companies, increased flexibility in investment, decision-making and hierarchical structure was just as notable as advances in technology and management. The old class barriers seemed moth-eaten and in places had already given way to differences in position and to symbolic distinctions whose gradations appeared easier to handle, less prone to trigger old-style clashes, and more conducive to orderly dialogue and negotiated agreement. Thus, even though the 'New Society' had been abandoned as a political project, France continued to be haunted by the vision that had lain at its heart. The 'central group' had developed its profile around the emergent middle classes of managers, white-collar workers, technicians and state employees, demonstrating its own dynamism and enhancing its social and cultural influence. Somehow or other, a compromise had been reached on the future of the countryside and on the role to be accorded to rural life in the process of modernization, while, spectacularly, the explosion of towns and cities carved change into the most familiar landscapes of everyday life.

The second new development, as 'legible' socially as the first though more gradual in its impact on the general mindset, was the eruption of greater prosperity. This was marked by very tangible advances in mass consumption, which most people experienced as an unprecedented source of pleasure, and which some even greeted as the annunciation of the sole attainable happiness. Consumption turned the rise in average earnings into a source of immediate profit, stimulating every appetite, breathing youthful vigour into people's forward planning, and ensuring the smooth development of leisure, the family, and even private life.

The last of our three new developments is the sense of cultural irresolution, betraying genuine disquiet with the – as yet only partially accepted – emergence of the greater social fluidity and increased prosperity to which we have just referred. The bedding-down of mass culture, the media strength orchestrated by a youthful television, and the elitist distancing of high or 'cultivated' culture all began to chip away at what had once been a shared stock of values and cultural practices. And this occurred despite the attempt to sketch out a policy for a public culture, and despite the characteristically French breadth of resistance and gift for subtle adaptation when confronted with imported cultural patterns common to all developed Western societies.

These three waves of innovation were sustained by the political atmosphere and the national ambitions of the time. They served to authenticate the modernizing challenge that had been laid at the feet of the French by the culmination of decolonization in 1962 – a challenge which most French people were willing to take up. At last, as de Gaulle expressed it, France would 'marry her time'. By all means – Pompidou seemed to add – let us modernize the country, but with moderation, respecting its traditional values of order, work and authority, and without damaging its primary institutions, private property, *grands corps*, lycées and territorial districts; let us by all means bring the country into line with international competition and its European future, let us make it as strong as the other developed nations that manage the affairs of the world. But let us do this without threatening its legacy and let us even, drawing strength from the consensus created around the republic's new institutions, delay confronting its old and harmful shortcomings, however irritating: persistent inequality, the abuse of power, social elitism, the inability to negotiate, the failure to rise to the challenge of mass schooling, or the invasion of paralysing statism.[1] Addressing a question frequently raised since the end of post-war reconstruction –

'can the new France be made to fit into the mould of the old France?' –
Stanley Hoffman noted that Pompidou's approach was to adopt 'a
strategy of adaptive restoration, not reform'.[2]

It is worth recalling that this general ambition, with these provisos,
was endorsed in the elections of 1969 and 1973 and that in 1974 a
majority of French voters made what was doubtless a rather more
reforming yet fundamentally not so very different choice by electing
Giscard d'Estaing. Yet such consistency and loyalty does not mean that
they had simply – or indeed nervously – come to terms with the
shortcomings we have just enumerated. By the time that the sociologist
Michel Crozier's *La Société bloquée* ('The Stalemated Society') had been
published in 1970, 'everybody now accepted it as a fact, however
reluctantly', and Crozier's book provided much food for thought in the
upper reaches of the administration, among large-scale employers, in
the trades unions and in Chaban-Delmas' entourage: French society
was certainly 'stalemated', trapped in a 'bureaucratic and paternalist
vice', while the French spent their time 'reinforcing even through their
recriminations the system from which they suffer[ed]'.[3]

Based on meticulous investigations into the workings of bureaucracy
in private companies and the civil service, Crozier's analysis attacked
the issue head-on, providing evidence of the difficulties and indeed the
powerlessness of many top civil servants, heads of companies, technicians and intellectual mandarins – all equally brilliant and competent –
in facing up to the demands of economic and social development now
firmly on the nation's agenda. His analysis also prompted disquiet by
demonstrating that centralizing bureaucracy, which was strongly attached to the gains it had made and to the rights which had been
bestowed upon it, and which its trades unions defended tooth and nail,
actually rubbed along very well indeed with the anarchic individualism
of claimants' culture, just as the rather more tranquil aristocracy of
trade got along with the civil service. Similarly, Crozier showed how
caste and managerial cadre, pressure group and decision-making
authority, a guaranteed income and overbearing management often
went hand in hand, cooperating wonderfully to extend the life of a
familiar pattern of French behaviour which, though now nearing exhaustion, remained all too fully operational. From this twofold observation, Michel Crozier drew a conclusion that was to influence a great
many 'decision-makers': in order better and more profitably to secure
the participation of everyone in the national effort, organizations
needed to move from this rigid bureaucratic pattern to a 'more flexible
and more tolerant [pattern] founded on mobility, competition and
negotiation. The struggle therefore should not be to rein in over-

powerful organizations but rather to ensure that they really do modernize themselves.'

The force of 'Pompidolian' persuasion ensured that modernization of this kind was indeed implemented in public and private enterprise. Yet it was not taken sufficiently on board to ensure its urgent introduction into the machinery of the nation's governance. After all, the implementation of such a complex task would have required a thorough overhaul of all command structures including, first and foremost, those of the state. This would have flown in the face of the conservatism of Pompidou's policy: there was no desire to rock the boat or to challenge authority by pushing through inconvenient reforms. A forthright appeal, however, was made to the existing mechanisms, and to people already in position, whom it was possible to convince of the country's need to modernize and whose power to take relevant action was considerably increased. Employers continued to be recruited from as narrow a social base as before: in 1973, only 12 per cent of employers, often the smallest, came from blue-collar, white-collar or crafts backgrounds, and this proportion had remained unchanged since the start of the century. In 1965, the CNPF, taking its lead from Georges Villiers, had swerved towards liberalism, very much against the grain. But Paul Huvelin, Villiers' successor as head of the CNPF, found a means of encouraging many employers to engage in negotiation of a less episodic nature, to accept the monthly payment of wages, and to introduce social welfare programmes: some even – at a push – were prepared to envisage business reform.[4]

The financial elites and the *grands corps* – as socially exclusive in their recruitment, as technocratically excellent, and as centralist in their approach to public service as ever before – were charged with cultivating collective power and with securing economic development before giving any consideration to the engineering of equality through changes to the tax system, or improvements to the machinery of welfare redistribution or the strengthening of such public services as hospitals, public transport, nursery schooling or old people's homes. In short, they were to risk exacerbating inequality by going for growth which, on its own, it was argued, via consumption and social mobility, would fuel the most effective of all possible redistribution processes. Here again, it was a matter of forging something new from old materials, by imposing central authority on regional notables, without allowing for any superfluous complicity, while holding a tight rein on both old-fashioned employers and over-corporatist pressure groups. And this course was to be pursued even if it meant turning a blind eye to job-hopping between the civil service, state enterprise and private industry (with, in some cases, even a spell of ministerial office), as well as to hopes of a cushy number in private enterprise – both of which tendencies were beginning to seize hold of the small world of the *énarchie*, the ENA-educated civil service elite.[5]

A generation of brilliant state administrators had thus diligently supported and then taken over from the handful of leading civil servants who had overseen the modernization of the country after 1945. This remarkable and uniquely French 'technostructure' was widely envied abroad. It could wield initiative and expertise and provide momentum, and it had never been found severely wanting in any respect: indeed, without it little could have been accomplished. Yet it had steered and managed the 'stalemate society' ruthlessly, and had prolonged, techno-logized, rejuvenated and hence extended the tradition of dependency *vis-à-vis* public authorities and, it goes without saying, had never had the good fortune to contribute to any reform of the state. At best, this 'technostructure' had strengthened its tutelage – especially over indus-trial policy and town planning – or had introduced changes into its role by undertaking a reform of state-owned enterprises in line with the recommendations of the 1967 Nora report. At worst, it had com-pounded the bottlenecks within certain institutions by supporting the corporatism of their staff – in television, for example, and especially in education. Above all, it had had little incentive to refine its interventions through negotiation with such counterweights and alternative power bases as could have taken part in the elaboration of policies: parliament had been humbled, regional bodies were suspected of 'Girondism', while local interest groups could simply be by-passed by Paris at the decisive moment. The fault-line between decision-making and represen-tative democracy gaped ever wider because, as Stanley Hoffmann put it, 'France is a society in flux, which has not yet found a way of institutio-nalizing the extension of its state.'

Even if the state was on the whole properly administered and embo-died a broadly shared aspiration for modernization and prosperity, France still found it uncomfortable to face concerns about its future and protests about the present state of affairs. For, as Stanley Hoffmann concluded, 'a consensus on economic progress is neither an agreement on common values nor an agreement on the structures and institutions of a new society'. However, the mass of questions that economic growth raised regarding both its very validity and the possibility of its exhaus-tion, weighed down by ecological concerns, issues of social exclusion and marginal grievances, was prevented from growing any further by the economic crisis that utterly transformed the situation, silencing all such questions. On the other hand, despite the efficiency of the repressive policies deployed under Raymond Marcellin, anti-establishment protest, with the echoes of May 1968 still ringing in everyone's ears, had ample room to prosper, to draw in the most diverse of groups, to interlace, as the jargon then had it, 'quantity' and 'quality'. It was in a position to focus simultaneously on all three types of new development that had seized hold of the country, and to challenge all those institutions, including trades unions, whose role – it could be alleged – was to betray the revolt. And it was able to maintain a state of confusion between the eternal populist combat of the 'weak' against the 'powerful', the new individual and group demands for autonomy or worker's management (*autogestion*), and the pseudo-revolutionary 'grand refusal' that was both cultivated and play-acted within the militant minority hothouse.

The list of rebels, all to a greater or lesser extent children of May '68, was inexhaustible: hard-up blue-collar workers feeling severely exploited; the first wave of immigrant workers now raising their heads above the parapet; farmers blockading roads and 'neo-rural' incomers at odds with wider society; small traders and craftspeople 'organized' into Gérard Nicoud's CID–UNATI; experts and managers furious at being excluded from decision-making; university and school students tangled up in the loops of the educational system; regionalists veering towards separatism; women doing battle for the right to abort; local district activists dreaming of grass-roots 'urban struggle'; hippies curled up in their counter-culture; angry young things inflamed by subversive rock; pioneering ecologists and anti-nuclear demonstrators. Yet however cacophonous and chaotic this list, it spelled out a litany of irrepressible disquiet that might easily have turned to wholesale revolt, to street clashes or to orchestrated media uproar.

The mistake that leftists made was to believe, as Jean-Paul Sartre wrote in 1973, that all that was needed was 'to organize the vast anti-hierarchical movement that everywhere challenges the institutions'.[6] The theorists of imprisonment, technocratic normalization and invasive structures – with Michel Foucault at their head – mistakenly believed that this society, in fact in a state of prolonged ferment, was a closed system destined to become increasingly one-dimensional and totalitarian. Morin, Lefort and Castoriadis, on the other hand, believed that the libertarian 'breach' that had been half-opened in 1968 would be forced further ajar by sustained battering. They all pooh-poohed the observations that Alain Touraine was then making about old and new social movements and which he later summed up thus: 'Society is action focused on itself, cultural production, but through the strife of social conflict.'[7] Touraine, a sociologist, itemized the defensive collective actions which, although on the decline, mobilized people more than ever before around issues of employment, salary, prosperity and even life-style, confronting a real and clearly identified power, and which also might always be taken up or 'coopted' by institutions, primarily the unions. Yet Touraine made a distinction between such actions and counter-offensive commitments – 'struggles for the reappropriation of society's power to act upon itself' – which opened out the scope of demands, going beyond what was socially instituted, advancing to address nature, desire, an appeal to mass communication or to straight-forward social relations. It was these commitments, even if they were still dressed up in a discourse and ideology that had been borrowed from earlier movements, that, Touraine concluded, were now most strongly rooted in society and pointed the way forward. In fact, the end of the 1970s would display first their impotent proliferation and then their crumbling, even though their social visibility and media presence increased. Yet due to the lack of sufficiently strong shared values and the persistence of former *blocages*, French society in 1974 clearly had scant comprehension of or control over the work and agitation that was focused upon it. And, equally clearly, the only response to social protest was a combination of defence of the established order and calls for reform.

If they could not agree as to the nature of the society that had afforded them a better standard of living, and if they found its hierarchies increasingly hard to stand, the French did at least have something that served to calm their strains and enabled them to trace a way forward: their pragmatic consensus on the way they were to be governed, founded on the acceptance of the institutions and rules of the Fifth Republic, and on the acknowledgement of the sovereign ideal of gran-deur that General de Gaulle had given the nation. And – even if some commentators already considered this to be antiquated – it was along the well-worn political fault-line running from right to left that the French were content to situate the power conflicts, social tensions and cultural rifts that continued to divide them.[8] Despite all their protests, and however bruised their souls, the French people, encouraged yet left unsated by economic growth,[9] still felt free enough in 1974 not to accept wholeheartedly – indeed, less than ever – the notion that elections were just 'a fool's game'.

Notes

The figures in brackets refer to the books listed in the bibliography. Unless stated otherwise, the place of publication is Paris.

1 CHANGE AND CONTINUITY

1 (17), chapters 8 to 10.
2 As related by General de Boissieu (176), p. 181.
3 (166), p. 236.
4 *Ibid.*, p. 89.
5 (163), pp. 310–11; Jean Charlot, 'L'Union des démocrates pour la République sous Georges Pompidou', in (175).
6 Jean and Monica Charlot, 'Persuasion et politique. Les campagnes de Georges Pompidou et Alain Poher', *Revue française de science politique*, 20, April 1970, pp. 230–1.
7 (166), pp. 193–5.
8 *Ibid.*, pp. 191–3.
9 (54), p. 102; (17) vol. I, p. 412.
10 Jérôme Jaffré, 'Georges Pompidou et les Français à travers les sondages: un président populaire', in (175).
11 *Ibid.* See also Alain Lancelot and Pierre Weill, 'L'Evolution politique des électeurs français de février à juin 1969 d'après les sondages de la SOFRES', *Revue française de science politique*, April 1970, pp. 249–81.
12 (163), p. 318.
13 (17) vol. I, pp. 415–16.
14 See (179), the essential work on this subject.
15 *Ibid.*
16 Quoted in Serge Berstein, 'Destins du centrisme politique sous la présidence de Georges Pompidou (1969–1974)', in (175).
17 (15), vol. II, pp. 51, 55, 95, 135, 141, 151.
18 (166), pp. 61–4.
19 This was remarked upon by R.-G. Schwarzenberg in *Projet*, September 1970, p. 92.
20 (163), pp. 330–3.
21 *Ibid.*, pp. 333–4.
22 *Ibid.*, pp. 337–9.

2 THE 'NEW SOCIETY', 1969–1971

1 (163), p. 375.
2 *Ibid.*, p. 376.
3 *Ibid.*, p. 392.
4 (17) vol. I, p. 432.
5 (163), pp. 403–4 and 450; (179), pp. 132–3.
6 (163), pp. 377–81.
7 *Ibid.*, pp. 407–11.
8 (180), *passim*.
9 *Ibid.*
10 (179), p. 136.
11 (163), pp. 369–75.
12 *Ibid.*, pp. 405–6.
13 Jaffré, 'Georges Pompidou et les Français à travers les sondages'.
14 (166), pp. 107 ff.
15 Christian Stoffaës, 'La Politique industrielle de Georges Pompidou en perspective', in (175).
16 *Ibid.*
17 Bernard Esambert, 'La Politique industrielle de Georges Pompidou', in (175).
18 Jacques Adda, Roland Colin, Gérald Collange and Monique Fouet, 'La Remise en cause des équilibres d'après-guerre, 1969–1973', in (174).
19 Stoffaës, 'La Politique industrielle' and André Giraud, 'Certaines décisions de Georges Pompidou dans les domaines du pétrole et du nucléaire', in (175).
20 Giraud, 'Certaines décisions'.
21 Stoffaës, 'La Politique industrielle'.
22 *Ibid.* and Roger Martin, 'Les Concentrations dans la grande industrie. Deux exemples: le verre et l'acier', in (175).
23 Stoffaës, 'La Politique industrielle', and Martin, 'Les Concentrations'.
24 Stoffaës, 'La Politique industrielle'; (163), pp. 382 and 442.
25 (163), pp. 349–50, and (17), vol. I, pp. 436–7.
26 Quoted in (163), p. 353.
27 (186), p. 368.
28 Françoise Piotet, 'La Négociation collective et le développement conventionnel', in (175).
29 Jean Bunel, 'La Mensualisation', in (175).
30 *Esprit*, May 1974.
31 Pierre Avril, 'Les Rapports du gouvernement et du Parlement', in (175).
32 (17), vol. I, pp. 440–1; (163), p. 362; (162), pp. 113–14.
33 (17), vol. I, pp. 442–3.
34 *Ibid.*, pp. 442–5; (163), pp. 392, 394, 397–8.
35 Jaffré, 'Georges Pompidou et les Français à travers les sondages'.
36 (17), vol. I, pp. 445–8 and 463–4; (163), pp. 398 and 401.

3 THE GOVERNMENT IN CRISIS, 1971–1972

1 (181), pp. 98–113 and 150–77; André Mathiot, 'Les Rapports du président de la République et du Premier ministre', in (175).
2 Quoted in (163), p. 425.
3 *Ibid.*, pp. 423–32.
4 *Ibid.*, pp. 411–17.
5 Charlot, 'L'Union des démocrates pour la République sous Georges Pompidou'; (163), pp. 355–6.
6 Charlot, 'L'Union'; (163), p. 399; (17), vol. I, pp. 450–1.
7 (1); Charlot, 'L'Union'; (163), p. 399.
8 Charlot, 'L'Union'; (163), p. 432.
9 Mathiot, 'Les Rapports'; (163), pp. 418–19.
10 Colette Ysmal, 'M. Valéry Giscard d'Estaing et les républicains-indépendants', in (175).
11 (166), pp. 192–3.
12 Jacques Duhamel, *Une stratégie, une doctrine, une morale*, CDP, 1971, pp. 7–8.
13 *Ibid.*, p. 5.
14 Serge Berstein, 'Destins du centrisme politique à l'époque de la présidence de Georges Pompidou', in (175).
15 (171), in particular pp. 265–74.
16 *Ibid.*, pp. 226–35; (17), vol. I, pp. 455–8.
17 (17), vol. I, pp. 458–9; (58), pp. 105–8; (60), pp. 262–70.
18 (17), vol. I, pp. 458–61.
19 *Ibid.*, pp. 453–71; (163), pp. 434 and 456–7.
20 Jean-Louis Quermonne, 'Le Référendum du 23 avril 1972: signification et portée', in (175); (181), pp. 61–73.
21 Recounted by Edouard Balladur, quoted in (163), p. 465.
22 (17), vol. I, pp. 469–71; (163), pp. 464–6; (181), pp. 109–16.

4 ENDGAME, 1972–1974

1 (163), p. 468.
2 *Ibid.*, pp. 468–70; (17), vol. I, p. 475; (181), pp. 116–19.
3 (163), p. 471.
4 (17), vol. I, pp. 475–7; (163), pp. 471–2.
5 Olivier Duhamel, 'La Gauche et la Ve République sous la présidence de Georges Pompidou', in (175); (182); (17), vol. I, pp. 478–80.
6 Ysmal, 'M. Valéry Giscard d'Estaing et les républicains-indépendants'.
7 Charlot, 'L'Union'.
8 *Ibid.*
9 *Ibid.*; (17), vol. I, pp. 480–1; (163), p. 479.
10 (163), p. 480.
11 Charlot, 'L'Union'.
12 Matiot, 'Les Rapports'; (17), vol. I, pp. 480–4; (163), pp. 483–4.
13 Charlot, 'L'Union'; (182).

14 (163), p. 483, as recounted by General de Bénouville.
15 Serge Berstein, 'Destins du centrisme'; (17), vol. I, p. 486; as recounted by Pierre Messmer at the FNSP (Fondation nationale des sciences politiques) Pompidou symposium.
16 Quoted in (17), vol. I, p. 487; (163), p. 485.
17 (17), vol. I, p. 487.
18 *Ibid.*, p. 488; (182).
19 (163), pp. 487–90.
20 (166), pp. 225–6.
21 (17), vol. I, pp. 489–91; (163), pp. 490–2.
22 Quoted by Charlot, 'L'Union'.
23 (17), vol. I, pp. 491–2; (163), pp. 492 and 493–5.
24 (181); Françoise Decaumont, 'La Réforme avortée du quinquennal', in (175); (17), vol. I, pp. 492–4; (163), pp. 493–5.
25 (166), pp. 160 ff.
26 (17), vol. I, pp. 497–9; (163), pp. 496–7 and 500–2.
27 (163), pp. 474–5.
28 (17), vol. I, pp. 496–7; (163), p. 500.
29 (17), vol. I, pp. 495–7.
30 *Ibid.*, pp. 495–6; (163), p. 499; (187), pp. 224–42.
31 Jaffré, 'Georges Pompidou à travers les sondages'.
32 (17), vol. I, p. 500.
33 *Ibid.*, p. 503; (163), pp. 508–10.

5 THE GROWTH-RATE SOCIETY

1 J. Fourastié, *Les Trentes Glorieuses ou la Révolution invisible de 1946 à 1975*, Fayard, 1979.
2 See (165), vol. III.
3 See Groupe 1985, *Réflexions pour 1985*, La Documentation française, 1964: the prediction was that GDP and household consumption would exceed 300 – taking 1960 as the base.
4 See above, chapter 2, and (166), chapter 5.
5 See Lionel Stoléru, *L'Impératif industriel*, Seuil, 1969, which served as a manifesto for this policy of industrialization, whereby the state, industrialists, workers and consumers would seek a balance between their powers and their aspirations for the general good.
6 On all their mechanisms and on the financial rules of the contemporary economic and social game, see Y. Bernard, J.-C. Colli and D. Lewandowski, *Dictionnaire économique et financier*, Seuil, 1975. On the main companies, see P. Allard, M. Beaud *et al.*, *Dictionnaire des groupes industriels et financiers en France*, Seuil, 1978.
7 For a good insider's account: J.-F. Picard, A. Beltran and M. Bungener, *Histoires de l'EDF, Comment se sont prises les décisions de 1946 à nos jours*, Dunod, 1985.
8 See A. Beltran and J.-P. Willot, *Le Noir et le Bleu, Quarante ans d'histoire de Gaz de France*, Belfond, 1992.

9 See C. Carlier, *Marcel Dassault. La légende d'un siècle*, Perrin, 1992: the perfect example of a durable alliance between a successful industrialist and the state against the background of the Fifth Republic.

10 See the brief account by M. Freyssenet and C. Omnès, *La Crise de la sidérurgie française*, Hatier, 1982, and, on the subsequent period, Ph. Mioche, 'La sidérurgie française de 1973 à nos jours. Dégénérescence et transformation', *Vingtième Siècle, Revue d'histoire*, 42, April–June 1994.

11 See J.-P. Daviet, *Une multinationale à la française. Saint-Gobain (1665–1989)*, Fayard, 1989, chapters 6 to 8.

12 However, the chronic weakness of the Bourse, which played a secondary role in investment financing, deprived firms of facilities for capital increases and the issuing of debenture loans. The stock exchange remained ill adapted to the ambitions of industry. This was illustrated in 1968 when BSN's takeover bid of Saint-Gobain collapsed. The Bourse only really revived after 1974.

13 The Debré–Haberer reform of 1966–7 had abolished the obsolete distinction between deposit banks and merchant banks. This speeded up mergers (for example, the one that created the BNP in 1966), boosted competition and hastened a shake-out of executive personnel. For its part, the former mutualist sector tasted success: indeed, Crédit agricole became one of the very first world banks. On this 'third banking revolution', see: H. Bonin, *L'Argent en France depuis 1880. Banquiers, financiers, épargnants dans la vie économique et politique*, Colin, 1989, chapters 3 and 12; and *La Banque et les Banquiers en France, du Moyen Age à nos jours*, Larousse, 1992, part four. For two specific examples, see: E. Bussière, *Paribas, l'Europe et le Monde (1872–1992)*, Fonds Mercator, 1992, and M. Meuleau, *Des pionniers en Extrême-Orient. Histoire de la Banque d'Indochine (1875–1975)*, Fayard, 1990. For a good geography of money, see J. Labasse, *L'Espace financier*, Colin, 1974.

14 See above, chapter 2, and S. Guillaume, 'Léon Gingembre, défenseur des PME', *Vingtième Siècle, Revue d'histoire*, 15, July–September 1987.

15 Evidence of this ambition is provided by the 1967 best-seller *Le Défi américain* by J.-J. Servan-Schreiber (Denoël): in order to combat the brain drain and the technological gap, especially in computer science, that the Americans were preparing to come and organize in Europe, Servan-Schreiber wanted France to become truly a part of the world 'technological community'.

16 For example, the medium-term 'physical–financial' model ('FIFI' for short), used from 1967 onwards in the preparation of the Sixth Plan and then broadly taught at rue Saint-Guillaume and at ENA (Ecole nationale d'administration), comprised 1,600 equations, involving 4,000 different parameters. From 1966 onwards, ZOGOL predicted the short term, STAR the short to medium term and from 1969 onwards DECA modelled self-financing behaviours. One further development was that some models were now directly designed by the special forecasting division of the finance ministry and no longer by the Plan alone. Moreover, the state created other research and forecasting bodies which had nothing to do with the Plan: for example, the Centre d'études des revenus et des coûts (CERC) in 1966 and

the Centre d'études de l'emploi established in November 1970 at INED. On the general evolution of planning, see the evidence collected by F. Fourquet, *Les Comptes de la puissance. Histoire de la comptabilité nationale et du Plan*, Encres-Editions Recherches, 1980.

17 On this little-studied question, see R. Gilpin, *La Science et l'Etat en France*, Gallimard, 1970, and P. Papon, *Pour une prospective de la science*, Seghers, 1983.

18 An early example: R. Aron, *Les Désillusions du progrès, Essai sur la dialectique de la modernité*, Calmann-Lévy, 1969.

19 See *Halte à la croissance?*, Fayard, 1972, and, for an early French discussion of the issues, R. Lattès, *Pour une autre croissance*, Seuil, 1972.

20 See D. Kergoat, *Bulledor ou l'histoire d'une mobilisation ouvrière*, Seuil, 1973; *Quatre Grèves significatives*, Editions de l'Epi, 1972; E. Maire, Ch. Piaget *et al.*, *Lip 73*, Seuil, 1973; M. Clavel, *Les Paroissiens de Palente*, Grasset, 1974; 'Les Grèves', special edition of *Sociologie du travail*, October–December 1973; F. Sellier, *La Confrontation sociale en France (1936–1981)*, PUF, 1984; C. Durand and P. Dubois, *La Grève. Enquête sociologique*, Presses de la FNSP/Colin, 1975; J.-D. Reynaud, *Les Syndicats en France*, Seuil, 1975, 2 vols; R. Mouriaux, *Le Syndicalisme en France depuis 1945*, La Découverte, 1994.

21 See (166), chapter 6 and above, chapter 2.

22 See O. Marchand and Cl. Thélot, *Deux Siècles de travail en France*, INSEE, 1991, p. 180. This work has confirmed and checked the most reliable figures. According to these calculations, the employment rate stood at 43.5 per cent in 1806, 50 per cent in 1900, 45.6 per cent in 1955 and 43.3 per cent in 1990.

23 The average employment rate for women rose from 36.2 per cent in 1968 to 38.7 per cent in 1975. Indeed, by 1975, two out of every three women between the ages of twenty and thirty and one out of every two between thirty and fifty-five were in work (see E. Sullerot, *Les Françaises au travail*, Hachette, 1973). There were 1,200,000 foreign workers in 1968 and 1,700,000 in 1972. In 1974, foreign immigrants numbered roughly 3,800,000, amounting to 7 per cent of the total population of France and 14 per cent of that of the Paris conurbation. Their numbers, which had risen considerably during the 1960s, were now levelling off: in 1974, following the introduction of stricter regulations, net immigration stood at 100,000 as compared to 180,000 in 1970. They included roughly 800,000 Algerians, 750,000 Portuguese and 570,000 Spaniards and Italians. See M. Amar and P. Milza, *L'Immigration en France au XXe siècle*, Colin, 1990; Y. Lequin, ed., *La Mosaïque France*, Larousse, 1988; O. Milza, *Les Français devant l'immigration*, Brussels, Complexe, 1988; G. Noiriel, *Le Creuset français. Histoire de l'immigration (XIXe–XXe siècle)*, Seuil, 1988; C. Wihtol de Wendel, *Les Immigrés et la Politique*, Presses de la FNSP, 1988.

24 In 1972, the average working week ranged between fifty-seven hours for farmers and employers in industry and commerce, forty-seven hours for members of the liberal professions and senior executives, forty-six hours for blue-collar workers, and forty-four hours for middle-ranking executives and white-collar workers. Fourteen per cent of blue-collar workers still worked

more than forty-eight hours a week, as against 20 per cent in 1968 and 25 per cent in 1962. The law enacted on 24 December 1971 lowered the number of legal overtime hours to five, and the standard working week was still forty hours long, as it had been since 1936. However, in 1972 the French working year still consisted of 1,957 hours as compared with just 1,767 hours in West Germany. The fourth week of paid annual holiday was introduced in 1969.

25 A number of contemporary documents are reproduced in M.-F. Mouriaux, *L'Emploi en France depuis 1945*, Colin, 1972. See also B. Brizay, *Qu'est-ce qu'un chômeur?*, Pluriel, 1979. Unemployment, though low, was deemed quite unacceptable since, ever since the Liberation, it had been the state's task to ensure full employment, and firms, broadly speaking, had 'externalized' unemployment. The experts of the Fifth Plan (1965–70) were the first to note with some astonishment the first warning sign of a crisis that was still a long way off: a gap in the forecasts of 600,000 people between the figure for the working population actually 'employed' and the working population merely 'available' (see R. Salais, N. Baverez and B. Reynaud, *L'Invention du chômage*, PUF, 1986).

26 See, for example, A. Guillerm and Y. Bourdet, *Clefs pour l'autogestion*, Seghers, 1975, and P. Rosanvallon, *L'Age de l'autogestion*, Seuil, 1976.

27 See the description in R. Linhart, *L'Etabli*, Minuit, 1978, and in J. Frémontier, *La Forteresse ouvrière: Renault. Une enquête à Boulogne-Billancourt chez les ouvriers de la Régie*, Fayard, 1971.

28 After the euphoria aroused prior to 1968 by the work of S. Mallet, P. Belleville and others, there was now a move to relativize the whole phenomenon and to reflect on the new social conflicts that it fuelled. See J.-D. Reynaud, 'La Nouvelle Classe ouvrière, la technologie et l'histoire', *Revue française de science politique*, June 1972.

29 See *Les Nouvelles Formes d'organisation du travail*, special edition of *Sociologie du travail*, January–March 1976.

30 See D. Bertaux, *Destins personnels et structures de classe*, PUF, 1977.

31 See F. Bon and M.-A. Burnier, *Classe ouvrière et Révolution*, Seuil, 1971, and A. Gorz, *Critique de la division du travail*, Seuil, 1974, both highly significant in this regard. An investigation focusing on 116 workers revealed an enormous variety in their voting behaviour, ideological commitments, trade union affiliations, religious beliefs and cultural practices: see G. Adam, F. Bon, J. Capdevielle and R. Mouriaux, *L'Ouvrier français en 1970*, Colin, 1970.

32 V. Giscard d'Estaing, *Démocratie française*, Fayard, 1976, p. 56. Obviously, this vision was either ignored or denounced by the political opposition: see *Changer la vie. Programme de gouvernement du Parti socialiste*, Flammarion, 1972, and, for the Communist version, C. Quin, *Classes sociales et Union du Peuple de France*, Editions sociales, 1976. Marxist sociology and political science continued to insist on the concept of the 'petty bourgeoisie': see C. Baudelot, R. Establet and J. Malemort, *La Petite Bourgeoisie en France*, Maspero, 1974, or N. Poulantzas, *Les Classes sociales dans le capitalisme aujourd'hui*, Seuil, 1974, both of which enjoyed a wide readership at the time. The first historical analyses appeared in G. Lavau, G. Grunberg and

N. Mayer, eds., *L'Univers politique des classes moyennes*, Presses de la FNSP, 1983, part two; C. Bidou, *Les Aventuriers du quotidien, Enquête sur les nouvelles classes moyennes*, PUF, 1984; *Les Classes moyennes*, special edition of *Vingtième Siècle. Revue d'histoire*, 37, January–March 1993.

33 The numbers of middle and senior managers, taken together, increased by 55 per cent between 1965 and 1973, as compared to an increase of just 12 per cent for wage-earners as a whole. Still generally excluded from decision-making within their firms, despite their intellectual and technical expertise, they had not yet reaped the full benefit of their key social position. Their 'malaise' and their increasing unionization were a subject of great interest among sociologists and the specialized economic press which, thanks to them, was enjoying great success: see, especially, J. Cheverny *Les Cadres. Essai sur les nouveaux prolétaires*, Julliard, 1967, and J. Dubois, *Les Cadres, enjeu politique*, Seuil, 1971. For a more scientific analysis, see L. Boltanski (121).

34 In 1962 there were 1,700,000 and in 1975 2,300,000 public service employees, not including workers in public-sector industry. See J.-F. Kesler, *Sociologie des fonctionnaires*, PUF, 1980, and F. Dupuy and J.-C. Thoenig, *Sociologie de l'administration française*, Colin, 1983.

35 As well as C. Thélot (125), see A. Darbel, 'L'Evolution récente de la mobilité sociale', *Economie et Statistique*, 71, October 1975.

36 Lyon, Marseille, Bordeaux, Nancy and Strasbourg had annual growth rates of about 1 per cent, but Toulouse and Nantes fluctuated between 1.6 per cent and 2 per cent, whereas smaller towns like Grenoble, Clermont-Ferrand, Tours, Orléans and Montpellier grew at rates of between 2 and 3 per cent.

37 The population of Montpellier, for example, with 211,000 inhabitants in 1975, had increased by 111,000 since 1954, with a huge expansion in service and high-tech industries. The Cannes–Grasse–Antibes conurbation, with 258,000 inhabitants, on the other hand, had increased its population by 117,000 over the same period by developing leisure and service industries and attracting people in retirement.

38 See 'Les Migrations intérieures entre 1968 et 1975', *Economie et Statistique*, 107, January, 1975. This mobility was involving people from further afield: in 1975, 30 per cent of immigrants in each conurbation came from the surrounding department, as against 40 per cent in 1968 and 50 per cent in 1962. But it was above all small and medium-sized towns that were affected: in 1975, 20 per cent of the population of towns with under 20,000 inhabitants were newcomers who had arrived between six and eight years previously.

39 See. F. Chaslin, 'Les Années de béton', *L'Histoire*, no. 102, July–August 1987; J.-P. Flamand, *Loger le peuple. Essai sur l'histoire du logement social*, La Découverte, 1989; M. Lescure, *Immobilier et bâtiment en France. (1820–1980)*, Hatier, 1983; and above all C. Topalov, *Le Logement en France. Histoire d'une marchandise impossible*, Presses de la FNSP, 1987.

40 It was in this grey area where private haste was covered by public power that the property and development scandals that punctuated the de Gaulle and Pompidou years with monotonous regularity had their breeding ground, with land development funds apparently used to finance party-political

activities and the election campaigns of the majority grouping, or to bribe local councillors or civil servants. The most famous of these scandals were the Aranda affair in 1972, the Garantie foncière scandal and the La Villette fiasco in 1971. See above, chapter 3, and G. Martinet, *Le Système Pompidou*, Seuil, 1973, chapter 5.

41 Lille–Roubaix–Tourcoing, Nancy–Metz–Thionville, Strasbourg, Lyon–Grenoble–Saint-Etienne, Marseille–Aix-en-Provence, Toulouse, Bordeaux and Nantes–Saint-Nazaire were the eight conurbations intended to counterbalance the crushing weight of Paris.

42 See D. Voldmann, ed., *Les Origines des villes nouvelles de la région parisienne (1919–1969)*, IHTP-CNRS, 1990, and R. Chenu, *Paul Delouvrier ou la passion d'agir*, Seuil, 1994. Other new towns were launched in the Nord (Villeneuve-d'Ascq), the lower Seine valley (Le Vaudreuil) and in the Lyon region (L'Isle-d'Abeau).

43 See A.-H. Mesnard, *La Planification urbaine*, PUF, 1972.

44 See (166), chapter 6. If the rise in rents had slowed down since 1954, largely thanks to inflation, letting new homes remained a profitable business: from a baseline of 100 in 1954, the building cost index reached 270 in 1963 while the rental index soared to 650. From 1974 onwards, however, the cost of buildings outstripped their rental profitability.

45 Home ownership increased from 36 per cent of households in 1954 to 43 per cent in 1968 and 46 per cent in 1974.

46 That is to say the boredom and dreariness of the new suburbs. The word *sarcellite*, inspired by the huge estates at Sarcelles to the north of Paris, first appeared in the press in 1961 and played a part in the success in the same year of the novel by Christiane Rochefort, *Les Petits Enfants du siècle* (Grasset).

47 Urban sociologists sought to analyse urban life and its rejection: see, for example, *Politique urbaine*, special edition of *Sociologie du travail*, October–December 1970. But they concentrated more on the wave of critiques, seeking to theorize them. See M. Castells, *La Question urbaine*, Maspero, 1972; H. Lefebvre, *Le Droit à la ville*, Anthropos, 1968 and 1972, 2 vols; F. Fourquet and L. Murard, *Les Equipements du pouvoir*, UGE-'10/18', 1976.

48 In the Paris region alone, planning permission for a total of 400,000 square metres was granted annually until 1968, but this rose to an annual average of 900,000 square metres between 1969 and 1975.

49 See M. Bonneville, *Désindustrialisation et Rénovation immobilière dans l'agglomération lyonnaise*, L'Hermès, 1975.

50 See the remarks on this 'vandalism' by M. Fleury and G.-M. Leproux, in their afterword to L. Réau, *Histoire du vandalisme*, Laffont-Bouquins, 1994.

51 When it came to the overhauling of the public transport system, on the other hand, it proved impossible to make up the lost ground completely, despite the opening in 1969 of a stretch of the first RER line between Nation and Boissy-Saint-Léger stations. It was not until December 1977, however, that Nation was at last linked to Saint-Germain-en-Laye.

52 See the articles in the *Nouvel Observateur* by the best spokesman for the countryside, A. Fermigier, *La Bataille de Paris*, Gallimard, 1991; the denun-

ciation of the *macropole* in *Le Monde* by A. Chastel, *Architecture et Patrimoine*, Imprimerie nationale, 1994; and M. Cornu, *La Conquête de Paris*, Calmann-Lévy, 1977. A summary was provided by B. Marchand, *Paris, histoire d'une ville (XIXe–XXe siècle)*, Seuil, 1993.

53 See P. Grémion, *Le Pouvoir périphérique, Bureaucrates et notables dans le système politique français*, Seuil, 1976.

54 *Une image de la France en l'an 2000. Scénario de l'inacceptable*, La Documentation française, 1971. On the history and achievements of DATAR, see the picturesque reminiscences of one of its directors, F. Essig, *DATAR, des régions et des hommes*, Stanké, 1979.

55 It is clear in both Brittany, where the 1960s movement around the issue of the region's economic interests, represented by CELIB, was overtaken by a more regionalistic 'Breton' movement led by EMSAV (see M. Nicolas, *Histoire du mouvement breton*, Syros, 1982) as well as in Occitanie where underlying regionalism was fuelled by linguistic and political militancy (see R. Lafont, ed., *Le Sud et le Nord. Dialectique de la France*, Privat, 1971, and A. Touraine and F. Dubet, eds., *Le Pays contre l'Etat. Luttes occitanes*, Seuil, 1981). For a more economically informed view of the question see, for example, C. Glayman, *Liberté pour les régions. Bretagne et Rhône-Alpes*, Fayard, 1971, and C. Beringuier, A. Boudou and G. Jalabert, *Toulouse Midi-Pyrénées. La transition*, Stock, 1972. For conciser views of the issue, see J.-F. Gravier, *La Question régionale*, Flammarion, 1970, and *Paris et le Désert français*, Flammarion, second edition, 1972; R. Dulong, *Les Régions, l'Etat et la Société locale*, PUF, 1978; and S. and C. Gras, *La Révolte des régions d'Europe occidentale de 1916 à nos jours*, PUF, 1982. In June 1972, there was another example: the committee for the development and economic expansion of the Rhône-Alpes region published a disenchanting and pessimistic balance-sheet looking back over ten years of initiatives and achievement. Its authors deplored the decline in the region's role in governing the economy while at the same time regretting the state's increasing disengagement: 'There is general scepticism', it concluded, since 'how can we be concerned, when we cannot ourselves be actors?' On the other hand, a mass of socio-logizing literature, echoed in the news magazines, boasted of the art and joy of living in the countryside, far from the rushing, mind-numbing life of the Paris area: see J. Planchais, ed., *Les Provinciaux, ou la France sans Paris*, Seuil, 1970.

56 See H. Mendras, *La Fin des paysans. Changement et innovations dans les sociétés rurales françaises*, SEDEIS, 1967, republished by Colin, 1970. At the time, this book prompted a lively debate.

57 See, for example, the very telling investigation into Ille-et-Vilaine in 'L'Exode agricole. Etude socio-économique', in *Notes et Etudes documentaires*, no. 3928, La Documentation française, 6 October 1972.

58 This creed prompted a great many investigations in the social sciences. In particular, see the excellent monographs by product and by region in M. Bodiguel, *Les Paysans face au progrès*, Presses de la FNSP, 1975, and, above all, the major multi-disciplinary investigation into Plozévet (Finistère), summarized in A. Burguière, *Bretons de Plozévet*, Flammarion, 1975.

59 See B. Lambert, *Les Paysans dans la lutte des classes*, Seuil, 1970.

60 M. Debatisse, *La Révolution silencieuse. Le combat des paysans*, Calmann-Lévy, 1963, stimulated considerable interest.
61 See H. Delorme, 'Les Années Chirac', in P. Coulomb, ed., *Les Agriculteurs et la Politique*, Presses de la FNSP, 1990, pp. 423–7.

6 THE OUTBREAK OF PROSPERITY

1 J. Dubois, 'Bleu comme compteur', in C. Sèze, ed., *Confort moderne. Une nouvelle culture du bien-être*, Autrement, 1994.
2 J. Baudrillard, *La Société de consommation, ses mythes, ses structures*, Denoël, 1970. See M. Ruffat, 'La Société de consommation et ses critiques. Pour une mise en perspective des années soixante', *Historiens de l'Europe contemporaine*, December 1993.
3 C. Villeneuve, 'Les Mémoires d'un caddie', *Le Nouvel Economiste*, 12 January 1981, and P. Beaudeux, 'Les Cinq Voitures du maître ouvrier', *L'Expansion*, October–November 1985.
4 5.4 per cent a year from 1959 to 1963, 3.8 per cent from 1964 to 1968. In 1974–8, it fell to 3.4 per cent.
5 It was a way of reasoning that was already obsolete, with the development of the Peugeot Mobylette and the VéloSolex in the 1950s and their subsequent retreat before the motor-car: 380,000 'Solexes' were sold in 1964 but just 198,000 in 1971.
6 J. Fourastié, *Machinisme et Bien-être*, Minuit, 1962; *Les Trente Glorieuses*; *Le Jardin du voisin. Essai sur les inégalités en France*, Pluriel, 1980 (with B. Bazil).
7 See (202).
8 The ratio between the average salary of a particular category of employee and the average salary of employees as a whole (set at baseline 100) in 1967 put senior managers at 363, middle managers at 170, white-collar workers at 88 and workers at 80. In 1973, the figures were 325, 156, 87 and 81 respectively.
9 As for people in business or the liberal professions, profits (indexed at 119 in 1974, taking 1970 as baseline 100) were concentrated in retail sales, and the legal, medical and paramedical professions: between 1970 and 1974, the average fiscal profit of notaries rose from 111,000 to 211,000 francs, that of advocates from 40,000 to 67,000, that of general practitioners from 61,000 to 87,000, that of physiotherapists from 28,000 to 45,000, and that of nurses from 17,000 to 34,000.
10 See E. Cohen, *L'Etat brancardier. Politiques du déclin industriel (1974–1984)*, Calmann-Lévy, 1989, and P. Rosanvallon, *L'Etat en France de 1789 à nos jours*, Seuil, 1990.
11 The figures in current (non-adjusted) francs climbed from 124 to 241 billion between 1969 and 1974, shared out between health-related benefits (36.2–37.3 per cent), old-age benefits (41.6 to 42.6 per cent), employment benefits (2 to 2.6 per cent) and family benefits, which were now falling with the end of the baby boom (20.2 per cent to 17.5 per cent).
12 See (200). This assessment broadly agrees with those produced by INSEE, which in 1975 conducted a study that showed that the richest 10 per cent of

households possessed 57 per cent of total assets, whereas the least well-off section owned only 5.5 per cent of total wealth. The 340,000 households with wealth in excess of 0.15 million francs thus owned 26 per cent of gross wealth. Of these 226,000 were aged over fifty and 31 per cent lived in the Paris region, 10 per cent on the Côte d'Azur and 7 per cent in the Rhône-Alpes region. INSEE concluded that, compared with France, the concentration of wealth was more acute in Great Britain, very similar in Belgium and the Federal Republic of Germany, but less marked in Sweden.

13 See J. Lepidi, *La Fortune des Français*, PUF, 1988. However, this trend began to turn around even before the crisis, with an increase in cash savings, which between 1970 and 1973 rose from 24 per cent to 30 per cent of the property income value. Average household saving, as a percentage of disposable income, stood at 18 per cent in 1975, as against 14 per cent in 1969.

14 In the Paris region alone, the number of supermarkets rose from 10 to 253 between 1960 and 1969. In France as a whole, the 1,000 mark was passed in 1968.

15 Radar, Auchan and Euromarché were also very successful, as were more specialist types of store, such as Bernard for meat products, Conforama and Darty for household electrical goods and FNAC. FNAC was founded in Paris in 1954 by André Essel and Max Théret and branches opened in Lyon in 1972. Expanding rapidly, FNAC moved from just selling photographic products to cover the whole range of cultural goods (televisions, records and even, in 1974, when its new shop opened in the rue de Rennes in Paris, discounted books), also organizing artistic events in order to sustain its turnover. Habitat, founded in 1973, applied the same principles to simple, well-designed and affordable home furniture. See also M. Roy, *Les Commerçants. Entre la révolte et la modernisation*, Seuil, 1971.

16 See P. Pynson, *La France à table (1960–1986)*, La Découverte, 1987.

17 Their invasion, hastened by Eminence, which dominated the market and whose sales doubled between 1969 and 1974, inspired J.-P. Aron, *Les Modernes*, Gallimard, 1984, pp. 273–87.

18 See D. Friedmann, *Une histoire du blue-jean*, Ramsay, 1987.

19 Little girls' dolls can be early fashion pointers: in 1972, Barbie, along with her wardrobe, first as an American import and later made by Mattel France, conquered 75 per cent of the market.

20 See B. de Roselle, *La Mode*, Imprimerie nationale, 1980, chapter 6, and G. Lipovetsky, *L'Empire de l'éphémère. La mode et son destin dans les sociétés modernes*, Gallimard, 1987.

21 Yet the size of homes remained very inegalitarian. In 1973, members of the non-working population had on average thirty-four square metres each, members of the liberal professions thirty-five, senior managers thirty, middle managers twenty-four, white-collar workers twenty-two, and blue-collar workers just nineteen. In the Paris region, one blue-collar household in three had less than fourteen square metres per person, whereas the rate for middle managers was one in ten and for senior managers one in twenty. The Fonds national d'aide au logement was established in 1971 to address such inequalities.

22 See R. Guidot, *Histoire du design (1940–1990)*, Hazan, 1994.
23 See C. Bertho, *Télégraphes et Téléphones. De Valmy au micro-processeur*, Librairie générale française, 1981, and C. Pinaud, *Entre nous, les téléphones. Vers une sociologie de la télécommunication*, Insep Editions, 1985.
24 In 1970 France was ranked sixth in the world for expenditure on advertising, but fourteenth for expenditure per head of population and thirtieth in terms of share of GNP. See M. Martin, *Trois Siècles de publicité en France*, Odile Jacob, 1992, and A. Cadet and B. Cathelat, *La Publicité*, Payot, 1968.
25 See the anthology compiled by M.-J. Jaubert, *Slogan mon amour*, B. Barrault, 1985.
26 See J.-M. and Ph. Benoit, J.-M. Lech, *La Politique à l'affiche. Affiches électorales et publicité politique (1965–1986)*, Editions du May, 1986.
27 See A. Hennion, *Les Professionnels du disque, Une sociologie des variétés*, A.-M. Métailié, 1981.
28 Leisure was for a long time taken to mean little more than non-work and perceived as a new opportunity for popular education and this is how it was analysed, especially at Annecy: see J. Dumazedier, *Vers une civilisation du loisir?*, Seuil, 1962, and *Révolution culturelle du temps libre (1968–1988)*, Méridiens Klincksieck, 1988; J. Fourastié, *Des loisirs: pour quoi faire?*, Casterman, 1970, or B. Cacérès, *Loisir et Travail du Moyen Age à nos jours*, Seuil, 1973. Developments in holidays and tourism led Edgar Morin and his colleagues to change this view: see, as an early example, 'Vacances et tourisme', *Communications*, no. 10, 1967.
29 In 1972, 24,500,000 French people went away on holiday. Of these, 4,500,000 went abroad, above all 'to the seaside': 1,500,000 to Spain or Portugal, 1,000,000 to Italy. Unlike anywhere else in Europe, a full three-quarters of these French holidays were taken between 14 July and 15 August. Holiday trips were spread between the seaside (55 per cent), the countryside (28 per cent) and the mountains (17 per cent).
30 See A. Ehrenberg, *Le Culte de la performance*, Calmann-Lévy, 1991, part two.
31 DIY and gardening, the passion for home improvements or, in some cases, for doing up one's second home, knew no social boundaries, their share of the average household budget tripling between 1968 and 1975, while the number of DIY enthusiasts tracked by the statisticians rose from four to nine million.
32 See G. Konopnicki, *La France du tiercé. Ordre et désordre d'une passion populaire*, La Manufacture, 1986, and (219), chapter 1.
33 See R. Hubscher, ed., *L'Histoire en mouvements. Le sport dans la société française (XIXe–XXe siècle)*, Colin, 1992.
34 Groupe d'Arras, *Le Partage des bénéfices*, Minuit, 1966.
35 H. Marcuse, *L'Homme unidimensionnel*, Minuit, 1966.
36 See (211).
37 See IFOP, *Les Français et de Gaulle*, Plon, 1971, pp. 90 and 299, and SOFRES, *L'Opinion française en 1977*, Presses de la FNSP, 1978, p. 97.
38 The law enacted on 13 July 1965 reformed the institution of marriage: a wife could now take a job and open a bank account without obtaining her husband's authorization. 'Paternal power' disappeared from the statutes in 1970, replaced by 'parental authority' attributed to both parents.

39 See L. Roussel, *Le Mariage dans la société française contemporaine. Faits de population, données d'opinion*, PUF, 1975, and M. Segalen, *Sociologie de la famille*, Colin, 1981.

40 On 13 October 1955, J. Derogy broke the silence with an investigation published in *Libération*, which was quickly followed by F. Giroud writing in *L'Express* in 1956. M. Auclair's book, *Le Livre noir de l'avortement*, which appeared in 1962, and an investigation by K. D. Kaupp in *Le Nouvel Observateur* in April 1965, relaunched the campaign. Throughout this period, Dr C. Escoffier-Lambiotte wrote frequent articles on contraception for *Le Monde*.

41 See N. Garcia Guadilla, *Libération des femmes. Le MLF*, PUF, 1981.

42 Yet by 1962, 40 per cent of practising Catholics were in favour of contraceptive methods. The Fédération protestante de France, for their part, came out in favour of contraception in 1969. See M. Sevegrand, *Les Enfants du Bon Dieu. Les Catholiques et la procréation au XXe siècle*, Albin Michel, 1995.

43 See J. Mossuz-Lavau, *Les Lois de l'amour. Les politiques de la sexualité en France (1950–1990)*, Payot, 1991, and G. Duby and M. Perrot, eds., *Histoire des femmes*, vol. V: *Le XXe Siècle*, Plon, 1992.

44 See Dr P. Simon, *Rapport sur le comportement sexuel des Français*, Julliard-Charron, 1972.

45 See J. Delumeau and D. Roche, eds., *Histoire des pères et de la paternité*, Larousse, 1990, part four, and M. Fize, *La Démocratie familiale. Evolution des relations parents–adolescents*, Presses de la Renaissance, 1990.

46 See M. Winock, '1963–1973: les folles années de la jeunesse', *L'Histoire*, no. 61, November 1983; 'Les Générations', *Vingtième Siècle. Revue d'histoire*, 22, April–June 1989; G. Paloczi-Horvath, *Le Soulèvement mondial de la jeunesse (1955–1970)*, Robert Laffont, 1972; O. Galland, *Les Jeunes*, La Découverte, 1985.

47 The term was introduced by J. Capelle, a chief education officer, in *L'Ecole de demain reste à faire*, PUF, 1966. Its entry into ministerial usage was made official in 1975 by R. Haby. On the way the machinery operated, its reform and on educational policies, see J. Minot, *L'Entreprise Education nationale*, Colin, 1970, and J. Capelle, *Education et Politique*, PUF, 1974.

48 Thus, 'teaching statistics' (*Statistiques des enseignements*) were published each year from 1967 onwards. There was also a boom in symposia and enquiries: for example, AEERS, *Pour une école nouvelle. Actes du colloque national, Amiens, 1968*, Dunod, 1968; OECD, *Examen des politiques nationales d'éducation, France*, OECD, 1971; *Propositions pour une modernisation du système éducatif français*. La Documentation française, 1975.

49 That is, in millions of francs, 4.9 in 1958, 16.8 in 1966, 26.1 in 1970 and 40.6 in 1974.

50 On this law, see S. Berstein (166), pp. 229–31.

51 See the account given by R. Rémond, then vice-chancellor of the university of Nanterre, *La Règle et le Consentement*, Fayard, 1979.

52 These figures lump together both French and foreign students. At the same dates, the numbers of students of French nationality were 187,000, 586,000 and 684,000.

53 The classes preparing pupils for entry to the *grandes écoles* remained strongly

Malthusian. In 1970–1, they catered for 32,000 hand-picked students, as compared with 21,000 in 1960–1. This represented a very modest expansion to an index of 155 in 1970 from a baseline of 100 in 1960, and indeed it was not until 1983 that the 200 index was reached. At the same dates (1960, 1970, 1983), the indexes for student numbers in higher education were 100, 308 and 434.

54 On the hopes raised by the vocational training provided for by the law enacted on 11 July 1971, see J. Vaudiaux, *La Formation permanente, enjeu politique*, Colin, 1974, and *La Formation permanente. Idée neuve? Idée fausse?*, special edition of *Esprit*, October 1974.

55 Many primary-school teachers, in response to the events of May 1968, merely reread C. Freinet, espousing a teacher-as-buddy stance and advocating libertarian teaching methods as against institutional pedagogy.

56 In 1970, roughly 64,500 students passed the 'A' series baccalauréat; 11,000 the 'B' series, 21,500 the 'C' series, 36,000 the 'D' series, 34,000 the 'E', 'F' and 'G' series: a total of 167,000 new *bacheliers*. This compares with totals of 49,000 in 1959 and 225,000 in 1981. On lycées, see G. Vincent, *Les Lycéens. Contribution à l'étude du milieu scolaire*, Colin, 1971, as well as his well-documented 'white paper', *Le Peuple lycéen. Enquête sur les élèves de l'enseignement secondaire*, Gallimard, 1974.

57 Sometimes building work went ahead too fast. The arson attack on the CES in rue Pailleron in Paris on 6 February 1973, in which twenty people, including eighteen children, lost their lives, brought to light a number of construction faults. The effort represented by the building programme, however, had no precedents.

58 The rapid failure of this third strand was recognized in 1971 by the Royer law, authorizing companies to offer apprenticeships to fifteen-year-olds who quite clearly could not complete compulsory schooling. Despite the outcry that this move sparked among teachers and opposition parties, it merely acknowledged this collapse, while aiming to usher in an era of realism and increased effectiveness in providing young people with timely vocational and careers guidance.

59 See A. Prost, *L'Enseignement s'est-il démocratisé? Les élèves des lycées et collèges de l'agglomération d'Orléans de 1945 à 1980*, PUF, 1986. On p. 201, the author concludes: 'The 1959, 1963 and 1965 reforms, which set out to ensure equality of opportunity in schools and the democratization of education have, in actual fact, organized the recruitment of the educational elite from among the social elite.'

60 See V. Aubert *et al.*, *La Forteresse enseignante. La Fédération de l'Education nationale*, Fayard, 1985, and R. Chéramy, *La Fédération de l'Education nationale*, Editions de l'Epi, 1974.

61 Published as *Les Héritiers* (Minuit, 1964), the investigation by P. Bourdieu and J.-C. Passeron into the French education system showed that the underlying causes of unequal opportunities at school and university were neither economic nor institutional but cultural.

62 Joseph Fontanet, a particularly bold minister, had grasped the challenge: 'Real equality of opportunity requires a range of educational provision, on condition that assistance is delivered to the weakest, in particular through

the systematic development of supportive teaching methods', he told the National Assembly on 5 June 1973.

63 In 1959, there were, for example, 67,500 teachers in secondary education – working either in lycées or in *collèges* – but this number had rocketed to 235,000 in 1972. In many cases they had been hastily recruited – 2,200 posts for *professeurs agrégés* and 7,150 posts for *professeurs certifiés* advertised for competitive examination in 1973, as against 1,543 and 2,600 respectively in 1959 – and the training they had received at university was uneven. See I. Berger, *Les Instituteurs, d'une génération à l'autre*, PUF, 1979; G. Vincent, *Les Professeurs du second degré*, Colin, 1967; P. Gerbod, *Les Enseignants et la Politique*, PUF, 1976. Two amusing accounts by young *profs* are particularly recommended: F. George, *Prof à T.*, UGE-'10/18', 1976, and C. Duneton, *Je suis comme une truie qui doute*, Seuil, 1976.

64 Two very widely read books became instant classics of exasperated and impotent pessimism: P. Bourdieu and J.-C. Passeron, *La Reproduction. Eléments pour une théorie de l'enseignement*, Minuit, 1970, and C. Baudelot and R. Establet, *L'Ecole capitaliste en France*, Maspero, 1972. In reaction to this, teachers discovered the approach to teaching set out in A. S. Neill, *Libres Enfants de Summerhill*, or returned to the work of C. Freinet. At the same time, these worries were compounded by teachers' concerns regarding their salaries, which remained low. For example, in 1971, 50 per cent of male senior managers in the private sector were better paid than a *professeur agrégé* at the end of his career and only 4 per cent were less well paid than a *professeur certifié*.

65 In 1974, 80 per cent of employers, academics and students felt that schools were failing to fulfil the role that they regarded as most urgent – to train students to do a job. See, among others, two critical but informative contemporary descriptions of the schooling system: J. Fournier, *Politique de l'éducation*, Seuil, 1971, and S. Citron, *L'Ecole bloquée*, Bordas, 1971. Subversive ideas also thrived at this time: I. Illich's first book, *Une société sans école* (Seuil, 1971), denounced what it termed the 'capitalists of knowhow', and alleged that public service schooling 'depersonalized' children. It conjured up a society in which the entire population would educate itself. In the space of a few weeks, the book sold 70,000 copies.

66 Ministère de l'Education nationale, *Rapport de la Commission d'études sur la fonction enseignante dans le second degré*, La Documentation française, 1972. See also R. Boudon, *L'Inégalité des chances*, Colin, 1973 (new edition, Hachette, 1985).

7 A SPLINTERED CULTURE

1 See J.-P. Rioux and J.-F. Sirinelli, eds., *La Guerre d'Algérie et les Intellectuels français*, Brussels, Complexe, 1991.

2 See, for example, the critical numbers of *Esprit* in November 1963, May 1967 and March 1973 as well as the November 1966 edition of *Les Temps modernes*. Weekly magazines such as *L'Express* and above all *Le Nouvel Observateur* played a major part in popularizing structuralist ideas. See the article that F. Furet wrote in 1967, 'Les Intellectuels français et le structuralisme', in *Preuves, une revue européenne à Paris*, Julliard-Commentaire, 1989.

3 All of these were published by Plon. See also the collection of texts by and about Lévi-Strauss edited by R. Bellour and C. Clément, *Claude Lévi-Strauss*, Gallimard 'Idées', 1979, and C. Clément, *Claude Lévi-Strauss ou la Structure et le Malheur*, Le Livre de Poche, 1985.

4 F. Jacob, *La Logique du vivant*, Seuil, 1970; J. Monod, *Le Hasard et la Nécessité. Essai sur la philosophie naturelle de la biologie moderne*, Seuil, 1970.

5 This description was used by François Dosse (227), vol. I, chapters 33–5.

6 See M. Foucault, *Dits et Ecrits*, Gallimard, 1994, vols. I and II; D. Eribon, *Michel Foucault (1926–1984)*, Flammarion, 1989; D. Eribon, *Michel Foucault et ses contemporains*, Fayard, 1994.

7 Roland Barthes, *Sur Racine*, Seuil, 1963, which was preceded by a sensational article published in *Les Annales ESC*, May–June 1960; Raymond Picard, *Nouvelle Critique ou Nouvelle Imposture*, Jean-Jacques Pauvert, 1965; Barthes replied with *Critique et Vérité*, Seuil, 1966, and took his analysis a step further in *Le Plaisir du texte*, Seuil, 1973. Also see R. Barthes, *Œuvres complètes*, Seuil, 1994, vol. II: *(1966–1973)*; L.-J. Calvet, *Roland Barthes. Un regard politique sur le signe*, Payot, 1973, and *Roland Barthes (1915–1980)*, Flammarion, 1990.

8 J. Ricardou, *Le Nouveau Roman*, Seuil, 1973; *Nouveau Roman: hier, aujourd'hui*, UGE-'10/18', 1972, 2 vols; A. Rykner, *Nathalie Sarraute*, Seuil, 1991. Nor should one ignore J. Bloch-Michel, *Le Présent de l'indicatif. Essai sur le nouveau roman*, Gallimard, 1973, which takes up the cudgels against this 'literature of boredom'.

9 See Ph. Forest, *Histoire de Tel Quel*, Seuil, 1995.

10 For an overview of this literature, see, for example, J. Lacarme and B. Vercier, *La Littérature en France depuis 1968*, Bordas, 1982.

11 In 1961, they had their successful, albeit glacial, cult film in Alain Resnais' *L'Année dernière à Marienbad*, with screenplay by Alain Robbe-Grillet.

12 See E. Roudinesco, *La Bataille de cent ans. Histoire de la psychanalyse en France (1925–1985)*, Seuil, 1986, vol. II, and Jacques Lacan, *Esquisse d'une vie. Histoire d'un système de pensée*, Fayard, 1993.

13 It is no accident that it was currently the fashion to analyse intellectuals as a social group. *Les Intellectuels* (PUF, 1962) by Louis Bodin, published in the popular 'Que sais-je?' collection, was the first book to promote this analysis. Then, in 1966 and 1971, Frédéric Bon and Marc-Antoine Burnier upset previously accepted classifications by highlighting in their *Les Nouveaux Intellectuels* (Seuil, 1971), a book crammed with all the rival ideologies and verbal tics of the time, the existence of technocratic and technical intellectuals.

14 See, for example, the vigorous anonymous critique contained in 'L'Idéologie technocratique et le teilhardisme', published by *Les Temps modernes* in August 1966. See also C. Cuénot, *Ce que Teilhard a vraiment dit*, Stock, 1972, and H. de Lubac, *Teilhard posthume*, Fayard, 1977.

15 Claude Lévi-Strauss responded to this point in *La Pensée sauvage*. Raymond Aron mounted a strong argument in favour of freedom, in *D'une Sainte Famille à l'autre*, Gallimard, 1969, then *Histoire et Dialectique de la violence*, Gallimard, 1973.

16 See his *Plaidoyer pour les intellectuels*, Gallimard, 1972. On Sartre's role as the

'philosophy teacher to the whole French people', who in 1964 turned down the Nobel prize and whom de Gaulle refused to 'send to the Bastille' during the Algerian war, see Paul Thibaud, 'Jean-Paul Sartre: un magistère?', in *Traversées du XXe siècle*, La Découverte, 1988, and Annie Cohen-Solal, *Sartre (1905–1980)*, Gallimard, 1985. On his 'leftism' at that time, see Ph. Gavi, J.-P. Sartre and P. Victor, *On a raison de se révolter*, Gallimard, 1974. See also the joint development of S. de Beauvoir in D. Bair, *Simone de Beauvoir*, Fayard, 1991.

17 The two volumes of *Lire le Capital* (Maspero, 1965), compiled with Althusser's authorization by the young philosophers Jacques Rancière, Pierre Macherey, Etienne Balibar and Roger Establet, included the best sections of the seminar held at the Ecole normale. See also Althusser's own fascinating memoirs, *L'Avenir dure longtemps*, Stock-IMEC, 1992, and a posthumous assessment by his loyal colleague Etienne Balibar, *Ecrits pour Althusser*, La Découverte, 1991.

18 This development was followed by a very new kind of press, which drew on Californian 'underground' experience to intervene in original ways in the intellectual debate. Apart from the daily newspaper *Libération*, launched on 5 February 1973, the best example of this is *Actuel*, founded in 1970 by Jean-François Bizot. See the series of conversations published in *Actuel*, *C'est demain la veille*, Seuil, 1973.

19 Louis Althusser, *Eléments d'autocritique*, Hachette, 1974; Jacques Rancière, *La Leçon d'Althusser*, Gallimard, 1974 (significantly, these books were published by 'bourgeois' publishers, and no longer by Maspero). Writing in *Esprit*, in January 1974, Jean-Marie Domenach denounced what he termed Althusser's 'vacuum-packed Marxism'.

20 Raoul Vaneigem, *Traité de savoir-vivre à l'usage des jeunes générations*, Gallimard, 1967, and Guy Debord, *La Société du spectacle*, Buchet-Chastel, 1967.

21 *La Vie quotidienne dans le monde moderne*, Gallimard, 1968, and *La Pensée marxiste et la Ville*, Casterman, 1972.

22 'Sociological intervention' was much valued at this time, involving both students and teachers in the study of the subversive potential of group dynamics – research that could tip over into psychodrama. Theorized by Georges Lapassade (*Groupes, Organisations et Institutions*, Gauthier-Villars, 1970, and *Le Livre fou*, Editions de l'Epi, 1971), such 'intervention' sought to arm a counter-cultural revolution. For a time it also agitated in favour of a non-directive, self-managing (*autogestionnaire*) approach to teaching, which took its inspiration from the work of Carl Rogers. Some, however, barricaded themselves behind a barely dusted-down Marxism: for example, N. Poulantzas, *Les Classes sociales dans le capitalisme aujourd'hui*, Seuil, 1974. For a broader view of sociology, see H. Mendras and M. Verret, eds., *Les Champs de la sociologie française*, Colin, 1988, as well as three contemporary collections: J.-D. Raynaud, *Tendances et Volontés de la société française*, Futuribles-SEDEIS, 1966; *Une nouvelle civilisation? Hommage à Georges Friedmann*, Gallimard, 1973; *Science et Conscience de la société. Mélanges en l'honneur de Raymond Aron*, Calmann-Lévy, 1971, 2 vols. Yet it would be a mistake to overlook the somewhat marginal impact of such writers as R. Boudon (*La Crise de la sociologie*, Droz, 1971) or F. Bourricaud (*Le*

Bricolage idéologique. Essai sur les intellectuels et les passions démocratiques, PUF, 1980), let alone the very marked influence of R. Aron (see N. Baverez, *Raymond Aron. Un moraliste au temps des idéologues*, Flammarion, 1993).

23 Sociology, often in the American mould, was at the heart of the strong boom then affecting all the social sciences. See *Le Développement des sciences sociales en France au tournant des années soixante*, CNRS, 1983, and *Mai 68 et les Sciences sociales*, Les Cahiers de l'IHTP, no. 11, CNRS, 1989. See, for example, on the consequences of May '68, A. Touraine, *Le Mouvement de Mai ou le Communisme utopique*, Seuil, 1968, *La Production de la société*, Seuil 1973, and *Un désir d'Histoire*, Stock, 1977; E. Morin, C. Lefort and C. Castoriadis, *Mai 68. La brèche*, followed by *Vingt Ans après*, Brussels, Complexe, 1988. The journal *Critique*, published since 1946 by Minuit, devoted a lot of space to the eminent role that the social sciences were now acknowledged to play.

24 See 'Rétro. La fortune d'un mot', *Universalia 1975*, Encyclopaedia Universalis, 1975, and A. Gorz-Michel Bosquet, *Écologie et Politique*, Seuil, 1978.

25 See their much later denunciation in L. Ferry and A. Renaut, *La Pensée 68. Essai sur l'anti-humanisme contemporain*, Gallimard, 1985, and T. Pavel, *Le Mirage linguistique. Essai sur la modernisation intellectuelle*, Minuit, 1988.

26 See P. Restany, *Le Nouveau Réalisme*, UGE-'10/18', 1978.

27 See 'Histoire et structure', in *Annales ESC*, May–August 1971.

28 In terms of publishing, in 1971 Pierre Nora launched a Gallimard series called the 'Bibliothèque des histoires' (note the use of the plural), while Jacques Julliard and Michel Winock launched Seuil's 'L'Univers historique'. See also Jean-Pierre Rioux, 'L'Histoire saisie par les médias', *Esprit*, September–October 1979.

29 J. Le Goff and P. Nora, *Faire de l'histoire*, Gallimard, 1974, 3 vols.

30 This history remains to be written, but C.-J. Bertrand and F. Bordat, *Les Médias américains en France. Influence et pénétration*, Belin, 1989, provides a starting-point.

31 Edgar Morin popularized sociological thinking in the article he wrote in the 6–7 July 1963 edition of *Le Monde*, following the *nuit des copains* on 22 June in the Place de la Nation (reprinted in *Sociologie*, Fayard, 1984). In December 1963, writing in *Les Temps modernes*, Bourdieu and Passeron were already calling him a dangerous manipulator. The whole debate that followed, involving A. Moles (*Sociodynamique de la culture*, Mouton, 1964), J. Baudrillard (*Le Système des objets*, Gallimard, 1968) and G. Debord (*La Société du spectacle*, Buchet-Chastel, 1967), is well summarized in Jean Cazeneuve, *La Société de l'ubiquité. Communication et diffusion*, Denoël-Gonthier, 1972. On the developments of mass culture, see E. Morin, *L'Esprit du temps*, vol. I: *Névrose*; vol. II: *Nécrose*, Grasset, new edition 1975.

32 See J.-P. Rioux, 'La France yé-yé des années 60', *L'Histoire*, no. 182, November 1994.

33 P. Nora, 'Le retour de l'événement', in Le Goff and Nora, eds., *Faire de l'histoire*, p. 217.

34 *Le Cinéma ou l'Homme imaginaire*, Minuit, 1956. Also, *Les Stars*, Seuil, new edition 1972.

35 See (233).

36 An investigation carried out by CNC (Centre national du cinema), on the 1962–74 period, found that the average number of times a year that blue-collar workers went to the cinema had dropped from eleven to four while senior managers, who had previously gone fourteen times a year, now went only eleven times. Above all, cinema had lost its 'routine' customers – those who had gone regularly on Saturday evenings or Sunday afternoons.

37 Jean-Luc Godard's cinema provides a superb overview of this: individualistic in *A bout de souffle* (1960), sombre in *Pierrot le Fou* (1965), yé-yé in *Masculin-Féminin* (1966), roaming the consumerist suburbs in *Deux ou trois choses que je sais d'elle* (1967), caught up in the cult of the car in *Week-End* (1968), prophetically revolutionary in *La Chinoise* (1967), embracing protest in *Cinétracts* (1968), and mixing reality and fiction in *Ici et ailleurs* (1976), which closed the cycle. See 'Spécial Godard', *Les Cahiers du cinéma*, 1991.

38 See F. Courtade, *Les Malédictions du cinéma français*, Alain Moreau, 1978; C. Ford, *Histoire du cinéma français contemporain (1945–1977)*, Editions France-Empire, 1977; P. de Comes and M. Marmin, eds., *Le Cinéma français (1960–1985)*, Atlas, 1985; R. Prédal, *Le Cinéma français depuis 1945*, Nathan-Université, 1991; C. Capdenat, 'Les Enfants terribles de la Nouvelle Vague', *Vingtième Siècle. Revue d'histoire*, 22 April–June 1989, pp. 45–51. The twenty-eighth Cannes Festival, held in May 1974, in the midst of the presidential election campaign, and chaired by a very elderly René Clair, provided quite an accurate overview of the situation: while Fellini's *Amarcord* testified to the vitality of a great film *auteur*, most of the offerings centred on reliable popular film stars: Jean-Paul Belmondo in Resnais' *Stavisky*, Marie-José Nat in Drach's *Les Violons du bal* and Sylvia Kristel in *Emmanuelle*, a straightforward blue movie that was highly successful at a time when porn films were just being launched. The history of cinema's place in contemporary French culture and imagination remains to be written.

39 See F. Cazenave, *Jean d'Arcy parle*, INA-La Documentation française, 1984; J. Beaulieu, *La Télévision des réalisateurs*, INA-La Documentation française, 1984.

40 See S. Bachmann, 'La Suppression de l'ORTF en 1974. La réforme de la "délivrance"', *Vingtième Siècle. Revue d'histoire*, 17, January–March 1988, pp. 63–72.

41 European political science was just beginning to look at the issue. As regards the 1974 presidential elections, see J.-G. Blumler, R. Cayrol and G. Thoveron, *La Télévision fait-elle l'élection?*, Presses de la FNSP, 1978.

42 See the analysis provided by one of those dismissed in 1968, J. Thibau, *Une Télévision pour tous les Français*, Seuil, 1970, as well as the useful anthology compiled by P. Besenval, *La Télévision*, Larousse, 1978.

43 This invasion was roundly denounced by Etiemble in *Parlez-vous franglais?*, Gallimard, 1973.

44 The first book, *Astérix le Gaulois*, published in 1961, sold only 6,000 copies that year. But by 1965, *Astérix et les Normands* had sold over a million copies.

45 Regarding this last-mentioned product (to which one should add OSS 117, Force M and Coplan), see E. Neveu, 'Trente ans de littérature d'espionnage en France (1950–1980)', *Vingtième Siècle. Revue d'histoire*, 10, April–June

1986, and *L'Idéologie dans le roman d'espionnage*, Presses de la FNSP, 1985. The revival of the French *polar* was so marked that questions were raised as to the genre's role in the social imagination: see F. Lacassin, *Mythologie du roman policier*, UGE-'10/18', 1974, 2 vols.

46 The role of money in the newspaper business was often denounced as a betrayal of the hopes of the Liberation. A different, distinctly French, tradition arose, designed to involve readers and encourage newspaper staff to form their own companies on the pattern provided by *Le Monde*; see, for example, J. Schwoebel, *La Presse, le Pouvoir et l'Argent*, Seuil, 1968.

47 See M. Martin, ed., *Histoire et Médias. Journalisme et journalistes français (1950–1990)*, Albin Michel, 1991, and C. Delporte, *Histoire du journalisme et des journalistes en France*, PUF, 1995.

48 Free sheets provided an extreme case of the mix between advertising, news and consumer interest. The first one was set up in Le Mans in 1962, though its example was rapidly followed in every French department and, in 1969, Sylvain Floirat launched *Un Jour*, a newspaper-cum-catalogue, pushed through 2,800,000 letter boxes. Worried by this development, 'paid-for' papers, especially outside Paris, mounted a counter-offensive, above all by producing weekend colour supplements.

49 As compared with, at the same dates, 6.1, 5 and 4.6 per cent on radio advertising and 0.3, 4.3 and 7.7 per cent on television commercials. See M. Martin, 'Le Marché publicitaire français et les grands médias (1918–1970)', *Vingtième Siècle. Revue d'histoire*, 20, October–December 1988, p. 88.

50 See J.-N. Jeanneney and J. Julliard, *Le Monde de Beuve-Méry ou le métier d'Alceste*, Seuil, 1979, and L. Greilsamer, *Hubert Beuve-Méry (1902–1989)*, Fayard, 1990.

51 See S. Siritzky and F. Roth, *Le Roman de L'Express (1953–1978)*, Atelier Marcel Jullian, 1979; M. Jamet, *Les Défis de L'Express*, Editions du Cerf, 1981; L'Express, *L'Aventure du vrai*, Albin Michel, 1979 (anthology of articles by personalities).

52 See L. Rioux, *Le Nouvel Observateur des bons et des mauvais jours*, Hachette, 1982; L. Pinto, *L'Intelligence en action: Le Nouvel Observateur*, A.-M. Métailié, 1984; *De Sartre à Foucault. Vingt ans de grands entretiens dans Le Nouvel Observateur*, Hachette, 1984 (anthology).

53 The far-left press, as anti-establishment and poor as it was, contributed to this eclecticism in its own way. Most visibly, *Libération*, formerly a Maoist tract, was relaunched as a daily in 1973, while *Politique-Hebdo* served as a mouthpiece for rebels thrown out of the PCF. Founded in October 1970 around Paul Noirot, it reached a circulation of 35,000. Its collapse paved the way for the launch of the journal *Politique aujourd'hui*. The 'underground' press, imitating its American counterpart, was extremely lively, though its audience remained very limited.

54 Significantly, France hesitated before giving itself over to the Beatles cult. The group's first concerts at the Paris Olympia in January 1964 were in fact relative flops, despite the support billing of Trini Lopez and Sylvie Vartan. But once the Europe 1 radio station had featured them on its *Musicorama* programme, their place on the airwaves was ensured and their second set of

concerts, at the Porte de Versailles sports stadium, was a triumph: presented as 'American stars', they completely eclipsed the Haricots rouges, Moustique and the Yardbirds.

55 See S. Coulomb and D. Varrod, *68–88, Histoire de chansons, de Maxime Leforestier à Etienne Daho*, Balland, 1987.

56 J. Sutter, *La Vie religieuse des Français à travers les sondages d'opinion (1944–1976)*, Editions du CNRS, 1984, 2 vols. All the data reported here come from the second volume.

57 Paul VI later said that France 'bakes the intellectual bread of Christianity'. The philosophers Jacques Maritain and Jean Guitton, as well as Father Yves Congar, Father Jean Daniélou and Father Henri de Lubac were consulted and their contributions stimulated a great many analyses and controversies. See, for example, Y. Congar, *Le Concile de Vatican II*, Beauchesne, 1984; René Laurentin, *Bilan du Concile*, Seuil, 1967; Henri de Lubac, *Entretien autour de Vatican II*, Editions du Cerf, 1985; and J.-F. Six, *Le Courage de l'espérance. Les dix ans qui ont suivi le Concile*, Seuil, 1978.

58 See E. Fouilloux, 'Jalons pour une histoire de dix ans', *Esprit*, special edition, *Les Militants d'origine chrétienne*, April–May 1977, and 'Le Choc de Vatican II', *L'Histoire*, July–August 1987.

59 Father S. Bonnet, a sociologist with great specialist expertise, raised this question in *La Communion solennelle. Folklore païen ou fête chrétienne?*, Editions du Centurion, 1969, and highlighted the strength of ancient rites and words in *Prières secrètes des Français d'aujourd'hui*, Editions du Cerf, 1976. See also J. Delumeau, ed., *La Première Communion. Quatre siècles d'histoire*, Desclée de Brouwer, 1987. The death of *religion populaire* then became a sought-after research topic: see, for the earliest findings, B. Plongeron *et al.*, *La Religion populaire. Approches historiques*, Beauchesne, 1976, and *La Religion populaire*, Editions du CNRS, 1979.

60 For a good example of this, see R. Pucheu, 'La Confession d'un paumé', *Esprit*, special edition, *Réinventer l'Eglise?*, November 1971.

61 See Clavel's highly significant *Ce que je crois*, Grasset, 1975.

62 A first-hand history of this movement is summarized in *Nous, chrétiens de gauche (1934–1978)*, special edition of *Lettre*, November 1977.

63 See J. Lestavel, *La Vie nouvelle. Histoire d'un mouvement inclassable*, Editions du Cerf, 1994.

64 A detailed sketch of these commitments is provided in 'A gauche, ces chrétiens', a report by the journal *Autrement*, February 1977. The press showed considerable interest: see, for example, 'L'Eglise vire à gauche', a special report produced by *L'Express*, 7 December 1970, and the hostile reaction of Maurice Druon, 'Une Eglise qui se trompe de siècle', *Le Monde*, 7 August 1971. In 1969, to combat what he saw as 'Marxization', Pierre Debray launched the Rassemblement des 'silencieux de l'Eglise', which succeeded in attracting 10,000 supporters to Versailles the following year.

65 In *Le Paysan de la Garonne. Un vieux laïc s'interroge à propos du temps présent*, Desclée de Brouwer, 1966. This sold 40,000 copies in the space of two months.

66 Many monographic studies confirmed this situation of poverty. See, for example, A. Delestre, *Trente-cinq Ans de mission au Petit-Colombes (1939–1974)*, Editions du Cerf, 1977.

67 In 1971, roughly 25,000 boys and girls were paid-up members of JOC-JOCF and the organization's monthly had a circulation of 50,000. The apostolic vocation of ACO was still insisted upon, though the hoped-for encounter was now with a Christ committed to the aspirations of workers engaged 'in struggle' against capitalist injustice. Moreover, despite the crisis affecting the Mission ouvrière and the Mission de France, worker-priests were making a comeback: in 1970 they numbered 287 and in 1974 756, above all in public works, construction and navigation. See P. Pierrard, *L'Eglise et les Ouvriers en France (1940–1990)*, Hachette, 1991.

68 See M. de Certeau and J.-M. Domenach, *Un christianisme éclaté*, Seuil, 1974, and, for a different perspective, E. Poulat, *Une Eglise ébranlée. Changement, conflit et continuité de Pie XII à Jean-Paul II*, Casterman, 1980.

69 As a corrective to this widespread feeling, the power of religious publishing was still very tangible – accounting for 7 per cent of all new books in 1969 – as was that of the Catholic press, mostly published by Bayard. In 1972, *L'Echo de notre temps* had a circulation of 1,200,000, *Clair Foyer* 400,000 and papers targeted at the younger audience had been rejuvenated, with the success of *Pomme d'Api* and *Okapi*, which had a circulation of 290,000, while *Télérama* had broken through to a circulation of 138,000.

70 Yet it was at the beginning of the 1970s that the first prayer rooms began to make their appearance in the immigrants' hostels (those run by SONA-COTRA, for example), in certain factories and on premises belonging to parishes.

71 See B. Philippe, *Etre juif dans la société française*, Montalba, 1979, and Pluriel, 1981, with a complementary bibliography, and D. Bensimon, *L'Intégration des Juifs nord-africains en France*, Mouton, 1971. In 1966, the Jewish community numbered a total of approximately 503,000 people, 62 per cent of whom lived in the Paris region and 23 per cent along the Mediterranean coast: see 'Les Juifs en France', *H Histoire*, no. 3, Hachette, November 1979, which includes a bibliography.

72 A number of Jewish shop-keepers, suspected of causing some of their female customers to disappear and of thus persevering in 'ritual crime', became the object of racist threats. The so-called rumour soon petered out, and E. Morin (*La Rumeur d'Orléans*, Seuil, 1970), writing shortly after the events, interpreted the affair as a consequence of the *banalisation* or increased matter-of-factness regarding the Jewish presence in French society.

73 See, for example, F. Delteil *et al.*, *Le Protestantisme, hier, demain*, Buchet-Chastel, 1974.

74 'Debout les damnés de Luther!' ran the headline of *Le Canard enchaîné* on 29 December 1971.

75 See the holy anger of two Protestant historians, P. Chaunu and F. Bluche, *Lettre aux Eglises*, Fayard, 1976.

76 See Institut Charles-de-Gaulle, *De Gaulle en son siècle*, vol. VII: *De Gaulle et la Culture*, Plon-La Documentation française, 1992, chapter 1; Institut Charles-de-Gaulle, *De Gaulle et Malraux*, Plon, 1987; Comité d'histoire du ministère de la Culture, *Journées d'étude sur la création du ministère de la Culture*, La Documentation française, 1995.

77 See J.-P. Rioux, 'Pompidou, Beaubourg et l'art contemporain', *L'Histoire*,

no. 175, March 1994. The President summarized his ideas on this issue in a 'Déclaration sur l'art et l'architecture' published in *Le Monde* on 17 October 1972 and reprinted in G. Pompidou, *Entretiens et Discours (1968–1974)*, Flammarion, 1984.

78 See *Vie culturelle et Pouvoirs, publics*, La Documentation française, 1972, p. 9; J. Duhamel, *Discours et Ecrits (1971–1973)*, Comité d'histoire du ministère de la Culture et La Documentation française, 1993; J. Rigaud (J. Duhamel's principal private secretary), 'La Politique culturelle. Bilan de deux années d'action', *Défense nationale*, February 1972; A. Girard, J.-P. Rioux and J.-F. Sirinelli, eds., *Les Affaires culturelles au temps de Jacques Duhamel*, La Documentation française, 1995.

79 See Ch.-L. Foulon, 'Des Beaux-Arts aux Affaires culturelles (1959–1969). Les entourages d'André Malraux et les structures du ministère', *Vingtième Siècle. Revue d'histoire*, 28, October–December, 1990.

80 See P. Emmanuel, *Pour une politique de la culture*, Seuil, 1971, and *La Révolution parallèle*, Seuil, 1975.

81 This milieu suffered from competition and was overtaken by crisis. On the relative failure of its historical models of intervention, see G. Poujol, ed., *L'Education populaire au tournant des années soixante. Etat, mouvement, sciences sociales*, Document de l'INJEP, no. 10, 1993.

82 See A. Chastel, *Architecture et Patrimoine*, Imprimerie nationale, 1994.

83 A. Malraux, *Le Miroir des limbes*, Gallimard, 'La Pléiade' collection, 1976, appendix.

84 See P. Gaudibert, *Action culturelle. Intégration et/ou subversion*, Casterman, 1977, and F. Jeanson, *L'Action culturelle dans la cité*, Seuil, 1973. On the example provided by Saint-Etienne, see D. Mandon, *Les Barbelés de la culture. Saint-Etienne, ville ouvrière*, Fédérop, 1976.

85 Formulated as early as 1969, and entrusted to Emile Biasini, the scheme met with a long opposition but finally led to the opening of the centre in 1976. See C. Mollard, *L'Enjeu du Centre Georges-Pompidou*, UGE-'10/18', 1976.

86 P. Bourdieu and A. Darbel, *L'Amour de l'art. Les musées et leur public*, Minuit, 1966; second edition (the most widely read), 1969. See also R. Abirached, ed., *La Décentralisation théâtrale*, vol. II: *Les Années Malraux (1959–1968)*, and vol. III: *1968, le tournant*, Actes Sud-Papiers, 1993 and 1994; J. Caune, *La Culture en action. De Vilar à Lang: le sens perdu*, PUG, 1992.

CONCLUSION TO PART 2

1 A. Peyrefitte was shortly to publish a detailed account of this in (193).

2 S. Hoffmann, *Essais sur la France. Déclin ou renouveau?*, Seuil, 1974, pp. 538–9. Chapter XII, 'L'Etat: pour quelle société?', written in March 1974, is remarkable for its force and lucidity.

3 M. Crozier, *La Société bloquée*, Seuil, 1970, p. 9.

4 See M. Lévy-Leboyer, *Le Patronat de la seconde industrialisation*, Le Mouvement social/Editions ouvrières, 1979; B. Brizay, *Le Patronat. Histoire, struc-*

ture, stratégie du CNPF, Seuil, 1975, and the investigation by A. Harris and A. de Sédouy, *Les Patrons*, Seuil, 1977.

5 See the pamphlet by J. Mandrin, *L'Enarchie, ou les Mandarins de la société bourgeoise*, La Table ronde, 1967; P. Birnbaum, *Les Sommets de l'Etat. Essai sur l'élite du pouvoir en France*, Seuil, 1977, and J.-P. Rioux, 'Ces élites qui nous gouvernent', *L'Histoire*, no. 147, September 1991 (with bibliography).

6 See J.-P. Sartre, 'Elections, piège à cons', *Les Temps modernes*, January 1973, p. 1108, as well as the highly significant report in the same issue of *Les Temps modernes*, 'Nouveau fascisme, nouvelle démocratie', May 1972.

7 See A. Touraine, *Un désir d'histoire*, Stock, 1977, p. 125; *Production de la société*, Seuil, 1973; and *La Société post-industrielle*, Denoël, 1969.

8 See A. Laurens, *D'une France à l'autre*, Gallimard, 1974.

9 See E. Morin, *L'Esprit du temps*, vol. II: *Nécrose*.

Bibliography

References (1) to (164) are taken from the previous volume of the Cambridge History of Modern France, *The Republic of de Gaulle, 1958–1969* by Serge Berstein. References (165) to (239) relate specifically to issues addressed in this volume. Unless stated otherwise, the place of publication is Paris.

1 G. Vincent, *Les Français 1945–1975. Chronologie et structures d'une société.* Masson, 1977 (a chronological guide with valuable commentary).
2 M. Belloc *et al.*, *Chronologies, 1946–1973.* Hachette, 1974 (shorter but useful).
3 *Annuaire statistique de la France.* Imprimerie nationale, volumes published annually (all the essential statistics).
4 INSEE, *Le Mouvement économique en France, 1949–1979, séries longues macro-économiques.* Imprimerie nationale, 1983 (provides the figures on French growth).
5 *L'Année politique*, published annually by Presses universitaires de France, then by Editions du Moniteur (indispensable chronicle and analysis of events).
6 R. Lasserre, ed., *La France contemporaine, guide bibliographique et thématique.* Tübingen, Niemeyer, 1978 (a bibliography of France).
7 Ch. de Gaulle, *Discours et messages*, vol. III: *Avec le renouveau, mai 1958–juillet 1962*; vol. IV: *Pour l'effort, 1962–1965*; vol. V: *Vers le terme, 1966–1969.* Plon, 1970 (a fundamental source).
8 Ch. de Gaulle, *Lettres, notes et carnets*: Plon, *Juin 1958–décembre 1960*, 1985; *1961–1963*, 1986; *Janvier 1964–juin 1966*, 1987; *Juillet 1966–avril 1969*, 1987 (a day-to-day account of de Gaulle's actions).
9 R. Rémond in collaboration with J.-F. Sirinelli, *Notre siècle, 1918–1988.* Fayard, 1988. Vol. VI of *L'Histoire de France*, ed. Jean Favier (the most recent survey of France in the twentieth century).
10 S. Berstein and P. Milza, eds., *Histoire du vingtième siècle.* Hatier, 1985–7 (vol. III of the textbook deals with the present period).
11 B. Droz and A. Rowley, *Histoire générale du XX siècle*, vol. II: *Depuis 1950*; vol. III: *Expansion et indépendances 1950–1973.* Editions du Seuil, Points Histoire series, 1987 (a synthesis).
12 Y. Lequin, ed., *Histoire des Français XIX–XX siècle*, vol. I: *Un peuple et son pays*; vol. II: *La société*; vol. III: *Les citoyens et la démocratie.* Colin, 1983–4 (twentieth-century France placed in the context of its long-term historical evolution).

13 F. Bédarida, J.-M. Mayeur, J.-L. Monneron and A. Prost, *Cent ans d'esprit républicain*. Vol. V of *L'Histoire du peuple français*. Nouvelle Librairie de France, 1965 (a remarkable study of French society and mentalities from the foundation of the Third Republic to 1962).

14 J.-P. Azéma, *De Munich à la Libération 1938–1944*. Editions du Seuil, Nouvelle histoire de la France contemporaine, XIV, 1979.

15 J.-P. Rioux, *La France de la Quatrième République*, vol. I: *L'ardeur et la nécessité 1944–1952*; vol. II: *L'expansion et l'impuissance 1952–1958*. Editions du Seuil, Nouvelle histoire de la France contemporaine, XV–XVI, 1980 and 1983 (indispensable guides to an understanding of de Gaulle's Republic).

16 P. Viansson-Ponté, *Histoire de la République gaullienne*, vol. I: *La fin d'une époque, mai 1958–juillet 1962*; vol. II: *Le temps des orphelins, août 1962–1969*. Fayard, 1970–1 (a pioneering study).

17 J. Chapsal, *La Vie politique sous la Ve République*, vol. I: *1958–1974*; vol. II: *1974–1987*. Presses universitaires de France, 1987 (the basic text).

18 Hugues Portelli, *La Politique en France sous la Ve République*. Grasset, 1987 (an interesting essay on the various stages of the Fifth Republic).

19 Ch. de Gaulle, *Mémoires d'espoir*, vol. I: *Le Renouveau, 1958–1962*; vol. II: *L'Effort, 1962*. Plon, Le Livre de Poche, 1970–1 (unfortunately unfinished vision of the Fifth Republic by its founder).

20 J.-L. Monneron and A. Rowley, *Les 25 ans qui ont transformé la France*. Vol. VI of *L'Histoire du peuple français*. Nouvelle Librairie de France, 1986 (a remarkable synthesis, well informed and analytical).

21 S. Sur, *La Vie politique en France sous la Ve République*. Montchrestien, 1987 (a useful and well-organized summary).

22 *Les Années de Gaulle, 1958–1974*. Special issue of *L'Histoire*, 102 (July–August 1987) (a remarkable collection of essays by leading specialists aimed at the general public).

23 J. Lacouture, *De Gaulle*, vol. II: *Le politique*; vol. III: *Le souverain*. Editions du Seuil, 1985–6 (an outstanding biography and an excellent work of history. Indispensable).

24 L. Noël, *La Traversée du désert*. Plon, 1973 (interesting on the transition period, May–December 1958).

25 L. Noël, *Comprendre de Gaulle*. Plon, 1972 (a defence of de Gaulle).

26 J.-R. Tournoux, *La Tragédie du Général*. Plon, 1967 (the inside story of the early days of the regime).

27 A. de Boissieu, *Pour servir le Général, 1946–1970*. Plon, 1982 (the view of de Gaulle's son-in-law).

28 C. Fouchet, *Mémoires d'hier et de demain*, vol. I: *Au service du général de Gaulle*; vol. II: *Les lauriers sont coupés*. Plon, 1971–3 (the memoirs of a loyalist).

29 E. Burin des Roziers, *Retour aux sources: 1962, l'année décisive*. Plon, 1986 (the record of the Elysée secretary general).

30 G. Pilleul, ed., *L'Entourage et de Gaulle*. Plon, Espoir series, 1979.

31 *De Gaulle et Malraux*, conference organised by the Institut Charles-de-Gaulle, 13–15 November 1986. Plon, Espoir series, 1987.

32 S. Cohen, *Les Conseillers du président: de Charles de Gaulle à Valéry Giscard*

d'Estaing. Presses universitaires de France, Politique d'aujourd'hui series, 1980.

33 IFOP, *Les Français et de Gaulle*, with an introduction and commentary by Jean Charlot. Plon, 1971 (the verdict of public opinion on de Gaulle and his policy from IFOP polls).

34 *Les Constitutions de la France depuis 1979*, with an introduction by J. Godechot. Garnier-Flammarion, 1970 (an essential source).

35 O. Duhamel and J.-L. Parodi, eds., *La Constitution de la Ve République*. Presses de la Fondation nationale des sciences politiques, 1965 (the judgements of constitutional experts on the regime).

36 J.-L. Quermonne, *Le Gouvernement de la France sous la Ve République*. Dalloz, 1980 (a fundamental text).

37 S. Sur, *Le Système politique de la Ve République*. Presses universitaires de France, Que sais-je? series, 1983 (a straightforward and useful summary).

38 D. Maus, *Textes et documents sur la pratique institutionnelle de la Ve République*. La Documentation française–CNRS, 1982 (a most important source).

39 D. Maus, *Documents pour servir à l'histoire de l'élaboration de la Constitution*. La Documentation française, 1987, vol. I (on the drawing up of the constitution).

40 J. Gicquel, *Essai sur la pratique de la Ve République*. Librairie générale de droit et jurisprudence (LGDJ), 1968.

41 P. Avril, *Le Régime politique de la Ve République*. LGDJ, 1967 (two critical accounts of the workings of the regime).

42 A. Chebel d'Appolonia, *L'Extrême Droite en France de Maurras à Le Pen*. Brussels, Editions Complexe, Questions au XXe siècle series, 1988 (a clear, up-to-date and complete synthesis).

43 P. Milza, *Fascisme français. Passé et présent*. Flammarion, 1987 (an analysis of the extreme right and its relationship to fascism).

44 R. Rémond, *Les Droites en France*. Aubier, 1982 (a classic work, recently brought up to date. The essential text on the subject).

45 J.-C. Colliard, *Les Républicains-indépendants. Valéry Giscard d'Estaing*. Presses universitaires de France, 1971 (the only work on the subject).

46 J. Charlot, *L'UNR, étude du pouvoir au sein d'un parti politique*. Presses de la Fondation nationale des sciences politiques, 1967 (the essential work on the party and a model study).

47 J. Charlot, *Le Phénomène gaulliste*. Fayard, 1970 (continues the preceding study).

48 J. Touchard, *Le Gaullisme 1940–1969*. Editions du Seuil, 1978 (interesting perspectives).

49 J.-Th. Nordmann, *Histoire des radicaux (1820–1973)*. La Table ronde, 1974.

50 J.-M. Mayeur, *Des partis catholiques à la démocratie chrétienne (XIX–XX siècle)*. Colin, U series, 1980 (the subject is approached from a European angle).

51 E.-F. Callot, *Un parti politique de la démocratie chrétienne en France, le MRP*. Rivière, 1978 (slightly disappointing).

52 F.-G. Dreyfus, *Histoire de la démocratie chrétienne en France, de Chateaubriand à Raymond Barre*. Albin Michel, 1988 (a well-documented study which

argues that only when christian democracy places itself on the right is it true to itself and guaranteed of a future).

53 O. Duhamel, *La Gauche et la Ve République*. Presses universitaires de France (key text).

54 H. Portelli, *Le socialisme français tel qu'il est*. Presses universitaires de France, 1980 (a very well-informed study which argues that French socialism is simply a form of neo-radicalism).

55 H. Hamon and P. Rotman, *La Deuxième Gauche, histoire intellectuelle et politique de la CFDT*. Ramsay, 1982.

56 M. Rocard *et al.*, *Le PSU et l'avenir socialiste de la France*. Editions du Seuil, 1969 (a programme rather than a history).

57 J. Mossuz, *Les Clubs et la politique en France*. Colin, Dossiers U2, 1966.

58 J.-P. Brunet, *Histoire du PCF*. Presses universitaires de France, Que sais-je? series, 1982 (an excellent account which says what needs to be said).

59 Ph. Robrieux, *Histoire intérieure du parti communiste*, vol. II: *1945–1972, de la Libération à l'avènement de Georges Marchais*. Fayard, 1981 (a precise, detailed insider account).

60 J.-J. Becker, *Le Parti communiste veut-il prendre le pouvoir?* Editions du Seuil, 1981 (on the PCF's strategy).

61 F.-O. Giesbert, *François Mitterand ou la tentation de l'histoire*. Editions du Seuil, 1977 (more enlightening on Mitterrand's union of the left strategy than C. Nay's superficial study *Le Noir et le Rouge ou l'histoire d'une ambition*, Grasset, 1984).

62 F. Bédarida and J.-P. Rioux, eds., *Pierre Mendès France et le Mendèsisme*. Fayard, 1985 (the last section deals with the Fifth Republic).

63 F. Mitterrand, *Le Coup d'état permanent*. Plon, 1964 (a fundamental text on the opposition to the Fifth Republic).

64 F. Mitterrand, *Ma part de vérité*. Fayard, 1969 (the events of 1965–9 as seen by the candidate of the united left in the 1965 election).

65 P. Mendès France, *Pour une République moderne, 1955–1962*. Vol. IV of *Œuvres complètes*. Gallimard, 1987 (a critique of the regime and an alternative strategy).

66 F. Bon, *Les Elections en France, histoire et sociologie*. Editions du Seuil, 1978 (an excellent, succinct survey).

67 A. Lancelot, *Les Elections sous la Ve République*. Presses universitaires de France, 1983 (a work of reference).

68 Association française de science politique, *L'Etablissement de la Cinquième République. Le référendum de septembre et les élections de novembre 1958*. Colin, 1960, Cahier de la FNSP, 109, *Partis et élections*.

69 François Goguel, ed., *Le Référendum d'octobre et les élections de novembre 1962*, Presses de la Fondation nationale des sciences politiques, 1965, Cahier de la FNSP, 142.

70 Centre d'étude de la vie politique française, *L'Election présidentielle de décembre 1965*. Colin, 1970, Cahier de la FNSP, 169.

71 *Les Elections législatives de mars 1967*. Colin, 1971, Cahier de la FNSP, 170.

72 *Les Elections législatives de 1968*. Imprimerie nationale, 1969.

73 F. Goguel, *Chroniques électorales*, vol. II: *La Cinquième République du général de Gaulle*; vol. III: *La Cinquième République après de Gaulle*. Presses de la

Fondation nationale des sciences politiques, 1983 (electoral analyses by one of the masters of French political science).

74 B. Droz and E. Lever, *Histoire de la guerre d'Algérie*. Editions du Seuil, Points Histoire series, 1982 (the best synthesis of the subject with a detailed bibliography).

75 L. Theis and Ph. Ratte, *La Guerre d'Algérie ou le Temps des méprises*. Mame, L'Histoire à l'épreuve series, 1974 (two historians analyse the contradictory evidence of fifteen protagonists).

76 Ch.-R. Ageron, *Histoire de l'Algérie contemporaine, 1830–1970*. Presses universitaires de France, 1970 (the issue placed in its historical perspective).

77 L. Terrenoire, *De Gaulle et l'Algérie, témoignages pour l'histoire*. Fayard, 1964 (the account of a Gaullist favourable to Algerian independence).

78 J. Soustelle, *L'Espérance trahie (1958–1961)*. Editions de l'Alma, 1962 (the account of a Gaullist who felt betrayed by de Gaulle's policy).

79 R. Salan, *Mémoires. Fin d'un Empire*, vol. IV: *L'Algérie, de Gaulle et moi (7 juin 1958–10 juin 1960)*. Presses de la Cité, 1974 (a work of self-justification which turns into a denunciation of de Gaulle's policy).

80 J. Massu, *Le Torrent et la digue*. Plon, 1972 (the memoirs of one of the principal actors in the Algerian drama).

81 B. Tricot, *Les Sentiers de la paix en Algérie (1958–1962)*. Plon, 1972 (the account of de Gaulle's closest collaborator on Algerian affairs).

82 R. Buron, *Carnets politiques de la guerre d'Algérie*. Plon, 1965 (the diary of one of the negotiators of the Algerian peace).

83 R. Girardet, *La Crise militaire française, 1945–1962*. Colin, 1964 (the essential book on the subject).

84 P.-M. de La Gorce, *La France et son armée*. Fayard, 1963.

85 M. Vaïsse, *Alger, le putsch des généraux*. Brussels, Editions Complexe, 1983.

86 H. Hamon and Ph. Rotman, *Les Porteurs de valises. La résistance française à la guerre d'Algérie*. Albin Michel, 1979 (the FLN's French support networks).

87 H. Alleg, *La Question*. Editions de Minuit, 1958 (the book which revealed the scandal).

88 P. Vidal-Naquet, *La Torture dans la République*. Editions de Minuit, 1972 (a committed account, written by an intellectual, which passionately denounces the use of torture).

89 P. Vidal-Naquet, *L'Affaire Audin*. Editions de Minuit, 1958.

90 *OAS parle*. Julliard, Archives series, 1964 (a collection of documents on the OAS).

91 *La Politique africaine du général de Gaulle (1958–1969)*, transactions of the conference organized by the Centre bordelais d'études africaines, the Centre d'études d'Afrique noire and the Institut Charles-de-Gaulle, Bordeaux, 20 October 1979. Pédone, 1980.

92 R. Bourgi, *Le Général de Gaulle et l'Afrique noire (1940–1969)*. LGDJ, Nouvelles Editions africaines, 1980 (Bibliothèque africaine et malgache, 33) (a very legalistic account of the subject).

93 F. Braudel and E. Labrousse, eds., *Histoire économique et sociale de la France*, vol. IV: *L'Ere industrielle et la société d'aujourd'hui (siècle 1880–1980)*. Presses universitaires de France, 1982 (an impressive survey written by the leading specialists).

94 M. Parodi, *L'Economie et la société française depuis 1945*. Colin, U series, 1981 (a clear, intelligent and rich study).

95 H. Bonin, *Histoire économique de la France depuis 1880*. Masson, 1988 (a convenient textbook which covers the ground).

96 J.-Ch. Asselain, *Histoire économique de la France du XVIIIe siècle à nos jours*, vol. II: *De 1919 à la fin des années 1970*. Editions du Seuil, 1984 (the principal stages in economic evolution).

97 J. Guyard, *Le Miracle français*. Editions du Seuil, 1970 (a study of growth and its effects).

98 J. Fourastié, *Les Trente Glorieuses ou la révolution invisible de 1946 à 1975*. Fayard, 1979 (an enthusiastic hymn to growth).

99 E. Malinvaud, J.-J. Carré and P. Dubois, *La Croissance française*. Editions du Seuil, 1972 (the basic work).

100 R. Delorme and C. André, *L'Etat et l'économie. Un essai d'application de l'évolution des dépenses publiques en France 1870–1980*. Editions du Seuil, 1983.

101 Ph. Brachet, *L'Etat-patron. Théories et réalités. Le rôle des entreprises publiques en France depuis la Libération*. Skyros, 1974.

102 H. Rousso, ed., *De Monnet à Massé*. IHTP–CNRS, 1986 (on the role of planning).

103 Y. Morvan, *La Concentration de l'industrie en France*. Colin, 1972.

104 J. Chombart de Lauwe, *L'Aventure agricole de la France de 1945 à nos jours*. Presses universitaires de France, 1979.

105 A. Gueslin, *Le Crédit agricole*. La Découverte, 1985.

106 B. Guibert *et al.*, *La Mutation industrielle de la France. Du traité de Rome à la crise pétrolière*. Collections de l'INSEE, 173–4, E-Enterprises series, 31–2, November 1975.

107 A. Cotta, *Inflation et Croissance en France depuis 1962*. Presses universitaires de France, 1974.

108 A. Prate, *Les Batailles économiques du général de Gaulle*. Plon, 1978 (the government's economic policy described by one of de Gaulle's collaborators).

109 P. Sorlin, *La Société française*, vol. II. Arthaud, 1969 (an overall assessment of social change written from a 1968 perspective).

110 J. Beaujeu-Garnier, *La Population française*. Colin, U2 series, 1982.

111 M. Gervais, M. Jollivet and Y. Tavernier, *La Fin de la France paysanne*. Vol. IV of *L'Histoire de la France rurale*, ed. G. Duby and A. Wallon. Editions du Seuil, 1977.

112 M. Roncayolo, ed., *La Ville aujourd'hui*. Vol. V of *L'Histoire de la France urbaine*, ed. G. Duby. Editions du Seuil, 1985.

113 F. Bloch-Lainé, *Profession: fonctionnaire*. Editions du Seuil, 1973 (the memoirs of a classic technocrat).

114 P. Birnbaum, *Les Sommets de l'Etat. Essai sur l'élite du pouvoir en France*. Editions du Seuil, Politique series, 1977 (a valuable analysis on the composition of, and relationship between, the political, administrative and economic élites under the Third, Fourth and Fifth Republics).

115 P. Birnbaum, *La Classe dirigeante française*. Presses universitaires de France, 1978.

116 H. Weber, *Le Parti des patrons, le CNPF (1946–1986)*. Editions du Seuil, 1986.

117 J. Capdevielle and R. Mouriaux, *Les Syndicats ouvriers en France*. Colin, 1970.

118 A. Barjonet, *La CGT*. Editions du Seuil, 1968 (asks why it was that the union undermined the May movement).

119 A. Bergounioux, *Force ouvrière*. Presses universitaires de France, Que sais-je? series, 1982 (a solid, well-documented account).

120 Y. Tavernier, *Le Syndicalisme paysan, FNSEA et CNJA*. Colin, 1969.

121 L. Boltanski, *Les Cadres*. Editions de Minuit, 1982 (a critical analysis).

122 A. Prost, *Histoire de l'enseignement en France (1800–1967)*. Colin, U series 1968 (a basic text).

123 A. Prost, *Histoire générale de l'enseignement et de l'éducation en France*, vol. IV. Nouvelle Librairie de France, 1982 (a complete account of the subject).

124 L. Roussel, *Le Mariage dans la société française*. INED, 1975.

125 C. Thélot, *Tel père, tel fils? Position sociale et origine familiale*. Dunod, 1982 (a study on social mobility, and its causes, in twentieth-century France).

126 M. Winock, *Chronique des années soixante*. Editions du Seuil, 1987 (everyday life in the period of French economic growth; a remarkable picture of French life during de Gaulle's Republic).

127 A. Grosser, *Affaires extérieures. La politique de la France 1944–1984* (a global analysis of France's foreign policy).

128 J.-B. Duroselle, *Histoire diplomatique de 1919 à nos jours*. Dalloz, 1971 (5th edition) (an essential text).

129 A. Grosser, *La Politique extérieure de la Ve République*. Editions du Seuil, 1965 (a remarkable analysis with penetrating insights for the time it was written).

130 Ph. G. Cerny, *Une politique de grandeur*. Flammarion, 1986 (the thesis is that de Gaulle's world policy had purely domestic goals).

131 L. Hamon, ed., *L'Elaboration de la politique étrangère*. Presses universitaires de France, 1969.

132 P. Gerbet, *La Construction de l'Europe*. Imprimerie nationale, 1983 (an overall survey, which includes France's policy).

133 E. Jouve, *Le Général de Gaulle et la construction de l'Europe 1940–1966*. LGDJ, 1967 (a substantial volume covering the essential areas of de Gaulle's policy).

134 G. Gozard, *De Gaulle face à l'Europe*. Institut Charles-de-Gaulle–Plon, 1976.

135 R. Poidevin and J. Bariéty, *Les Relations franco-allemandes 1815–1975*. Colin, 1977 (places de Gaulle's German policy in an overall framework).

136 J. Binoche, *L'Allemagne et le Général de Gaulle 1924–1970*. Plon, 1975.

137 J.-B. Duroselle, *La France et les Etats-Unis des origines à nos jours*. Editions du Seuil, 1976.

138 M. Error, *De Gaulle et l'Amérique, une amitié tumultueuse*. Plon, 1973.

139 R. Lescop, *Le Pari québécois du Général*. Montreal, Boréal Express, 1981.

140 M. Mourin, *Les Relations franco-soviétiques 1917–1967*. Payot, 1967.

141 S. Cohen, *De Gaulle, les Gaullistes et Israël*. Alain Moreau, 1974.

142 M. Couve de Murville, *Une Politique étrangère 1958–1969*. Plon, 1971 (the

unrevealing and uncritical testimony of France's principal foreign policy executant during de Gaulle's republic).

143 H. Alphand, *L'Etonnement d'être. Journal 1939–1973*. Fayard, 1977 (the memoirs of a great diplomat, a crucial source for the period).

144 Jean Doise and M. Vaïsse, *Diplomatie et outil militaire 1871–1969*. Imprimerie nationale, 1987 (the essential text on military policy, remarkably clear and well informed).

145 R. Lothar, *La Politique militaire de la Ve République*. Presses de la Fondation nationale des sciences politiques, 1976.

146 R. Rémond, *Le Retour de de Gaulle*. Brussels, Editions Complexe, 1985 (13 May and the change of republic viewed by the most knowledgeable specialist on twentieth-century France).

147 O. Rudelle, *Mai 58, de Gaulle et la République*. Institut Charles-de-Gaulle–Plon, 1988 (how de Gaulle's vision of the republic can explain his strategy in May 1958).

148 A. Dansette, *Mai 68*. Plon, 1971 (a useful narrative).

149 E. Morin, C. Lefort and C. Castoriadis, *Mai 68: la brèche, suivi de vingt ans après*. Brussels, Editions Complexe, 1988 (a new edition of the first on-the-spot interpretation of the May events, together with the authors' reflections twenty years later).

150 *Mai 68*, special edition of the journal *Pouvoirs*, 39 (1986) (published papers of a colloquium on the various interpretations of the events).

151 H. Hamon and Ph. Rotman, *Génération*, vol. I: *Les Années de rêve*; vol. II: *Les Années de poudre*. Editions du Seuil, 1987–8 (the life paths of the actors of 1968, before, during and after).

152 M. Grimaud, *En mai, fais ce qu'il te plaît*. Stock, 1977 (the testimony of the chief of police on the events).

153 E. Balladur, *L'Arbre de mai, chronique alternée*. Atelier Marcel-Jullian, 1979 (a curious novel-testament of one of Pompidou's closest collaborators in May 1968).

154 R. Aron, *La Révolution introuvable, réflexions sur la révolution de mai*. Julliard, 1968 (a very critical judgement on the May movement).

155 M. Crozier, *La Société bloquée*. Editions du Seuil, 1970 (a sociological explanation of the May movement).

156 A. Touraine, *Le Mouvement de mai ou le communisme utopique*. Editions du Seuil, 1968 (an attempt to construct a theory of protest).

157 Ph. Alexandre and R. Tubiana, *L'Elysée en péril, 2–30 mai 1968*. Fayard, 1969 (government's response to the May crisis, as seen by two journalists).

158 J. Massu, *Baden 68*. Plon, 1983 (the testimony of de Gaulle's interlocutor on 29 May).

159 Ph. Alexandre, *Le Duel de Gaulle–Pompidou*. Grasset–Tallandier, 1970 (a journalistic account of the conflict between de Gaulle and his successor).

160 G. Pompidou, *Pour rétablir une vérité*. Flammarion, 1982 (posthumous fragments of Pompidou's memoirs dealing particularly with his relations with de Gaulle from the Liberation to 1969).

161 M. Jobert, *Mémoires d'avenir*. Grasset, 1974 (the testimony of a close collaborator of Pompidou).

162 M. Jobert, *L'Autre Regard*. Grasset, 1976 (continuation of the above).

163 E. Roussel, *Pompidou*. J.-C. Lattès, 1984 (an accurate biography).
164 M. Winock, *La Fièvre hexagonale. Les grandes crises politiques 1871–1968*. Calmann-Lévy, 1986; reprinted by Editions du Seuil, Points Histoire series, 1987 (the crises of May 1958 and May 1968 portrayed within an overall assessment of French political crises).

GENERAL WORKS

165 Institut Charles-de-Gaulle, *De Gaulle en son siècle*. Plon–La Documentation française, 1991–2, 'Espoir' collection, 7 vols. (the proceedings of the international symposium held in 1990: an essential reference).
166 S. Berstein, *La France de l'expansion*, vol. I: *La République gaullienne (1958–1969)*. Seuil, 1989. English translation, Cambridge University Press, 1993 (the previous volume in this series).
167 M. Winock, ed., *Histoire de l'extrême droite en France*. Seuil, 1993 (a valuable recent review by outstanding specialists).
168 J.-F. Sirinelli, ed., *Histoire des droites en France*. Gallimard, 1992, 3 vols. (a monumental work covering all aspects of the subject).
169 S. Berstein and Odile Rudelle, eds., *Le Modèle républicain*. PUF, 1992 (on the Fifth Republic as compared with previous republics).
170 S. Berstein, *Démocraties, Régimes autoritaires, Totalitarismes. Pour une histoire politique comparée du XXe siècle*. Hachette, 1992 (a comparison of the Fifth Republic with the regimes of other industrial countries).
171 A. Bergounioux and G. Grunberg, *Le Long Remords du pouvoir. Le Parti socialiste français, 1905–1992*. Fayard, 1992 (relations with the government as seen from within the PS).
172 J.-F. Kesler, *De la gauche dissidente au nouveau Parti socialiste. Les minorités qui ont rénové le PS*. Privat, 1990 (the birth of modern socialism).
173 M. Vaïsse, *Histoire des relations internationales depuis 1945*. Colin, 1990 (a review that summarizes the most recent work of specialists in the field).
174 Jean-Marcel Jeanneney, ed., *L'Economie française depuis 1967. La traversée des turbulences mondiales*. Seuil, 1989 (of fundamental importance on the transition from economic growth to crisis).

POLITICS

175 'La Présidence de la République de Georges Pompidou. Exercise du pouvoir et pratique des institutions' (the most noteworthy collection of studies on this subject, compiled to mark a symposium organized by the Fondation nationale des sciences politiques, regrettably as yet unpublished, but to which the present volume owes a great deal).
176 *Georges Pompidou hier et aujourd'hui*. Neuilly-sur-Seine, Breet, 1990 (the proceedings of a commemorative symposium, though largely hagiographical).
177 M.-A. Burnier, ed., *La Chute du Général*. Editions et publications premières, 1969 (an analysis of the conditions surrounding Pompidou's accession to the presidency).

178 R.-G. Schwarzenberg, *La Guerre de succession. Les élections présidentielles de 1969*. PUF, 1969 (the same subject).

179 S. Rials, *Les Idées politiques du président Georges Pompidou*. PUF, 1977 (a book remarkable for its erudition and sensitivity).

180 P.-B. Cousté and F. Visine, *Pompidou et l'Europe*. Litec, 1974. This can be supplemented by the proceedings of a very useful symposium: Association Georges-Pompidou, *Georges Pompidou et l'Europe*. Brussels, Complexe, 1995.

181 F. Decaumont, *La Présidence de Georges Pompidou: essai sur le régime présidentialiste français*. Economica, 1979 (the best study on the development of institutions).

182 *Les Partis politiques et les Elections de mars 1973*, a *Le Monde* 'Dossiers et documents' supplement, 1973.

183 F. Goguel, *Chroniques électorales; la Cinquième République après de Gaulle*. Presses de la FNSP, 1983 (lucid electoral analyses).

184 G. Pompidou, *Le Nœud gordien*. Plon, 1974 (an essential work, written in 1968–9, shedding light on the views of the future president).

185 G. Pompidou, *Entretiens et Discours (1968–1974)*. Plon, 1975, 2 vols. (an important tool).

186 J. Chaban-Delmas, *L'Ardeur*. Stock, 1975 (rather lifeless memoirs by the serving prime minister from 1969 to 1972).

187 J. Charbonnel, *L'Aventure de la fidélité*. Seuil, 1976 (interesting information from a minister in Pompidou's government).

188 L. Hamon, *Vivre ses choix*. Robert Laffont, 1991 (the memoirs of a left-wing Gaullist close to Chaban-Delmas, who acted as spokesman for his government).

189 J.-M. Jeanneney, *A mes amis gaullistes*. Presses-Pocket, 1973 (the reasons behind a split).

190 C. Fouchet, *Mémoires d'hier et de demain*, vol. II: *Les lauriers sont coupés*. Plon, 1973 (on the refusal of a loyal Gaullist to become a 'Pompidolian').

191 F. Mitterrand, *La Rose au poing*. Flammarion, 1975.

192 F. Mitterrand, *La Paille et le Grain*. Flammarion, 1975 (these two books, by a man poised to become the head of the left opposition, chart the socialist recovery and criticize the Pompidou government).

193 A. Peyrefitte, *Le Mal français*. Plon, 1976 (a survey of French society by a former UDR general secretary and government minister under Pompidou).

194 M. Poniatowski, *Cartes sur table*. Fayard, 1972 (or 'how to trounce one's Gaullist allies'!).

195 L. Vallon, *L'Anti-de Gaulle*. Seuil, 1969 (a virulent pamphlet attack on Pompidou by a left-wing Gaullist).

196 J. Vendroux, *Ces grandes années que j'ai vécues*. Plon, 1975 (the memoirs of de Gaulle's brother-in-law, following his resignation from the UDR).

ECONOMY, SOCIETY AND PROSPERITY

As well as the works cited on pp. 361 and 366–7 of (166) and in (174):

197 *Annuaire rétrospectif de la France. Séries longues 1948–1988*. INSEE, 1990 (all the statistics, however dusty).

198 Ph. Ariès and G. Duby, ed., *Histoire de la vie privée*, vol. V: *De la Première Guerre mondiale à nos jours*. Seuil, 1987 (many fresh insights).

199 J.-Ch. Asselain, *Histoire économique du XXe siècle. La réouverture des économies nationales (1939 aux années 1980)*. Presses de Sciences politiques and Dalloz, 1995, chapter 2 (a clear examination of the international context).

200 A. Babeau and D. Strauss-Kahn, *La Richesse des Français. Epargne, plus-value, héritage*. PUF, 1977 (the first reliable assessment).

201 B. Bruneteau, *Les Paysans dans l'Etat. Le gaullisme et le syndicalisme agricole sous la Ve République*. L'Harmattan, 1994 (very up-to-date).

202 CERC, *Les Revenus des Français*, Albatros, 1977 (the first CERC report, which caused a surprise).

203 CERC, *Les Revenus des Français: la croissance et la crise (1960–1983). Quatrième rapport de synthèse*, La Documentation française, 1985 (dry but exhaustive).

204 P. Coulomb, H. Delorme *et al.*, eds., *Les Agriculteurs et la Politique*. Presses de la FNSP, 1990 (a symposium that reviews the situation).

205 L. Dirn, *La Société française en tendances*. PUF, 1990 (well analysed and soberly commented figures).

206 *Données sociales*, INSEE, 1974 and 1987 (two mines of official statistics with comments).

207 J. Dupâquier, ed., *Histoire de la population française*, vol. IV: *De 1914 à nos jours*. PUF, 1988 (a good textbook).

208 J.-F. Eck, *Histoire de l'économie française depuis 1945*. Colin, 'Cursus' collection, 1990 (very clear).

209 B. Esambert, *Pompidou capitaine d'industries*. Odile Jacob, 1994 (by the former industrial adviser to the president).

210 J. Klatzmann, *L'Agriculture française*. Seuil, 'Points-Economie' collection, 1978 (clear and measured).

211 H. Mendras, *La Seconde Révolution française (1965–1984)*. Gallimard, 1988 (a meticulous observation of developments).

212 G. Noiriel, *Les Ouvriers dans la société française (xixe–xxe siècle)*. Seuil, 1986 (the best textbook, with a rich bibliography).

213 Ph. Pinchemel, *La France*. Colin, 1981, 2 vols. (the essential geographical overview).

214 H. Rousso, ed., *La Planification en crise (1965–1985)*. Editions du CNRS, 1987 (insights into the end of the golden age of the plan).

215 Y. Tavernier, M. Gervais and C. Servolin, eds., *L'Univers politique des paysans dans la France contemporaine*. Colin, 1972 (a major contemporary symposium, which influenced many decision-makers).

216 Y. Trotignon, *La France au XXe siècle*, vol. II: *Depuis 1968*. Dunod, 1984 (rather schoolish, but with a wealth of significant details).

217 M. Verret, *L'Ouvrier français*. Colin, 1979 and 1982, 2 vols. (an unusual far-reaching approach).

218 D. Woronoff, *Histoire de l'industrie en France. Du xvie siècle à nos jours*. Seuil, 1994 (particularly valuable are pp. 537–93, and a good bibliography).

219 P. Yonnet, *Jeux, Modes et Masses. La société française et le moderne (1945–1985)*. Gallimard, 1985 (a stimulating sociological approach).

EDUCATION, CULTURE AND BELIEFS

As well as (123), which remains of fundamental importance:

220 C. Bellanger *et al.*, *Histoire générale de la presse française*, vol. V: *De 1958 à nos jours*. PUF, 1976 (exhaustive description).

221 J. Bourdon, *Histoire de la télévision sous de Gaulle*. Anthropos-INA, 1990 (an indispensable thesis).

222 J. Bourdon, *Haute Fidélité. Pouvoirs et télévision (1935–1994)*. Seuil, 1994 (the control of the 'small screen').

223 C. Brochand, *Histoire générale de la radio et de la télévision en France*, vol. II: *1944–1974*. La Documentation française, 1994 (a major collection of documents).

224 G. Cholvy and Y.-M. Hilaire, ed., *Histoire religieuse de la France contemporaine*, vol. III: 1930–1988. Privat, 1988 (comprehensive).

225 G. Delannoi, *Les Années utopiques (1968–1978)*. La Découverte, 1990 (the intellectual repercussions of May 1968).

226 V. Descombes, *Le Même et l'Autre. Quarante-cinq ans de philosophie française (1933–1978)*. Minuit, 1981 (a packed overview).

227 F. Dosse, *Histoire du structuralisme*. La Découverte, 1991 and 1992, 2 vols. (in-depth account).

228 Institut Charles-de-Gaulle, *De Gaulle et les Médias*. Plon, 1994 (a symposium: studies and first-hand accounts).

229 J.-N. Jeanneney and M. Sauvage, eds., *Télévision, nouvelle mémoire. Les magazines de grand reportage (1959–1968)*. INA-Seuil, 1982 (looking at the television with the eyes of an historian: a pioneering book).

230 F. Jouffa, *Vinyl fraise. Les années 60*. Michel Lafon, 1993 (on *yé-yé* culture: anecdotal, nostalgic and encyclopaedic).

231 J. Le Goff and R. Rémond, eds., *Histoire de la France religieuse*, vol. IV: *Société sécularisée et Renouveaux religieux (xxe siècle)*. Seuil, 1992 (a clear perspective).

232 R. Mehl, *Le Protestantisme français dans la société actuelle*. Labor et Fides, 1982.

233 Ministère de la Culture et de la Communication, *Pratiques culturelles des Français en 1974. Données quantitatives*. La Documentation française, 1974, 2 vols. (the first statistical investigation).

234 J.-L. Missika and D. Wolton, *La Folle du logis. La télévision dans les sociétés démocratiques*. Gallimard, 1983 (an early overview).

235 P. Ory, *L'Entre-deux-Mai. Histoire culturelle de la France (mai 1968–mai 1981)*. Seuil, 1983 (on two contrasting eras).

236 A. Prost, *Education, Société et Politique. Une histoire de l'enseignement en France de 1945 à nos jours*. Seuil, 1992 (collection of topical articles).

237 J.-F. Remonté and S. Depoux, *Les Années radio (1949–1989)*. L'Arpenteur, 1989 (anecdotal but useful).

238 R. Rieffel, *La Tribu des clercs. Les intellectuels sous la Ve République (1958–1990)*. Calmann-Lévy–CNRS Editions, 1993 (specialized and meticulous).

239 J. Verger, ed., *Histoire des universités en France*. Privat, 1986 (a sociological approach).

Index

Maps and tables are indicated by bold numbering.

The Cambridge History of Modern France

Other titles in the series include:

The Republican Experiment, 1848–1852
MAURICE AGULHON
  Translated by Janet Lloyd
  ISBN: 0 521 28988 2

The Rise and Fall of the Second Empire, 1852–1871
ALAIN PLESSIS
  Translated by Jonathan Mandelbaum
  ISBN: 0 521 35856 6

The Third Republic from its Origins to the Great War, 1871–1914
JEAN-MARIE MAYEUR and MADELEINE REBERIOUX
  Translated by J. R. Foster
  ISBN: 0 521 35857 4

The Decline of the Third Republic, 1914–1938
PHILIPPE BERNARD and HENRI DUBIEF
  Translated by Anthony Foster
  ISBN: 0 521 35854 X

The Fourth Republic, 1944–1958
JEAN-PIERRE RIOUX
  Translated by Godfrey Rogers
  ISBN: 0 521 38916 X

The Republic of de Gaulle, 1958–1969
SERGE BERSTEIN
  Translated by Peter Morris
  ISBN: 0 521 25239 3